SIGNS OF THE AMERICAS

SIGNS OF THE AMERICAS

A Poetics of Pictography, Hieroglyphs, and Khipu

EDGAR GARCIA

The University of Chicago Press   CHICAGO AND LONDON

The University of Chicago Press, Chicago 60637

The University of Chicago Press, Ltd., London

© 2020 by Edgar Garcia

Published 2020

Printed in the United States of America

29 28 27 26 25 24 23 22 21 20   1 2 3 4 5

ISBN-13: 978-0-226-65897-1 (cloth)

ISBN-13: 978-0-226-65902-2 (paper)

ISBN-13: 978-0-226-65916-9 (e-book)

DOI: https://doi.org/10.7208/chicago/9780226659169.001.0001

The University of Chicago Press gratefully acknowledges the generous
support of the Division of the Humanities at the University of Chicago
toward the publication of this book.

Library of Congress Cataloging-in-Publication Data

Names: Garcia, Edgar, 1983– author.
Title: Signs of the Americas : a poetics of pictography, hieroglyphs,
and khipu / Edgar Garcia.
Description: Chicago ; London : The University of Chicago Press,
2020. | Includes bibliographical references and index.
Identifiers: LCCN 2019019112 | ISBN 9780226658971 (cloth : alk. paper) |
ISBN 9780226659022 (pbk. : alk. paper) | ISBN 9780226659169 (e-book)
Subjects: LCSH: Picture-writing—Latin America. |
Picture-writing in literature.
Classification: LCC P.3.L29 G373 2019 | DDC 411—dc23
LC record available at https://lccn.loc.gov/2019019112

♾ This paper meets the requirements of ANSI/NISO Z39.48–1992
(Permanence of Paper).

FOR THE ANCESTORS CROWDING THE ROOM—
GRANDMOTHERS AND GRANDFATHERS

Origin, although an entirely historical category, has, nevertheless, nothing to do with genesis. The term origin is not intended to describe the process by which the existent came into being, but rather describe that which emerges from the process of becoming and disappearance. Origin is an eddy in the stream of becoming, and in its current it swallows the material involved in the process of genesis. That which is original is never revealed in the naked and manifest existence of the factual; its rhythm is apparent only to a dual insight. On the one hand, it needs to be recognized as a process of restoration and re-establishment, but, on the other hand, and precisely because of this, as something imperfect and incomplete. There takes place in every original phenomenon a determination of the form in which an idea will constantly confront the historical world, until it is revealed fulfilled, in the totality of its history. Origin is not, therefore, discovered by the examination of actual findings, but it is related to their history and their subsequent development. The principles of philosophical contemplation are recorded in the dialectic which is inherent in origin. This dialectic shows singularity and repetition to be conditioned by one another in all essentials.

—**Walter Benjamin,** *The Origin of German Tragic Drama*

When amnesia began to sow shadows in our memory, we went to our ancient lakes, seeking in the depth the faces we had lost. We saw through the mist of the ages that they were blurred and no longer the same. We reached the ancient bed of a river, facing the mountain of granite. We shouted for the echo to give back to us the names and the voices that had departed . . . leaving us empty. We came down from the hills, along the trails and roads, dragging our roots against the thorns, the snow, and the fire. We inquired after our destiny, but no one wanted to understand us because our signs were so strange. . . . We descended to the bottom of the sea, where the stars descend to their nests, to ask if the heavens know where we are headed or where we come from. . . . *Know, those who have been immolated, for in this region you will be the dawn and you will also be the river. . . .*

—**Miguel Méndez,** *Pilgrims in Aztlán*

CONTENTS

ILLUSTRATIONS

Color Plates (following page 158)

Black-and-White Figures

PREFACE
Threshold Magic

When the *New York Times* reported on the Society of Independent Artists' costume ball of March 11, 1921, the outfit that received the lengthiest copy was the Uruguayan artist Joaquín Torres-García's poem overalls. While harlequin, futurist, primitivist, folkloric, and cross-dressing garbs each received some words in the short article, Torres-García's sartorial poetry attracted relatively extensive description: "[he] had New York City outlined on his costume, the Woolworth Building on one leg down town, the Metropolitan Tower on the other, he sat on the Bowery, the Times Building was on his chest just above Forty-second Street, and the Bronx ran uptown on the back of his neck" ("Greenwich Village"). The overalls hung on Torres-García's frame with the same baggy absurd colonial excess with which the city extended itself over the forests, fields, streams, wetlands, salt marshes, and beaches of the island. Whereas Walt Whitman had once found in the native Lenape name *Mannahatta* "a word, liquid, sane, unruly, musical, self-sufficient . . . nested in nests of water-bays, superb" (585), Torres-García's poem outfit (fig. 1) recaptured the modernist deceptions of Whitman's bombast: the outfit mimes the borough of Manhattan spread sloppily over the island, the unruly colonial urbanism that had crowded out the Lenape people, and the strategic spatial code of modernity that alienates the signifying of a native *Mannahatta*. The Venezuelan poet, art historian, and curator Luis Pérez-Oramas writes that Torres-García's overalls marked "the disappointment, even the failure, of his time in America . . . disguised as a 'human ad, a decoy'" (*Arcadian Modern* 24). As such, Torres-García's outfit is an emblem of historical alienations. It is thus another installment in the saga of world loss that anthropologist and cultural historian James Clifford calls "the 'serious poem' of cultural history," quoting Giambattista Vico, to describe how signs, figures, tropes, and even foppish outfits form the substance of

FIGURE 1 Joaquín Torres-García, "Overalls Poem" (1921). Hand painted and worn to the Artist's Ball (Society of Independent Artists) at the Waldorf Astoria Hotel, New York, 1921. Photograph: Courtesy of the Estate of Joaquín Torres-García.

our everyday realities in the wake of colonial violence (*Writing Culture* 10). The "serious poem" of colonial history is the outfit that anyone who walks those sprawling urban streets wears—a symbol of dislocation, dispossession, and defeat.

Yet when Torres-García's overalls marked an anthropological impasse, when they made dress a wearable sign of what Claude Lévi-Strauss, long ago, called "a circle from which there is no escape—the first thing [that] we see as we travel round the world [which] is our own filth, thrown into the face of mankind" (43, 38), they also drew attention to the rollicking dislocation of signs from their ordinary circuits of legibility. This meeting of cultures in an unequal context creates the consciousness of conflict and contradiction that the Cuban anthropologist Fernando Ortiz calls "transculturation," in which the tensioned and often hostile interaction of different cultures encourages each cultural system to try to capture the terms of the other, but only to find that the intercultural convergence creates new meanings for signs. From the tensioned interaction of cultures emerges a dynamic sense of cultural contingency and social transformation. In this light, the most profound contradiction of Lévi-Strauss's *Tristes Tropiques*—quoted above—is that its form outpaces the melancholia of its contents. While the book sags with a lament for the catastrophe of European global mobility—"I hate traveling and explorers," it famously begins, it enacts its mourning by means of a "transient efflorescence" (7). Even the "streets of New York," Lévi-Strauss writes, give a sense of transpositions or slippage points, incomplete makings, anticipations, and situations "which do not yet exist as objects"—rather, they are "signs of activity" whose situational nature in colonial power trips up on the imperfectability of that power (79–80). His prose animates itself in an implicit idea that the structure of the sign—that fundamental unit of language and culture—is not a thing in the world but a situation in which the slippage points of things are revealed. Signs are relational, and their relations are always being made, contested, and negotiated. Therefore, the "serious poem" of cultural history is not only a representation of loss. As Torres-García writes, "*Signo: Estructura*" and "*lo temporal no és més que símbol*"[1]—which is to say that, if *time is a symbol*, symbols are expressions of the unstable temporal thresholds in which they find themselves, and those temporal thresholds are expressions of the symbols through which time finds its meanings. The signs of our "serious poem" of colonial historicity reflect those histories while giving form and content to them.

Walking through the entryway of the Waldorf Astoria, what else should the disillusioned Uruguayan wear but the immense artificial landscape of empire? Still, when that landscape takes on the easy disposability of overalls, it anticipates removal, change, and "transient efflorescence." While it cannot move backward to an origin in the Lenape *Mannahatta*, it can make "origins" into what Walter Benjamin—poetic theorist of historical experience (that is, a thinker who highlighted the value of the imagination in understanding history)—calls "an eddy in the stream of becoming" (*Origin* 45). For Benjamin, history is something other than an archive, something other than a container of content. It is a swirl of present makings and creative possibilities. And it is in the form, not only the contents, that such "transient efflorescence" of signs in time makes itself perceptible. For instance, in Torres-García's painting *Indoamérica* (fig. 2),[2] the geometric aesthetic of pre-Incan Andean pictography casts the alphabet into a native visual design, suggesting that this peripheral type of signifying (i.e., pictography) is not so peripheral. Here, it recalls the graphic writing of concrete poetry, in which the visual shape and patterning of words affects their semantic and phonetic values. But more subtly, the intercalation of writing and image also suggests that words have depth of field, that they are a part of the material world, transmitting and transforming it, even as the material world stages the conditions in which signs make meanings. The underlying message is that the "serious poem" of pictographic writing can transform how we view and experience the world, its materials and events, including those events that would appear to have superseded indigenous pictographs and native lands.

FIGURE 2 Joaquín Torres-García, *Indoamérica* (ca. 1937). Photograph:
Courtesy of the Estate of Joaquín Torres-García.

The world in which pictographs appear is usually imagined as a collection of boundary points. A presumption about their limited legibility
restricts their intellectual ambit to questions of racial or national positionality: as in, what race or nation is intrinsically closer or further away
from these things? (Typically, as in *Tristes Tropiques*, this idea is traced
in terms of how far the modern world has come from such things.) Such
positions comprise a meaningful part of the historical index for pictography, which is to say, the fact of colonialism and its archival logic of
supersession. Yet importantly, those positions also change when cast
in the aesthetic forms—the distinct troping and figuration—that such a
seemingly antiquated sign system as the pictograph provides. From the
vantage of the signs of the Americas, Torres-García's outfit is a sign of
waiting pictographic transpositions and efflorescences.

This book unravels how such sign types become thresholds of meaning in modern and contemporary poetry, storytelling, art, and law. Focusing on four sign types—pictography, petroglyphs, hieroglyphs, and
khipu—which this book calls "unnatural signs," it examines these signs
in their dislocation, transiting in and giving meaning to contemporary
happenings, effectively challenging the "*tristes*" of Lévi-Strauss's colonialist melancholia over an enfeebled subalternity. The double nature of

the claim is essential: the story of how these signs suffer the ramification of the modern world is well known. They are subject to expropriation, misuse, and mistranslation. That story can never go away, nor should it, because it is an ongoing story of unhinged racial hierarchies and hidden social manipulations. Less known, and the story that this book tells so as to empower the very sites that Lévi-Strauss presents as powerless, is how these signs also create systems of knowing and being well into the twenty-first century. Pictography is not a dead language, lying flat in archival tombs. I aim to show that those tombs have always been cenotaphs, empty signifiers for a signifying system that is very much alive, energetic, responsive, and indeed unnatural in its ability to continuously redefine the nature of its world. The key to doing that is to focus on the semiotic and aesthetic forms of these signs, and to observe how these forms have moved across languages and cultures to create contemporary experiences, insights, and relations.

When Torres-García walked into the Waldorf Astoria dressed as a disposable Empire City, hoping thus to shed some of that city's imperialist psychogeography, he practiced something akin to what Benjamin calls "threshold magic" or "profane illumination." With these terms, Benjamin refers to the practices of inverting seemingly natural mimetic orders upon themselves, using aesthetic *form* to work the *content* of history into more pliable political agency. As Benjamin also calls it, this is a technique of "anthropological materialism," a means of immersing oneself in the aesthetic contours of an object of analysis, in order to reveal its contradictions and turn these innervated or embodied contradictions into sources of critical poetic inspiration (*Arcades Project* 214; *Selected Writings*, vol. 2, pt. 1, 209, 217). Through the presencing of visual and poetic forms, the contents of history could be loosened from imperial norms and brought into a mutable (because vulnerable) now: from the ruins of history, the imaginative itineraries of historical experience.

To be sure, Benjamin recognizes the risk involved in such creative criticality. His "Theses on the Philosophy of History" read, "to articulate the past historically does not mean to recognize it 'the way it really was . . .' It means to seize hold of a memory as it flashes up at a moment of danger" (*Illuminations* 255). Benjamin sees the danger involved in creative engagements with historical objects—but he also foregrounds the necessity of such engagement. The danger has been imposed on us, who must live through the racial violence that would keep these signs silent. In that regard, their moment of danger *is* now—amid the persistent colonial interdict that has defined these signs as off limits and retrograde. But, if their moment of danger is *now*, then it is all the more urgent to seize the poetics of these signs, to hear the echoes of their historical music in our midst. Benjamin's "eddy in the stream of becoming" is also a flow pulling away from colonial historiography, churning in the forms that continue to define the diverse worlds that surround and suffuse us. The critical point of Benjamin's "profane illumination" is that history is not unidirectional, captive to the forward force of the pseudo-Hegelianism of linear time leading inescapably to modernity and accelerated capitalism. His flows of time are heterogeneous, with currents, countercurrents, variant imperatives, and ever-shifting possibilities moving in all directions—including the threshold of the Waldorf Astoria when framed in the disposability of Torres-García's poem outfit.

The problem of such temporal heterogeneity rushes through Torres-García's works and is the breaking wave of conceptual questions at the heart of the book in the reader's hands: how are these signs subject to normative positions, spaces, and temporalities of history while they shape those positions, spaces, and timescapes as well? That is, how are signs technologies of the social body in both senses of the term *techne*: subjectivizing the body while making available its discrepant fashionings? How are the signs of the Americas aesthetic thresholds or "serious poems" of cultural history in the fullest sense? And by what failure of the conception of the sign as (Saussurean) index of content do we strain to see history formed and transformed in semiotic and aesthetic thresholds? To draw forcefully on the Benjaminian poiesis of historical experience: how is history more than an archive, more than its collected contents? How is it also a totalizable act of present making, a sign that signs—like people—are active at the scene of their becoming, *then* and *now* in the *nows* of our *thens*? And how does that mimetic reserve nonetheless compel us because it constrains us, grounding us in material presences that must signify the fragmentary histories we might wish to flip transversely, into contemporary streams and unnatural becomings? How are the signs of the Americas a source of poetics in the realest sense, limited by material conditions that they also define, organize, and enliven? How are these signs indeed worlds, absorbing us into their realities (whether we perceive them or not)? How are they here and now?

ACKNOWLEDGMENTS

This book is sharper because of its interaction with the following people. At the University of Chicago, I've had the blessing of an intellectual atmosphere that has nourished its concepts and thinking. In particular, it has grown in conversations with Lucy Alford, Lauren Berlant, Larissa Brewer-García, Claudia Brittenham, Adrienne Brown, Bill Brown, Dipesh Chakrabarty, Maud Ellmann, Leah Feldman, Frances Ferguson, Rachel Galvin, Adom Getachew, Timothy Harrison, Kirsten Ihns, Patrick Jagoda, Alison James, John Kelly, Florian Klinger, Jonathan Lear, Steven Maye, Josephine McDonagh, Mark Miller, W. J. T. Mitchell, John Muse, Deborah Nelson, Sarah Nooter, Julie Orlemanski, Stephan Palmié, Mark Payne, Sarah Pierce Taylor, Andrei Pop, Eric Powell, Srikanth Reddy, Na'ama Rokem, Marshall Sahlins, Zachary Samalin, Victoria Saramago, Geronimo Sarmiento Cruz, Jennifer Scappettone, Richard Strier, Christopher Taylor, Sonali Thakkar, Kenneth Warren, John Wilkinson, and Evan Wisdom-Dawson. James Chandler deserves special thanks for the depth and extent of his engagement with the book's development and conceptual design. Ramón Gutiérrez deserves special thanks for the extent of his intellectual and professional mentorship.

The Chicagoland Junior Faculty Working Group was a crucial support for this project—key in that group has been my conversation and collaboration with Harris Feinsod. Other Chicago friends important for this work are Daniel Borzutzky, Peter Coviello, and Nasser Mufti. My longstanding collaborator, Jose-Luis Moctezuma, also merits special thanks.

Outside of Chicago, important interlocutors for this project have been Rosa Alcalá, Chadwick Allen, Arturo Arias, Birgit Brander Rasmussen, Vicki Couzens, Nilanjana Deb, Kristin Dykstra, Jonathan Eburne, Merve Emre, Michael Golston, Olivia Guntarik, Len Gutkin, Roberto Harrison,

Matthew Hofer, Virginia Jackson, Steven Justice, Donee Lepcha, Jerome McGann, Anne Middleton, Fred Moten, Julieta Paredes, Yopie Prins, Diane Rothenberg, Jerome Rothenberg, Lucia Sa, Glyn Salton-Cox, Craig Santos Perez, Andrew Schelling, Jonathan Skinner, Kathleen Stewart, Michael Angelo Tata, Michael Taussig, Massimiliano Tomba, Gerald Torres, Rodrigo Toscano, and Cecilia Vicuña. As I was acquiring image permissions, I received gracious responses and feedback from Alurista, Carla Alvarez, Francisco Aragón, Stuart Bernstein, John Borrows, Cecilia de Torres, Eleonora di Erasmo, Jennifer Dunbar Dorn, Bettina Erlenkamp, Victoria Fedrigotti, Molly Haigh, Nicholas Hurley, Rushing W. Jackson III, Justin Katko, AnaLouise Keating, Elise McHugh, Kara Newby, Simon Ortiz, Vanessa Pickett, Piper Severance, Eric Singleton, Karen Van Hooft, Gerald Vizenor, and Melissa Watterworth Batt. At its beginning, the project relied on the belief and vision of Wai Chee Dimock, Langdon Hammer, and Anthony Reed at Yale University, as well as Barbara Tedlock and Dennis Tedlock at the University at Buffalo (SUNY). And, at its end stage, the project was nourished by the rigorous but supportive words of its (then) anonymous peer reviewers, Doris Sommer and Roberto Tejada. The advice of two anonymous peer reviewers at *Publications of the Modern Language Association*—where an article version of chapter 3 appeared as "Pictography, Law, and Earth: Gerald Vizenor, John Borrows, and Louise Erdrich"—was also decisive. Amberle Sherman, Joseph Wallace, and Lisa Wehrle provided intelligent and incisive edits. To all of these people, I am profoundly thankful.

I would also like to thank Alan Thomas and Randolph Petilos at the University of Chicago Press for their care in bringing this book into publication. My research assistant, Serin Lee, also deserves a special note of gratitude for helping to bring the book's many parts together, as do the staff members in the departments of English and Creative Writing at Chicago—Racquel Asante, Angeline Dimambro, Starsha Gill, Jessi Haley, and Lex Nalley. Thanks to Anne Walters Robertson, Dean of the Division of the Humanities, for the additional subvention in support of the book's publication. Vice Provost Melissa Gilliam and Regina Dixon-Reeves also merit sincere thanks for their manifold and ongoing support.

At an institutional scale, this work matured in research trips and conversations made possible by fellowships at the Beinecke Rare Book and Manuscript Library at Yale University, the Yale Club of San Francisco, and the Institute for Critical Social Inquiry at The New School; as well as the Provost's Postdoctoral Fellows Program and the Neubauer Family Assistant Professor Program at the University of Chicago.

But most importantly, I am grateful for the intellectual journey that I found with my partner and best friend, Alexis Chema.

INTRODUCTION
Unnatural Signs

It is a popular misconception that the era of the pictograph has come to a close. That says less about the pictograph than about our inability or reluctance to read such signs. The study of literature in the West largely stands on the premise that literature begins with letters. Anything otherwise—such as the weaving stories of khipu or Andean knot writing; texts of image, object, and sound amalgamated in Mesoamerican hieroglyphs; or the complementary visual and mnemonic cues of pictographic inscription found throughout the native Americas—is treated as a relic of a preliterate and preliterary past. The ongoing poetics of these signs are obscured by a cultural logic of the archive as a final resting place, despite their literary output continuing into the twenty-first century. It is appropriate, then, for the seeds of this book to have sprouted in the discolored, wrinkled, and disintegrating papers of the special collections library at UCLA. There, with the dim light of the reading room casting an academic achromasia on a stack of stories written in pictography and "fonetik" spelling, I developed the thought that these objects were incorrectly set in a preservational past tense: protected from the peril of the present and prevented from disclosing future horizons. This thought was brought about by the provenance of the pictographs on my desk, written by the eccentric early twentieth-century Spanish American rodeo cowboy turned anthropologist and poet named Jaime de Angulo, who collaborated with such seemingly disparate figures as Pomo basket weaver William Ralganal Benson and modernist poet Ezra Pound. In his papers, the cultural logic of the archive was forced to compete against its contents. Here, rather than what Diana Taylor has called the "absencing" of the archive, were pictographs inspiring poetry about ongoing social tensions, confrontations, and collaborations—"repertoires" and "scenarios," as she puts it, of ongoing social life (22–28). Rather than symbolize simply cultural loss, the textual activity of these pictographs sparked fully contemporary modalities, logics, affects, pedagogies, and thresholds of encounter.

The archive and the act of curation are twin modes of making time in cultural history. This book participates in both modes—digging deep in archives to curate a renewed understanding of the signs of the Americas—but it resists some commonplaces about how such work is conceptualized. While the act of curating intends to bring things out of the past into the experience of contemporary encounter, it sometimes struggles to disentangle ideas of supercession or evolutionary development from its sense of history. For instance, when pictographs are presented in literary scholarship, they are typically at the beginning of an anthology of American literature, captured in an evolutionary chronology that culminates in the written word, suggesting that pictographs precede (and are eradicated by) the alphabet and its literary products. Even when a contemporary pictographic work such as N. Scott Momaday's 1969 *The Way to Rainy Mountain* appears in the *Norton* or the *Heath* anthologies of American literature, its pictographs are neatly excised. More experimental (and indigenously oriented) anthologies—such as Jerome Rothenberg's *Technicians of the Sacred*, Gordon Brotherston's *The Sun Unwound*, or Cecilia Vicuña's *Oxford Book of Latin American Poetry*—intersperse pictographs throughout their pages to distort an evolutionist chronology. But they do not explain how pictographs are on comparable semiotic, aesthetic, or temporal footing as the alphabet (exemplifying the challenge of a multisemiotic account of the literatures of the Americas). In the world of art curation, the Metropolitan Museum of Art stands out for its recent decision to display more than one hundred native artworks in its American Wing, alongside pieces by Alexander Calder, Mark Rothko, and Isamu Noguchi. This act makes strides to unfix the native objects from the ethnological looking glass of "deep time"—yet the challenge in succeeding with that will be to teach viewers and readers how it is that native materials signify and give meaning to the objects around them, how they are more than a mirror for the works of Western artists. How, in other words, do the signs of the Americas illuminate their non-native others? How do they carry distinct rhythms or patterns that capture the temporal experience of surrounding objects and viewers? How might *these signs* see *their viewers*—to create thus what Mark Rifkin calls "indigenous orientations" (1)? In what ways do their forms subsume and affect because—as Rifkin suggests—they organize an experience of space and time? This book furthers the effort of asking such questions by showing how the manifold uses of such sign systems as pictographs, hieroglyphs, and khipu—by indigenous and nonindigenous writers and artists—continue to make meaning, responsively shaping contemporary happenings and concerns, untwisting thus forms of ongoingness that resist historical supersession and cultural evolutionism.

In no uncertain terms, the poet I encountered in Special Collections at UCLA conceived of pictographs as antithetical to archival absencing. "You reach the stage of the symbol, of our pictograf of the little man, you think you have at last reached pure meaning," writes de Angulo, "but you have only landed in the midst of almost pure form; you have reached the mathematical symbol, the algebraic expression of a curve!" ("What"). Drawing on the theories of linguistic anthropologist Edward Sapir, de Angulo describes the pictograph as a starting point for meaning, an instance of "pure form," which gives way to a "poetic indeterminacy" that stands in contrast to the historically specified knowledge that we sometimes expect from products of a literary past (Friedrich). The pictograph is not so much an object of analysis as it is a means of expressing what analysis is possible or relevant—more like a mathematical constant than an inert artifact from a foregone past. For de Angulo, pictographs are not signs of a past captured in its representations; they are devices for making new representation, meaning, and perception. This idea is nowhere better ramified than in his pictographic translations of fellow Spanish poet Federico García Lorca's "deep song" (plates 1 and 2).

García Lorca's poem invokes a spirit of *duende*—the spirit of mortal danger that inspires Andalusian "deep song" or *cante jondo*—which de Angulo translates into a stand-alone icon with an arrow shooting beyond the page. Depicting mortality salience as a shooting arrow, flying to the unknown space beyond the page's margin, the pictograph's visual language bears the translator's underlying aims. For him, death does not represent a terminus. Rather, it gestures toward a world beyond the page—a world of continued interactions and creative makings. The apparently moribund signifier of pictography points toward an envisioned existence that brings together Spanish, American, and American Indian systems of poetic signification. In casting transnational literary movement within pictographic design, de Angulo relays the meaning of transnational movement through an indigenous vector, by which overused notions of a "singular modernity" or a homogeneous world culture (Jameson) are sent flying from the page into the signs, tropes, and forms that Chadwick Allen has called the "trans-indigenous."

Allen's notion of the "trans-indigenous" characterizes indigenous cultures as "ongoing processes rather than finished outcomes . . . this *trans*- signifies *across*, *beyond*, and *through*, suggesting sustained movement, but also *changing* or *changing thoroughly*, suggesting significant metamorphosis" ("Productive" 240). While partly motivated by the transnational pulls in social life (pulls that do not necessarily draw native cultures into transnational capital), "trans-indigenous" signifies more comprehensively the presencing of native cultures in the metamorphoses of historical experience. Rather than the primordial signal outside of time (the allochronicity, to invoke Johannes Fabian's resonant term) that the colonialist episteme demands of native people, the conception of "trans-indigenous" demarks those ironies by which constituted worlds could stay transitive, present to ongoing processes, and animated by the material histories they wish to flip into sites of sovereign native worlds. This point is emphasized in Mark Rifkin's study of "temporal sovereignty," which points out that sovereignty is not only a spatial prerogative—it is a right to exist in the accidents, disparities, contingencies, and changes of time, as well as to shape and define those temporal multiplicities (2–6). World-making practices are profoundly temporal. Therefore, a consideration of the signs of the Americas prompts us to ask: how do these signs create the world historical moments in which they appear? How, for instance, do pictographs give historical orientation and temporal form to the same colonial acts that would seek to silence them? To answer such questions requires recognition that indigenous channels have focalized and vocalized the meanings of worlds and heterogeneous world semiotics. The sign, as particular locus of language and culture, offers a place in which to observe the transitive meaning making of indigenous cultures in indigenous and nonindigenous contexts.

In this book, I bear down into such vectors and channels, tracking how indigenous signs play an integral but unrecognized role in shaping world poetics, those linguistic arts that give rhythm and form to the experience of worlds. My purpose is to make that role conspicuous, to lay bare the semiotic and poetic patterns of the indigenous Americas that impact contemporary North American and Latin American poetry. Such hemispheric philology is prefigured in the literary spatial field of the "poetry of the Americas." Sylvia Wynter (1997), Charles Bernstein (1999), Ramón Saldívar (2006), Jahan Ramazani (2009), José David Saldívar (2011), and—most recently—Harris Feinsod (2017) have laid the groundwork for considerations of poetic form forged across the cultures and nations of the "trans-American" hemisphere. But these works have missed a connection with analyses of how the hemisphere's native sign systems bear poetic worlds too. The problem is a temporal mismatch: whereas studies of the poetics of indigenous signs have focused on moments of colonial encounter—as in the works of Rodolfo Kusch (1971), Walter Mignolo (2003), Gordon Brotherston (1992), Miguel León-Portilla (2002), Joanne Rappaport and Tom Cummins (2011), Birgit Brander Rasmussen (2012), and Matthew Cohen and Jeffrey Glover (2014)—studies of the contemporary world poetry of the Americas have presupposed a modernity that is lettered, capitalistic, urban, and singular. The works that engage with the poetics of indigenous signs have focused on the past, while those that are situated in the present have focused too little on indigenous signs. This mismatch has had the unintended effect of archiving the indigenous while normalizing mestizo and hybrid cosmopolitanisms as world historical vanguards. Allen's work updates these hemispheric circuits to reckon with their native articulation, exploring the tension between transnational and trans-indigenous. And my work builds on that effort by examining how signs do not exactly interact in a singular world system but carry world systems of their own—that is, worlds against the one world of world literature.

As Diana Taylor notes, the archive of the hemispheric Americas has served to manage who gets to be in the singular "now" of Western imperial time, and, in so doing, relegates repertoires of non-Western cultural performance to the past tense. Ontological ambivalence informs Taylor's sense of repertoire: when cultural analysis discredits the totalizable worlding of indigenous repertoires, it produces a renewed colonial archive, a type of "'absence studies,' disappearing the very populations it pretends to explain" (34). To restructure a study of the Americas within its indigenous worlds, she focuses on the fracture between the ontological and epistemological—"the *is/as*" divide—that a singular conception of world historical existence bears. This fracture exploits a distinction between reality and imagination in order to perpetuate a racialized time, in which some people are in the *real* world of a Western rational and capitalistic present time while others are delayed in the *enchantments* of a strictly symbolic and mystified premodernity. This divide is usually attributed to G. W. F. Hegel, imputing to him the conception of linear progressive time that dominates modernist thought. Yet, even in Hegel, such a time scheme is troubled by incommensurabilities: negations of negations and "breaks in continuity" (qtd. in Anderson, *Lenin* 105). Hegel himself was ambivalent about the singularity of time amid so many fracture points in how people actually experience time. In the context of the Americas, such incommensurabilities are perceptible only when distinct temporal schemes are seen as more than conventional; that is, when cultures are afforded ontological parity. Bolivian scholar of the Andes Javier Sanjinés points out that when we affirm the reality of the cultural repertoires we set out to understand, the field of analysis becomes temporally unstable, covered with cultural "embers" that can set fire to a world, becoming the live and intense events that our cultural objects always already are.

De Angulo's arrowed entity is one such ember (plate 2), pointing beyond the page at a world it seeks to define in terms of itself. The poem suggests that the world should be redefined in terms of the pictographic arrow—"land/of death without eyes/but arrows" (plate 1)—but the pictograph itself enacts that redefinition. Dominating the spatial field of the page, this pictograph (plate 2) also captures its temporal coordinates: instead of the step-by-step process of a poem whose letters form words turned into poetic lines and stanzas, García Lorca's poem is translated into a stand-alone icon that shows its every angle at once. The pictographic arrow then channels that total immediacy to the page's margins, as if to break our gaze and make us look away from the icon into the world that surrounds the poem. Its immediacy points then to our reality. But the gap between those two domains is not bridged—the surrounding world and the icon are irreparably separated. Still, the icon brings us to this threshold of reckoning the difference between worlds. The sign thus introduces a directive by which the time of the archive is split open to other kinds of experience.

Temporal Heterogeneity: Rhythms and Arrhythmia

In 1992, the quincentenary of Christopher Columbus's arrival to the Americas, the Sioux legal scholar and theologian Vine Deloria Jr. put the world historical problem of such temporal tensioning in prosodic terms: "From an Indian point of view, the general theme by which to understand the history of the hemisphere would be the degree to which the whites have responded to the rhythms of the land—the degree to which they have become indigenous. From that perspective, the judgment of Europeans is severe" (429–30). Deloria's use of the figure of "rhythm" to describe historical experience puts that experience squarely in the domain of those institutions that create the temporal patterns of everyday life. Here, rhythm is not subordinated to an "empty, homogeneous time"—as Benjamin is often quoted, out of context and misconstrued with this phrase (Benjamin, *Selected* 4:402); it is time in its plurality. That is, there are various and discrepant social and ecological practices that induce temporal experience, including ones that are autochthonous to the American hemisphere. While capitalist culture encourages all rhythms to be subsumed to labor time, and thereby to absorb all life into the lockstep of the commodity, it is constantly disrupted and challenged by such voices as Deloria's that abide in other temporal patterns. And Deloria's main point is that such temporal discrepancy is available to all people, when they engage with these diverse rhythms.

Crucially, Deloria does not promote an abandonment of historical knowledge. Instead, he wishes to redefine the concept of historicity when it is syncopated in the rhythms of non-Western ecology, arts, religion, music, poetry, literature, law, and science. Such syncopation reveals the contingency and incompletion of Western progressive modernity culminating in the neoliberal world market. Despite its most dramatic claims to have ended history, the failure of capitalist culture to hide such contradictory voices as Deloria's reveals its inability to eliminate them. The political articulation of such temporal conflict has been refined among contemporary Bolivian scholars such as Sanjinés, whose country constitutionally ratified a "plurinational" and "post-neoliberal" Andean state in recent decades. At the supposed end of history, a plurinationalism emerged there to negotiate the competing means of organizing historical experience among indigenous, nonindigenous, mestizo, migrant, and itinerant people. In Marxist discourses, this confluence appears in the debate on the question of "formal subsumption." These discourses have been inspired by historian and philosopher Dipesh Chakrabarty's call to take on cultural difference while holding fast to Marx—to articulate a "subaltern studies . . . [that situates itself] at the juncture where we give up neither Marx nor 'difference,' for . . . the resistance it speaks of is something that can happen only *within* the time horizon of capital, and yet it has to be thought of as something that disrupts the unity of that time" (95)—that is, to use the sobering political GPS of materialist critique to "provincialize Europe." The use of a European philosopher's ideas (i.e., Marx) in provincializing European historiography is not an impasse but a manifestation of the very temporal heterogeneity that motivates calls for the reorganization of cultural life. It is from this "arrhythmia," as historian and political theorist Harry Harootunian has called it, that the pliability, porosity, and "asymmetries and possible discordances" of time can be asserted (55). With that assertion, the forms of worlds other than the Western one can be seen to subsume (because they affect) the living dynamics of present events. In indigenous studies, the question of temporalities is related to rhythm because, as Rifkin notes, rhythms denote "patterns of consistency and transformation that emerge immanently out of the multifaceted and shifting sets of relationships that constitute [varied temporal] formations and out of the interactions among those formations" (2). Time is not a container but a means of becoming and interacting—and it is most clearly delineated in those acts that disrupt and reorient temporal norms. Deloria likewise dares his readers to think indigenously, which is not to appropriate indigenous thought but to reckon with the disruption that indigenous thought—even in translation—provokes in the cadences of contemporary reality.

Proposing that this interactivity is channeled through the poetic structures and conceptual rhythms of signs, this book analyzes their ongoingness by way of such poetic tropes as metonymy, metalepsis, amphiboly, catachresis, and analepsis. These tropes induce a relational mode that resembles, because it informs, the social conditions of their use. Poetic tropes render the ways in which people understand their realities, affecting not only aesthetic discourses but acting as constellating force to contemporary transculturations. And, in an increasingly global era, tropes serve to give meaning to relational systems whose ever-incipient globality need not be necessarily identical with global capital. As I argue in the first chapter (building on discourses on formal subsumption, as well as on the writings of Bolivian-Andean theorists of temporal heterogeneity), current conceptions of poetics in studies of world literature limit the possibility of finding indigenous worlds in translation. World form is regularly taken to be synonymous with "singular modernity," a global capitalist model of "one, and uneven" (Jameson and Moretti qtd. in Warwick 10). Yet such a model presupposes the very homogenization that it sets out to analyze; or, as anthropologist Marshall Sahlins put it, Immanuel Wallerstein's influential world-system model "becomes the superstructural expression of the very imperialism it despises—the self-consciousness of the World-System itself" ("Cosmologies" 416). Restructuring that search through anthropologist June Nash's idea of "counterplots," or literary form understood as temporal repertoire (*Mayan* 2, 34–36, 222–23), in chapter 1 I show how temporal systems as seemingly distant as those found in the "Aztec Priests' Reply" of 1524 and the Aztec sunstone reverberate in the experimental poetics of their translators—Gordon Brotherston, Jennifer Dunbar Dorn, and Edward Dorn—subsuming the world of the translators into a Mesoamerican one. Focusing in particular on an Aztec poetic form of dis-identification—what we would call "metalepsis" but which is known as *inamic* in the Nahuatl language—I reposition translation itself within the conceptual boundaries set out for the materials to begin with by their original speakers: a Nahuatl poetics of nonidentity recaptures translation itself in a Nahuatl world of endless dis-identification.

Translation itself is fraught, bearing evidence of interpretive limits and intercultural miscommunication. But the story told in the following pages is not about what fails to get across. The story told here traces the residual legibility of cultural materials in translation, showing how the animation of worlds in intercultural, cross-temporal, and transindigenous motion lays bare an aesthetics of indigenous "survivance"—to quote Anishinaabe poet and scholar Gerald Vizenor—as well as a survivance of indigenous aesthetics (*Manifest* 14). "Survivance" is Vizenor's neologism to describe the persistence of native cultures amid their colonial fragmentation; it combines survival and resistance to communicate the possible totalizability of native forms in colonial and postcolonial contexts. Implicitly, it critiques the idea of the untotalizable fragment, whereby translation is impossible and poetic form has no "ontological legitimacy"—to quote Debjani Ganguly in an allied discourse in postcolonial studies (79–83). The totalizable fragment is the necessary concept for considering how poetic form scales into the encompassing experience of time that we call "world."

To render this concept, the questions asked in this book have to do with the possibility of disclosing semiotic and poetic survivance in translation. What persists of pictographic meaning when it appears in the historical palimpsest of de Angulo's archive? What of its worlding breaks through that archive with enough shaping force that the meeting point between text and reader becomes an actual site of syncopating world formations? How does fractured form or temporal heterogeneity, then, inform the experience of reality? And does that syncopated temporality affect readers, including those unaware of how pictographic inscription works? Does the pictograph look forward, in its own way, to indeterminate and still undisclosed future horizons? If so, how do the other sign systems of the Americas, such as khipu, hieroglyphs, and petroglyphs, inflect the time horizons of past, present perfect, present, future, and future anterior with their own meanings and desires? How does a seemingly defunct sign remain historically interactive—even amid its archival silencings, colonial interdicts, and transcultural corrosions?

Pictographic Time

De Angulo had some version of these questions in mind with his wish to land the pictograph "in the midst of almost pure form." He explains that "pure form" signifies formal indeterminacy: "in that picture-word meaning is the all important factor, but form is not completely excluded. It is reduced to a minimum, but it is still there. . . . Meaning is very closely associated with chance, while form is not. Meaning demands acrobatic performance, which form, staid form, is seldom ready to produce" ("What" 20, 31). This notion that form works by receding into meaning (which, in turn, gives way to new form, hence to new meaning) derives from the writings of Edward Sapir. While Sapir has been inaccurately associated with an impoverished notion of linguistic relativism or even determinism (i.e., the so-called Sapir-Whorf hypothesis), in fact a notion of "poetic indeterminacy" was central to Sapir's grand theory of language, as poet and anthropologist Paul Friedrich, one of Sapir's great commentators, emphasized. The difference is that Sapir's relativity hypothesis does not refer to language as such, but to *poetic* language: "the poetic potential of language—not logic or basic reference—most massively determines the imagination." Poetic language means the formal, syntactical, metaphoric, and musical twists by which language becomes self-aware. At that moment when the sign as such becomes visible, audible, or otherwise perceptible to its users, poetic form creates what Friedrich calls "parallactic positions" on language use. These are sightlines onto the meaning of meaning making—by which signs become "rhythmically self-conscious" (5, 16–17, 23–28).[1] The deep structure of language—the condition that all languages share—is not deterministic relativism but rather the ability to constantly reformulate what the structure of language is amid its present contexts. This means that, for Sapir and Friedrich (and de Angulo), all language is poetry when it becomes self-aware; and poems wish to be the event of language becoming self-aware.

Pictographic literacy depends on arts of memory and performance, or mnemonics and improvisation, two things that do not typically come to mind when one thinks about how to read. But in making creativity present in the scene of reading, pictographs amplify the eventhood of language, and thus are of particular interest in relation to the idea of the self-awareness of poetry. Despite the consensus, this type of literacy is not archaic, simplistic, preliterate, or incomprehensible. A variety of pictographic literacies are found throughout the Americas, some of which are in use to this day. The first ethnographies of the pictograph—Henry Rowe Schoolcraft's *Information Respecting the History, Condition, and Prospects of the Tribes of the United States* (1851–57) and Garrick Mallery's compendious *Picture-Writing of the American Indians* (1888)—were clear about one thing: they are "signs depicting the chief objects of *stanzas* committed to memory" (Schoolcraft qtd. in Severi's *La Memoria Rituale* 175). The mnemonics of pictography were the subject of studies in the early twentieth century—by Aby Warburg (1923) and Erland Nordenskiöld (1928)—that were particularly interested in the relation between image and memory.[2] That linkage, however, served to exclude a discussion about the *poetics* of the pictograph. The Warburg-influenced Gombrich school transformed pictography into a manner of visual art, "a script for the illiterate" (Gombrich, "Action" 382),[3] "purely conceptual, not narrative" (Frankfort qtd. in Gombrich, *Art* 124). The pictograph is thus taken as synonymous with visual style, a manner of imaging, such as it is described in the writings of image theorists W. J. T. Mitchell (27–31) and Hans Belting (32–33).[4] These conceptions of the pictograph overlook the central importance of poetics that Schoolcraft signaled—with his mention of "*stanzas*"—as key to its meaning making.

One of the principal characteristics of pictographic use is its close association with oral performance—as argued in studies by Nancy Munn (1973), M. Jane Young (1988), Hertha Sweet Wong (1992), Gordon Brotherston (1992), Whitney Davis (1992), Walter Mignolo and Elizabeth Hill Boone (1994), and Carlo Severi (1993, 2012), in addition to the experimental allegorical ethnography edited by Mihnea Mircan and Vincent W.J. van Gerven Oei (2015). This close association between icon and oral performance implies that pictographs have a distinct poetic system. Put simply, the icons are performance prompts for individuals who know what sound and sense each image is meant to elicit. Hill Boone writes, "pictorial histories are closer to being scripts . . . their relation to their readers is closer to being that of a play's script to its actors . . . pictorial histories were read aloud to an audience, they were interpreted, and their images were expanded and embellished in the oration of the full story. The pictorial histories were painted specifically to be the rough text of a performance" (71). Such a description in itself illustrates the fecund workings of pictographic writing. A mnemonic system based on visual cues, it leaves ample room for improvisation to meet the needs of a given moment. Those needs, from which the meaning of a given text typically emerges, themselves emerge from the social relations that come together at the scene of performance. Thus does pictography create semantic resonance between icon, performer, and social context. These metonymic relays—from sign to social atmosphere and back to the sign—have distinct philosophical implications throughout the native Americas.

In the Pueblo context where de Angulo learned about pictography, the link between memory and performance has ecological resonances.[5] In her study of Zuni pictographs, Young describes their cognitional space as an ecological metonymy, or a system in which mnemonics and performance string together not only social contexts but also the other-than-human world in which performances take place (see fig. 3). That is, because a pictograph does not act as isomorphic link between a sound and alphabetical letter (or, for that matter, a concept and ideogram)—but instead acts as a mnemonic cue that prompts remembered, flexible textual wholes existing off the page—the experience of the narrative spreads into a local environment through visual associations between the pictograph, rock art, pottery, fetishes, dances, and even natural features of the landscape and its nonhuman inhabitants. She describes this braid of diffuse associations, stringing together abstract and salient entities, as a kind of metonymy—the trope in which concrete figures transit to more abstract domains (159–73, 185).[6] Like metonyms, or the trope that circles from a sign to an atmosphere and back to a sign, pictographs loop together visual, mnemonic, interpersonal, and environmental factors into a text of shifting texture. That is, this is a special type of metonymy in that it does not disperse into abstraction. It weaves back into its text the visual, mnemonic, social, and environmental threads working as

FIGURE 3 Pictographs from Newspaper Rock State Historic Monument, Utah (present day). Photograph: Jim Unterschultz, Wikimedia Commons.

interdependent agents. While the reader of a pictographic text can refabricate the text—changing it in response to the shifting social pressures of a new performance, new rhetorical network, or new cultural and physical landscape—those objects, networks, and landscapes also thread back into the pictographic meaning, shaping it and its reader in accord with *their* needs and desires.[7] In this way, pictographs are vehicles of poetic indeterminacy and contextual metamorphosis.

If such metonymic entities lurk in de Angulo's pictographic form, then his translation of death into arrowed deictics—"land/of death without eyes/but arrows//(wind in the lanes/breeze in the alamedas)" (plate 1)—appears all the more self-aware about its semiotic specificity. The "arrows" paraphrastically turned into "wind" and "breeze" literalize metonymic dispatch: the poem moves from icon to environment, from the arrow on the page to the coursing realities beyond the page's margins. Those coursing realities in turn give the sign a sense of poetic indeterminacy, a breezy freedom in the winds and alamedas of the world. But for the poem to have that indeterminacy, it must move through the determinate threshold of pictographic metonymy (i.e., the sign creates the mediation by which it is creative and indeterminate). So we have a redoubled circularity, which Young calls the "dynamic ambiguity" of pictographs (154), but which I specify as a relationality that is generated by, and generates, its ongoingness. Each pictograph bears the marks of both memory and imagination, compressing time into the event of reading while these mnemonic and creative cues express new possible relations. Time is compressed into the event of recitation that, mediated by the sign's creative function, opens time to new enunciations, contacts, and relations.

This circular trope, wending ongoingness through the weft of the social relation, is the subject of the book's second chapter, which reads de Angulo's poems alongside the pictographic poems of the Acoma Pueblo poet Simon Ortiz's *Spiral Lands*. Ortiz calls the ongoing relationality of native poetry an "active relationship" between speakers and contexts, as well as between speakers and language as such: Puebloan poetics elicits the "sacred nature of language, [when] you realize that you are part of it and it is part of you, and you are not necessarily in control of it, and that if you do control some of it, it is not in your exclusive control" (*Song* 6). Ortiz characterizes language as an active agent in poetry and thus complicates the act of worlding that the first chapter attributes to the temporal structure of a poem's form.

As Ortiz sees it, a poem's capacity to subsume experience is self-emergent. In having language itself effloresce the relational network of the pictograph, Ortiz extends the relational agency of the pictograph still further to nonhumans. He provides thus a ground from which to study interspecies kinship as a poetics, as an instance of signs becoming self-aware. For de Angulo, the social form of poetic speech was similarly nonhuman. "It is necessary to lose one's own humanhood," he writes (*Reader* xiv), and wishes "that the earth would constantly return" (Duncan, *Poet's Mind* 236), while expecting that the metonymic relays of pictographic speech would enact such recursive "return" of nonhuman agency: "the psychic life of the community is like an immense sluggish stream, a procession of trees, of animals, of stones, none of them quite clear from the others, but rather here the claws of an eagle, and there the green leaf of a tree; here a human face, there something going like a puff of wind" (*Coyote's* 47–48). Yet when relations are reconfigured in the interspecies kinship of the pictograph, the racial line that separates Ortiz and de Angulo is blurrier, if not also noisier. The noisiness of racial difference rises from an impoverished wish: while we might wish to refute the ontological premises of race, its force in structuring social realities prevents us from doing so. Still, we might find a less impoverished position if we affirmed, in tandem with critiques of racialization, ontologies that alienate race. When a poetics of kinship blurs the hierarchical distinctions of qualified life and unqualified nonlife, this poetics alienates—if provisionally, yet powerfully—the biopolitical tiers on which racial lines are drawn.[8]

The question of how pictographs frame social, legal, political, and ontological mediations continues into the third chapter, which explores

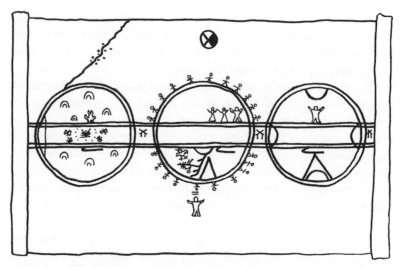

FIGURE 4 John Borrows, "Scroll One: Daebaujimoot." Pictograph from his *Drawing Out Law: A Spirit's Guide* (2010), p. 3, © University of Toronto Press. Reprinted with permission of the publisher. Courtesy of John Borrows.

the work of three Anishinaabe writers: poet, novelist, and scholar Gerald Vizenor, Canadian legal scholar John Borrows, and poet and novelist Louise Erdrich. For these Anishinaabe writers, the pictograph helps to contest the juridical grounds of native dispossession. In theorizing Vizenor's authorship of the Constitution of the White Earth Nation in 2007–8 to be coextensive with his creative uses of pictographic amphiboly, this chapter develops the political resonances of pictography beyond—as de Angulo has it—indeterminacy. Related more closely to legal multiperspectivalism, Vizenor's uses of pictography resound with those of Borrows. In his *Canada's Indigenous Constitution* (2010), Borrows advocates for a multijuridical legal culture, in which forms of indigenous counsel and council are recognized as jurisprudentially legitimate. As a way of creating that multijuridical culture, his book of legal case studies, *Drawing Out Law* (2010), uses pictographs to articulate law as a locus of shifting contexts and perspectives (fig. 4). His underlying claim is that pictographic indeterminacy can consolidate public spheres and political communities with special ability to adjust over time, to meet present social pressures, and to negotiate "inter-societal" collaboration. The way in which pictography changes the meaning of community into a site of contextual and collaborative meaning making is a conceptual thread that weaves the present book more deeply into a study of intersubjective voicing. Erdrich's book of pictographic council, *Books and Islands in Ojibwe*

Country ([2003] 2014), discloses how such voicing involves nonhuman participants, directing attention to the biotic relational circuitry of the petroglyphs and lichenoglyphs of the islands of Lake of the Woods between Minnesota and Ontario. In this way, she reveals how pictographic reading is a means of, as Borrows puts it, "provid[ing] guidance about how to theorize, practice, and order our association with the earth, and [it does] so in a way [that] produces answers that are very different from those found in other sources" (qtd. in Pomedli 227–8).

Also engaged with theories of native constitutionalism in Edmund Burke, Lisa Brooks, Seyla Benhabib, and Elizabeth Povinelli, this chapter examines uses of Anishinaabe pictography in contemporary legal contexts, challenging the notion that the law must necessarily inhere in alphabetical isomorphism, let alone in the colonialist inscriptive norms of the nation-state. Explaining how pictography elicits a loosened relation between sign and signified, this chapter further develops a semiotic theory of non-isomorphy to analyze uses of pictography in Borrows's advocacy of jurisgenerative multiperspectivalism; in Vizenor's conception of social irony and ironic constitutionalism; and in Erdrich's figuration of ecological literacy and reciprocity. Offering the pictographic metonym a jurisgenerative valence, this chapter shows how the perspectival shifts of pictographic metonymy change the law and offer colonial legalities new entanglements on which to trip themselves up.

To see the pictograph affecting jurisgenerative practices requires a different conceptual framework from the one in which pictography is typically seen. Whereas the pictograph has been seen as a strictly archival object with attenuated potential, whose fragmented condition at best expresses colonial superordination, its continued creative effects necessitate some reckoning. It prompts us to ask how the historical fragment might scale itself into totalizable experiences of history. These effects are more than reparative. They carry the possibility for the creation of comprehensive worlds and the contradiction of worlds. Always marked by the history that rendered it a fragment, the pictograph nonetheless arrives with a kind of totalizability that can organize its fragmentary origins. To conceptualize such a totalizable fragment, this book builds on Samuel Weber's masterful illumination of Benjamin's theory of the suffix of possibility, "-able" and "-ability." The totalizable fragment does not propose a universalized totality. Rather, it suggests that the fragment has movement within it, a tendency to mediation that involves not only past moving into present but the expectation of future difference as well. It is not only self-aware, it is aware of its past from a future to come— a "transient efflorescence" from the confident perspective of a future secured.

Totalizable Fragments

The fragment that can scale into a world enlivens its biographical and historical contexts as transitions mediated by the fragment. De Angulo was an exile anarchist; like García Lorca, he was of the generation of leftist Spain that resisted the global expansion of fascism in the early twentieth century. As Benedict Anderson notes, one of the tenets of that transnational resistance was to look to indigenous cultures for groundswell against what de Angulo called "RECAPIM (the REactionary CApitalist IMperialist complex)" (G. de Angulo 369).[9] In García Lorca's poetry, that groundswell of resistance taps into the social ecology of *cante jondo*, a type of impassioned voicing with historical origination in Arab Andalusia. In de Angulo's works, it is sourced from the pictography of the US Southwest. He arrived at that source by way of a labyrinthine path that spans the Americas: on arriving from Europe in 1905, he was first a rodeo cowboy on the North American Plains, then a prison guard in British Honduras, a firefighter in San Francisco, a medical doctor and psychologist for the US Army, a fruit fly researcher at Stanford University, and a rancher in the Big Sur mountain range. In these movements he studied languages and linguistics, including Mandarin Chinese, Otomi, Chiapanec, Zapotec, Taos, and a dozen native Californian languages. He also studied ethnomusicology, recording and transcribing indigenous songs, and in the process demonstrating a preference for the music, language, and culture of the Achumawi or Pit River tribe of northeastern California. Like Lévi-Strauss, his aesthetic sensibility made him magnetic to artists and scholars alike: Alfred Kroeber introduced him to the nascent anthropological milieu gathered around Franz Boas, Paul Radin, Edward Sapir, and Ruth Benedict; Pomo basketweaver and storyteller William Ralganal Benson introduced him to the cosmologies of native California, as did Tony Luhan to the ceremonial societies of New Mexico's Pueblos; and through the bohemian world of the San Francisco Bay Area, he became a correspondent and collaborator with Robinson Jeffers, Jean Varda, Harry Partch, Henry Cowell, Henry Miller, Carl Jung, Ezra Pound, Marianne Moore, William Carlos Williams, and Blaise Cendrars, as well as an instructor in linguistics and folklore to Robert Duncan and Jack Spicer.[10] Yet, unlike Lévi-Strauss, de Angulo resisted the notion that such intercultural encounters were trapped "in a circle from which there was no escape" (*Tristes* 43). While most of his publications in the 1920s and 1930s were technical, focusing on language morphology, at the end of his life he tried something different. In 1948–50, as he was treated for the cancer that killed him, in a large-scale pictographic project of story, song, and ethnography that he called *Old Time Stories* he directed his energy to the notion that the world was "a parabola going out to no center . . . mercurial with coexisting possible universes" (Duncan, *Poet's Mind* 234). In such a world of multidirectional absorptions and illuminations, there were no foregone *tropiques* to lament; native cultures framed the very contexts in which they appeared, and thus they resisted and reframed the normative categories of racial nationalism by which they were suppressed.

This postwar project—the core of the archive held in special collections at UCLA—was multisubsumptive in the fullest sense: stacks of ethnographic notes, scores of indigenous songs, stories, and animal myths interspersed with drawings or (as he suggested) pictographs, and his own poems were all performed in a series of Berkeley-area evening radio broadcasts. This project aimed to shift thought away from the midcentury climate of nationalist xenophobia and toward intercultural collaboration. He wrote to Pound:

> Nothing has exasperated me more than the romanticism of the Indian, the Hiawatha and Chief-Bull-Sits-in-His-Pants sort of stuff. . . . I welcomed this opportunity to show the children (i have always been in love with the little sons-of-bitches) what *real* Indians were like, how unromantic, how realistic, how tolerant. i never cud make the anthropological world accept my thesis that so-called primitive man had as much logic as we, only did not choose to employ logic all the time (after all, the meta-logical thinking is as *valid* as the logical) maybe i cud put it in a book in the guise of children's stories and it amused the cynical and bitter part of me to think that i wud be fooling them, the damned pious Christians . . . here i wud be preaching agnosticism to their children, right under their noses, and the children wud laugh with Oriole at Foxboy when he wails at the lack of consistency in the Creation stories . . . What better way to teach a child religious tolerance . . . and by God, it worked! (qtd. in G. de Angulo 423–24)

As he says, the broadcasts were well received, rebroadcast by popular demand when his cancer prevented him from making new shows. Through the efforts of Pound and Marianne Moore, they were then published posthumously as the bestselling and still-in-print *Indian Tales*. But it is a heavily edited work. The stories are redacted and simplified, de Angulo's idiosyncratic phonetic spelling is normalized, most of the ethnographic details and indigenous-language songs are removed (excised, as it were, to an invisible archive), what few pictographs are included are framed as illustrations (rather than as the metonymic speech prompts that they are), and its live texture as a radio soundscape is altogether lacking.

These shortcomings alone merit the reconsideration of the work in its full form that I provide in the second chapter.[11] But the most trenchant missing element is the presence of the poet, whose effort to produce a pictographic prosimetric narrative about animal transformations was strangely actualized in his physical body.

With surprising literality, de Angulo became an instance of pictographic metamorphosis. The hormone therapy that he received for his cancer gave him an intersexual body, a physicality that he relished for its sexual radicalism. Duncan, who was his typist and live-in nurse in these years, remembers seeing de Angulo—who called this intersex self "Orlando," after Virginia Woolf's transtemporal transgender protagonist—stripped to the waist, "and he had female breasts, of course . . . he had become a hermaphrodite in that sense. Another aspect of Jaime was that he was also a transvestite . . . and Jaime's transvestite was a male lesbian" (*Poet's Mind* 234).[12] The poems that he writes about his transition riff on what anthropologist Carlo Severi, in his study of pictographic performance, calls the "complex" and "chimerical" body of the performer (*Chimera* 207, 281). Severi's point is that the ecological metonymy of pictographs attaches to the person who strings together the images, references, contexts, and environmental associations. Because these elements are always changing, they give a sense of transformation to their speaker: the "metamorphoses of the locutor," as Severi puts it, take place in the eyes of their audience (*Chimera* 199, 222–26). And in de Angulo's case, the metamorphosis was more than perceptual. His poems of this period—discussed in chapter 2—lay bare the pained genitalia, night sweats, and somatic discomfort of actual sexual transformation, and thus give a heightened sense of wounding to the metamorphoses of the pictographic locutor. While de Angulo's masquerading as Woolf's hero carries sure signs of idealization, who could deny such signal dreams to a person experiencing their body's anomalousness? The anomaly is a concept Gilles Deleuze and Félix Guattari developed in thinking about transformation as a scene of crossed borders. As such, transformation is a phenomenon of "bordering," bringing attention to the intensity of holding in one's body the possibility of other bodies (243–45). This possibility rearranges the relation between real and symbolic states: rather than forming an opposition, the real and symbolic are mutual aspects of a process of virtualization—which does not mean the dispatch into abstraction, but rather the connection between material things and their possible forms. A material thing is not a closed circle. It is precarious, dangerous, and intense because of its communicability with other things, bodies, and states. The pictographic locutor is as exposed to this as anyone else. But, in the particular framework of pictography, the resonances of anomaly take on a special meaning.

In his work on Benjamin's odd tendency toward nominalization using "the German suffix *-bar*, which in English would have to be translated as -able (or -ible)"—"Criticizability," "Translatability," "Citability," "Reproducibility," "Recognizability," and "Impartability"—Weber distinguishes Deleuze's conception of the virtual from Benjamin's. If Deleuze "describes 'structure as the reality of the virtual,' one could say that Benjamin construes the virtual as the reality of structure—here [in such nominalizations], that of the concept" (39). Benjamin's use of the suffix specified that concepts and their names carry their possible realization inside them. Because this possible realization is always an instance of becoming something else, concepts and their names each come with "incommensurable, unique infinitude." For Benjamin, the linguistic fragment is not spoken "through," it is spoken "in," "or more precisely: each language imparts itself *in* itself, it is in the purest sense the 'medium' of imparting" (Benjamin qtd. in Weber 41). If each piece of language is the domain within which it imparts its meaning, then each such imparting is a world designating itself. In the world of de Angulo's pictographs, the changed body of sexual metamorphosis (as well as its physical porousness to cancer) imparts its meaning within the "pure form" of the pictograph, which is to say within its "formal indeterminacy," or what de Angulo elsewhere called "the algebraic expression of a curve." Duncan recalls:

> Jaime, when he was dying, wanted more and more to tell about what he thought was the reality that was going to be there when he died. And he said he understood what it was the Indians were talking about. The model could be found in contemporary physics. Jaime would draw a parabola that went out into endless space, and say this is it: "I pass into this, and go back into the universe . . . there's no center, there's no center in the universe," he said, "get it out of your head." (*Poet's Mind* 230, 234)

With his head bent toward death, de Angulo was recalcitrant in his anarchism. There is no center on which to mount the transcendent ego, only parabolas imparting their totalizability among humans, nonhumans, and the nonliving material phenomena of multiple spiraling cosmic orders. Inasmuch as these totalizabilities impart in the fragments of language, their pictographic figuration gives language a means by which to scale itself into the experience of decenterings, parabolas, and indeterminacy. Pictographic metonymy is a field of possible incommensurabilities mediated in pictographic metonymy.

When it is used to disturb social norms, such incommensurability can be described as *unnatural*, inasmuch as such signs as pictographs, petroglyphs, hieroglyphs, and khipu have indeed served to signal-jam the dominant, apparently natural social semantics of gender, race, kinship, life, world, humanity, and identity. Unnatural signs are signs that introject creative thresholds in seemingly ineluctable causal relations. They make cusps out of boundaries and jostle contingency into the infallibly true. They are instances of what Sanjinés calls "embers of the past" thrown into the present. Drawing on Benjamin's political theory alongside Aymara and Quechua philosophy, Sanjinés points to the heterogeneous temporality in his own critical method, which is a compound of critique in modernity (Benjamin) and coloniality (indigenous studies). In each of these critical traditions, racialized time is the source of social domination. Time is therefore the domain to disrupt. And Sanjinés does that by threading the parallels between Benjamin and the Andes.[13] In this way, he sets fire to the staid conceptions of historical progress by which imperial violence is rationalized.

Along those lines, my own experience of the materials in this book began with its hemispheric sources, which taught me how and why to read Benjamin. Positioned in the ellipses of what fellow Central American literary scholar Arturo Arias characterizes as the double-eccentricity of Central American Americans—alienated in a US racial hierarchy as Latinos, yet also alienated from Latinidad as non-Mexicans and non–Puerto Ricans—my work emerged as a wish to understand how the inheritances of this predominantly indigenous region inflect themselves in contemporary "cultural remittances" that seek to understand historical origination in spite of many layers of enforced blockage (xii–xv). As Benjamin would say, what is happening with migration from US war zones in Central America is *illuminated* by the vying histories of domination, suppression, and subversion embedded in a sense of a Central American past and present. Benjamin's concept of "illuminations" is a touchstone for his ideas about how language can carry multiple worlds or temporal densities, to which Sanjinés gives political fire in his translation of "illuminations" as "embers." But such elements of redemption are subtly present in Benjamin as well, who sourced his idea of "illuminations" from rabbinical literature on messianic time. In Germany in the 1920s and 1930s, to write about the "angel of history" was to break with racialized conceptions of the progressive rationalist time of the state and to introduce animating principles of heterogeneity and contingency into the process of historical unfolding (*Selected* 4:392). The illuminating angel is a signal-jam in the index of nature; it is an unnatural being by whose presence the meaning of being is recast.

Unnatural signs are of a piece with what Mignolo calls "languaging": a conception of creative language as a rupture to imperial cultural norms. The strangeness of the neologism "languaging" is in itself instructive because it gives a sense of eccentricity to the Argentine semiotician's point that a sign is nothing other than its use, and that its use can be a tactic for being and belonging in the strangeness of transcultural encounters: "languaging [is] thinking and writing between languages . . . moving away from the idea that language is a fact (e.g. a system of syntactic, semantic, and phonetic rules), and moving toward the idea that speech and writing are strategies for orienting and manipulating social domains of interaction" (*Local* 226). Any creative use of signs depends on the designative structures it sets out to disrupt; therefore, "languaging" refers to the disruption as well as the situation that made the disruption necessary. To rework Benjamin's angel of history, the angel of language in the Americas does not escape history. Rather, it elicits breaches in the temporal contradictions of historical experience. Similarly, in the present book, such a term as "pictograph" refers to the struggle for meaning that obtains around such a sign as the pictograph, capturing the formalist, ideological, and critical-theoretical discourses that these signs bear: formalist, in that these signs convey themselves *in* distinct patterns of expression and perception; ideological, in that these patterns complexly intertwine *in* the imperialist apparatuses by which they circulate; and critical-theoretical, in that this threading of reality *in* signs makes possible the project of unthreading and rethreading totalizability—the project called decolonizing poetics.

In the fourth chapter, I relate that project to Mayan hieroglyphs, with special attention to how their formal features integrate the temporal contradictions of decoloniality. It tells the story of how poets Charles Olson and Alurista each studied Mayan glyphs, finding in them a means to integrate political contradiction in a Mayan philosophy of parallelism. The philosophy of parallelism associated with the glyphs is called *kajulew* in K'iche' Mayan, which anthropologist Dennis Tedlock translates as "mythistory," or the interpenetration of mythic and historical times. As he and others have pointed out, that interpenetration does not resolve into synthesis. Mesoamerican mythistory is like a weaving with intersecting threads, in which the threads of mythic and historical times depend on one another but produce no unifying third position by which to resolve antinomies or contradictions (Leon-Portilla, *Aztec*; Tedlock, "Toward" 185–86; Hull and Carrasco; Maffie 143, 156–57, 168). The threads are suspended in a state of complementary intensification. Olson's and Alurista's encounters with the glyphs are tangents in a nonsynthesizing dialectic that is designed, as Tedlock describes it, "to find the traces of divine movements in our own actions . . . [and remain] always alert to the reassertion of the patterns of the past in present events" (*Popol Vuh* 58–60). With temporal heterogeneity spread like a braided mat around them, Olson and Alurista—partially moving in Mayan time, partially in the circuits of American empire—enact the diversity of movement by which Mayan time performs its dynamism. They demonstrate that Mayan time has movement within it, movement by which the calamity of the conquest is recontextualized as a continuity of Mesoamerican worlds.[14]

A prevalent misconception about Olson's understanding of Mayan signs is that it smuggled conceptions of natural language (McCaffery 45–57; Billitteri 115–87; Mackey 128). The argument is that—like Pound with Fenollosa's ideogram (see Bush and Benn Michaels) or the philosopher Cratylus with his "natural correctness of names" (Sedley 18), or, for that matter, Vachel Lindsay and Sergei Eisenstein on Mexican and Egyptian hieroglyphs (Hansen, *Babel* 93)—Olson conflated surface with meaning. This is simply not the case. A closer analysis of his prosimetric ethnography *Mayan Letters* (in addition to portions redacted from the final publication) reveals that Olson's semiotic prosody of the glyphs was one of "conjunction and displacement" (66–67). In his poetics of identity in difference, incommensurable parts do not synthesize but instead remain in constant alternation and intensification—in keeping with Mayan poetics of complementary duality, which this chapter distills from the words of the Mayan daykeeper or diviner Andrés Xiloj Peruch. Quite the opposite of self-evident iconicity, the glyphs give to Olson's poetry a sense of lingering in the thresholds of difference, where figures carry traces of discontinuity and polyphony, and not fixed transcendental identity.[15] (See figs. 5 and 6.) I am helped in my analysis by Tedlock's many writings—but especially his posthumously published *Olson Codex*, a book that situates Olson in the Mayan cosmos through which he moves and extends from Mexico to Black Mountain College in North Carolina. Tracing formal resemblances in the pedagogy at Black Mountain, I find these Mayan dialectics in the crashing limens of Cy Twombly's *Poems to the Sea*, a series that blurs the line between writing and painting while keeping each element discontinuous from the other. While art historians have tended to focus on what Roland Barthes called the "ductus" or visible chirography of Twombly's paintings ("Cy"), I focus on their intermedial syntax to describe their relation to the temporal tensioning of visual, syntactic, and phonetic elements in Mayan writing.

With regard to Alurista, whereas studies of his poetry have focused on problematics of identity in set racial categories (Bruce-Novoa, *Chicano Poetry* 69–95; Klor de Alva, "California"; Pérez-Torres 180; Arteaga), this chapter argues that Alurista's bilingualism does not toggle simply

FIGURE 5 *The Mayan Dresden Codex*, the oldest surviving book of the Americas (ca. thirteenth century). In the lower right of one page is a scene of ritual sacrifice and offering that Charles Olson translates as his "fish-glyph." Photograph: © SLUB Dresden/Deutsche Fotothek/Henrik Ahlers.

between English and Spanish idiolects—that is, between the indices of Anglo and Latino identity; it also calls on a hieroglyphic iconicity to break norms of identity formation. In *Spik in Glyph?* (1981), the words of poems are broken into floating letters whose assemblage in loose syntactical units shores up the contingency of the racial signifier "spic." This is the non-isomorphism of Mayan parallelism applied to the concept of race. In making race syntactically discontinuous with itself—an instance of irruptive "spikking" or languaging—Alurista draws out the frangibility of race thinking and translates the fragments of racial embodiment into a stutter-like performance: "wood u nut/rather/b/bean, being? be in/born than b/dye/in, ing? ang/s/t, angst?" (17). This performance

FIGURE 6 Charles Olson's tracing (1951) of what he considered *the* prototypical glyph of the *Mayan Dresden Codex*. Works by Charles Olson published during his lifetime are held in copyright by the Estate of Charles Olson; previously unpublished work are copyright of the University of Connecticut. Used with permission. Photograph: Archives and Special Collections, University of Connecticut Library.

disarticulates identity, breaks it into self-negation, a kind of identity in nonidentity, whose philosophical model was the Mayan glyph.

Hemispheric Negativity

The most striking realization of a sign's ongoingness is its ability to account for its own loss, to prefigure and manage the meanings of its negativization, to bear negativizability. There are traces of this in de Angulo's poetry. His radio program, *Old Time Stories*, takes place in a world of animals becoming other animals, where human personhood disappears into the becomings of nonhuman others. He dramatizes his entry into that world in a hybrid letter-poem announcing his cancer, whose addressee has a sense of impossibility to it. "To all my friends," it begins, calling together a group that can only cohere in the imagination. The virtuality of all of his friends is suspended over the chasm of the situation: the poet is set to disappear into the "serene" atmosphere of a poem (fig. 7). In his theorization of apostrophe, Jonathan Culler encourages readers to be clear about its basic impossibility: the "most radical, embarrassing, pretentious, and mystificatory" trope in poetry is the one in which the poet pretends to talk to an absent being or thing, human or nonhuman

```
                                                        2    II

     berkeley 16 july

to all my friends who have writn and sent me books and socks, and most of all
their love which so warmed the cockles of my heart: THANK YOU, thank you, i hav
just com back home and i am going to answer EVERYBODY
                                                    so, they tuk me to the
hospital in an ambulance, sum ten dayz ago--but they did not do much to me at the
hosp....only a litl torture just tu keep me in gud training....by the way, that
Fort Miley Veterans Hospital is the most wonderful i hav ever seen....a cheerful
place, everybody nice and cooperating, no red-tape, very gud food, and the consul-
ting physicians and surgeons are men eminent in the profession........but the
best of hospitals is no place for me who am in a hell of a hurry to finish my
manuscript and put everything in order before i die.....bekoz death iz around the
corner, no kidding...the doctors laff ar me and say "want to take a bet you'll se
next Xmas ?" but that wud be a stupid bet: how wud i collect it ?
     so here i am back, in my room, with the wonderful view of San Francisco Bay
and all my papers are spread on the bed, and my right leg is so swollen that it
looks like those cases of elephantiasis, but i still can take a few steps to the
bath-room    there iz nothing that can be done....for sum reazun the boring thru
the prostate wont heal, it keeps on bleeding, blood regurgitates back into bladde:
then blood clots stop the catheter, so i hav to take the catheter out and put a
new one in....Nancy and i hav become adepts at it, but poor girl is getting worn
out waiting on me, nursing, feeding....what a darling patient thing she is

          i dont suffer TOO MUCH acute pain...at least i keep most of it do
          with narcotics....wel, that's the story....thank you all, dahling
          i wil soon answer everyone

               but honestly, i am geting a litl bit fed up with life
               i'd like to go...as soon as i get all these thingz in
               order.....i hate messes
                                       LOVE YOU ALL
she came into my dream
tall and young with hair of gold and glaucous eyes            j
and made love to me
boldly

thank you my dear thank you
but why make love to an old man why

i am Death she said smiling
who waited for you these many years
and now i will take you to my home among the swinging stars
where the swirling atoms dance in sarabands
where there is no time no space no joy no pain
only that which is
serene......come, my love

tall and young with hair of gold and glaucous eyes
```

FIGURE 7 Jaime de Angulo, manuscript (1950). Jaime de Angulo Papers (MS 14), Special Collections and Archives, University Library, University of California, Santa Cruz.

(*Pursuit* 151). In an apostrophe the poet calls on the sentience of objects, implying that they live in a world in which signs are not abstracted from things in the world but interfused with them (149–71). Still, if apostrophe makes nothing appear, its actions capture objects in impossibility actualized: in apostrophe things are in negative relation to themselves, virtual but completely absorbed in their virtuality. In the self-elegy of de Angulo's letter-poem, this virtual negative is imagined to be coextensive with the poet's reality, coursing through the spirals in the page's margins into the disappearance of the poet from life. Likewise, the poem's figuration of death recalls the poet's figures for ecological metonymy: parabolas, swirls, and swinging stars. In these efforts, de Angulo wishes to capture the meaning of his self's own loss, to be a bearer of negativizability.

Negative circumstances become an aspect of efforts of negativizability, but that does not mean that they then go away. Death prompts de Angulo's effort to experience the negative as a source of possibility, or impossibility virtualized, but that does not stop him from dying. In a similar way, such negativization happens to signs when they change into other signs, disappearing in the material instability of linguistic change. When signs change into other signs—in workaday transformations, transcultural corrosions, or violent interdicts—signs also get lost, disarticulated, disappeared, and destroyed. That the destruction of signs and their communicable rhythms supports a people's domination is a truism of empire. The concept of a totalizable fragment necessitates itself because the archives of the Americas are fragmented in strategies of occlusion and elimination. The fragments are a trace of what was not meant to survive. But they did, and today they bear a survivance that tracks multiple temporal densities at once. In his prolegomenon to *The Origin of German Tragic Drama*—a comparable attempt to capture the historical experience of a world apparently foregone and "esoteric" in its temporal ruination (Germany in its baroque throes following the Thirty Years' War)—Benjamin affirms that "these ideas can still survive . . . even if [their] exemplary character can be admitted only in respect of the merest fragment." Benjamin makes no attempt to deny the "murky," "imperfect and incomplete" condition of the historical archive. On the contrary, its fragmentary quality fires his insights on how its "process of becoming" is coextensive with its "disappearance": "Origin is an eddy in the stream of becoming, and in its current swallows the material involved in the process of genesis" (42–46). Weber glosses this passage as an example of Benjamin's valorization of the unfulfilled, his so-called dialectic at a standstill—another instance of Benjamin finding potentialities held in "a complementary if conflictual interplay of becoming and passing-away" (134–36). That reading describes the breach but does not reckon with the breaking point. Once again, the signs of the Americas prefigure and adjust Benjamin: in various practices of resistance to colonial super-ordination, this breaking point (when a sign is in a state of emergency, bent toward elimination) has been captured as a source of possibility. This capture does not make colonial negativity go away; it catches it to introject emergence into disappearance, origination into fragmentation.

On that note, the fifth chapter of this book investigates what anthro-pologist Michael Taussig has called "the death space of signification," or the act of language that "challenges the unity of the symbol, the tran-scendent totalization binding the image to that which it represents" (*Sha-manism* 298). Taussig refers to linguistic practices that he saw in the Co-lombian Amazon in the 1970s and 1980s, where shamans were tasked with healing people who were suffering from the violence and terror of the rubber extraction business. Existentially threatened by neocolonial governance, the shamans ritualized erasure and negativization to break apart the dominant symbols of that governance, interpolating in the gaps of these signifiers new concretions of space, time, being, and belonging. Taussig's "death space" refers both to the state of emergency in which these shamans worked their magic and the magical practices of erasure, cancellation, blanking, and gapping by which they made that emergency into scenes of emergence. This is a contextual conception of shamanism, actively involved in shaping historical experience. But it also proposes that shamanism is a set of linguistic practices that depend on the pliabil-ity of signs. Pushing into that pliability, this chapter examines the lateral movement of shamanic technique across neoliberal borderlands into the writings of Gloria Anzaldúa and William Burroughs, two writers whose signal methods of cutting and canceling text were derived from encoun-ters with folk healing. The comparison of this apparently incompatible pair is meant to further problematize our reception of authors who carry different positions and temporal densities but encounter comparable challenges in the same set of linguistic techniques. In Burroughs's *Yage Letters*, his cut-up technique emerges from the same emergency in the Amazon that Taussig describes, only a couple of decades earlier. In Anzal-dúa's "Coatlicue State," the states of emergency that irrupt in the racial-ized US-Mexico borderlands lead to her practices of self-disarticulation (*Borderlands*); the colonial signifiers that she embodies require the de-rangement and destruction by which a body might break itself apart and congeal some selfhood beside the colonial self.

Such a reading reframes Anzaldúa's field-defining mestiza intersec-tionality as a position not of identity formation but of identity deforma-tion. This reading aligns with recent scholarship that takes stock of the thematic messiness of her archive to revisit her position in postcolonial feminist historiography (Bost; Keating). The Anzaldúa of the archive is rangy in ways that the paradigm of intersectional identity alone does not showcase. For the present book, the slipstream of the Anzaldúa "that thematizes urban dwelling, spirituality, science fiction, shape-shifting, illness . . . spirits, animism, sickness, diabetes, computer technology, gravity, and archival environments . . . her labor, her writing process, her filing system, even her computer and printer" is of principal interest (Bost 626–27). Yet one need not preclude the other. Anzaldúa prompts readers to ask: what can the discourse of intersectional subjectivization learn from negative poetics and vice versa? What happens to this discourse when cast in the light of a poetic technique that disconnects, deranges, and destroys in order to capture political negativizability?

Khipu Time

The sixth and final chapter of this book delves still deeper into the present worlds of absence, investigating a sign without significations, a semiotics without semantics. Khipu or quipu, the yet undeciphered Andean writing consisting of knots in a series of strings, presents a special case study of a sign system with a tangible aesthetic framework but without a Rosetta Stone, as it were, to crack open the meaning in the form (see plate 9). Logical analyses of the knots have concluded that they are arranged in a binary code akin to computing sequences (M. Ascher and R. Ascher); that this system—built of knots of varying types, shapes, and sizes, sequenced in colored patterns on strings of varying length pendant from a primary code—has numeric, syntactic, and semantic aspects; and that these aspects conveyed a wide range of information. Brotherston writes that the khipu was used for "mathematics, calendar, liturgy, narrative, and even spatial mapping," that "by means of the quipu, messages were sent to and from the capital specifying date and address . . . and a continuous check was kept on such tiny details as individual absences from work, the offspring of a llama, and the last stick of firewood." Evidently the colonial proscription on khipu was motivated by the "fact that the enormous empire of Tahuantinsuyu [the Inca] was minutely regulated and described by this medium" (*Book* 77) (see fig. 8).

In spite of the interdict, the aesthetics of the medium remained so embedded in Andean cultures that scholars have recomposed the indigenous media concept of khipu, called *quilca*, which is specifically tactile: "identifiable," Galen Brokaw states, "in terms of the materiality of the media" ("Semiotics" 175). Khipu was a writing system defined in the tactility of its vehicle, the cords and knots shifting between a reader's fingers. Yet, while such scholarly reconstruction has made available the

FIGURE 8 Depiction of a *Quipucamayoc* or "Khipu reader" in Quechua noble-man Felipe Guamán Poma de Ayala's *Corónica* (ca. 1615). Compare with Vicuña's performed poetry of interwoven khipu sociality (plate 10).

aesthetics and semiotics of khipu, the fact is that the knots remain undeciphered. Nobody today can read the knotted writings of Tahuantinsuyu. Still, the negativized knots of the Incas have been anything but a
blank in contemporary poetry and arts. Their poetics of tactility hold a
prominent place in the Chilean poet Cecilia Vicuña's multimedia "metaphors in space" (*Saborami* 165): her installations, sculptures, weavings,
and performances that thread audiences in the aesthetic tactility of khipu
(see plate 10). The question is: how, then, does this sign work its effects
across the deeply cutting interdict? How is a semiotics without semantics effective?

Vicuña's use of khipu erodes the conceptual hierarchy that separates
materials from meaning, earth from world, signs from their significations. Her works bear a poetic form that confronts colonial erasure with
the very materials that have endured that erasure: "the quipu that remembers nothing, an empty cord/the heart of memory," she writes, "[is]
the earth listening to us. . . . Piercing earth and sky/the sign begins/to
write from below, seeing the efface" (*QUIPOem* q.8–12). To be sure, the
concept of an *unnatural* sign exhausts itself here, asking that the present
book revalue itself in light of a poet whose "unnatural" significations are
enmeshed in the natural materials of the signs. Relating Vicuña's khipu
to Paul Ricoeur's concept of anamnesis—or the necessity of forgetting in
order to experience remembrance—this chapter argues that the absences
of the colonial archive intensify, rather than diminish, the affective economies of memory. The dominant trope for this concept is analepsis, the
tropological inverse of metalepsis: unlike metalepsis, which connects
abstract and salient entities, in analepsis that connective tissue has been
lost and, therefore, must be imaginatively created. The immediate context for such retroprojective re-creation was Vicuña's exile from Chile
after the capitalist coup of 1973, a time in which "politically, magically,
and aesthetically [she wished] to make an object every day in support of
the chilean revolutionary process" (*Saborami* 12). Naturally, the values
that she attributes to this process are opposed to capitalism: nonindivid-
uation, amorphous collectivity, selfless disinterest, and an ecologically
rooted version of materialism. Yet to develop such values, she must confront the erasures, spatial alienations, and temporal distances that capitalism perpetuates in the ideology of the free market. In that absencing
and distance is the analeptic intensification of her khipu creativity. Amid
the forceful silencing of the colonial-cum-capitalist archive, her most
revolutionary act is to be creative in its materials.

Interlocking this intensification with the relational circuitry of native
Andean worlds (as described by Vicuña and Peruvian anthropologist

Marisol de la Cadena in conversation with Justo Oxa, a Quechuan school-teacher in Peru), this chapter theorizes a "natural sign" distinct from the natural sign of the Western episteme. Not the isomorphic sign that Michel Foucault discusses in *The Order of Things*—that is, the natural sign of ecclesiastical philosophy whose iterability was infinite but whose reference was singular, referring always to a Christian God and his works— the sign of Andean khipu is heterogeneous in nature: as de la Cadena remarks, "in the prose of the [indigenous Andean] world, where there is no separation between the event and its narration, eventfulness can be ahistorical. Far from the events not having happened, this means that events are not contained by evidence as requirement" (116). To explore this end of historicity in temporal heterogeneity, which is the culminating point of the present book, this chapter draws on the interconnected writings of Friedrich Nietzsche, Pierre Klossowski, and Foucault—or, more specifically, Klossowski's Nietzsche as read by Foucault—on fabulation. Following de la Cadena's cue, I situate Foucault in an indigenous conception of mediation because doing so helps to translate that conception, while also transposing new meanings into Foucault's writings, and into Saidiya Hartman's sense of the "critical fabulation" necessitated by certain archives (11). In situating Foucault's "prose of the world" within khipu semiotic reciprocity, de la Cadena allows us to reposition Foucault, putting his words to work new meanings in khipu. Moreover, such a reading helps us to see that the political dynamism of Vicuña's khipu is not only that it is creative but that it affords creative potential for the khipu itself—that it "stakes out a space of its own creation" (*QUIPOoem* q.131–32). In its creativity the khipu implicates new poetic makings in the material contents of a living khipu archive.

Tracing the life of signs beyond their archival entombment, in ways that implicate contemporary makings in the native worlds of the Americas, brings us back to the story of Joaquín Torres-García. In his Benjaminian exploration of a Latin American city without name, *La Ciudad sin Nombre*, activities, experiences, and interactions are construed within the visual chirography of pictography (fig. 31). The correspondences of handwriting, sign, and creativity give his movements in the nameless city particularly physical analeptic pulls. In this work, the city is that which exhausts itself in the poetics of a sign that preceded even the cities of the Inca: the pictographs of ancient Tiwanaku (ca. 800 CE). As artist and scholar César Paternosto notes, the aesthetic immediacy of the pictographs of Tiwanaku (in present-day western Bolivia) makes it so that their ancientness flattens at the same touch that also activates their massive temporal density. In a final analysis of Torres-García's movements in urban analepsis (moving through cities with dense native temporalizability), this book augments studies of hemispheric modernity and postmodernity, which have departed from the idea—made commonplace by Ángel Rama—that contemporaneity depends on a "lettered city." Arriving once again to the works of Bolivian scholars Sanjinés and René Zavaleta, especially their conception of post-neoliberal plurinational statehood in the Andes, this book's conclusion proposes that temporal heterogeneity could also be a model for the changing migrant states of the United States and Europe in need of "nonindivisible" nationalisms and temporal alternatives to progressive liberalism that are socialist in nature. Why Bolivia and the Andes? As Sanjinés and Zavaleta point out, drawing on the earlier works of the Peruvian philosopher José Carlos Mariátegui, the Andes offer post–Cold War models for integrating indigenous cultural and jurisgenerative practices in a non-Soviet socialist political project. It is a working model for how the signs of the Americas might organize socially equitable political life.

In response to such a model, this book itself works in a global circuitry of cultural difference—connecting tropes, figures, sign systems, poets, and concepts across a hemispheric domain of varying temporal densities, working from the purported periphery inward to showcase the centrality of the apparently peripheral. Because the book has diverse directional flows, or performed subsumptions, it will be helpful to provide its core map in a visual format. It is designed to be semiotically ranging and geographically ambitious, beginning with the pictographs and petroglyphs of North America and winding its way through the hieroglyphs of Mesoamerican Mexico and Central America to conclude with the shamanism, khipu, and pictography of the Andes in South America:

	Sign Form	Trope	Figure	Poets and Writers	Concepts
Ch. 1	translatability	metalepsis	parallel	Aztec priests and Dorn	subsumption/ rhythm
Ch. 2	pictography	metonymy	curve	Ortiz and de Angulo	kinship
Ch. 3	pictographs/ petroglyphs	amphiboly	law	Vizenor, Borrows, and Erdrich	multiperspectivalism
Ch. 4	hieroglyphs	metalepsis	body	Olson, Twombly, and Alurista	difference
Ch. 5	none	erasure/ catachresis	shaman	Anzaldúa and Burroughs	absencing
Ch. 6	khipu (quipu)	analepsis	textile	Vicuña and Torres-García	presencing

This scope represents a semiosphere or suite of ontological modes constituted by the distinct and describable poetics of indigenous signs. Here, my implication in the book's analytical object is most undeniable. In studying the signs of the Americas, I have come to see the book as a pictograph or "picture-puzzle"—to quote Theodor Adorno on the *Denkbild*—that is meant to "get thought moving" (qtd. in Richter ix). In this regard, the book is evidence of the very "cultural remissions" that Arias points to as the inescapable effect of Central American migrations in the Americas: the voices of those movements are traced by a colonial remembrance they will never accept because of the broader impact that cultural inheritances and efflorescences have in a lasting imagination. But, more generally speaking, this pictograph of the book also represents an intellectual method that combines poetics and semiotics—the study of signs in their intercultural uses—that could be called a kind of anthropological philology.

Anthropological Poetics

As I discuss in the book's afterword—dedicated to my mentor and friend the ethnopoetics scholar Dennis Tedlock, who passed away during its writing—an anthropological poetics can disclose the movement of unnatural signs and other natures in our midst. Since the 1970s, such anthropologists as Tedlock, Taussig, Clifford, Renato Rosaldo, Donna Haraway, Roy Wagner, Nestor García Canclini, Talal Asad, Stephen Muecke, Stuart McLean, Michael Jackson, Anand Pandian, and Kathleen Stewart have reckoned with the disciplinary poetics of anthropology, taking to task such concepts as form, figuration, representation, narrative, intimacy, and voice. Wagner, for instance, worried that his emphasis on the structuring power of figurative language would make ethnology into metaphor, "turning kinship and ritual into literature, and us [anthropologists] into literary critics" (*Symbols* 10). Feeling that literary studies has much to gain in a grand bargain with anthropology, I invite, through the present book, literary scholars to a disciplinary anthropology of poetics, by which we could make metaphor into a kind of ethnology and thus affirm the worlds and earths of the tropes we set out to disclose.

To be sure, poets writing in the wake of the "writing cultures" movement—particularly those of the language school, indigenous background, and ethnopoetic inclination—translated anthropology's transdisciplinary flashpoint into a way to animate their writings, putting into practice such concepts as reflexivity, textual thickness, play, ritual, and kinship. These intersections overlay their literary creations with a kind of interdisciplinary noise, challenging what a literary object is and what objects we elect to think of as literature. The problem is that literary studies has been slow to theorize this transdisciplinary noise. This book amplifies such noise in order to trouble disciplinary norms of literary studies—especially the study of poetry and poetics—while also tuning into that trouble as a strategy of interpretation. Advocating such a *tuning in* in terms of "*antropoesía*," poet and anthropologist Renato Rosaldo describes poetry as a language act that does not so much represent an event as it aims "to *be* the event itself." Quoting the French philosopher and literary scholar Jean-Jacques Lecercle, he advances the idea that such an event "is a violent irruption, or intervention, in an established world. This irruption . . . cancels the time of the current situation and marks a new foundation of time; the only event that aptly accounts for it is 'revolution'" (102–3). Conceptualized as temporal irruption, the literary object reveals itself to be the event it in fact is, porous in its conditions and possibilities.

My predisposition to trouble the poetics of the Americas is meant to highlight tensions within debates about the intercultural literacy of indigenous cultures. One of the striking features of indigenous criticism since the 1990s has been its proliferation, which contradicts what seemed at an earlier time to be an inevitable progression toward homogenization and cultural disappearance—the unstoppable movement toward monoculture that made Lévi-Strauss's *tropiques* so *tristes*. In the final book of a trilogy that has been the touchstone of the "writing cultures" movement, Clifford remarks how drastically the "power relations and discursive locations" of indigenous cultures shifted in the period between 1988 (when he published *The Predicament of Culture*) and 2013 (when he published *Returns*). In this period, the inability of the United States to sustain global hegemony after the fall of the Soviet Union—an inability that Clifford traces out in the fraught military ventures after 9/11—signifies the interaction of the globalizing process with worldwide decolonizing energies. "Both," he argues, "have worked to decenter the West, to 'provincialize Europe,' in Dipesh Chakrabarty's words" (*Returns* 6). Concomitant with this multidirectional transformation of the political climate of the planet is the historical momentum of "indigenous becoming." In courtrooms, classrooms, textbooks, art practices, literature, land protests, and museums the temporality of indigenous identity shifted from one that was fatalistically past-oriented to one that looks to the present and future of "adaptive traditions" and "new pathways in a complex postmodernity" (*Returns* 1–10). From that vantage, the following pages point out the pathways by which native signs never stopped making the worlds of the Americas, indeed by which these signs made significant inroads into the diverse poetries of North and Latin America—even amid the throes of the xenophobic nationalist fevers that continue to this day to shake our shared globalities.

Writing alongside the historical shift that Clifford describes, Māori scholar Linda Tuhiwai Smith remarks in her touchstone *Decolonizing Methodologies* that postpositivist critiques of research practices do not go far enough to legitimate the world alternatives of indigenous cultures. To legitimate such realities, she calls for expressive and representational practices to be endowed with world-shaping power: "story and story-teller," she writes, "both serve to connect the past with the future, one generation with the other, the land with the people and the people with the story" (145). As she has it, narrative consolidates private intimations into public meanings, individuals into groups, groups alongside other groups, and conceptions of whole worlds into the accidents of every-day being. Her suggestion is that the acts and artifacts of linguistic exu-berance that ramify existential orders ramify worlds outside of Western norms, interconnecting people beyond the familiar narratives of colony, nation, and capital—indeed, in the multitensioned realities that Chad-wick Allen calls the "trans-indigenous." Yet whereas narrative is often privileged for its world-forming power—for instance, anthropologist Mi-chael Jackson remarks, "storytelling is a quintessentially intersubjective activity that brings the social into being" (*Politics* 16), or, for that mat-ter, in Lévi Strauss's fixation on plot as the primary structure of human cognition—my work argues that such phenomena occur with special dy-namism in the eventhood of poetics. Tuhiwai Smith dares her readers to rethink the world from its grassroots networks, involving the stories that have been easy to deny within Eurocentric frameworks. The story of what *happens* to such poetics is well known; they are subject to misuse and so on. But that is only one side of the story. The other side, which Tuhiwai Smith urges scholars to tell—and which I tell in the following pages—is what the poetics underlying such stories *do* in, and to, the worlds they create for themselves and that we, as their readers, come to inhabit too. This focus on the active worlding of native poetics—especially in the world-making work of rhythm and temporal orientation—gives us a nar-rative for native and minority Latinx and Latin American poetics of the Americas that is not one of passive victimhood but instead one of active engagement, shaping and complicating such categories as race, gender, kinship, and environment into the twenty-first century. That is, if tropes and figures affirm worlds and earths, then an interrogation of native signs need not bear Lévi-Strauss's colonialist melancholia. Like a blazing con-stellation, these signs continue to cast meaning over the landscape of human thought, even dispelling the murky inheritances of colonial his-toricity in contemporary existence.

To bring such activity to light is to reckon with what Deloria calls "the rhythms of the land"—the poetics of the lands of the Americas—even where these rhythms appear to make arrhythmic worlds in as unusual a sign system as pictography, by as unexpected a maker as de Angulo, with as surprising an intertext as García Lorca's *duende*, and to as unbelievable an outcome as his physical metamorphosis. To write a story of the poetics of the Americas in response to the semiotic rhythms and conceptual habitats native to this hemisphere requires that we tweak our expectations of what the scale, scope, materials, and outcomes of analysis should be. To start to tweak our literary values in this way, this book begins at the beginning, with the first documented act of poetic resistance to European colonialism in the Americas: the Aztec priests' reply to their attempted interpellation in the recently conquered city of Tenochtitlan. In telling the story of how the poetic form of their speech premeditated translation, I argue that we can only reckon with the Aztec priests' integral worlding or rhythms of reality—spoken in 1524, transcribed by Bernardino de Sahagún in 1564, and translated for English readers by Gordon Brotherston, Jennifer Dunbar Dorn, and Ed Dorn in 1964—if we scale our conception of worlding *down* to attend to the world-forming work of poetic form, in this case metalepsis.

1

WORLD POETRY AND ITS DISAVOWALS

A Poetics of Subsumption from the
Aztec Priests to Ed Dorn

In 1524, three years after the fall of Tenochtitlan, a group of Aztec priests were called to one of the main squares of that great city-state to publicly denounce their ancient beliefs before a council of Catholic friars. A glance around the square would have given the changed social order no shortage of iconic resonance: the destroyed architecture of the conquered Aztec empire was in process of being replaced by the colonial-style buildings of a newly founded City of Mexico. What had once been the most populous autonomous municipality of the Americas was now not more than a diminished dependency of an unknown foreign power far across the cold, sword-white sea. Feeling thus that their entire way of existence was under threat of extinction, the Aztec priests devised a plan. They would respond to the requisite interpellation with their own interpolation, calling on the people in the square to remember that the worldview that had ruled Tenochtitlan could yet disavow the newfound glory of the Franciscans. Composed in the patterns of classic Aztec or Nahuatl poetry, what became known as the "Aztec Priests' Reply" is the earliest documented instance of a poetics of the Americas raised in resistance to European colonial power.

> What we say here is for its own reason
> beyond response and against our future.
>
> Our revered lords, sirs, dear ones,
> take rest from the toil of the road,
> you are now in your house and in your nature.
> Here we are before you, subjected,
> in the mirror of yourselves.
> Our sovereign here has let you come

you have come to rule
as you must in your own place.

Where is it you come from
how is it that your gods have been scattered
from their municipal centers?
Out of the clouds, out of the mist
out of the ocean's midst you have appeared.
The Omneity takes form in you
in your eye, in your ear, in your lips.
So, as we stand here,
we see, we address,
the one through whom everything lives,
the night   the winde
whose representatives you are.

And we have felt the breath
and the word of our lord the Omneity,
which you have brought with you.
The speaker of the world sent you because of us.
Here we are, amazed by this.
You brought his book with you, his script
heaven's word, the word of god.

And now what. How is it,
what are we supposed to say
what shall we present to your ears? (Dorn, *Derelict* 323–24)

In a stunning rhetorical parry, the Aztec priests cast the arrival of the Europeans as a cipher from their indigenous god to them. In the strange-bodied foreigners, they see "the one through whom everything lives,/ the night   the winde/whose representatives you are/ . . . /our lord the Omneity." In so translating the invaders into a cryptogram from their native god, Ehecatl (the night wind), they privilege themselves as the interpreters of the events unfolding—the unparalleled destruction, disease, waste, and war. They are the semioticians of a world in which the arriving conquistadors are mere signs. With these signs, the Aztec priests compose a speech that centers their language, metaphors, themes, landscape, and cosmos. If these Spaniards are, as they say, a mirror for them ("Here we are . . . in the mirror of yourselves"), this is the looking glass of polished obsidian famous throughout Mesoamerica for its dark reflections, forming images as if in a night storm or a cloud of smoke, whose name was Tezcatlipoca or smoking mirror. The Spaniards are an instance in which to reflect on darkly shining Aztec significations.

The problem in this particular case is that such an encounter as described above might not have happened in that way at all. Bernardino de Sahagún, the Franciscan missionary known as the first anthropologist of the Americas, recomposed the event in 1564, forty years after its supposed occurrence in a time before he had even arrived to New Spain. Based on a hodgepodge of written and oral reports, his historical reconstruction—hidden in the archives of the Vatican for nearly four hundred years—could have been transcribed first in Nahuatl and later translated to Spanish or, just as likely, first transcribed in Spanish and later translated to Nahuatl. In that forty-year interim, traces of the original "speech"— in the public square before the friars and populace of Tenochtitlan— could have moved through various Nahua memories, arriving in amalgamated form to its transcription in 1564; or, just as possibly, it could have been transcribed in translation by Spaniards in 1525, only later to be translated back into Nahuatl. The latter possibility poses the special problem of imagining Spaniards translating and transcribing an oral utterance they could have only scarcely grasped in 1525. More likely, the Spaniards recorded the event, making cursory note of a speech, which Sahagún later (forty years after its utterance) asked his Nahua students to recompose.

In any case, the speech as we have it today is an intersection of voices, memories, imaginations, and entextualizations, whose heterogeneity— though entangled in the lettered archives of colonial administration—still indicates absorption in speech patterns that distinguish themselves from that administration. For instance, the diphrastic sentence—"what are we supposed to say/what shall we present to your ears"—stages its "unlettered" voicing by dramatizing its orality ("to say") and its aural context ("your ears"). Its parallelist speech pattern, the diphrastic structure of twinned elements (oral/aural//mouths/ears), organizes these markers of orality and aurality. Remarking such speech cues, J. Jorge Klor de Alva argues that the dialogic relationship between Sahagún and his native informants enfolds Sahagún's entire work into the dialogic norms of native vocalization (*Work*). Structured into a parallel sentence, the phrase invokes a philosophical tradition of dialectical dualism found throughout Mesoamerica. Here, the dualism organizes the experience of having to explain the dualism to a colonial other. It is a philosophical institution outside of which the Spaniards stand, looking in, rather than the other way around.

Moreover, the transcription is a text that organizes its own contradictions. The translation at hand (the collaborative work of Ed Dorn,

Jennifer Dunbar Dorn, and Gordon Brotherston) expands the reach of the poem's dialectical dualism: in their commitments to anticapitalist and proindigenous activism (more on this below), these translators introduce another instance of encounter. Karl Marx's concept of "primitive accumulation," or the observation that capitalist systems emerged from the surplus of the colonial expropriation of indigenous people and lands (873–940), appears here as a feature of the translators' critical relationship to the text. That is, these Marxian translators convey their political commitments through a primal scene of capitalist accumulation, which was selected for translation because its native worlding anticipates and resists the gross theft by which colonialism gives way to capitalism. And if the text carries inside itself a dialectic that centers native world process, the very scene of primitive expropriation in which the Aztec priests are called upon to participate looks forward to its later translations and mediations, capitalist or otherwise, incorporating these changes into a theory of Nahua time.

While such a work as the Aztec priests' speech might be described as a palimpsest, the stratigraphic nature of that metaphor does not capture the active conflicts between form, time, and historicity that are vivid in the text. As historian of Mesoamerica Matthew Restall notes, these apparently archaic native texts are often very canny about their temporal "continuity," building into their form "patterns of repetition" by which a never-uniform time of war, conquest, and cultural fragmentation could be revealed to be so many consolidations of a native historiography (41). Arturo Arias pulls this claim into the present moment, with his observation that the Mesoamerican story of creation—the *Popol Vuh*—is almost ubiquitously impactful on contemporary writings by Central Americans and Central American Americans. As such, its cosmogony gives coherence and communal identity to a region whose very names—Mesoamerica and Central America—seem captive to colonial and Cold War historicities. This predominantly indigenous region is embedded in the cultural objects by which it circulates: "we can see a new, eccentric design emerging from the movement of a heterogeneous group through old patterns of representation" (xv). The design Arias describes is eccentric because it is located amid Central American war, genocide, migration, diaspora, exile, and internment, at the fringe of capitalist governmentality, while also defining itself and its accumulative other by way of Mesoamerican patterns and poetics. These cultural rhythms are historically responsive to the active conflicts in which they find themselves, but they are also responsible for making meaning of such historical experience.

This chapter examines how such theory-bearing form acts with the characteristics of what Javier Sanjinés calls "embers of the past," or historical objects liable to make ontological conflagration upon touch. As he puts it, these embers make fires because they "[introduce] doubt into the rectilinear course of modernity . . . [reopening] the gap—the hiatus, Jacques Lacan would call it—between the symbolic and the real" (27). He then points out that that chasm gives way to Lacan's third relational entity, the Imaginary, by which people enact their capacity to create new forms of existence (see Castoriadis 70). But those forms of existence are precisely the kind of worlding that scholars have had a difficult time recognizing when it comes to such speech acts as that of the Aztec priests. To bring that kind of worlding to the fore, this chapter emphasizes that the imagination-inspiring hiatus is made possible by the persistence of Mesoamerican time in its poetic and conceptual rhythms. Those rhythms bear worlds capable of contesting the uniform conception of world history in capitalism. They contest a singular modernity and, in their philosophical specificity, give meaning to the fractures of such a speech act as that of the Aztec priests, even in its most mediated version at the hands of Brotherston and the Dorns.

World Duress

Scholars have struggled to see world heterogeneity in the poetic form of such an enunciation as the "Aztec Priests' Reply" because most scholarship of world poetics presumes a singular capitalist world system in its analytical framework. This interpretive lopsidedness will be familiar to literary scholars. As the field has turned to analyze transnational and transdisciplinary circuits, it has held as truisms certain theories about how cultural repertoires create worlds. *Worlds* itself is a word that complicates as much as it evokes. Debjani Ganguly points out how little and how much the word does in its complex relation to global distributions of labor, shared sense of cultural immanence, residues of Martin Heidegger's *Dasein*, and ecological damage endangering human being-in-the-world. "World" signifies world system or *globe*, cultural making or *worlding*, activity of abiding or social *milieu*, and *planet* too. Her description of this four-part matrix lays bare some of the shortcomings of conceptions of "worlding":

> The world as spatial amplification and systemic interconnection across the globe through the circuits of informational capitalism; the world as an aesthetic remainder of the globe that resists the space-time compression of global commodity circuits; the world as an ethical site of human relationality and humanitarian connectivity; and the world as a self-contained totality analogous to a Leibnizian monad whose many

parts are compossible with each other and that is not reducible to the materiality of the actual world we inhabit. (69)

My purpose in this chapter is to show how Ganguly's latter three instances of ontosemiotics—worlding, milieu, and planetarity—are not necessarily subsumed into the first, capitalist modernity. To do so, this chapter takes as an object of analysis the discourse on the Marxian concept of "subsumption," or the debate as to whether there is a temporal exterior to a global capitalist distribution of labor and management of surplus.

In this analysis, I engage with critical readings of Marx that have complicated political economy with an account of cultural difference. While I argue that capitalist hegemony is not inescapable, Marx remains crucial, inasmuch as he offers a systematic critique of how material exploitation has created what Yellowknives Dene political scientist Glen Coulthard calls the "entangled relationship between capitalism and colonialism" (8)—that is, between logics and practices of accumulation and state violence. Still, the logic of accumulation need not subsume the logics by which it is analyzed: the repeated failure of capital to silence noncongruent cultural characteristics reveals its accidental and incomplete nature. This contingency is most perceptible where capital meets resistance from other cultural modalities. That coming into consciousness of cultural contradiction has animated the subsumption debates among a spectrum of scholars from North and South. I focus on the writings of Dipesh Chakrabarty, Harry Harootunian, Massimiliano Tomba, and René Zavaleta—as well as commentaries by anthropologists June Nash, on the scales of habitus, and Marshall Sahlins, on the structure of the conjuncture—to include in the account of resistant temporalities a reckoning with the rhythms and syncopations of poetry.

The critique necessitates itself because the paradigm of a singular capitalist temporality is implicit to current conceptions of worlding in the study of world poetry. This chapter wishes to show how poetics in particular bear world systems other than the capitalist one, which logically integrate events, materials, and people into themselves—to describe how words working in the poetic and semiotic system of the Aztec priests respond to a scene of primitive accumulation, while also creating experiences and realities with fully integral cultural insides (or ontosemiotics). As literary studies expands in polyglot, transnational, and intercultural considerations of literary value, it now faces the question of how to see the worlds that make up our shared globalities without reconstituting a world system that constrains those networks as evidence only of colonial, national, and transnational capitalist scrim.

The problem is familiar enough. The challenge of valuing the plurality of existential modes that crisscross the planet has compelled scholars to normalize a framework of analysis that cannot affirm worlds outside its own. I mean the common conception that the multiple cultural and political systems of the world are contained in a uniform economic system. Most influentially described by Immanuel Wallerstein, world-system theory holds that Western capitalism constitutes a world economy within which there is a division of labor that transcends political entities and cultural structures. Wallerstein hence suggests that this system constitutes its own kind of culture, a "geoculture," by which he means the world-economic system when it becomes self-aware (23–29, 60–75). The problem is that, in conceptualizing an economic system as an integral culture, world-system theory normalizes a provisional economic center as the cultural totality of the planet. For Wallerstein, this world culture is the liberalism that established itself as the European centrist norm after the French Revolution. The culture of the citizen subject, emerging from the North Atlantic after the eighteenth century, subsumes all cultures of the planet into its geocultural singularity by virtue of its subjugation of non-Western people and their ways of making their lives. This is a classic valorization of market liberalism tracked to a racialized model of developmental time, moving from precapitalist primitive to neoliberal modernity. As Argentine Mexican philosopher Enrique Dussel puts it, "capitalism, liberalism, dualism (without valorizing corporeality), and so on are *effects* of the management of this function [of citizen subjugation] which corresponded to Europe as center of the world-system: effects that are constituted through mediations in systems that end up totalizing themselves" (16). The perverse effect of a world-system theory is that it phenomenologically introjects an accumulative world economy as the singular mediation the instant any culture comes into contact with the phantasmatic economic entity known as "the West." Or, as Sahlins puts it: "World System theory becomes the superstructural expression of the very imperialism it despises—the self-consciousness of the World System itself" ("Cosmologies of Capitalism" 416).

While literary studies that have dealt with world literature or world poetics have held a range of positions to Wallerstein's theory, those positions often rely on a magnified scale of analysis that enlists the geocultural worlding it sets out to critique. A straightforward way of noting this is to remark how often studies of world literature scale *up* in their critical concepts. For instance, Wai Chee Dimock notes that such a polyvalent category as genre requires "scale enlargement for [its] analysis" (5), echoing such conceptions of sociological enlarging as Susan Stanford Friedman's planetarity of literary interdependence, David Damrosch's global circulation of literary semantics, Franco Moretti's trees and waves of literary accumulation (or his direct sourcing of the concept of the "one and unequal" world system from Fredric Jameson's conception of a singular modernity), Jahan Ramazani's transnational geometry of postcolonial poetic form, and Pascale Casanova's world republic of literary prestige. By the same token, the idea that some substratum other than exchange value can be a source of linguistic exuberance that exceeds globalized capital reenacts a big singular history thesis. In this regard, Pheng Cheah's work helpfully identifies worlding as a temporal phenomenon, but points to its excess as a possible source of political transcendence: "The persistence of time is infrastructural to capital and cannot be destroyed. As an enactment of the opening of worlds by the coming of time, world literature points to something that will always exceed and disrupt capital" (11). To be sure, the manifold temporalities of storytelling that Cheah refers to as "time" do serve to disrupt capital. But to suggest that they do so by virtue of a notion of worldwide spiritualized time only summons the globalist specters we might wish to exorcise—if not the older ghosts of enforced progress lurking in quasi-Hegelian developmental time. Any world that must accumulate or exceed in order to resist instates measures of excess that constitute certain accumulative logics of capital.

Scaling up, in itself, is not the problem. We need such scales to address planetary crises and animate transnational political collaborations, as well as to deploy those collaborations to reckon with the violence of transnational capital, as the authors of the volume edited in response to humanities-based critiques of the world system have affirmed (Palumbo-Liu et al.). However, when we create critical geocultures by coupling cultural morphology to a world economy we risk totalizing world capitalism as a norm. Of course, capitalism is a world norm—but it is a situated norm, or what Coulthard might call a "grounded normativity," implicated in other relations, obligations, and normative practices. This is to say: the culture of the commodity is not the only world norm. Even if it is the case that the morphology of the commodity fetish implicates itself in planetary biosystems, as environmental historian Jason Moore argues, webs of life have their own ways of reticulating objects and subjects into their worlds too. Anthropologist Anna Tsing describes how even fungi have tactics for disarticulating capitalist strategies—tactics reminiscent of Michel de Certeau's conception of living practices of political resistance. Even spores demonstrate resistant agency in their practices of everyday life, and such is likewise the case with cultural acts and artifacts. If anything, the precarious worlding of world capitalism compels us to make visible the alternative reserves in our midst, to challenge ourselves with the unusual reality of other realities, to derive from those challenges a sense of contingency and plurality in our planetary historiographies, and perhaps to make such contingencies tactically effective for the heterogeneous flourishing of cultural and biotic makings.

Poetics of Subsumption

The cultural critique of political economy was mobilized in the works of Sardinian Italian Antonio Gramsci and Peruvian José Carlos Mariátegui. In the context of the Americas, Mariátegui's perspective is dominant. Like Gramsci, Mariátegui noticed that the crisis of incipient capitalism did not singularly originate in northern Europe; rather, capitalism and socialism had multiple versions, genealogies, temporalities, spatializations, contradictions, and themes, depending on local conditions and cultures. Just as Gramsci glimpsed the inadequacy of the Comintern's western European repertory for addressing the problem of the subaltern peasantry in southern Italy, Mariátegui saw that the "historical presuppositions" of western European Marxism could not comprehend the multilayered reality of Latin America, which involved an indigenous past that was not actually past and whose present conditions were a complex interaction of indigenous communalism, colonial feudalism, and transnational capital. Harootunian calls this Mariátegui's sense of "stratigraphic history, with its vertical embodiment of coexisting layers of different historical societies from Peru's past inscribed in the present, the most important historical residues [being] those representing the original Andean communities" (16, 143). Harootunian's metaphor of stratigraphy helps to introduce Mariátegui's distinct sense of Andean historical experience as an interaction of multiple temporalities of production: communal farming and kinship redistribution alongside global-market-oriented agriculture and mining operations. But the geological metaphor falls short of escaping the figure of a palimpsest, which emphasizes superordinate layers in a singular spatial density. As Harootunian notes, Mariátegui had the unique notion that political economy could articulate "contemporaneous noncontemporaneity (expressing synchronous nonsynchronicity)," from which the seeming totality of capitalism could be disarticulated in the totalizations of other cultural practices (16). Jaime Hanneken notes that one of the distinct sources of such critical syncopation for Mariátegui was myth. Reading him alongside Argentine political theorist Ernesto Laclau, she notes that Mariátegui's sense of mythic time affined temporal form and content, to accord to myth the contemporary life that it has in structuring personal and communal experience, as well as in developing critical perspectives and political positions (18–22). As Sanjinés puts it, "the gods are signs that meddle in historical time, that contradict it and make it incongruent with itself" (102). Mariátegui thus granted to the gods and their myths their own gravitational density within the ambits of Marxian critique. These signs can pull things into their meanings—and thus participate in those temporal heterogeneities that complicate the question of subsumption.

Harootunian explains that Mariátegui's "contemporaneous noncontemporaneity" thus necessitates a distinction between real and formal subsumption. Real subsumption is what Fredric Jameson calls the "singular modernity" of worldwide capitalism, a condition of totalized capital that brings everything and everyone into what Antonio Negri characterizes as the single floating body of enforced co-presence (Hardt and Negri 288; see Tomba 145). Real subsumption would have us interpret the Aztec priests' reply as an exemplum of the floating body of the commodity relation extending itself, like a ghost over the waters of the earth, ever already arrived to where it was going.

Tellingly, Marx called this state of being the "illusory community" of capitalist time, a notion of unsubstantial substance that Massimiliano Tomba distills in his reflections on the "phantasmagoria" characteristic of capitalist society in Marx's writings (46–52). Such a description points to a basic contradiction in real subsumption: that it is not exactly real at all. The concept transforms the bodies it wishes to emancipate into a bodiless singularity, all bodies everywhere into not bodies at all, not aggregates of contradictory and autonomous material histories, values, and aleatory social, cultural, and physical ecologies—nothing other than the ghost or floating phantasmagoria of capital. Against this spectralization, Harootunian argues that Marx never meant to make so many ghosts. He never meant for real subsumption to be descriptive but rather to be a heuristic, not a thing in history but a way of comprehending histories, not an object but a possible situation. Real subsumption is a way of seeing that is subordinate to "formal subsumption." Drawing on Marx's ethnographic analyses, Harootunian explains that "subsumption was first and foremost expressed as form, with diverse manifestations, which often prefigured a specific content and invariably outlasted its moment."[1] Marx's theory of how social forms subsume one another was not anchored to a general predictive outcome of the commodity relation but rather was "consistent with views that disavowed a unitary model"; it was a general way of interpreting how systems of production and relation integrate one another (8–9, 18–19). Key here is the idea of mutual interaction and integration. Harootunian takes formal subsumption to imply that there is no singular present in world historical existence. World historical existence consists of multiple temporal schemes, cultural stratagems, and ontological modalities acting on one another, configuring fragmentary systems of contingent production and relation, in which it is not always the case that exchange value obtains (18, 20). Subsumption is multidirectional, calling for analyses that illuminate the multiple pasts that bring contradictory presents into being, bringing to light "embodied untimely temporalities announcing their unevenness and difference" (17).

In Latin America, such analyses of cultural difference have been theorized in terms of identitarian commitments to subordinated difference that can disrupt a dominant state structure. Anne Freeland provides a handy bibliography of such models: "transculturation (Fernando Ortiz, Ángel Rama), hybridity (Néstor García Canclini), heterogeneity (Antonio Cornejo Polar), subalternity (John Beverley, Ileana Rodríguez, Alberto Moreiras, Gareth Williams, et al.)," in addition to "[Alejo] Carpentier's tropical Baroque aesthetic" and Álvaro García Linera's "state-society relation" (in which the incommensurability of social relations within a virtual or always only "apparent" state is a mark of their antistatist achievement) (65–66). Freeland is the English-language translator of the Marxist Bolivian politician and philosopher René Zavaleta Mercado, who offers a critique of these identitarian positions as always reinscribing the centrality of a world system on whose periphery or in whose unfulfilled metonymy such positions stand subordinated and expectant. In their emphasis on difference as such, these positions remain on the margins of the reality of the modern nation. In distinction, Zavaleta emphasizes a "disruptive contingency" of plural centers that he calls "*abigarramiento*" or "motley society." The motley refers to temporal overlap, in which each overlapping portion not only is its own whole but can absorb into its wholeness surrounding entities. The purpose is to give creative force to those "embers of history," as Sanjinés calls them, by recognizing their dangerous enkindling of nearby things. There is no utopia implicit in *abigarramiento*—it is a risk in its porosity. Yet, as such, it is a resource for recognizing countersubsumptions or multiform subsumptions moving and absorbing in various directions, creating the kinds of contingencies that are sources of political and social possibility.

This sense of porosity is key for understanding the self-position of the Nahuas in the speech: "what are we supposed to say," they ask; "what shall we present to your ears?" The questions they pose are something akin to: what subsumption against colonial subsumption and how? How will the effectiveness of their signs subsume those of their colonial others? How will their world cast the materials and events it encounters into itself, and also attend to the contradiction that emerges in doing so? As they see it, it is their task to cast their motley others into *their* world as representatives of it: "the night   the winde/whose representatives

you are." The notion of representation is not only a referent in the Nahuatl sentence, it is also emphasized by the particularly Nahuatl style of
parallelist representation: "*xiptlava, amipatilloa*," reads the Nahuatl that
is translated as "representatives," but which means more exactly "image,
spokesperson" (Sahagún 146–48).[2] At the levels of reference and frame—
that is, content and form—the arriving Spaniards are absorbed into a
parallelist Nahuatl world. In that phrasal turn are more than the contents
of differential identity; therein are the rhythms of a universe unto itself.
Here, I venture to push the concept of formal subsumption into a consideration of poetic form, noting that myth and the times of the gods do not
travel merely as content, that they come implicated in narrative and poetic forms, and that these forms also shape historical experience. While
the works of Harootunian and Tomba give ample explanatory power to
metaphors of rhythm, their analyses focus on how practices of material
production affect the experience of time. Mariátegui and Zavaleta and
Sanjinés after him are more considering of the aesthetics of time—the
"aesthetic forms" that also affect "the temporal conditioning that guides
our thoughts" (Sanjinés 11). Yet none of these scholars has explored the
impact that poetry—the art of linguistic temporalization—can have in
situations of temporal heterogeneity. In suggesting that poetic form can
induce temporal conditions in formal subsumption, I take a cue from Caroline Levine's twinning of poetic and institutional rhythms (49–80). The
parallelism of the Aztec priests' speech ("*xiptlava, amipatilloa*"—"image,
spokesperson") is an institution-bearing form, carrying the density of Mesoamerican religion and philosophy. As I will explain, its nonsynthesizing
dialectic is a conscious expression of the very temporal heterogeneity
into which it is hailed to make its sense of history.

The priests' reply therefore presents readers with the ontological problematic that requires us to disentangle our reading practices from the
globalist prosodies of literary studies. In elaborating how its poetics invites us to rethink our relation to a globe that has never been singular
and that continues to lay bare the limits of plausible unity, the worlds of
the Aztecs' poetic making reminds us that relational units are not only
effective when they circulate globally. Their speech requires us to scale
our sense of cultural expressivity and ontological effect *down* from its
exaggerated position in the symptomology of global capitalism—down
into the world-making effects of poetic language. After all, implicit in the
speech is an insistence that the poetic performance of the Aztec priests
could cast changes in their world even as it was partially in tow to conquest wars and colonial reorganizations. And it bears a notion that language in particular has the capacity to alter a colonial world that beckons
them with its contingencies. To hear that power to subsume requires that

we scale our attention down to the poetics with which they cast their world, into a poetic formalism emerging from their formal subsumption of surrounding events.

Anthropologist of Mesoamerican cultures June Nash conceptualizes the ethnographic value of such a downward scaling into literary form, as it informs and is informed by reality, with what she calls "counterplots." Counterplots are structuring principles that "sustain an alternative vision to that offered by capitalist development . . . [that] are still integrated into an indigenous cosmology and a syncretic religious paradigm that provides them with a framework for resistance to colonialism and domination" (*Mayan Visions* xviii, xix).[3] The value of counterplots is that they reveal resistances internal to the subjects and objects of indigenous cosmologies, providing cosmographies to map the ambits and happenings of diverse worlds. Reckoning with the worlds outside of the world of transnational capital, counterplots reveal both the persistence of the indigenous worlds and their integral quality. They show how cultures pattern structuring principles that incorporate change, eventuation, contradiction, and difference. In the attention paid by the Nahua speakers to the form of their speech, it is evident that it is not just narrative that plots reality: poetic tropes and rhythm do as well.

This conception of emplotment is of a piece with Chakrabarty's drawing on Heidegger's ideas of belonging and dwelling—especially as these states of being are grounded in fragmentariness—to provincialize European historicity. Chakrabarty takes Heidegger's concept of worlding to be a type of being in the "now" that is never fully there. That is, there is a "plurality that inheres in the 'now,' the lack of totality, the constant fragmentariness, that constitutes one's present." In our efforts to contravene these fragmented worldings, we wish to belong and dwell in "historicist or ethnographic mode[s] of viewing that involve the use of anachronism in order to convert objects, institutions, and practices with which we have lived relationships into relics of other times" (243). But those relics defy the archivist desire to have them signify "other times." They carry their own signification, undermining historicism while producing pasts too heterogeneous to keep whole present "nows." By the same token, the form of the Nahuatl speech carries its own signification that is not subsumed into a colonial archive—rather, it bears those signals that insist that "other temporalities, other forms of worlding, coexist and are possible" (Chakrabarty qtd. in Hanneken 22). If we read closely—even in translation—we can see that it subsumes events and happenings into a Nahuatl cosmos: "The Omneity takes form in you/in your eye, in your ear, in your lips," the Aztec priests say, explaining to their audience (in the public square, in Sahagún's library, in the correspondence of the

English-language translators, in the circulation of the present book) that they are nothing other than the handiwork of a Mesoamerican creator. Like the fragmentary body of eyes, ears, and lips evoked in their apostrophe, the power to constitute reality depends on the broken nature of time itself, always available to worldings in a fragmentary plural; yet, in this case, that fragmentariness is also an expression of an "Omneity" constituted in rupture.

What Nash offers to Chakrabarty's sense of worlding in rupture—and what is important for my claim that poetics produces integral qualities for heterogeneous "nows"—is the idea that such fragmentations are more than incidental or phenomenological. They are plotted as well. By plot I do not mean narrative causality. In line with Nash's notion of plot, I refer to the effect that language has on temporal experience more generally. Noting that her conception of counterplot is related to habitus, she tweaks Bourdieu's fulcrum from its exaggeration of the market logic in bodily habituation in order to look, instead, at such embodied or innervated habits as "the minimal unit for reproducing and generating cultural repertoires" (*Mayan Visions* 221). The minimalization of habitus to a unit of cultural reproducibility offers a broader spectrum for what cultures can ramify as, how they communicate, and where that communication extends cultural repertoires into new existential and embodied modalities—let alone how the repertoire might take on spontaneous, indeterminate, and unexpected movements. Influenced by broader trends in indigenous studies that affirm the reality-shaping relational work of stories, songs, art, and metaphor,[4] Nash's point is that indigenous cultural emplotments give rhythm to encompassing worlds. They are more than just local customs: they delineate and define "worldwide interactive spaces" of a "global ecumene" (*Mayan Visions* 221), and can do so because whole worlds embed in the dynamics of cultural and social rhythm.[5] To be clear, the emphasis on cultural rhythm operating at a minimum—not maximum—scale of expression does not minimize its effect. It showcases how the world making of culture is scalar, generating world repertoires even in poetic patterns whose apparent smallness hides the ability to format larger cosmographic and cosmological dimensions. Poems and the rhythms of storytelling carry whole worlds that can affect the worlds that surround them.[6]

Within this translocal scale of multidirectional interaction operating at a minimum scale of cultural expressivity, the story of indigenous cultural repertoires is not just what happens to them when the economies of colonialism or worldwide capitalism cross their cultural boundaries;[7] rather, their story also involves what they do to the diverse social orders they encounter and how they integrate the partial "now" of the intercultural event into their patterns of existence. To be clear, the question here is one of scale: while the large scale of Wallerstein can tell the story of how colonial networks gave way to capitalist flows, it cannot describe the activity of cultural units situated in local networks, carrying a layer of social and cosmic organization that requires a shifting of scales—to borrow global historian Jacques Revel's term (*jeux d'échelles*)—into the world-making work of the poetics of the resistant Nahuatl voices. Only with such an approach will we hear in the poetics of the speech the Nahua counterplot or counterpoetics or more simply rhythm—which is more than contrast or counter, which is a world unto itself—that casts the Franciscans' plots into itself. As we will now see, those patterns of expression and perception carry an integral Nahua reality.

The World-in-Metalepsis of the Aztec Priests

Regardless of whether the speech as we see it above was composed in the inner chamber of a ruined temple of Tenochtitlan in 1524, in Sahagún's study in the makeshift colonial library of Tlatelolco in 1564,[8] or in the exchanges between Brotherston and the Dorns in the late 1960s and early 1970s, the fact remains that the speech distinguishes itself in Nahuatl expressive patterns that carry their own reality. The source for these expressive patterns could have been either written or oral reports of the speech as it was given in 1524, the twenty or so years of ethnography that Sahagún had conducted at that point in compiling his *General History of the Things of New Spain* (i.e., the Florentine Codex), or the critical stances of his indigenous students at the Colegio for whom the transposition into European "discursive frames" was tensioned by "the content of their memories as well as in the way of remembering and transmitting them" (Mignolo 203–4); most likely, it is some combination of these sources (as well as the pro-native commitments of its English-language translators) that gives the speech its recognizable Nahuatl poetics.

Stated prosodically, the speech begins with, and throughout consists in, the classic Nahuatl poetics of syntactic reversal called parallelism. That of which the arriving Spaniards are said to be "image and representatives" is itself a diphrastic pairing: "the night   the winde," or (in Nahuatl) "*in ioalli in ehecatl*." Such a phrasing derives its poetic dynamism from the tension between internal continuities and discontinuities of sound and sense—its parallelism. In this phrase, the semantic and sonic similarities of the two Nahuatl words—"*in ioalli in ehecatl*" (repeating the bracket structure "in" and "l" sounds, while differentiating those two brackets with the contents of the words)—make up what Roman Jakobson, in his analysis of parallelism, called the "poetic artifice consist[ing] of recurrent returns" (399). These returns to a thing that has changed typically connote moods of tension and opposition that are resolved by the unified theme of the poetic enunciation, evoking fragmentation to confirm a dynamic sense of solidity across difference. In Mesoamerican culture, where such pairs structure artistic expression widely, the theme by which such pairs are unified does not connote unity exactly. Such pairs take hold in a cosmology structured around a concept of complementary duality, a dialectics in which objects do not synthesize but remain in constant alternation and mutual dis-identification (Hull and Carrasco; León-Portilla, *Aztec Thought*; D. Tedlock, "Toward" 185–86). Here that dual structure is emphasized, as it is in many Nahuatl parallelisms, by the use of the reduplicated Nahuatl demonstrative "*in*," which means "this" in English. This "*in . . . in*" serves as a metapragmatic marker for the structure of poetry, inasmuch as the word for poetry is expressed in the reduplicated demonstrative, "*in xochitl, in cuicatl*" or "this flower-this song."[9]

Philosopher James Maffie has called this deep structure of poetic parallelism by its Nahuatl name of "*inamic*" or complementary pairs, pointing out that such common Nahuatl pairs as "night wind" or "*in ioalli in ehecatl*" (or, for instance, flower-song, feather-serpent, flower-war, above-below, inner-outer, order-disorder, stone-flower, jaguar-eagle, fire-water, deer-bird, smoke-mirror, root-branch, and so on) are not to be understood as opposites that balance each other out, which would require a third position of the middle. They do not prefigure the multicultural hybrid or concept of *mestizaje*. Their peculiar significance is that they are interdependent dyads, mutually emergent partners that "define, complement, [and] condition" one another, yet remain in perpetuity incommensurable with one another. Such poetics of endless identity in dis-identification serves, in turn, to affirm a "cyclical back-and-forth" between paired items that carries meanings of "self-emerging and self-transforming" form. Because the items in an *inamic* pair do not synthesize, assimilate, or sublate into a singularity—as we might expect of quasi-Hegelian-style dialectics—their diversity is maintained as mutable distinction, a negativizability of negativity, in which a thing is never identical with itself (in a more canny Hegelian mode). It is somewhat like Hegelian mediation, if the identity of things were kept unfinished (in a process of emergence by way of a dialectical other into which it is never resolved), if things are seen rather as the mediality or "movement through which [a] world constitutes itself" (Weber 36). In *inamic* dialectics, paired items bear an inner virtuality that Maffie calls the Aztec "world in motion" (156–57, 168, 143).[10]

The dyads that express this "media theology" (Weber 36) or "theology without a teleology" (Sanjinés 112)—in which the mediality of items is kept suspended as a signal of their ongoing totalizability—in the Aztec priests' speech are lords-gods; clouds-mist; sky-water; eyes-ears; eyes/ears-lips; human-god; breath-word; script-word; and night-wind. These serve as the basis for a second tier of parallels, in which pairs mirror other pairs: lords-gods/human-god; sky-water/breath-word; breath-word/world-earth; eyes/ears-lips//one lip-two lip; celestial-divine/perishable-mortal; and sky-water/hearts-flesh. But the most significant of such ateleological theology-bearing medial dyads occurs in that line "the night   the winde"—the moment at which the speech declares a continuity between its "self-emergent and self-transforming" form and the deity presiding over such continuity in discontinuity, casting time as an entity that has Nahua movement in it. Announcing that the conceptual framework of Nahuatl parallelism will structure their speech, the priests declare that their traditional patterns of perception and interpretation remain a living and viable model for comprehending the events unfolding in the lands of Tenochtitlan. Their emplotment will cohere the events of the previous years into the Aztec world that it still is. In such a paradigm, the seeming defeat of the conquest is not more than the emanation of their two-part divinity, the night-wind, which is both a theonym (one of 360) for the earth-god Tezcatlipoca and an allusion to the spirit-god with which Tezcatlipoca is paired in *inamic* opposition, Quetzalcoatl (who is also known as Ehecatl Quetzalcoatl or wind feather-serpent) (Miller and Taube 164). The *inamic* deity of dialectical process presides over the speech, which is a mediation of mediality—its deity is a media concept through which the events unfolding in Tenochtitlan are understood.

In interpolating the events of the conquest into something that is thus meaningful within the Nahua cosmos, the priests conquer conquest to an extent, becoming not its victims but its superintendents. They affirm a dyadic world in motion, where power has shifted back and forth between Aztec and Spaniard, yet that is a world for which they are the privileged interpreters. In this respect, there is no better translation for the presiding Nahua deity than the Dorns' and Brotherston's "Omneity," inasmuch as the all-encompassing beinghood taking form in their speech is the twin-form divinity manifest in the oppositional nature of the total colonial encounter. In their speech, colonial conflict is subsumed under dyadic mediality. In that respect, the formal effects of that deity's temporal configuration—*inamic*—are perhaps productively translated with the classical concept of *"rhusmos,"* a pre-Socratic dialectic that classicist Glenn Most identifies as the social configuration of *"rhuthmos"* or rhythm. As he explains, Democritus used this "dialectical form of *rhuthmos*" to express the "configuration" between poetic rhythm and the rhythms of everyday life, as well as rhythms that interpenetrate perception and imagination (252). *Rhusmos* was a concept by which form could scale between poetic and social instances, but it was importantly not associated with fixed or consistent form. Émile Benveniste explains that *rhusmos* is a conception of "form in the instant that it is taken upon by what is moving, mobile, fluid." It is rhythm its in historical instances, drawing special attention to temporal movement when it occurs in the transformation of signs into other signs—when form refers not to the selfsame sign but to its dynamic ability to configure itself in, and configure the meaning of, changing situations and differing contexts (Benveniste qtd. in Hallyn 59–60). One way in which we might think about that continuum between signs and their social configurations is as rhythm in its metaleptic instances, when signs find themselves transposed in new situations. The metalepsis of the Aztec priests' speech is organized by the *inamic* poetics that stage the new differential encounter between Aztec and Spaniard in the dialectic of a never-synthesizing, and thus ever-moving *rhusmos* of Mesoamerican cosmology.

Viewed as an active configuration or *rhusmos* of *inamichuan* (pl. of *inamic*), the very meeting of Aztec and Spaniard takes on meanings of mutual emergence, endless dis-identification, interdependence, and transformation. Throughout the speech, the priests emphasize that the arrival of the Spaniards is embedded in the purposes of their indigenous god, even claiming that the new Catholic god is a gift from "the night   the winde": "And we have felt the breath/and the word of our Lord the Omneity/which you have brought with you./The speaker of the world sent you because of us." The Nahua priests tell the Spaniards that "the night the winde . . . the Omneity" and his interpreters mediate whatever world the Spaniards have arrived from. Thus, while it may seem as if the Nahuas have lost everything in the colonial war, those battles have been nothing more than a syncretic transformation determined by their living god, the god of an oscillating process of dis-identification and *inamic* reality giving rise to itself. In the end, "the night   the winde" controls the meaning of reality, to which his priests welcome those present at the public square, the colonial library, its archive, and its translation. In thus reframing the encounter, the Nahuas affirm a world that is confirmed, not impoverished, by the interactions and conflicts of the so-called conquest, a world that is struggling yet to comprehend conquest but that knows that its dynamic movements signal a Tenochtitlan that is still alive. By the end of the speech, when the Aztec priests promise to resurrect the god of Tenochtitlan, they have in a sense already done so. As I have mentioned, Tezcatlipoca's name translates as "smoking mirror," which is another way of saying obsidian mirror: in representing the Spaniards as a mirror ("Here we are . . . in the mirror of yourselves"), which is to say an entity actively refracting lit faces in its knapped facets of obsidian darkness, the Spaniards are an element of Nahua reality. This dark mirror—a symbol itself of parallelist relationality—mediates its images and experiences, forming and transforming subjects and objects, while its diphrastic divinity absorbs all present events into its smoky wholeness.

To be sure, the defensive posture of the speech only magnifies how profoundly its deliverers felt the need to secure a world under threat. Their defense reminds us how real the violence of the Spanish colonial project was, subjugating populations, destroying and superseding municipal architecture and ordinance, reformatting regimes of knowledge, and reconstituting existential orders. Situated within this large-scale structural transformation, the speech has to make certain assumptions about how language works, if it imagines itself as an effective corrective to the situation at hand. It has to assume that the colonial conditions are not comprehensive enough to preclude poetic affirmations; that colonial culture is not totalized and that the Aztec world still can be elicited—in actual and virtual ways—in the "minimal" cultural expressivity of a speech. The speech must believe in its ability to bring into perception a world it recalcitrantly rules. Present objects are features of a situation unfolding in Mesoamerican terms.

In this way, the priests' speech anticipates what I call the totalizable fragment. For them, the cosmos can be enacted in the discrete unit of the poetic pairing. Such a seemingly insignificant phrase as "the night   the winde" avows a world against colonial rule. We can imagine an audience in 1524 receptive to such world avowal, trained to its patterns of expression, embodying the institutions and habitus of endless dis-identification. Such an audience would not have to struggle to see that the Spaniards represent one item in the dualistic itemizing wholeness of *inamichuan*. Needless to say, that is not the audience that presents itself to the speech today. Today, readers are forced to reckon with its fragments out of context. Still, if all we do then is describe the distance of that original context, then we reproduce what Sahagún had in mind when he claimed the speech for the colonial archive. What Diana Taylor calls the " 'preservation' [that] served as a call to erasure . . . a safe strategy for handling dangerous materials" hits close to home: the colonial archive "preserved 'diabolic' habits as forever alien . . . the studied, scholarly distance functioned as repudiation" (41). Such repudiation (even when tucked into the celebratory logics of cultural difference) is disheartening inasmuch as the Nahuas explicitly set out the terms by which their words can be received as a living and world-bearing performance of poetic totalizability. The speech challenges us to read it outside of the past tense, as more than a relic of a lost world. And it provides the resources with which to do so—that is, to interpret its transtemporal heterogeneity in terms of Nahuatl media theories.

To a certain extent, we have already started to do that, insofar as *in-amic* poetics have forced here a reconsideration of what a world system is. The way in which worlds absorb worlds in multiple directions forces a reconsideration of what Ganguly refers to as "global form." In the case of the Nahuas' speech, form globalizes itself by means of a dialectical poetics that elicits a native world in perpetual motion. Whereas the friars demanded that the Nahuas recognize the natural subordination of Indians within a Catholic ecumene, the Nahuas make that ecumene contextual, its nature unnatural, and its totality frangible when positioned inside their totalizable mediations of time, space, and reality. To be clear, the point here is that what happens when totalities come to oppose one another is already answered for by the oppositional poetics of the Aztec priests' speech. In its self-splitting syntactical effects, the speech subsumes the events of the conquest into a temporality in which their god of a world in motion holds dominion. In this way, the ruins of Tenochtitlan signify the split ontology of Tezcatlipoca-Quetzalcoatl, their ancient and still-arriving host of a world in dyadic oscillation. With their words as our starting point, we can then see how that split ontology also determines speech effects when the speech leaves its sixteenth-century context.

As its English-language translators in 1968 knew, the speech has as much to say about political resistance as it does about mediality and translation. To bring out its political metapragmatics, the Dorns and Brotherston translated the speech in such a way that not only translates the Nahuatl content into the English language but transmits the English language into Nahuatl poetic form. I want to stay with this phrase, "the night   the winde," because its unusual spacing and orthography have a special import in the translation—together pointing to two distinct poetic traditions. First, the spacing of the line underscores the parallelism of *inamic* pairs—as expressed by the doubled demonstratives that frame the Nahuatl, "*in ioalli, in ehecatl*"—which takes us into the Nahuatl tradition of mutually emergent and complementary counterforces. While Tezcatlipoca was known as "Yoalli Ehecatl," presenting that theonym within the doubled demonstrative "*in . . . in*," or "this . . . this," signals parallelism as a present frame of reference: *this* paralleled with *this*. The deictic uses of this demonstrative could refer to *this* night and *this* wind present at the enunciation, *this* night and *this* wind present in some kind of iconographic text that is being actually pointed to by the transcribers in Sahagún's library, or—as is likely in any scenario—the cosmology of *this* night and *this* wind into which all audiences to the speech act are presently convoked. It is not *that* night and *that* wind that are spoken of here; the deictics indicate a present frame of reference. Moreover, in addition to making Tezcatlipoca presently demonstrative, in that frame of reference, the wind (*ehecatl*) is also emphasized as an aspect of Quetzalcoatl. In his aspect of Ehecatl, Quetzalcoatl assumes the regenerative powers of the wind, spreading rain and seed over the earth so its vegetal life will continue. But the association with the wind goes beyond meanings of fertility. Quetzalcoatl's association with the wind is also related to primordial acts of human cultural making: kindling fire, turning breath to speech, and making music with flutes (Maffie 284–87). In his relation to wind, Quetzalcoatl is known as the progenitor of language and the arts. *This* wind then indexes the act of writing. And, here, that act is translated into the orthography of Anglophone prosody, scoring a second poetic tradition: spelled "winde," the word evokes the wind's figural history in English poetry, as in such poems as the sixteenth-century song of the ceaseless "Westron Wynde" and John Donne's wish to "find/What winde/Serves to advance an honest minde." The lines from Donne serves to recall a time when the vowel in "wind" was long, so rhymed with "find" and "mind." In gesturing at such pronunciation, the translation signals an early modern soundscape comparable to the estranged sound that sixteenth-century Nahuatl would have for Nahuatl speakers today. In this regard, it presents its English-language readers with something of a temporal contradiction: its voicing is distant because it is archaic, yet it is also intimate because that archaism is familiar. That affective tension of temporalities recalls Harootunian's conception of "arrhythmia," or the syncopation by which the intimacies of a dominant temporality are pulled into hiatus. The hiatus here is a gap between signs and signifieds, a rupture in the essential integumentation of language, through which the mythopoetic language-maker Quetzalcoatl is given freedom of movement.[11]

As the progenitor of language, Quetzalcoatl gives special meaning to the idea of interdiscursive representability.[12] The colonial friars who are said to be "representatives" of Quetzalcoatl are so not only because Quetzalcoatl is the "Omneity" or all-god but because the very activity of abstract representation is a special aspect of this all-god. No matter whom they proclaim to represent, in representing they always already represent Ehecatl-Quetzalcoatl, original breath of language. Quetzalcoatl's domain extends beyond the Nahuatl language into the mediations by which conceptual thought gives rise to itself. He rules language as such, meaning of course that he rules the languages of his translations. His translators are attuned to this reality. By virtue of the ambiguous use of "whose" in the final line of the stanza, the pronominal first-person plural voice of that sentence could represent the priests in 1524, or Sahagún and his students in 1564, or the collaborating translators of 1968. Here's how: echoing the interweaving of Nahuatl pronouns that occurs in the original speech,[13] in the translation "whose representatives" can be taken to mean either to mean "you Spanish friars who are representatives of Quetzalcoatl," "we Aztec priests, who stand here, see, and address, and represent," or "you Quetzalcoatl who is represented in 'the night   the winde.'" And, if the latter is a possible referent for the passage, then representation *qua* Quetzalcoatl subsumes all other instances of representation into his semiotic domain—including the deictic trace of the translators signaled by the loudly prosodic translation of "the winde." The loudness of the translated term "winde" locates translation itself within the act of representation that Tezcatlipoca-Quetzalcoatl rules.

As I have suggested in terms of poetic tropes, the way in which Tezcatlipoca-Quetzalcoatl captures the center of the poem's polyvalent voicing is called metalepsis. If the priests' utterance is something like the work of art in the era of colonial translatability, Tezcatlipoca-Quetzalcoatl captures that translatability into a Nahuatl era by means of metalepsis, a trope that shifts positions between subjects and objects, in a manner that echoes the alternations of *inamic* pairs. If relations shift as an *inamic* pair, as the speech suggests, then the metalepsis by which Tezcatlipoca-Quetzalcoatl overtakes the poem—after lying hidden in the secret archive of the Vatican for four hundred years—is the awakening of a deeper ontological transit point disclosed in Nahuatl poetics. Sylvia Wynter describes the subsuming power of such slips with her claim that the Americas are themselves a deeply "poetic" invention, the result of a European "transumptive chain" or metalepsis of conquest. For Wynter, the metalepsis of the Americas was the redistribution of power that the slippery semantics of racial ideology enabled (141–63). Interestingly, Wynter draws on Harold Bloom for her notion of colonial transumption. For Bloom, transumption (Latin for metalepsis) is a type of "figurative interplay" that aims to spirit moments away from staid tropes. It is a "trope-undoing trope," related to psychic conditions of "introjection or crossing[s] of identification" (Bloom 105–6). In a colonial context, the aim of metalepsis is to alienate native images, metaphors, and figures with the crisscrossing introjection of colonial ones. Still, such crisscrossing is not necessarily colonialist. The same "trope-undoing trope, which seeks to reverse imagistic priorities," can serve to alienate colonial norms, transuming countercolonial materials into the experiential world. Thus does Wynter note that metalepsis is also a transgressive trope in the Americas, making available poetic worldings against given imperial hegemonies, nows against colonial nows, indeterminacies against a seemingly natural order of dominion.[14] The same intrusive transumption—the trope-undoing tropology—by which the ideology of race becomes the colonial reality of the Americas nourishes transgressions against that reality. Tezcatlipoca-Quetzalcoatl's syntactic slipperiness in the speech shows us that metalepsis can create countercolonial worlds as readily as it makes colonial ones, casting motley colonial others into native worlds as representatives of those worlds.

Moreover, even in translation, *inamic* pairs self-theorize their transhistorical movement. As Maffie notes, "although devoid of any stable, permanent created structure, [reality's] ceaseless becoming—and hence the becoming of the cosmos and all its contents—are nevertheless characterized by an enduring, *immanent* rhythm or pattern; namely, agonistic *inamic* unity" (139). The structure of Aztec or Nahua time is such that it is always disclosing itself in a contested ongoingness, capturing beings into rhythms that are always conjunctural, to draw on anthropologist Marshall Sahlins's classic apothegm (*Islands of History*). For Sahlins, the structure of the conjuncture is a means of affirming indigenous realities in their historical unfolding: the structure of their history and the histories of their structure. Here, however, the unfolding of Aztec reality has its own sense of conjunctural structure that obtains in, and designates the meaning of, its temporal and discursive movements. Maffie explains that the *inamic* unity of Aztec reality is not a thing in itself. It is a process of constant unfolding, combining action and meaning into a "special kind of unity . . . in which [each] component is *essentially* interrelated, interdependent, co-related, interactive, and ultimately defined in terms of [the] other component" (150). Every poetic instance of the speech orchestrates surrounding actions into its meaning. From this theoretical foothold, the complex temporality of *our* version of the speech of the Aztec priests—entangled in the three moments of 1524, 1564, and 1968—consolidates structures of constant unfolding that organized the speech in the first place. The historical dislocations that make the speech difficult to contextualize give it its resonance in the "world in motion"— the Nahua space-time with its agonistic fragmentary now, the temporal heterogeneity—that it sets out for itself. To return to the organizing problem of this chapter—that is, what to make of the colonial mediation of the speech—we see that that mediation is already indigenized. The speech is constituted in a designative framework that is always already becoming indigenous by virtue of its conjunctural structure. By looking outward from the conceptual rhythms native to the speech, we see that its poetics prepared it to always recapture itself in its own terms. "The night   the winde" demarcates a poetic act whose meaning coheres when those transhistorical embers burst and send sparks flying into an atmosphere of time still in motion and surrounded by combustible

materials. "The night the winde" is a rhythm illuminated by the situations it sets aflame.

A Conjuncture of the Sun

An image of the Aztec world in motion appears in Edward Dorn's drawing for an unpublished collection of poems made in Mexico, "Mexico
Scrapbook," around the time that he, Jennifer Dunbar Dorn, and Gordon Brotherston translated the "Aztec Priests' Reply" (*Derelict* 330). The
drawing (plate 4) is based on the Aztec sunstone, with which readers
will probably have some familiarity. The massive basalt calendar—on
which the glyphs representing shifting world ages circle, like a cosmic
serpent, around the face of the sun god, Tonatiuh[15]—appears in Mexican and Mexican American art, signifying allegiance to what José David
Saldívar calls the psychogeography of "Greater Mexico." Its most celebrated reworking is Octavio Paz's *Sunstone* (1957), a book-length poem
whose single sentence begins in the same way that it ends—"a crystal
willow, a poplar of water,/a tall fountain the wind arches over,/a tree
deep-rooted yet dancing still,/a course of a river that turns, moves on,/
doubles back, and comes full circle,/forever arriving:"—conveying with
that poem-ending colon the poem's perpetual rebeginning (11). As in the
Aztec priests' speech, in Paz's poem a world in motion curls like a snake
around a stone of time, gripping it while traversing its surface. Yet for
Paz the indigenous was always constituted within the nation form, an
elemental expression of standard Hegelian historical destiny.

In Dorn's drawing that elementalism is construed differently: that circularity is seen in the arrow curled upon itself, akin to the prodigious serpent of the ouroboros, rejuvenating itself in its pursuit of itself. But here
the figuration of a world in motion is also marked in the symbols that
swirl around the snake-like arrow. These symbols are chemical equations
that signify the entropy of stars making energy, a catalytic process called
the carbon-nitrogen-oxygen cycle used by stars much hotter and less ef-
ficient than our sun.[16] In playing on themes of accelerated solar entropy,
Dorn invokes the basic meaning of the calendar stone, which tracks the
movement of cosmic eras across deep scales of time, scales that the stone
characterizes as moving suns. Noting that entropy (*tlazolli* in Nahuatl) is
a central meaning of the Aztec moving suns, Maffie writes: "Disordering,
degenerating, disintegrating, deranging, and decomposing forces are meta-
physically fundamental and ineliminable. This gives rise to one of the
defining characteristics of human existence: the Fifth Sun-Earth Ordering is a perilous habitat for humans. It is 'slippery,' as a Nahua proverb
recorded by Sahagún puts it" (167). Life amid the moving suns is slippery

because it falls inside systems trying to make themselves more stable, thinking with each step that they are making themselves more stable but only to create new unstable systems. That is, just when we think we have order, we find disorder; when we capture identity, we are seized by difference; just as we find meaning, discrepancy; with unity, plurality; in rest, motion; being, beings; structure, conjuncture; negativity, negativizability. In the Aztec world in motion, such systemic instability does not connote chaos. As the arrow pointed to itself in Dorn's drawing suggests, order depends on a constant movement—much as the balance of a person's walking depends on a constant tumbling forward (one of Maffie's metaphors)—of which the procession of the suns is meant to remind us (138). To convey this meaning of balanced imbalance, Dorn's "Mexico Scrapbook" interweaves his sunstone into an assemblage of drawings, photography, poetry, and collage (plates 5 and 6). The photograph in plate 5 shows his child in early walking stages bathed in the sun's light, learning to balance imbalances beneath the unbalanced balancing act that is solar entropy. Likewise placed beneath that burning sun, the scene in the collage of plate 6 traces the outline of the ceiba tree in plate 5, the tree on which the child walks, centering a relief of the sunstone in its boughs. In these pieces, the idea of cosmic entropy inflects the meaning of the scrapbook: assemblage brings together the traces of a trip to Mexico as something that cannot cohere into precisions of personhood or society.

In the political atmosphere of twentieth-century Latin America, national historical destiny converged with developmentalist economic models and, conversely, pro-indigenous, anti-imperial resistance movements (Saldaña-Portillo). In this world, Dorn's commitments were, as Robert Creeley puts it, "painfully, movingly, *political*" (qtd. in Dorn, *Derelict* 18). Dorn translated the poetry of, and materially contributed to, guerrillas in Latin America and Indian resistance movements in North America. While Dorn has therefore been characterized as a poet committed to addressing the exploitation and inequalities of racial capitalism, he nonetheless remained skeptical about identifications that reinscribed imperial historicities (Western capitalist or Soviet Marxist) in which all self-reckoning must be had. This was a most grotesque form of egoism to him: "I listen to anti-state arguments that strike me as stupid also," he writes in a commentary on his photo-essay ethnography (with Leroy Lucas) of Shoshone Indians, "I've got a note: the world and the uselessness of national boundaries. With the provision that any kind of one world idea is usually a trick of misunderstanding of what to be a whole world is. One world is not necessarily a whole world. . . . It has to be far more radical and far more subversive than that" (*Poet* 28). This far more subversive act, upon which his political commitments depended, was the recognition of nonperipheralizing, autonomous, self-centering worlds: "They're not trying to overthrow national life. . . . They're simply trying to be Indians" (*Poet* 11). That pull is enough to take into *inamic* conjuncture the world of the scrapbook, its inhabitants, and their political conflicts.

In Dorn's scrapbook, the poetry of conjuncture makes itself felt in the unsteady footing that drawings, poems, photographs, newspaper clippings, and collages hold in a medium whose cogency depends on the disarticulated ephemera of everyday life. In the scrapbook, items stand together yet, as a result of their manifold momentariness, also fall apart from one another, each page moving along, like Dorn's sun-washed son, in an art of controlled falling. Dorn distills this art of controlled falling in the poem written alongside the sunstone embossed in the collage:

> None of the words in English
> have such delicate temporal boundary
> They stop in poverty
> or go on forever
> because false revolution
> comes right around
> to the Biggest
> in the eyes of the
> Smallest   (*Derelict* 340)

The poem is about precision and control, wishing for a type of language that does not distort itself in the service of "false revolution." This is in keeping with Dorn's poetry in the late 1960s and early 1970s, which disentangled itself from the influence of Charles Olson by virtue of a skeptical attitude toward what Robert von Hallberg calls the "exploratory" mode of Olson's poetry (198). Unlike Olson, Dorn does not set out to survey and document fields of knowledge. His mode is a reflexive turn from exploration, exploring the problems of exploring. From cautious self-reflection Dorn wished to create a fulcrum of humane art on which to balance the identitarian excesses of political aesthetics and the imaginational poverty of aesthetic depoliticization. The challenge that animates such poetry is the vulnerability of language to ideological manipulation. In this poem, the intimacy of critique riles inside a language that cannot communicate the historical scale or "temporal boundary" of the ephemera that surround it. Rather, the poem suggests that the ephemera have what it takes to express the scale necessary for a humane poetics. In the scrapbook, these ephemera include a drawing of a ceiba tree, the Spanish word "úle" for natural rubber (i.e., *hule*), and the embossed sunstone of plate 6. As Dorn seems to have known, the ceiba (*ceiba pentandra*) is of a piece with the sunstone, insofar as each symbolizes Mesoamerican space-time: the sunstone depicts the Aztec world ages, and the ceiba is the Mayan world tree or *axis mundi* where upper and lower worlds meet.[17] Dorn conjoins these two symbols with the Spanish word for rubber, *hule* (i.e., "úle"). Because the ceiba does not produce rubber, we must find what connects the drawing, sunstone, and word elsewhere. The connection is to be found in the word's Nahuatl etymon, *olli*, a word for rubber that is related to the Nahuatl word for movement, *ollin*. The etymological link results from the flexibility and bounciness of rubber, used throughout pre-Columbian Mesoamerica for the famous ceremonial ballgames. In classic Mesoamerica, the ball's movement in the game was seen a ritual reenactment of the sun's movement through the sky and underworld, the *axis mundi* of the ceiba. Moreover, such movement invokes a central religious motif that is echoed in the Aztec name for the current world age of the sunstone, *Nahui Ollin*, meaning literally "Four Movement." *Nahui Ollin* is a slippery and elastic era prone to earthquakes and entropy (Miller and Taube 186, 144, 42–43, 70–71). This was the era in which the Aztec priests spoke their world poetics to the Spanish friars, while slipping into various temporalities configured nonetheless in the rhythm by which those slips patterned the same art of declivities that Dorn calls the art of "simply trying to be."

In the midst of its ephemera, the poem's self-critical attitude is rendered as a controlled fall. That is, the poem tellingly lacks the precision it desires, coming up short in its ability to find footing in its analytical object. Its situation is far too complex: "Biggest," "Smallest," and "false revolution" float around one another in a stream of predicates and prepositions that wash away the self-assurance of the causal conjunction, "because." Here, the intimacy of Dorn's critique is a recognition that the Mesoamerican poetics that reveal to him his lack of precision cannot also be a way for him to achieve that precision. They can only disclose his distance from the object. This is what he called the "secret, inward, resistance" of native materials when they traverse cultural lines—or when they are traversed upon by an *exploratory* mode (Dorn qtd. in Dresman 92). But in falling away from the material he also comes closer to it. Mutual dis-identification is, after all, a central meaning of the parallelist or *inamic* poetics that casts the Nahuatl world in motion. Viewed—like the meeting of Nahua and Spaniard in the Aztec priests' speech—as an active manifestation of *inamichuan*, his precipitous falling away from the cultural material recalls the contrapuntal complementarity that tips the Nahuatl world into its motion. This paradoxical situation, in which Dorn's distance is a type of nearness, is enabled by material that can subsume him without itself being subsumed. It is a world poetics that emerges from the poetic forms of its native sources. In his translation of those forms, it is not exactly the case that he recaptures them from one colonial archive for another. We can see also that Tenochtitlan lives on in the flaking embers of its linguistic forms: *inamic* poetics subsumes, because it transumes, its translator while he floats like a flaking bit of kindle into the slippery night airs of Mesoamerica.

Part One

PICTOGRAPHIC METONYMS

2
PICTOGRAPHIC KINSHIPS

Simon Ortiz's *Spiral Lands*
and Jaime de Angulo's *Old Time Stories*

In 2010, a comrade of Dorn's in the Indian Nations of North America collaborated with the German artist Andrea Geyer on a project titled *Spiral Lands*, inspired by the pictographic "ledger books" of the nineteenth and early twentieth centuries, in which "the 'writing' on top of 'writing' on top of 'writing' . . . illustrate a literal translation of a battle over signification" (*Spiral* 175). The centerpiece of this collaboration between the Acoma Pueblo poet Simon Ortiz and Geyer is the photograph of the "Newspaper Rock" shown in figure 3 of the present book's introduction. It serves as a centerpiece because the collaboration—like the palimpsest of petroglyphs called "Newspaper Rock"—involves multiple artists, writers, happenings, and layers of inscription. Geyer's images, on which Ortiz's poems are superimposed, are interspersed with musings on the written word from Ortiz and Geyer, as well from the Mvskoke-Creek poet Joy Harjo (specifically, from her own collaboration with photographer Stephen Strom) and the Cherokee artist Jimmie Durham's lectures on the practice of art as revolutionary struggle. These musings reflect on the continuum between breath, voice, writing, and rock art. "There are voices inside of rocks, shallow washes, shifting skies," reads a quote that carries a central motif, "they are not silent" (*Spiral* 175).

The figure of voices lurking in rocks is familiar for Ortiz. His poems collected in the omnibus *Woven Stone* return to it frequently: "Look the plants with bells/Look the stones with voices," "they will come,/singing, dancing/bringing gifts,/the stones with voices,/the plants with bells," "'chiseled'/into mind or memory stone—/into thoughts of sound itself," "Below are dark lines of stone,/fluff of trees, mountains/and the Earth's people—all of it,/the Feather in a prayer," "Little Wren, this morning, quickly/make me a song/made of sandstone clefts,/a bit of yucca growing there," "What is it but stone,/the earth in your mouth" (46, 49, 52,

122, 134, 202). In these poems the figure of a speaking stone represents the petroglyphs in the US Southwest. These stones with voices appear again in *Spiral Lands*, where they wish to understand their place in a historiography that includes nonhuman beings, even stones and rocks: "Carved, painted, over and again—hundreds—ends tucked and ends floating. . . . They move inward, coil around the center of their speaking, and then move out again. A motion that carries the gentle force of continuity like breath" (179). The force of the simile here is tellingly weak; "like breath" suggests that it is not breath but something analogous to it, something else presenting itself *as* breath. The petroglyphs or rock writings are not exactly voices in a human sense. They move with the slow coiling *rhusmos* of a snake, whose rhythm of being is felt in the multiple layers of pictographic text (spanning thousands of years, involving countless cultural histories) inscribed in the long duration of the rock. The melee of signification is a slow temporality of snakes pressing their form through the rock into the scene of reading.

The poem therefore presents itself in a conscious contradiction: while the meanings of these glyphs might be lost, their way of making meaning remains to give form to those illegibilities. Even through the silences of the rock, the snake presses its "gentle force of continuity." Ortiz writes: "We do not know what they mean, but we know they are involved in their meaning . . . I've never been sure./What it is./A scene . . . I want to know but maybe I'm not to know" (*Spiral* 178). Still, even as he admits his pictographic illiteracy, he calls on the pictographs to shape his sense of loss and disconnection from the glyphs: "I turn my gaze to the morning sun and see that the walls of the canyon show figures hovering above the line of the trees. Life-size they stand painted and packed into the walls. Suddenly I feel a gaze returned. Some of them have little creatures sitting beside them or on their shoulders. I sit down. *Herds of sheep run along*" (*Spiral* 178). Turning away from the rock art, he sees its figures leaping over the trees and looking back at him, becoming the material bodies of a surrounding landscape. While elusive as a galloping herd of sheep, the glyphs gallop like such sheep across a landscape; which is to say, in the poem, the petroglyphs absorb the contents of a landscape into their aesthetic configuration, even while their meanings remain evasive. This chapter examines what that configuration is exactly, and how it connects signs to environments—glyphs to snakes, sheep, stones, and breath. "The Land is," Ortiz writes, "The Land speaks—speaks back to you and you can listen" (*Spiral* 181). With special attention to the contexting function of pictographic reading, this chapter argues that such encounters as the one described by Ortiz carry special conceptions of kinship that involve signs in the worlds of agential nonhumans.

FIGURE 9 Simon Ortiz's poem superimposed on Newspaper Rock in *Spiral Lands*, his collaboration with German artist and photographer Andrea Geyer (2011). Courtesy of Simon Ortiz.

Moreover, in the poem that Ortiz and Geyer superimpose on the photograph of Newspaper Rock, a sense of kinship captures even the colonial historicities of rock writing—creating complex interspecies interactions and networks (fig. 9). As he puts it, these interspecies kinships involve "even the fact of conquistadors, conquistadors." The poem reads:

I've never been sure.
What it is.
A scene.

Variety, like a carnival. Or a state fair. A doing. Something happening.
And how old is it? It is fairly contemporary in some aspects and details.
Even the ride-like spirals. And the zig-zag contraption figure. Snake loops.

Buffalo. Mountain sheep. Kaahs-kuh. The name of an elder uncle. Elk.
Antelope. Deer. Goat. And horses. A number of horses. One or two with riders.
And the horses I figure are recent. Since Spanish conquistador times at least.

So it doesn't figure.
Sometimes, no.
Footprints, for example.

And snake tracks.
And a mark like time.
Or something magic.

I want to know but maybe I'm not to know. Being within the culture
sometimes is:
Not knowing and accepting it's okay. Knowing you're within is knowledge enough.
You're part of all that has taken place: buffalos, mountain sheep, elks, antelope, deer, goats, horses, their riders, even the fact of conquistadors,
conquistadors.
                                                                (*Spiral* 181)

The poem thickens its context by translating environmental elements into
signs, rendering footprints, snake tracks, and natural striations in the rock
into significations left behind by movements of the natural world. Those
significations are presented here for the reader, in the curls and ligatures
of alphabetic inscription. In much the same way as the "sign" in classical
antiquity was conceptualized as trace or evidence of the emergence of an
expression (Mannetti 14; Most and Laks 252), the sign here is held in a
suspended state of emergence or emergency, coming from animal worlds
into human perception. Such ecology of semiotic emergency is what the
Anishinaabe scholar Niigaanwewidam James Sinclair calls the "network
of intellectual and physical pathways" that petroglyphs bear, the "complex ecological and spiritual systems [embedded] in particular places"
(8).[1] The petroglyphs do not represent landscapes so much as they bear
the trace of the emergence of those never-inert landscapes in the midst
of their readers. Ortiz anticipates Sinclair's idea that petroglyphs are
living ecological networks in an early essay. Titled *Song, Poetry, and
Language—Expression and Perception* (1978), it casts poetic meaning as
the end product of interactions between Ortiz, his father, their spirit fa-
miliars (Mountain Lion and Deer), and the ecological terrain through
which they all move. The occasion is a hunting trip in which Ortiz realizes that hunting songs are prototypical of ecological poetics, inasmuch
as a successful catch depends on sympathetic reciprocities between the
song and the animal world—that is, the mimesis of songs entrances and
captures the mimetic spirit of animals. Yet, more than just Frazer-style
sympathetic magic, the takeaway from such reciprocity is the fusion between expression and the perception of a nonhuman world. This type of

singing brings into focus "the totality of what is around," when there is "no division between that within you and that without you as there is no division between expression and perception" (*Song* 10, 8). In such songs, the "sign" is a scene of dynamic interaction between humans and nonhumans—a kind of kinship that is expressed as a contexting function.

Ortiz himself calls this interactive conception of the sign "context," and explains that for him context is how poems perceive and express relationships. A poem "is made substantial by its context," he writes, "The meaning that it has for me is that I recognize myself as a person in an active relationship—the hunting act—with Mountain Lion, the spirit friend and guide, and Deer. It is a prayer. A prayer song . . . I express myself as well as realize the experience" (*Song* 6, 5). Kinship with other-than-humans is a recurring theme in native poetries. But Ortiz refers to something more specific than interspecies communing. He talks about poetry as a form of attention that brings into the light the interspecies milieus that bring poetry into being. The content of his poems is shaped by the contexts they set out to describe.

Still, context in the Americas is more than animals and landscapes; this context involves colonial history. As his poem about Newspaper Rock tells, the scene of pictographic reading involves "even the fact of conquistadors." It involves the scrim of five hundred years of colonialism that made the pictographs into an alien or eccentric sign system. Insofar as the poet intends to thicken context, then, that context must include the conditions in which a native poet—even when writing in the pastoral remove of a nature poem—must reckon with material subjugations of native people, cultures, and languages. Even conquest must appear in the kinships of context. Yet, if this contexting function is ruled by the special aesthetic configuration of the pictograph—if the contents of a historical archive change when cast in the forms of indigenous knowledge systems, if the snake indeed presses its rhythms into the reading scene—then even "the fact of conquistadors" is absorbed into the forms of attention specific to the pictograph.

Those pictographic forms of attention or styles of perception prioritize the emergence of ecological reciprocities. In them, the colonial sign is caught in the larger spiral through which language is a trace of vital movements in an environment. In this way, even English becomes an indigenous language: "We can make use of English," Ortiz writes, "and determine for ourselves how English is to be a part of our lives socially, culturally, and politically." To think that indigenous resistance must only ever be opposing is "an internalized colonized mode of thought" of a piece with discourses of identitarian difference that reinscribe people in the margins of reality. "English language writing can work to our advantage when we write with a sense of Indigenous consciousness" ("Speaking-Writing" xiii–xiv). These words appear in a larger debate in American Indian studies on the proper context of native literature. Showcased in a volume edited by Jace Weaver, Craig Womack, and Robert Warrior, Ortiz's position in that debate is that the context of indigenous poetics is not diminished but is fulfilled in its reckoning with colonial reality. "The struggle against colonialism," he writes, is that "which has given substance to what is authentic" (256). The editors of that volume understand Ortiz's words to mean that he "brilliantly lays claim to English as an Indian language instead of the omnipresent cliché that Indian people are the victims of English" (xviii). Yet the way in which he does so—with recourse to the poetics of a pictographic spiral—nonetheless troubles the boundaries around the English language. English becomes a trace of deeper movements in a field of ecological relations created by pictographic literacy. If English is context for Ortiz, it is context shaped by the nonhuman feedbacks of pictography.

As I suggest, in *Spiral Lands* these feedbacks are figured in the spiral, an ambidirectional curve that emanates from a point, moving farther away as it revolves from that point to which its curving line always leads back. It is the sign conceptualized as always emergent from rocks and galloping sheep, the land speaking for itself, even in those instances where the poet appears to turn away in frustrated speech from the land. Such ambidirectional movement of signs through environments and changing social contexts prompts such questions as: what happens to the meaning of a pictograph in its movements through the fissures, interstices, dislocations, and destabilizations of intercultural circulation? How does intercultural circulation affect its meaning, and, in turn, how does the self-emergent sign throw light upon the meaning of intercultural circulation? If, as scholar of Zuni petroglyphs M. Jane Young suggests, "the particular meaning articulated in a given moment" of pictographic reading "depends on the context, the situation, in which meaning is given voice," how do those situations inhere in the particular contexting function of the pictograph through which they are articulated? How are the situations of pictography pictographic?

In this chapter, I argue that such situations can be understood as pictographic when we consider the contexting function of pictography—its way of emphasizing the role that the reading scene plays in what is read and how it is read. In this way, its contexting function is fulfilled and amplified by the range of contextual situations it takes into its ambit, "even the fact of conquistadors." This ecological metonymy—as Young characterizes it—is a contexting function in search of contents, absorbing those contents into its semiotic ecology. To examine this absorption, this chapter offers an extended close reading of one spiral-like figure in Jaime de Angulo's writings. This figure exemplifies colonial historicity—after all, de Angulo is a Spanish American anthropologist. Yet in those writings that history is recast, by way of the pictograph, into a temporality akin to the spiral of Ortiz's works. This comparative arc, moving from Ortiz to de Angulo back to Ortiz, is meant to demonstrate how the pictograph bears intercultural legibilities and kinships. By way of pictographic kinship, or the style of ecological attention fostered by pictographic contextualism, the poetics of these two writers can be seen as traces of that broader "network of intellectual and physical pathways" that Sinclair finds in the petroglyphs of the Americas.

Old-Time Parabolas

The strange story of de Angulo could begin in many places. But with regard to its double entanglement in modernist poetics and anthropological discourses, it begins in California. De Angulo appeared in the scene of anthropology by way of an accidental meeting with Alfred Kroeber on Christmas Day, 1918. The war had just ended, returning First Lieutenant de Angulo home to Carmel, California, where national optimism had taken hold. The United States had made its first mark on the fields of Europe militarily, and now, it seemed, it was time to do so intellectually as well. For such a scholar as Kroeber, as well as Edward Sapir, to whom Kroeber would soon introduce de Angulo (in correspondence, at least)—members of the first generation of American anthropologists to receive doctorates under the instruction of Franz Boas at Columbia University—this meant an opportunity to disentangle the discipline from its European trappings.

Boas dismissed the cultural evolutionism and biological determinism that had fueled ethnological racism in the previous century (Stocking, *Race* 264). He stressed extensive collection of ethnographies that would demonstrate a cultural pluralism to contravene the racial evolutionism of nineteenth-century ethnology—those long-lived inheritances of quasi-Hegelian progressive time (Leeds-Hurwitz 2).[2] As suggested in this book's introduction, Sapir—one of Boas's earliest students—believed that the cultural feature by which the elemental forms of social life could be revealed was poetic language, especially in its tremendous "variety of formal patterns" (125, 131). De Angulo could not agree more, writing in his unpublished supplement to Sapir, "[n]ot economy is the mainspring of language, or of fashion, or of some forms of art, but rather the spirit of play, the delight in patterns of form" ("What" 324). Focusing on human social organization as an offshoot of poetic form, de Angulo's "formalism" interconnected linguistics, poetics, and anthropology—each no more than a fractal extension of the deeper dialectic of form in the varied patterns of human making.

Yet in spite of his spirited engagement, a recurrent issue for his minders in the discipline was that de Angulo was completely untrained. Kroeber brought him into the anthropological fold because de Angulo had been doing large amounts of fieldwork, independently learning native languages and transcribing stories, through a casual network of friends from tribes of northern California, guided purely by his poetic understanding of the culture concept. As it turned out, professional anthropologists had little patience for de Angulo's poetic enthusiasm. Kroeber eventually dismissed him an intellectual eccentric: "De Angulo has quite unusual intellect along with an unstable personality. He gets tremendous pure enthusiasms as a result of which he works some aspect of science through then drops it. . . . Emotionally he is inclined to be vehement and infantile" (Kroeber and Sapir 384–85). Kroeber touches on de Angulo's aestheticism; as Robert Brightman puts it, "enthusiasm for the deployment of artistic sensibilities and mediums" led his research, an enthusiasm that "prefigured disciplinary preoccupations with reflexivism that emerged in the 1980s" (184–85). Preoccupied with the poetics of intercultural encounters, making him effectively a poet of context, de Angulo was doing "writing cultures" a half century before the "writing cultures" debate made vogue such concerns.

The "writing cultures" debate of the 1980s—its eponym the *Writing Culture* volume edited by James Clifford and George Marcus (1986)—was an interdisciplinary debate about anthropological genre. Ethnographic realism naturalized the space, time, experience, and outlook of the anthropologist, and thus instantiated the anthropologist's dominant position over their object of analysis. Drawing on Mary Louise Pratt's notion of the "contact zone"—"the space in which peoples geographically and historically separated come into contact with each other and establish ongoing relations, usually involving conditions of coercion, radical inequality, and intractable conflict" (qtd. in Clifford's *Routes* 192)—Clifford aimed to decolonize anthropological research by unfixing it from the realist representation of fieldwork. To call attention to the inequities of fieldwork realism, Clifford and "writing cultures" writers applied strategies of reflexivity, multilayered representation, intercultural voicing, dialogic textual construction, and fictocritical modes. One problem, however, was that in Clifford's writings the contact zone was not the jarring site of uneven encounter with an exotic and subordinated other; it was—as Clifford Geertz later put it, somewhat unfairly—"a reserved, middle-distance spectator moving uneasily through a hall of mirrors . . . not among castaway 'natives,' or indeed any 'peoples' at all, but among . . . ethnological exhibitions, tourist sites, art-show seminars, museum consultancies, cultural studies conferences, travelers' hotels . . . consequential collages [and] real life magic boxes." Becoming a kind of superordinate expression of the colonial palimpsest to which it claimed opposition, the new multimodal genre of anthropological writing was akin to the assemblage, collage, décollage, and decoupage of the high modernists.

In his accidental imbrication of high modernist aesthetics and the anthropological project, de Angulo effectively got "there" first. Yet he distinctly does it from the angle of poetic form, and never lets go of the native ontologies embedded in those forms, in a way that perhaps prefigures Renato Rosaldo and his works of "antropoesía." Like the poet-anthropologist Rosaldo, de Angulo manipulated figures, tropes, and poetic hermeneutics to create conscious contradictions in the intercultural encounter of the anthropological scene—to enact that "irruption" that Rosaldo says makes possible new temporalizations and worlds (101). More than just what Clifford wryly called his "deep hanging out" (qtd. in Geertz), this was anthropological deep text achieved in poetic forms of expressive contradiction, activating the tension points of interculturality while giving space to native poetic and philosophical systems.

This mode played itself out in the series of radio broadcasts that de Angulo performed on the listener-supported Berkeley radio station KPFA in 1949. Called *Old Time Stories*, the 95 fifteen-minute segments combining narrative, myth, poetry, and music, are—as Wendy Leeds-Hurwitz puts it in her disciplinary biography of de Angulo—"the real synthesis of his years of work with the various California Indian groups" (268). Largely based on his fieldwork with Pit River (Achumawi and Atsugewi), Shasta, Eastern Pomo, Karok, Paiute, Modoc, Sierra Miwok, and Kalapuya tribes—most of which was unpublished and unremunerated— *Old Time Stories* translates and adapts the themes, poetic structures, musical elements, and ethnographic details (such as hut-making, basket-weaving, and bow-stringing techniques) of the indigenous cultural systems of northern California. But it is not a typical ethnography. In it, the necessary journey that Lévi-Strauss so loathed (i.e., "I hate traveling and explorers") is rendered as a journey of animals into the worlds of other animals (*Tristes* 7). If de Angulo's *Old Time Stories* is transcultural encounter, its historicity is anything but realist; rather, it is a kind of historiography in which time and animal worlds interact. The ethnographer, his family, and close friends are presented as a pack of animals traveling the California countryside on their way from their home in the inland woods to visit friends on the coast. The ethnographer is something like a Wolf-Coyote hybrid, his wife (the anthropologist Lucy Freeland aka Nancy de Angulo) is "Antelope-woman," his daughter (Gui de Angulo aka Gui Mayo) is "Oriole-girl," and his friend William Ralganal Benson (the celebrated Eastern Pomo basketmaker and storyteller) is "Turtle Old Man" (*Shabegok* 104). Along the way, they meet such groups as the "Gazelle People," "Hawk People," "Crane People," "Grass People," and "Flint People," loosely based on indigenous groups of northern California, who tell about their societies and cultures. Rather than reify these cultures as an analytical object, this nonhuman fictocritical ethnography immerses its writer in the nonhuman worlds of the cultures he sets out to describe. Rather than tell the story of how Benson told him the Eastern Pomo story of the creation of the world, de Angulo's ethnography takes place in that mythopoetic world, in which animal people preceded the human people, in which animal storytellers had the world-making power of gods, and in which all these events are inscribed in the poetic forms that inform their reality.[3] Distinct from what we might expect from a mythic understanding of reality, these mythopoetic frameworks do not introduce repetitive certainty in the narrative. On the contrary, their enunciative multiplicity—shifting in the tellings and movements of each version's teller—encourages a kind of flexibly accepting skepticism, "mercurial with coexisting possible universes" (Duncan, *Poet's Mind* 234), whose end affirmations embrace the imagination and its ontological impacts.

One of the important stories in this mythistorical world is of a visit that "Old Man Coyote" makes to the Hawk People. This ethnographic scene is interlaced with a song sung by one of the Hawks, named Pis'wis'na, which in the manuscript is accompanied by a drawing of the singing hawk (fig. 10). In this story the anthropological and poetic range of *Old Time Stories* gives pictographic shape to its historical contents. History here is formed in its mythopoetic instances—it is a mythopoiesis that consists of animal worlds and colonial encounters. This begins when Old Man Coyote, which is a mask for de Angulo, recounts the Hawk's song, which is about losing oneself in a mask, whereby the narrative anxiously reflects on the limits of its reflexivity:

> I am Pis'wis'na, the Hawk.
> I am myself.
> I thought I was myself
> But I am only a head.
> I am a head crying in the desert. (*Indian* 152)

The hawk doubts its declaration that it is a hawk because, in Old Man Coyote's voicing, it is not fully itself. The song thus proposes ethnographic representation as a source of doubt and derangement. What, it asks, can such a song transmit when that transmission moves through the different bodies and cultures of its audiences? How does that transmission affect

FIGURE 10 Jaime de Angulo's pictographic drawing (ca. 1950) of the Hawk
People's hut, in which Pis'wis'na sings a song to Old Man Coyote and his traveling
family (published in *Indian Tales* 18). Jaime de Angulo Papers (Collection 160),
UCLA Library Special Collections, Charles E. Young Research Library.

the self-reckoning of the object's maker? And who or what, if not the
object's maker, presents itself before us when that ethnographic object
completes its intercultural transit? And what, amid these transits, *is* this
voice that can carry so many embodiments?

These questions bear political problematics. As de Angulo knew,
there are real people behind these cultural objects. The person behind
Pis'wis'na's song was the Modoc healer of native northern California
named Kate Gordon, in whose healing ceremony at Alturas de Angulo
participated in 1925. "Why you no sing?" he says Gordon shouted at him.
"*Canta, canta!*," she cries, imploring him to join her in the song that
serves as a source text for the Hawk's song (Gordon's song later appears
as de Angulo's poem titled "Old Kate's Medicine Song") (*Indians* 70):

> Without a body I am
> i am the song
>
> Without a head I am
> i am the head
>
> i am a head without a song
> i am rolling down the hill (*Coyote's* 65)

The scene of Gordon's singing—in which de Angulo perhaps felt the strange alienation of singing her song, like a Coyote pretending to be a Hawk—appears in de Angulo's more straightforward ethnography of native groups in Alturas, California, in the 1920s, *Indians in Overalls*. In that book, Gordon's "Medicine Song" has traditional and contextual significances.[1] Its immediate context is the deportation of Modoc Indians to Oklahoma after the Modoc Wars of 1870s (victims of so-called clearances by "gold bug" whites). A Modoc woman, Gordon would not have been allowed to return to California until 1909 (she lived in Oregon), after whites had exhausted mining operations in the area (Dunbar-Ortiz 127–30). This state of exception proved foundational, as deputy assistant attorney general of the United States John Yoo invoked the Modoc clearances in 2003 as precedent for his infamous Torture Memos. The bodies subjected to enhanced interrogation in the contemporary "War on Terror," the bodies with no claim to their own bodies, were prefigured in the 1865 *Military Commissions* and 1873 *Modoc Indian Prisoners* legal opinions that declared open season on Modoc life (Dunbar-Ortiz 224; Byrd 226–27). In this light, Gordon's song takes on the grave expression of what it is to exist in the state of exception: without a body, without a head, without a song, she is nothing other than the unqualified physicality she bears in the eyes of judicial power. This is all the more striking in consideration of her archival afterlife, where again she remains incomplete, a few words and characteristics in the writings of others. Still, across her invisibilities, she has a historical persistence in the endurance of her song. While the song is vexed by bodily disappearance, it affirms its ability to register that disappearance in its singability. Her "*canta!*" comes across as metaleptic, leaping from the scene of the healing ceremony into the histories of colonial terror that require the healing work of such a song.

This is to say: Gordon's song is not dispirited or defeated. Sung in 1925, in the wake of decades of colonial depradation, the song's every line repeats its first-person assertion of being, one that culminates in the only action in the song, when she says that she is "a head without a song . . . rolling down the hill." Prevalent throughout the storytelling cultures of native North America, a "rolling head" song is typically embedded in a ghoul story, in which a dead person's head vengefully chases its enemies to eat them.[5] The attitude underlying Gordon's song is thus revanchist, intending to reclaim losses—loss of body, being, and belonging in California—and directed against the occupying US military forces. Gordon's song—which de Angulo sings in session 43 of *Old Time Stories*, "laua'awátsa sálílúlúadánmi [head only, I roll down the hill]"[6]—is anticolonial in context, yet its content is shaped by the rolling head trope of rollicking political recapture. What gives this mythic trope its historical "substance" is, to use Ortiz's words, "the struggle against colonialism" ("Towards" 256).

With Gordon's song as its primary context, we can return to Pis'wis'na's song with a clear view of its confluence in colonial history, revanchist mythopoetics, and the pictographic sign that puts these elements into dialogue. These multiple flows are channeled in *Old Time Stories* through an overarching sense of textual mutability, a fluid sense of form in which myth, ethnography, history, and poetry flow into each other. To the extent that de Angulo's symbol for such fluctuation was the pictograph (as I have argued in this book's introduction), the pictograph serves as a channel for the work's transdisciplinary multimodality. In this way, the pictographs of *Old Time Stories* deploy scenes of animal metamorphosis as a code for a poetics of textual flux. The animals are metonyms for the work's formal techniques by which history is rendered in its mythopoetic instances. This is more than just temporal heterogeneity, it is temporal heterogeneity defined by the totalizability of the mythic animal world and its metamorphoses.

In figure 10, for instance, Pis'wis'na enters the scene in three curls that recall de Angulo's metonymic figures for pictography: decenterings and parabolas. Those figures come to life by virtue of contemporary engagement with the sign: that is, a sign is never so alive as when it is the source of indeterminacy that de Angulo references with his pictographic parabolas. Like Ortiz's "sign" that is a scene of dynamic interaction between humans and nonhumans, de Angulo's spiraling figure comes to life by virtue of contemporary engagements with the creativity of the sign, the creative work that follows the prompt, "*canta*." With regard to this contemporaneity, Young—who focuses on the pictographs of the Southwest with which de Angulo was familiar[7]—uses the concept of metonymy to describe how the pictograph weaves social contexts into mnemonic scripts. Like a metonym, which uses a salient entity to refer to an abstraction, a pictograph uses an image to refer to a text of some kind, be it a narrative, song, or some other performance. In the space between the image and the text, between the mnemonic prompt and its performance, there is room for improvisation to meet the demands and desires of a current moment. The adjacency of memory and improvisation has, as Young puts it, a "compression" effect: it makes a pictograph's reader "aware of the presentness of the past . . . [by virtue of a pictograph's] ability to evoke stories of the myth time and consequently to make the past coexistent with the present" (153). Anthropologist Nancy Munn calls this the "transgenerational continuity" of pictographs (213), the way in which they connect present time to pasts at all tiers of relationality, human and nonhuman. This historiographical promiscuity introduces a sense of responsibility in scenes of pictographic reading: if the structure of feeling elicited by the pictograph compresses historical time into the mythic time of animals (as de Angulo's *Old Time Stories* does), then the bounded subjectivity in which a person builds an ethical life is not limited to their individualistic or even human-centered self. The temporality of the body in pictographic reading consists of the times of its various human and non-human speakers, those entities that are understood to be speaking through the "enunciative apparatus" of the pictograph (Culler, *Theory* 16, 34).

I cite Jonathan Culler's conception of voicing because it approximates a translation of what we can call pictographic multivocality. But I depart from it inasmuch as it is stuck to certain assumptions about what constitutes a voice in a poem. Culler's critique follows a line of thinking that emerges from critical attitudes in deconstruction toward presence and the alphabet. That is, Culler's conception of voicing targets a written tradition in which what we see on the page is supposed to have one-to-one sonic correspondence with what a poet wrote, reifying a textual stability homologous with alphabetical isomorphism (*Theory* 35, 176, 223). In its emphasis on the stability of selfsame signs, the critique lacks appreciation for signs that render subjects and objects in states of persistent mutability. Jean-Luc Nancy has noticed this aporia in the critique of voice with his idea that the "open extension" of voice must be something other than speech, if its politics are to achieve any kind of intercultural scalability. For Nancy, voice is an integral, sublingual vibrational channel in which language takes place (48). But it seems to me that this conception of voice goes too far in the other direction, undercutting the distinct forms of attention and relation created by particular signs. While the KPFA broadcasts are certainly worth listening to—for their fine musical grain and quality of Benjaminian-storyteller layering (Benjamin's own radio broadcasts are a revealing intertext), as well as for the eccentric quality of de Angulo's Caribbean English accent, a trace of his early years in British Honduras—the soundscape is organized by the "enunciative apparatus" of pictography and the special relations this apparatus makes (Culler, *Theory* 16, 34). The primary characteristic of pictographic reading is multivocality and the multiple temporalities that inhere in multiple voices. Each enunciation is conditioned by the experience and memory of previous enunciations, which in turn are themselves shaped by the presence of new voices in the agglomerate plenitude of never singular or self-stable time. In the reading of a pictographic text, each voice is the embodiment of its many speakers—human, nonhuman, and mythic—integrated in a system (akin to Gordon's imperative to *sing*) by which these many speakers are prompted to speak again.

Pictographic Kinships

This conception of voice becoming always other voices redounds to where Pis'wis'na's song goes next. In a sequence of unpublished and unrecorded sections of *Old Time Stories* we see Pis'wis'na's song grafted onto a new metamorphosis. The hawk—who was also an anxious ethnographic mask for the coyote—now becomes a werewolf troubled by the process of transformation in which it comes into being. In drawings and poems, the body "without a head"—Deleuzian indeed, in its animal-becomings, yet always linked to a historical context in its association with the rolling head songs—is shown to be Coyote's (see plate 3 and fig. 11). The animal form for the ethnographer-poet is now decapitated, while new voices rearticulate the song for new settings and situations. The new setting is an exchange of letters with Dorothy Pound and Ezra Pound, with whom de Angulo initiated a correspondence while Pound was at St. Elizabeths Psychiatric Hospital and he was at Fort Miley Veterans Hospital. "My name is Jaime de Angulo. I am here with cancer of the prostate," he wrote in his wryly melodramatic first letter, "so here goes, altho i have absolutely nothing to say. . . . I imagine that you are lonely. So am I" (G. de Angulo 384). The irony of his letter is that for having nothing to say, in these last years of his life, he produces his massive *Old Time Stories*, a portion of which takes place in the letter exchanges with the Pounds (moreover, at this time he also translates García Lorca and writes his lengthy supplement to Sapir, "What Is Language?"). In one of the letters to the Pounds—accompanying the drawing in figure 12—he reveals what is happening to Coyote, who is transformed now into a "Werewolf":

Werewolf
i came upon him in the dawn
lying at the edge of a wood
moulting his form
he turned and i saw his face so full of pain
that i fled   (qtd. in G. de Angulo 385)

Metamorphosis has patently linguistic registers in the poem: "moulting form" sounds like de Angulo's description of the pictograph as "acrobatic performance, which form, staid form, is seldom ready to produce" ("What"); the Werewolf's "turning" recalls de Angulo's descriptions of poetic indeterminacy as a curvilinear "parabola going out to no center . . . mercurial with coexisting possible universes" (Duncan, *Poet's Mind* 234); and the painful flight with which the poem ends mirrors the

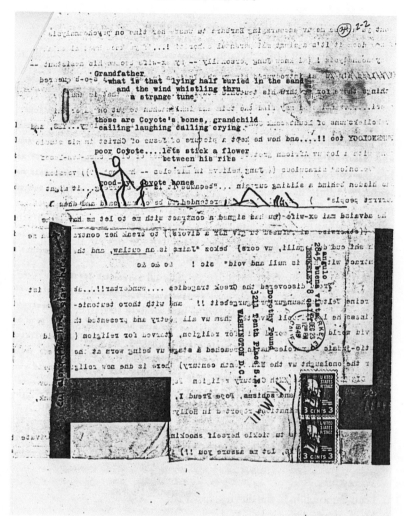

FIGURE 11 Jaime de Angulo's pictographic drawing (ca. 1950) of a headless Coyote appears in a typed letter to the Pounds. Jaime de Angulo Papers (MS 14), Special Collections and Archives, University Library, University of California, Santa Cruz.

metonymic leap from text to body, the leap by which his poems about metamorphosis instantiated in the author's real-life physical transformation. This poem that depicts a dynamic event of transformation also takes as its primary figure a kind of emblem of historical transformation. As plate 3 and figure 11 show, here the half-erased, "moulting" icon of Coyote is changing into a Werewolf. Seeing the change, a child asks his grandfather, “What is that lying half buried in the sand/and the wind whisting there/a strange tune”; to which the grandfather responds, “those are Coyote’s bones, grandchild/calling laughing calling crying.” In the poem for Pound in which this same icon is called “Werewolf” that transformation is complete: Coyote is a lycanthrope, the creature is a species of archaic shapeshifting folklore.

The most famous werewolf of modernist folklore is no doubt Freud’s “Wolf Man,” the Russian aristocrat Sergei Pankejeff through whom Freud articulated his notions of infantile neurosis, the primal scene, and the value of dreams in interpreting the unconscious. While de Angulo was a reader of psychoanalytical literature, he did not give much credence to mental interiorities. Even the above poem is all surfaces moving surfaces, more interested in temporal structure (the dawn, the moulting, the turning, the flight) than mind. In this regard, it recalls the readings of postcolonial lycanthropy that the Warwick Research Collective (WREC) gives of post–Cold War Russian novelist Victor Pelevin. WREC is particularly invested in Leon Trotsky’s conception of temporal density, in which

je l'ai surpris

FIGURE 12 Jaime de Angulo’s pictographic drawing (ca. 1950) of a werewolf in a reclined position, grimacing at its transformation. Jaime de Angulo Papers (Collection 160), UCLA Library Special Collections, Charles E. Young Research Library.

societies do not move necessarily through evolutionary frameworks of material progress because they can exploit the technological and cultural developments of other cultures—this is what Trotsky calls "combined and uneven development." Thus does world historical temporal heterogeneity consist in an "amalgam of archaic with more contemporary forms" (qtd. in WREC 6). In their readings of the contemporary werewolf novels of Pelevin, the collective finds in the strange archaic therianthrope a "structure of feeling" about such historical amalgamation. Pelevin uses the incongruity of the werewolf to express anxiety that "originates in traumatic transformations of local ecologies by imperialism or modernisation." The werewolf is the emblem of forceful incorporation and the converse "indigenous resistance" that presided over its originary articulation amid the clearances of the commons in eleventh-century Europe, that presides over the "critique of neoliberal capitalism" in Pelevin's anti-oligarchic post-Soviet fiction, and that takes hold in various "conjuncture[s] of fading and emergent regimes" of which de Angulo's 1949 was but one (WREC 98, 102). It is entirely possible that Pound's presence in de Angulo's critique of a postwar "RECAPIM (the REactionary CApitalist IMperialist complex)" introduced the very conditions by which such critique contradicted itself in its irreality. Postwar American empire was an incongruous continuity of antifascist political attitudes and the remnants of wartime fascism (that Pound represented), creating spectral correspondences for which the only workable metaphors appear to have been those of phantasmagoria and the supernatural. This is the same temporal potentiality that can be found in Freud's Russian aristocrat, if he is seen in the violence of his historical context (ca. 1910 in collapsing czarist Russia). Pankejeff was indeed a wolfman inasmuch as he was—like de Angulo's werewolf—an expression of the "conjuncture of fading and emergent regimes" (that is, the Russian aristocracy and the emergent Soviet socialist state).

The mythopoetic world of the werewolf is typically construed as a premodern fixation, stuck on enchantments with which the modern, secular, rational, and historically reflexive era has done away. This temporal construction depends on the myth that myth is monomythic—singularly and uniformly repetitive, unreflective, and historically unspecific. In actuality, there are plenty of mythological systems with built-in skepticism and historicity. Contemporary Mayans, for instance, have a conception of myth that anthropologist Dennis Tedlock translates as "mythistory," or myth as a means of participating in the process of historical unfolding. In such myth, people find "traces of divine movements" in their actions and, in turn, remain "alert to the reassertion of the patterns of the past in present events" (*Popol Vuh* 58–60).[8] This sort of historically responsive mythic system is echoed in anthropologist Michael Taussig's writings on the tactical uses of skepticism in certain magical regimes ("Viscerality"); or, to address the myth that the secular state ordains itself without recourse to mythology, in his writings on the oscillation between literality and metaphoricity by which myths are in turn ideological and critically reflexive. They are ideological when literal, indistinguishable from reality itself; then a poet or artist comes along to reveal their metaphoricity, the pliable relation between signs and things, which thus breaks the spell of the magic of the seemingly real and intractable state (*Magic of the State* 186). These versions of myth as a way of thinking that is skeptical, reflexive, and historically specific revisit the writings of Max Horkheimer and Theodor Adorno on the "dialectic of Enlightenment," which posited that Enlightenment philosophy was captive—in productive and unproductive ways—to the very magical thinking it condemned. The verso of this point, which the writings of Tedlock and Taussig bring to light, is that myth exerts a shaping force on historical forms and configurations.

De Angulo's werewolf exemplifies such a reading of myth and its poetics. It expresses a historical conjuncture at which voices of the past were endangered by the same contemporary energies that would seek to give them life. In his translation of the poem, Pound appears as a voice out of his time desperate to lay hold of this mythistorical werewolf's tail:

> At least best hv/ got so far   but hv/ had to twist his
> tail
> Werewolf   in selvage I saw ,
> In day's dawn shifting his shape .
> In leaf-fall he lay but in his face
> such pain , I fled agape ,
> Tho' he slept yet.
>   DAMB/ too many in's
>   left in it , and I dunno
> if can unkink the tail and keep any sort of lock.
>   ("Letter" [1949])

Pound wishes to incorporate the creature into an antiquated poetic jargon, but the creature shifts itself in that jargon, abiding in it for an instant before separating itself into its virtuality. In laying hold of its virtuality or future possibilities, the creature and the historical multiplicity it embodies escape Pound's grasp. While it is held in the form of Pound's translation for an instant, it also keeps its translatability in suspension. What Munn would call its "transgenerational continuity" is configured toward the future, carrying into the future the possibility for other temporal spheres and densities to interrelate. Whatever elements of empire, fascism, or deleterious modernization Pound represents are twisted into a broader ecology of ongoing kinships. While the historicity of these kinships is therefore mythic, inasmuch as their historical specificity is related to the metamorphic body of the werewolf shifting its shape, this mythic dimension remains conditioned in all particulars by historical conditions. Italian anthropologist Carlo Severi calls this pictographic interrelation of history and myth the "chimera principle" of pictography, noting that pictographs connect scenes of reading to broader mythological themes and relate the meanings of those themes to contemporary happenings (*Chimera* 1–23). Here we can see how such a principle is a species of historicization, bringing together not just bodies in space but bodies in temporal instability. The restlessness of bodies in the poem is a built-in resource to resist Pound's grasp, and to return to that ongoing imperative to sing the song anew, and thus to lay hold of future possibility.

If Gordon is still to be heard in this song, her "*canta*" now must remind its listeners that the relation between law and violence in the state of exception extends into contemporary moments. Her "*canta*" was sung in response to what Benjamin called "lawmaking violence," and just as Benjamin related such violence to its "possible righteousness," the song's persistence in its translations carries forward the imagined healing work of Gordon's imperative "*canta*" (Benjamin qtd. in de Wilde 198). Trenchantly, Benjamin characterized such possibility as a kind of "mythical violence . . . with the goal of preserving 'mere life' . . . its possible righteousness . . . the fulfilment of which is postponed to an unforeseeable future" (de Wilde 198). In Jacques Derrida's reading of Benjamin's idea of the state of exception, such mythical postponement serves to protect an important unrepresentability in the social order, a virtuality that activates responsibility for new bodies, shapes, and forms that might enter and pass through it (de Wilde 198). It is a wish to have a sign that does not resolve into any selfsame sign, whose law is a preservation of possible lawless belonging. In de Angulo's works, the relation between such a sign and the law is as that of the pictograph and its kinships—a werewolf shifting its shape to renew the possibility of new shapes and their future possible righteousness. For instance, when he expresses his desire to "lose [his] humanhood" and "his wish that the earth would constantly return," there is a reckoning with the possibility of other bodies and temporalities (*Reader* xiv; Duncan, *Poet's Mind* 236), an anarchism that extends into nonhuman domains. This must be so because the construct of the human is the signifier by which the racial purity of empire is policed. In protecting the purported purity of the human, the torture and clearance of undesirables or "non-humans" preserves self-homogenizing racial communities.⁹ The human carries the symbolic logic of colonial terror. To denounce the human is thus to divest such a certain signifying logic of its exclusionary power. In its place, de Angulo wishes that the earth should return. This return of the earth as assemblage to countermand the human is the kinship construct of these works—a manifestation of Benjamin's sense of mythic righteousness and a continuation of Gordon's imperative to sing.

In de Angulo's writings, Gordon's imperative remains dynamic because its various manifestations constitute an always alternating otherness whose horizons are vexingly open ended. In his aptly titled *The Metamorphoses of Kinship*, Marxist anthropologist Maurice Godelier argues that the affective bonds of kinship are animated by the perception of difference—when we feel ourselves interpolated in the otherness of others, for better or worse. This morphology of being-in-other is what anthropologists have diversely referred to as "dividual," "partible," or "fractal" personhood (Strathern; LiPuma; Wagner); "mutuality of being" or "mutual persons" (Sahlins, *What*); and "multispecies assemblages" (Haraway, *Staying* 160–61). The definitive difficulty of "being-in-other" is that it exposes interior states to the flux and conflict of shifting and always differing exteriorities. The metamorphoses of kinship are neither benevolent nor unrisky. Kinship is a being and becoming on the edge, existentially and psychically available to the unpredictability of an always alternating otherness, whose danger is manifest by its immanence. Kinship reminds one that they are other; that the policing of dominant signifiers will always fracture in the fissured nature of the sign-work that constitutes groups; and that community therefore can never be simply the homogeneity of the human. When de Angulo describes the kinship of metamorphosis he does not eke out a special place for the human in it. His kinship is an assemblage of parts diffusing into the privileged becomings of other beings. He writes:

> The psychic life of the community is a confused mass of thinking, feeling, emotions, perceptions, where everything is blended, warm and full of diffused gentle light . . . thus life flows by, as passionless as possible, like an immense sluggish stream, a procession of trees, of animals, of stones, none of them quite clear from the others, but rather here the claws of an eagle, and there the green leaf of a tree; here a human face, there something going like a puff of wind. What's the use of arranging it all in order? (*Coyote's* 47–48)

The interspecies diffusions of kinship, partible and blended at the same time like a true chimera, give rise to a sense of affinities that are not so

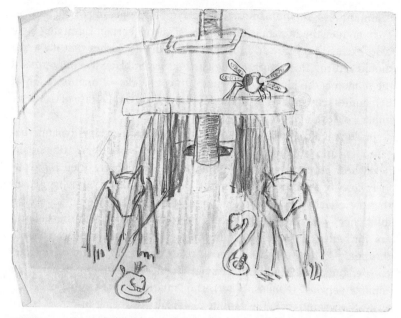

FIGURE 13 Jaime de Angulo's multiform kinship voicing is here depicted in a pictographic drawing (ca. 1950) of animals guarding the entry to the winter hut, in which Coyote has his exchange with Pis'wis'na (see fig. 10). Jaime de Angulo Papers (Collection 160), UCLA Library Special Collections, Charles E. Young Research Library.

elective. At the very least, it is not only a human poet who gets to do the choosing. It is not exactly that de Angulo brings Pis'wis'na, Coyote, Werewolf, Pound, and Gordon together in his poetry. These beings also pull at the disarranged whole. The catastrophe of colonialism is not exempt from this disarranged whole. If pictographic voice is the ever-becoming stream of multiplicity, that ever-becoming stream moves through the broken bodies of racial horror. Yet that horror must abide in a world in which it does not get to elect its sources of reproduction.[10] There are other beings and forms at play (fig. 13).

De Angulo came to be embodied by some of these other beings. While I cite Derrida where provisionally useful, critiques of presence have less of a hold in my analysis than they might have had, had this book been written in decades past: planetary precarity compels us to take seriously embodied ontologies of organism and breath (and to seek out those cultural repertoires that enact such ontologies). But that precarity is not so much new as historically uneven. Toxicity and ecological violence ordained the so-called progress of civilization and heralded colonial superordination

(Sahlins, *Stone*; Scott). In this regard, de Angulo was keen to consider how his cancer might be treated not only with hormones but with poetics, rhythms, and temporal configurations as well. And his turn to poetics appears to be a moment in which to engage the problematic possibility that nonhuman affinities and molecular networks might have no need for human participation in the kinship configuration. How to articulate oneself in that?

As I've mentioned, to treat his cancer de Angulo took hormones, which grew out his breasts, and had an orchiectomy, all of which served to trouble his gender. But he also saw this troubling as the final realization of "a polymorphic sexuality that operates in more than two genders," that involves as well "Moose, fox, pine tree and ocean [that] might also be genders" (Duncan, "Aug 1 1969").[11] The idea that gender fluidity obtains in nonhuman embodiment recurs throughout *Old Time Stories*. In one of the radio broadcasts he sings his translation of a Pit River song, in which animal heteromorphia is associated with his own body slipping into such change: "hermaphrodite/vulture . . . I flap my wings" (session 42). In less happy instances, this physical elision is related to the cancer itself, the molecular thing that is killing the poet, a nonhuman entity gnawing at the poet's humanhood. Such transpositions reckon with the possibility that the earth's constant returns have no special concern for a poet's life:

> little birds who sing in the night
> little mice of the fields, little mice,
> stop nibbling, listen to me, the Poet,
> I'm talking about a faun, a faun who was crying . . .
> > they aren't listening!
> little frogs, charging litl frogs,
> the color of baby crap, so pretty, so charming
> cease for a moment croaking at the edge of the pond
> listen to the story of a faun, a lycanthrope . . .
> What's a lycanthrope?
> He is a were-wolf, and this one . . .
> but please listen to me . . . I'm a Poet
> couac couac kwissli croak
> what is it a poet? Is it good to eat?
> They don't listen to me! Moon, oh, beautiful moon,
> moon
> round as a golden tittie, more beautiful than the
> > mistress of Solomon
> moon my mother listen to me, I'm a Poet . . .

Mother, mother, bring me my balls, i left them in the drawer
yes darling and be quiet your forehead is all sweaty
I'm the moon
I'm listening to you

(qtd. in G. de Angulo 406)

While the creatures of the poem are unconcerned with the poet's apostrophe, it is not quite the case that voice as such has dropped out of the poem. The poet's voice is there to mark off the overwhelming voices of other beings. The poet can hardly get his voice in edgewise because these others are so busy chattering, singing, nibbling, and croaking away. The poet tries to recite his Werewolf-Coyote poem but, as *that* poem suggests, its materials are not in the poet's control. Amid the autonomous and multiform metamorphoses of the poem, "the Poet" disappears. Yet here that disappearance is directly linked to the physical effects of cancer and its therapy: in a feverish sweat, the poet realizes that their genitals are gone and their breasts have risen like a moon in the night. In linking the physical effects of cancer to sublunar animal ecologies, the poet suggests that the cancer, too, is a kind of animal moving through the body, interrupting a fantasy of creative control, flipping the paradigm of apostrophe so that nonhumans control the imaginative relation between the symbolic and the real. Cancer was de Angulo's elemental other. It is at once an inescapable physical condition and a being changed in the force that myth exerts on its conditions. In this case, the myth is associated with an ecological totalizability extending across bodily difference and historical incongruity—a kinship of the werewolf, archaic because of the displacements of colonial history, but intimate because those displacements could not stop its singing in times of needed healing. In that singing, the poet finds deeper transits of animal ecologies by which he can let go of his pesky humanhood.

Kinship Spirals

While the pictograph is a source of possibility for social orders, it complicates understandings of authenticity or origination in those orders. Ortiz's emphasis on "even the fact of the conquistadors, conquistadors" troubles the relation between indigenous significations and their colonial historicities (*Spiral* 181). It is not only the case that "English [is] an Indian language" (Weaver, Womack, and Warrior xviii); the pictograph is also a source for English-language social and intellectual possibility—involving even the fact of de Angulo. This temporal twist is what I understand to be the significance of the figure of the spiral in *Spiral Lands*. As I propose in the next chapter, the singular authenticity regime of settler liberalism cannot see how the "battle over signification" can be won by any force other than itself. Arriving to that battle twisted in the poetics of the pictograph, Ortiz sees in that "spiral, a symbol, a world in motion"—a world in which virtual possibility pluralizes its presents and pasts, in which creativity affects our experience of historical change. Along these lines, he asks, "are these figures in the past or in the present?" (*Spiral* 178, 179). The conceptual heart of the question is a test on origination, in which origin is not the seed of the present deposited in an inaccessible past; origin becomes a metonym through which various agents both human and nonhuman move today, affecting both present and past, indeed through which the tree of the signs of the Americas continues to reseed literary and historical fields. In that "ecological metonymy," even the visage of inaccessibility is one creative density among others. The accumulated blockage of what Walter Mignolo calls "colonial semiosis"—which is a type of nonsemiosis, or a semiotics of semiotics that have ceased to exist, or that exist in conflict with dominant signifying practices (*Darker* 7–25)—is subordinated to the poetics of the pictograph because, as Ortiz points out, the semiotics of semiotics that have supposedly ceased to exist continue to make a noise, possibly even one that resonates in their mythic significations. In this case, that noise resonates in its poetics that contextualize the very forces that have tried to erase its poetics of context. Its noise is a noise that grounds the noise of "colonial semiosis." This point needs special emphasis because it is not just that native poetics compete with their colonial circulation or noncirculation in "empty, homogeneous time" (Benjamin, *Selected* 4:402). At a deeper level, that whole competition can be colligated by the poetics of some such sign as a pictograph.

Performing such configuration or *rhusmos*, Ortiz's poem about Newspaper Rock is a collection of rhetorical doubts that are valued as the kind of speculation that pictography makes possible—or, as he puts it, "admirable projection." He writes: "I want to know but maybe I'm not to know. Being within the culture sometimes is:/Not knowing and accepting it's okay. Knowing you're within is knowledge enough" (*Spiral* 175, 181). While he says he does not know what the pictographs mean, he depicts his not-knowing as a pictographic epiphenomenon. The secondary effects of pictographic imagination are referenced in the poem by the uses of the word "figure." It is used to mean both a written symbol—"the zig zag contraption figure"—and the poet's doubts and speculations—"the horses I figure are recent . . . So it doesn't figure. . . ." (181). With these speculations the poet suggests that the spiral figure makes possible future figuration. And the most striking instance of such spiraling figuration occurs in the second-person address—"You're part of all that has taken place"—which is ambiguously oriented toward either the reader or the glyphs. In blurring the figure of the glyph into its reader, Ortiz extends figurability to involve that reader. Present readers then are a part of "all that has taken place" with the glyphs—its ecological and colonial configurations, "buffalos, mountain sheep, elks, antelope, deer, goats, horses, their riders, even the fact of the conquistadors, conquistadors"—becoming a part of that mythic kinship by which the relational pathways remain open. The visual menagerie of the rock is synonymous with the existential and psychic exposures of kinship, the webs that reach across the ruptured boundaries of history and its violences.

Because the poem encourages readers to think about interspecies and interdiscursive menageries in terms of kinship, it also implicates such readers in the responsibility of kinship—what Benjamin characterized as "possible righteousness" for the new bodies, shapes, and forms that might enter and pass through a social order of expansive belonging (de Wilde 198). That is, the stone on which the pictures appear is also "a part of all that has taken place." Therefore, to consider the poem's deep contexting requires that we reckon with the ecological conditions of Newspaper Rock. The rock itself is in the desert of southeastern Utah, near the four corners where Utah, Colorado, Arizona, and New Mexico meet. It seems, from its palimpsest of designs (figures carved into the desert varnish, a dark tawny coat of manganese-iron that has collected on the sandstone, combining Anasazi, Diné, Pueblo, Fremont, Spanish, and Anglo figures and significations), that the rock has been an intercultural transit point for thousands of years. Yet in more recent times, that rusty patina has become a reminder of environmental violence, since the surrounds were a site of heavy uranium mining during the Cold War, which contaminated the lands and exposed Diné people to fatal levels of radon (Brugge, Benally, and Yazzie-Lewis). Ortiz introduces this aspect of *Spiral Lands* by quoting the poet, artist, and activist Jimmie Durham: "revenues from natural resources wander into the pockets of private corporations instead of their rightful destinations and lands are left behind polluted." In such radioactive historiography, the spirals of *Spiral Lands* involve the deep time of radioactive waste in their resonating afterimage: "a picture as culture, controlling history as an afterimage for the future" (*Spiral* 176, 177). That future is captive to an ongoingness of toxicity for which we are all now responsible. In such deep ecological contamination, there can be no ruptured boundary between humans and planet. Situated in that context, the petroglyphs carry a message of human waste into the far future. Yet—if we understand the pictograph to be a sign that foregrounds its contexts—these deep time markers of waste are also traced in the poetics of ecological metonymy. To echo Ortiz's words, *even the fact of radioactivity, radioactivity* is captive to the poetics of a sign that points us always back to the ongoing life of the environment in which it appears.

In anticipation of my engagement with Povinelli's works in the next chapter, here her conception of the "Desert" as a "scarred space" of modernity is illuminative. Her "Desert" is the crisis of life when confronted with ecological finitude, "a scarred meeting place where each can exchange conceptual intensities, thrills, wonders, anxieties, perhaps terrors, of the other of Life, namely the Inert, Inanimate, Barren. In this scarred space, the ontological is revealed to be biontology . . . [the Desert] is the affect that motivates the search for other instances of life in the universe and technologies for seeding planets with life" (*Geontologies* 17). Rather than a place of inert lifelessness, the desert is where the desertification of voice ends, calling forth the "possible righteousness" of the seemingly lifeless. The Desert calls for the kinds of conceptual intensities that can address the drama of life confronting its limits in barren, possibly toxic rocks. Povinelli adds that such confrontation intensifies human affirmations of the life of nonliving things, producing a disposition she calls "Animist." From ecological precarity emerges the feeling that "all forms of existence have within them a vital animating, affecting force . . . [a position] that can see life where others would see the lack of life" (17, 18). Such *extremis* is absorbed into de Angulo's and Ortiz's forms of radical inclusivity—their modes of "possible righteousness" and their beings of metamorphosis that summon the responsibilities of kinship.

In the passages of *Woven Stone* that imagine "stones with voices," ideas "'chiseled'/into mind or memory stone," or "the earth in your mouth," Ortiz finds voices in the physical ecology of the pictograph. In doing that, he interpolates the histories and happenings around those stones into the pictographic significations of the stones—involving even conquistadors and human waste. Even if he must approach the pictographs by way of their mediation in anthropological apparatuses—arriving to them through histories that include colonial maladies coextensive with de Angulo—the pictograph integrates those mediations into its meanings. It is a sign in which many bodies of radically varying type are configured to reckon with the situations that bring them into collective assemblage.

Such a process is mirrored in the paintings of Joe Herrera, the Cochiti Pueblo artist whose configuration of Puebloan iconography in abstract expressionist style results in works in which the influence of such painters as Marsden Hartley and Paul Klee (both influenced by the native iconography of the American Southwest) is absorbed in a pictographic aesthetic (plate 7). This aesthetic both is mediated in colonialism and capturing of those mediations. The spiral in Herrera's painting moves inward from the abstract fields of color and line at the edges of the canvas, leading the viewer's eye to the animals (two eagles and a rabbit) swirled into a chimera in the painting's center. This movement from abstract expression and even fetishized flatness to animal kinship is glimpsed, as well, in the figure adjacent to the rabbit: a kachina or spirit being represented in partially abstract style. Suggesting that abstraction is the aesthetic form from which the painter is working his way into the painting's heart—the spirit animals and kachina—the painting foregrounds contemporaneous art market demands for flatness and abstraction. Nonetheless, the spiral remains a line leading from market norms back to the spirits and animal powers. While showing evidence of market orientations, the dominating orientation in the painting is indigenous—a spiral guiding its viewers to its center. In that center, spirits of sky (eagles), earth (rabbit), and inner worlds (kachina) interact as if to remind viewers of the necessary righteousness of form: colonial and capitalist mediations must find their relation to the life of the stones in the southwestern desert toward which they are already pulled.

These stones and their pictographic aesthetic remind viewers that they—the viewers—are involved in an ongoing aesthetic whose assembly remains in process. That open-endedness is an invitation for the audience but also a source of responsibility in the face of intense and persistent danger. Even if the voices of pictographs are not voices in a strictly human sense, their presence is not sublingual or vibrational. Their vocalization is very much a trace of structuring patterns in the desert, whose lifeworld implicates us all. Rather than a single voice crying in the wilderness, it is a composite assemblage meant to remind readers of the assembly-like qualities of life itself: not exactly *vox* or voice in the wilderness, this is a complex expression of multiform vocality or *os clamans in deserto*. Such ecological expansions involve other-than-human kinships in a special kind of poetic form. This metamorphic form offers models for the human imagination to comprehend the nonhuman poetics of kinship. When Ortiz says, "You're part of all that has taken place," it is not solace as much as it is disturbance to the boundaries of subjectivization. To be a part of so much is to be on the edge, exposed to an always alternating otherness that may have no special felicity conditions for human belonging. The difficulty of organizing a social community—with jurisgenerative and life-sustaining practices—out of such radical inclusivity is the subject of the next chapter. It will continue the examination of the ongoing uses of the pictograph, but turn more deliberately to its uses in the law—especially in its uses as amphiboly, the trope of organized ambiguities.

3
PICTOGRAPHY, LAW, AND EARTH

Gerald Vizenor, John Borrows,
and Louise Erdrich

When he wrote the principal draft of the Constitution of the White Earth
Nation (CWEN), the Anishinaabe poet, novelist, and scholar Gerald
Vizenor surprised some by including a clause to protect ironic speech.
As he understood it, the need for creating the only "constitution of governance in the world [with] specific reference to the protection of literary and artistic irony [was that] for native storiers, protection of this
freedom could not go unstated" ("Up Close").[1] Of course, his is not the
only constitution in the world with a specific clause to protect expressive freedom. But his clause is unique in that it makes irony a conceptual
flashpoint for freedoms of expression. The fifth article of the constitution
reads, "the freedom of thought and conscience, academic, artistic irony,
and literary expression, shall not be denied, violated or controverted by
the government" (Vizenor and Doerfler 65). The Abenaki scholar Lisa
Brooks suggests that Vizenor's defense of irony is a means of transposing dissent into a domain common to all: humor (69–70). Inasmuch as
humor is a universal phenomenon, dissent must be universally recognized. Yet humor is hardly uniform. What is humorous to one person
could harm another or fail to have anything to do with artistic dissent.
Injurious humor can be outside the ambit of dissent, and dissent often
happens without recourse to humor. In considering why irony is presented as that from which the flames of dissent burst, a more vital spark
is found in figural ambiguity. Irony is a trope of disorientation, creating
indeterminate positions in language that foreground conceptual indeterminacy. Jokes rely on such disorientation, but other kinds of discourse—
including poetics, politics, and the law—rely on it as well. In this chapter,
I analyze how aesthetics and politics interact in Vizenor's constitutional
irony, with close attention to his and other Anishinaabe writers' uses of

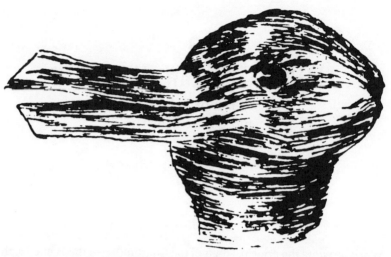

FIGURE 14 The Duck-Rabbit illusion from *Fliegende Blätter* (1892).

pictography: a sign system whose poetics foreground social ironies, and whose social ironies merge with questions of legal sovereignty.

Irony is typically understood as an antiphrastic trope, which works by pulling words away from their usual sense, or an amphiboly, an ambiguous use of language that reveals the duplicity of all language. Linda Hutcheon has argued that irony is more than simple antiphrasis; its full meaning depends on an "account [of] the inclusive and simultaneous nature of ironic meaning" (59). In her description of it, ironic antiphrasis is cast into the light *as* antiphrasis, putting the whole illusion of irony into view for what it is: an incoherent statement made to appear coherent. She explains her argument by referring to Ludwig Wittgenstein's reflections on the duck-and-rabbit optical illusion in his *Philosophical Investigations* (fig. 14). As she understands it, Wittgenstein's point is that the illusion does not prompt us to see the duck or the rabbit separately, or the duck and the rabbit together as some kind of animal hybrid. Rather, it prompts us to see the whole image as a visual problem that does not resolve into any one thing. Wittgenstein's optical illusion thematizes incoherence in the same way irony does. When irony brings to light the seeming coherence of incoherent elements, it creates "a differential aspect [from] ducks and rabbits" (62; see 184–96, 59–62). Irony induces a scene of differences participating, because irrupting, in one another at various levels of speech.

The irruptions are dramatized in the very syntax of Vizenor's clause defending irony. That is, irony sticks out in the way that the clause is phrased, awkwardly interrupting the syntax. What should be written either as "academic and artistic irony and literary expression" or as "academic, artistic, and literary expression" is instead interrupted by the appearance of irony: "academic, artistic irony, and literary expression." The awkward phrasing is an English-language problem. In the Ojibwe language, which exhibits freer ordering of its adjectives, making it possible to treat adjectives as clauses in their own right (Rosen 158–68), such phrasing is not unusual. If we consider irony's interruption here as the introduction of Ojibwe expressive patterns, in which irony could be modified by both "academic" and "artistic" in a conjoined clause, then the word "irony" enacts that which the constitution signifies: a stirring to life of native creative freedoms. The grammatical disruption makes irony a means of resisting colonial order. Moreover, if we consider that irony might be modified by both the adjectives "academic" and "artistic," as the roving use of adjectives in Ojibwe allows, then irony is presented as the amphibolic, "both/and," antiphrastic trope that it is typically understood to be. Yet in presenting irony doing the very thing that it is supposed to reference, Vizenor's clause takes on Hutcheon's note of irony's self-aware self-reference as well. Irony becomes self-ironizing, throwing into the light the contradiction of writing a constitution under an ironic spell.

Irony lets us see the contradictions of writing an Anishinaabe constitution in the English language—or, for that matter, the contradiction of writing any constitution that intends to resist the exclusionary norms of federated statehood. Its grammatical disruption marks both its interpolation within and its resistance to colonial order. Like Wittgenstein's optical illusion, Vizenor's clause defending irony opposes things to emphasize difference as such. But it emphasizes that this ironic differencing is related to political organization in an indigenous context—or, as Vizenor elsewhere puts it, "sovereignty is transmotion and used here in most senses of the word motion; likewise, the ideas and conditions of motion have a deferred meaning that reach, naturally, to other contexts of action, resistance, dissent, and political controversy. The sovereignty of motion means the ability and the vision to move in imagination and the substantive rights of motion in native communities" (*Fugitive Poses* 182). Instead of opposing colonial power with some version of sovereignty that reproduces colonial statehood—some version of the Westphalian model of ultimate authority within a closed territory—Vizenor imagines a type of sovereignty that is not circumscribed by territorial closure. While territorial rights are an inescapable necessity for native communities—whose sovereignty is eroded by territorial theft, and whose territorial "dispossession" was ideological elimination of the "native commons" and its values of noncapitalist communalism, ecological attentiveness, "reciprocity, nonexploitation, and respectful coexistence" (Coulthard 12–13)—Vizenor's point is that territorial reclamation need not be cast in those settler colonial models by which it was dispossessed. If, as political theorist Seyla Benhabib notes, "sovereignty is a relational concept . . . an ongoing process of constitutional self-creation," its iterations could relate to the state negatively. Sovereignty could be constituted in practices of "jurisgenerative" critique and confrontation, making inclusive collectivities that move away from the conservative norms of nation states (12, 19–21) as well as from the demands for staid cultural authenticity that settler liberalism places on native sovereignty claims. That is, in the context of native sovereignty claims, creative jurisgenerative practices trouble the rubric by which the validity of those claims is often assessed: the idea of an indigeneity untouched by history, accident, and change. As Mark Rifkin notes, "the performance of stasis is the condition of possibility for being accorded status as proper Indians" (6; see Barker; see Povinelli, *Cunning*). Whereas the recognition of native sovereignty typically involves a sense of non-ongoing, ahistorical, and racially unchanging being, Vizenor's emphasis on irony in articulating the self-determination of a community gives that community the inflection points of historical transformation: conflict, motion, imagination, action, dissent, difference, and complexity.

The necessary social irony of writing a constitution is remarked as early as Edmund Burke—with his notion that the inscription of the ancient (unwritten) English constitution established principles by which individual experiences would be subordinated to the rationalistic self-surety of the written word. Such legal rationalism occasions a paralysis in legal thought; the law's letter stands in the way of that which could not be rationalized or perfectly enunciated—that is, the ever-shifting relations between individuals and institutions (Pocock). Like Vizenor, Chadwick Allen situates such questions of legal transitivity in his consideration of the dynamics of native sovereignty: his conception of the "trans-indigenous" frames indigenous cultures as "ongoing processes rather than finished outcomes . . . this *trans-* signifies *across, beyond,* and *through,* suggesting sustained movement, but also *changing* or *changing thoroughly,* suggesting significant metamorphosis" ("Productive" 240). While partly motivated by the transnational pulls in social life (pulls in which native people need not orient themselves to the national), "trans-indigenous" signifies more comprehensively the presence of native cultures in the metamorphoses of historical experience. Instead of being the primordial signal outside of time (the allochronicity, to invoke Johannes Fabian's term) that the colonialist episteme demands of native people, the conception of "trans-indigenous" demarks those ironies by which constituted worlds could stay transitive, present to ongoing historical processes, and animated by the material histories they wish to flip transversely into sites of native sovereignty—even if such affirmative flips become instances of controversy (Allen, *Trans-Indigenous* xxxii). Vizenor's irony, which challenges notions of the indigenous as a staid ahistorical category, is one means of expressing and eliciting such jurisgenerative transpositions. And, as I argue in this chapter, the poetics of social irony are homologous to the poetics of a sign system long understood to be outside present time: pictography. Rather than a primordial sign system superseded by the alphabet and its rationalistic self-surety, the pictograph is a deft technology for reading the movements and changes of contemporary social life, including those that would appear to have rendered the pictograph as nothing more than a trace of colonial supersession.

The appearance of irony in CWEN turns the constitution into a question that, in its open-endedness, creates a relational possibility outside the authenticity regimes of multicultural recognition: while declaring the sovereignty of the White Earth Nation, it asks, to what extent does this sovereignty depend on or resist colonial norms? Irony does not let Vizenor dissipate the colonial content of constitution writing. After all, he is authoring a system of territorial closure and exclusionary membership—the White Earth Nation. Rather, irony reveals how such nation making could involve critical unmaking. Like Wittgenstein's rabbit-duck, Vizenor's irony threads disorientation into its sense of sovereignty, simultaneously bringing a nation together while pulling apart presumptions of its absolute authority or its single, correct way of seeing things.

This technique is of a piece with strategies of disorientation in his critical, autobiographical, fictional, and poetic writings. A trickster writer, Vizenor relishes breaking norms, collapsing genres, eliciting contradiction, and inhabiting difference. In one of his earliest books of poetry, *Summer in the Spring*, these tendencies quicken in the uses of Anishinaabe pictography or picture writing. To explain how pictography can bring social ironies to life—forms of life animated by constitutional irony— this chapter looks to the Anishinaabe legal scholar John Borrows, whose book of legal case studies, *Drawing Out Law: A Spirit's Guide* (2010), is written with pictographs. The pictograph, Borrows suggests, is distinctly capable of eliciting the kind of structural indeterminacy needed for flexible jurisprudence. In his view, multiperspectival thinking could enable the practice of a federal legal culture conducive to indigenous law. And pictographs are his technology for generating such multiperspectival thinking. For Vizenor, the Anishinaabe pictograph is likewise jurisgenerative, yet he concerns himself more with how social irony coalesces in the visual, poetic, narrative, and aesthetic components of pictography:

Anishinaabe pictographs, he writes, are "not objective collections and interpretations of historical facts or pedagogical models . . . [but] dream circles, visual images and oratorical gestures showing the meaning between the present and the past: word cinemas in the lives of the tribal people of the woodland" (*Summer* 15). In unraveling the complex meaning of Vizenor's and Borrows's pictographs, this chapter moves from a general analysis of pictographic writing to its legal implications, which for Vizenor are inextricable from the pictographs' aesthetic and sensual forms. To conclude, I argue that those jurisgenerative aesthetics are made environmental in the Anishinaabe novelist Louise Erdrich's *Books and Islands in Ojibwe Country*, where an engagement with native petroglyphs inspires reflection on ecological reciprocity.

Trunk and Branch: Constitutional Pictography

Hutcheon's reference to Wittgenstein's icon is an apt means to extend the discussion of pictography into legal considerations. Much as Hutcheon reckons with Wittgenstein's icon to develop her concept of irony, Borrows and Vizenor turn to pictography because it is a sign system that makes its meaning from a loosened relation between a sign and its meaning. Unlike the alphabet, in which letters correspond isomorphically to sounds that aggregate into words and abstractions, pictographic literacy works by mnemonic cues that are also instances of creative prompting. These cues prompt remembered narratives existing off the page, that are subject to change based on a reader's memory or this reader's creative response to social and environmental pressures present at the scene of reading. Scholar of Mesoamerican iconography Elizabeth Hill Boone therefore notes that pictographs are not just devices of memory storage, which is how Aby Warburg and Erland Nordenskiöld characterized them in early twentieth-century studies. Rather, what these early anthropologists missed is that pictographs are also devices of poetic improvisation (Hill Boone and Mignolo 71).[2] As I have mentioned, in her study of Zuni pictographs M. Jane Young thus discusses them in terms of visual metonymy (154, 159–73, 185). Conceptualized as metonymy, pictographs are revealed to be the poetic device that they in fact are: like metonyms, or the trope that circles from a sign to an atmosphere and back to a sign, pictographs loop together visual, mnemonic, interpersonal, and enviromental factors to create a text of shifting texture. Always available to refabrication in response to the varying social pressures of a new performance, new rhetorical network, or new cultural and physical landscape, pictographs are vehicles of poetic indeterminacy and contextual metamorphosis.

It is as a legal vehicle of contextual variability that Borrows values pictographic literacy. What he calls "Anishinabek literacy" (*Drawing* x) is a theory of justice based on pictographic writing and reading. He proposes this theory of justice in his nonpictographic analysis of indigenous constitutionalism in Canada, *Canada's Indigenous Constitution*. In this work, he calls for a multijuridical legal culture in which indigenous constitutions are not secondary to the federal Canadian system—that is, a multilegal legal culture that recognizes indigenous juridical systems and the ways those systems are communicated. In the present situation, totemic and kinship allocation, environmental stewardship, Earth's legal personhood, rights that are reciprocal with responsibilities, collaborative judgment and sentencing, and contextual analysis are a few of the indigenous legal principles that find themselves relegated to "the bottom of the legal hierarchy, labeled as simply customary" when confronting the federal Canadian legal system (56). One of the reasons why indigenous legal norms are dismissed is that their oral recitation is seen as unreliable, the mnemonic aides that support that recitation as illegitimate, and the role of the imagination as corrosive to the law: "stories, songs, ceremonies, feasts, dances . . . wampum belts, masks, totem poles, medicine bundles, culturally modified trees, birch bark scrolls, petroglyphs, button blankets, land forms, and crests" are but a few of the many legal devices unaccredited in federal courts (57). Basically, anything that is not the written word has no legal standing, as legal standing depends on the isomorphic stability of words written with alphabets.

Borrows argues that this one-to-one correspondence or isomorphism between the letter and the law leads to limitations and exclusions in legal thinking. At an institutional scale, the monojuridical legal culture of federated Canada is continuous with the self-surety of the written word.[3] In this culture, certain kinds of evidence are inadmissible in courts of law—for instance, treaty claims based on a history recorded by wampum. Yet behind the problem of evidence is a deeper problem of sociological affordances: the juridical prestige of the alphabet naturalizes the lowliness of the memories, perceptions, negotiations, exchanges, imaginations, expressions, and relations allowed by nonalphabetic types of communication. In a legal culture singularly fixated on the letter of the law, pictographs come to register an insignificant and unreliable semiotic aberration, the selfsame signal out of time expected of native people, rather than a sign system that creates authentic forms of ongoing social life. This precludes, in turn, political possibilities uniquely afforded by the pictograph.

In her analysis of Vizenor's constitutional work, Brooks points out the paradoxical situation in which North American federal constitutions were prefigured in, and likely influenced by, the native constitutions of the Americas that are now denied legal standing on the basis of the native semiosis by which they came into being. She refers not only to the constitution of the Haudenosaunee confederacy written on wampum belts, which prefigured the US constitution, but also to the many other types of "council books"—such as the Ki'che' Mayan *Popol Vuh* or Anishinaabe birch bark scrolls—that governed forms of social life throughout the hemisphere, each of which is connected to a larger network of a "long 'continental' literary tradition of constitutional literature" (49). She calls this the trunk and tree of constitutionalism in the Americas, citing the prominence Craig Womack gives to native significations: "tribal literatures are not some branch waiting to be grafted onto the main trunk. Tribal literatures are the *tree*, the oldest literatures in the Americas, the most American of American literatures. [They] *are* the canon" (qtd. in Brooks 51). Yet, as she notes, the difficulty in seeing this tree is that the semiotic traditions at its root remain obscured. Without making a place for such signs as pictographs in the understanding and practice of law, there can be no relevant multijuridical legal culture, no political affordances to contest the legal hegemony of the written word.

Emphasizing this, Borrows structures his book of case studies, *Drawing Out Law*, around sixteen self-designed pictographs that he calls "scrolls" (xiii). Each of these scrolls introduces a story that culminates in a legal problem explored in a combination of dialogue, dream interpretation, mythical and spiritual storytelling, animal visions, indigenous and common law analysis, and philosophical reflection. Instead of telling readers what to think or how to judge, he encourages readers to perceive how the indeterminacy and imaginative exploration induced by the "scrolls" can support the practice of law: "legal traditions are often at their most relevant when they continually change and address ideas their creators did not necessarily envision. . . . I hope readers feel empowered to remember and develop their own interpretations of what they see and read in images . . . to look through them into the larger issues they encounter" (xiii). Borrows calls this perspectival shift "Anishinabek literacy," which he describes as a shift into reckoning with shifting perspectives, a transposition of legal authority into the context of ambiguous, individual perceptions and interpretations (x). The foundation of this legal literacy is in the images or scrolls that preface each case study. These pictographs and the stories that follow them are meant to elicit the legal innervations lurking in their readers. In bringing those divergent, contradictory, and conflictive embodiments of the law into view, the materials produce a literacy that is more than lettered: the pictographs organize the multiple sources of authority in a legal conflict into a scene of active interpretation, and thus compose a dynamic constitution that is nonconstituting.

The Storyteller: Interpenetrating Literacies and Legalities

Borrows's book begins with a scene of instruction in pictographic reading. A young attorney dreams about a cave in which, the next day, he finds his grandmother awaiting him. In the cave's walls, which are lined with petroglyphs, there are dozens of pictographic birch bark scrolls. The scene forms a metonym that brings the attorney to remark that "this cave itself is something of a scroll" (41). His grandmother unravels a scroll, which shows an otter ascending several cosmic layers (fig. 15), to explain how its pictographs are to be read: the images correspond with opportunities for articulation that are commensurate with, as the grandmother puts it, the "development of choice" and "agency." This, she says, is when "it gets really interesting . . . [when] the scrolls expand in scope [to] teach about knowledge that's necessary to face many issues in life which have dependence at their root" (42). She explains that dependence is often a mirage that emerges when people "have not yet properly developed or used choices available to them" (42). Because they elicit a framework of choice—a pictograph's reader has room to interpret and adjust its meaning to meet the demands of a present social moment—pictographs dispel the seemingly ineluctable force of a given social condition. The grandmother calls this function of the scrolls a feature of "Anishinabek law" and adds that she thinks "communities and nations could also take counsel from what's found in here" (42).

The concepts of choice, indeterminacy, and agency, particularly within the "scrolls' wider implications involving nations and peoples," captivate the attorney, who considers how they would ramify in the complex legal debates about the Canadian Indian residential school system; the issues of children's rights, adoption, and assimilation that emerge from the history of that system; how these issues are implicated in questions of abortion and women's rights; and the misuses of legal agency to stifle indigenous people and "terminate their development" (46). Agency alone, he concludes, is an insufficient political tool: "couched in the language of agency, the liberty and security of the majority was held out as a reason to override minority rights" (46). Nonetheless—not ignoring this problem of exclusionary agency that Benhabib calls "democratic closure" (19)—his grandmother's ideas about the pictographs resonate with him, particularly the pictograph-inspired notion that "you have a choice about what laws you should follow as you climb through life" (*Drawing* 47).

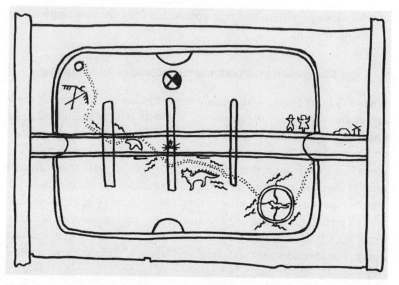

FIGURE 15 John Borrows, "Scroll Three: Pauwauwaein," a pictograph showing an otter ascending several strata of beings. Pictograph from his *Drawing Out Law: A Spirit's Guide* (2010), p. 30, © University of Toronto Press. Reprinted with permission of the publisher. Courtesy of John Borrows.

Her words come into fuller meaning the next day when, at the University of Toronto, where the attorney teaches, he must speak in a lecture series called "Choices: Aboriginal Peoples, Canada, and the Law." Lecturing before him are two indigenous professors whose political positions are diametrically opposed. One compares Canada's treatment of indigenous people to the Nazis' treatment of Jewish people to make the point that the law can abet the arbitrary rule of one people over another, legalizing genocide; and the other makes the point that, without the intervention of European ideas and technologies in the "Stone Age" world of precontact aboriginals, the indigenous societies of the Americas would have remained totalitarian backwaters. When the young attorney steps to the podium, "as thoughts of his visit to the cave [pass] through his mind," he begins by pointing out to the audience that they have just heard "two very interesting stories," remarking that "stories provide perspective for judgment" and that they "can reveal a range of choice in structuring thoughts, behavior, and relationships" (62, 63). Stories of any kind, even polemical ones, provide necessary perspective for understanding complex situations. Yet the problem with the stories that they have heard, he continues, is that neither acknowledges the basis for their decision making:

Despite the differences in these stories, they are similarly deficient in one significant respect. They largely portray Indigenous peoples as passive objects in their relationship with others. They depict them as people who are acted upon, not those who are much given to action. Yet Indigenous peoples were active agents in their history. They made their own decisions in the face of the circumstances they encountered. The events and ideas they confronted, while greatly challenging, were not fixed and immovable. . . . The same observation can be applied to Indigenous peoples today. Indigenous peoples in Canada continue to use their stories and exercise their agency in response to their ever-changing circumstances. (63)

The attorney points out that each story is based on a power to structure the world, a power that neither of the previous lecturers takes seriously. While these scholars disagree with one another, this power brings them together in the shared effort of producing native narratives. The issue is not whether to agree or disagree with one position or another, but rather to recognize that in choosing a narrative a world comes into being. The question then is: what kind of world do people wish to live in?

As he speaks these words, the attorney remembers the otter. In directing his audience to the concept of narrative decision making, he realizes a deeper meaning of the otter's journey. That is, it is not simply the case that people move through a world empowered to choose its material conditions. The possibility of choice is a consequence of power; who gets to choose what and how they get to choose it determines even the way in which people conceive their choices. He goes on to argue that just as the otter moves through a hierarchy of beings with their own power differentials, "[l]aw also has a vertical orientation that builds relationships hierarchically and thereby forges how we interact with each other. As such, those interested in law as it relates to Indigenous peoples must be attentive to its underlying aggregation of power and principle to understand its influence on their legal status. They must scale these heights and plumb these depths to appreciate the problems that Indigenous peoples experience in raising certain legal arguments and receiving appropriate remedies" (68). The power hierarchy structures the possibility of choice. And, still, the otter's journey is instructive in that it happens at all. Its movement through the cosmic tiers defended at each level by supernatural beings mirrors that of "First Nations and Indigenous communities . . . climbing against steep challenges within the Canadian legal culture" (66)—yet the fact that the otter climbs into the sun means, as well, that those challenges are not insurmountable: "We all face social, political, legal, economic, and spiritual contexts that constrain the degree to which we can truly do what we want." The attorney concludes, "nevertheless, the conditions in which we find ourselves are not fixed or immovable. They are subject to change and movement by a series of individual and collective actions over time and place. . . . Canada is a work in progress, and Indian agency must be respected as an important element in the continued construction of the country" (66, 68). This is more than a rallying cry. Inasmuch as the lecture extracts a scene of decision from a seemingly intractable conflict, the lecturer shows how stories have the power to reframe the conditions for choice. The attorney's lecture thus mimes the otter's journey, in that it encounters the polemics of power with a strategy of containing those polemics while redirecting power into his—the final storyteller's—shaping hands. In terming Canada a "work in progress" he implies that such a strategy could apply, as his grandmother suggests, to the construction of "communities and nations."

If Borrows advocates a multiperspectival approach to Canadian jurisprudence, he does not do so only to diversify legal opinions. More important, he dramatizes this multiperspectival approach as evidence of how a multijuridical culture operates. In particular, he uses the otter's story to reconfigure "Anishinabek literacy" in a legal context. "Anishinabek literacy" does not so much work within federal ideologies of law as it does subsume and shape those ideologies, presenting itself as the many-tentacled system by which indigenous law and Canadian federal law can relate. In this respect, "Anishinabek literacy" is not some branch to be grafted onto the multijuridical trunk of Canadian law—to paraphrase Womack's words—rather, it is the multiperspectival trunk through which a multijuridical culture effloresces. Through "Anishinabek literacy" the attorney comes to perceive the flowering of multiple legalities in the apparently uniform Canadian rule of law:

> We continue to occupy a physical and jurisprudential world that is made up of intermixed layers of ancient and recent origin. The interdependence of these elements for the diversity of life on the land cannot be over-emphasized. To look just on the surface, and think that what you see from horizon to horizon is all that is needed to survive, is to misunderstand your place on the ground [on] which you stand. To scale its heights—to learn its lessons—one must be alive to the underlying structures that support the visible and not-so-visible world around you. (72)

If it is the case that a multijuridical culture emerges from a multiperspectival approach, if "inter-societal" law is brought to life through "Anishinabek literacy," then the legal framework for "inter-societal" collaboration depends on a kind of semiotics (70). In this case, the sign system that teaches people how to read for multiple perspectives is pictography. Because the meaning of a pictograph changes over time, because its meaning can be adjusted by its readers to meet present social pressures, because those adjustments that readers make sit alongside the lingering memory of the previous iterations of a pictograph's meaning, because memory intermixes with invention and imagination in a pictograph's recitation, and because pictography is thus associated with the concept of metamorphosis, a sense of ongoingness, and the affects of being-in-other, it is the sign system through which Borrows builds his constitutional vision of mutually interpenetrating legal systems. Based on its function of "encouraging interpretive scope" (71), the pictograph produces the kind of world in which nondominant memories, perceptions, imaginations, and relations could implicate themselves in the legal and social hierarchy. The pictograph transforms that hierarchy into a series of circular movements—represented in figure 4 of the present book's introduction, the first pictograph of Borrows's book—that metonymically twist the distinctions of up and down, inside and out, and here and there to new conformations. Its three globe-like circles mirror one another, marking a homology between them that is broken by the discrepant figures inside and outside the globes. These figures—of little human-like bodies—repeat across the scroll, changing positions. The interchanging positions of the figures across the globes present a cosmography that is different from the tiered hierarchy in the otter's journey. Here, rather than stand in prescribed positions in a cosmic hierarchy, the figures appear in various possible relations to the interconnected spheres. If "Anishinabek literacy" had a representative icon, it would be something like this one, in which legal positioning consists of multiplicity, multidirectionality, interdependence, and "intermixed layers."

As in Vizenor's uses of irony, Borrows's visual cosmology creates a space of legalistic difference; but this is a difference that is different from differential *identity*. In his drawing, the similarity of the three spheres draws attention to the differently positioned figures inside and around the spheres. In and around the spheres, differences participate in one another at various intermixed levels. These intermixed levels seem associated most obviously with the multijuridical culture Borrows advocates. Yet they also offer a rich visual representation of how such multijuridical multiperspectivalism relies on difference in a relational mode. Beyond affirmations of a multiply oriented legal system, his pictographs make difference a central component of *collectivity*. His emphasis on the political value of difference recalls the writings of Theodor Adorno, particularly Adorno's last meditations on the destabilization of the "I" that inheres in states of difference: "the relationship of subject and object [that] would lie in a peace achieved between human beings as well as between them and their Other, [where] peace is the state of differentiation without domination, with the differentiated participating in each other" (247). Adorno arrives at this idea in a longer meditation on subjects and objects. His aim is to complicate the illusory retreat into inner life that the idea of subjectivity enables. According to Adorno, that retreat is illusory because subjectivity is completely interpenetrated by such objects as law, language, culture, and material history. "The dialectical primacy of the object" implies that every person, insofar as they conceive of themselves as a discrete subject, is alienated from their fundamental objecthood (253). It is only through the apperception of their own nonidentity that subjects rid themselves of the "subjective spell," the mystification that keeps people from seeing their being-in-other (254). That apperception, which he calls a kind of peace, is facilitated by a mindset welcoming of difference, when a person experiences the otherness of their objecthood without trying to dominate those objects. Such apperception is all the more intensified when the objects that constitute subjectivity involve, as Borrows puts it, "a physical and jurisprudential world that is made up of intermixed layers of ancient and recent origin," emphasizing the important "interdependence of these elements for the diversity of life on the land" (*Drawing* 72). When the boundaries separating up and down, inside and out, left and right are eroded, the illusory separability of individual subjects is revealed. The special spin that pictographic literacy puts on this revelation, and with which Adorno did not concern himself, is to emphasize its ecological dimension. The poetics of pictographs "give us knowledge of the earth that is impossible to get from other sources," Borrows writes (*Drawing* 72). That knowledge is not as powerfully doled out in any one story as it is in the way in which the stories come together, break apart, and fuse again in his book and outside it. That process is what Vizenor has in mind when he conceives of irony as an irruptive locution necessary for constituting a society in difference and disjunction. To further explore this process of communal self-differentiation, this chapter turns to the poetry that Vizenor wrote with pictographs. His poetry further informs the role that pictographic literacy might play in the creation of legal and political entities, especially ones entangled in nonhuman webs.

New Word Cinemas and Wood Theaters

The pictographs that appear in Vizenor's books come from Frances Densmore's early twentieth-century ethnographies, *Chippewa Music* and *Chippewa Music II*. In Densmore's ethnographies, documented songs are presented alongside the mnemonic icons with which they were then associated. Vizenor explains what these pictographs mean to him in a collection of "Ojibwe lyric poems and tribal stories" titled *Summer in the Spring*. This slim book, first published in 1965, anchors each of its untitled poems and short stories to pictographs collected by Densmore. However, there is a loose relation between the songs associated with the pictographs in Densmore's books and the poems and stories linked to them in Vizenor's: Vizenor's poems are not translations of the songs in Densmore's ethnographies. They are his inventions. This is in keeping with Vizenor's understanding of the poetics of the glyphs, which Vizenor describes in the book's introduction as "not objective collections and interpretations of historical facts or pedagogical models . . . [but] dream circles, visual images and oratorical gestures showing the meaning between the present and the past: word cinemas in the lives of the tribal people of the woodland" (*Summer* 15). Like Borrows, Vizenor sees the pictographs as a source of shifting perspectives, mutable utterances, changing contexts, and alternating poetic agency. But he adds to this poetics of indeterminacy a sense of temporal, spatial, and imagistic multiplicity as well.

In his description of the poetics of the pictographs, language loosens itself from fixed relation to present or past, opening the experience of time to ongoing flow, in which multiple temporal frameworks combine into an experience of synchrony and diachrony, or structure and change. Such flow recalls what Rifkin terms "temporal frames of reference" (x) or those "collective frames [that] comprise the effects on one's perception and material experiences of patterns of individual and collective memory, the legacies of historical events and dynamics, consistent or recursive forms of inhabitance, and the length and character of the timescales in which current events are situated" (ix). Rifkin emphasizes the necessary multiplicity of such temporal orientations in the lived experience of time, because this living multiplicity and the complexity it engenders is precisely what is denied to indigenous people when they are consigned to that singular present moment of settler colonialism that requires them to exist in an inaccessible past. In Vizenor's reorientation of the pictographs, they coordinate the modern technological framework of "cinemas" with the apparently timeless world of the "woodland." Likewise, they relate the diachrony of history to the repetition of "dream circles" to show us the "meaning between present and past." Vizenor implies therefore that pictographs themselves have the capacity to orient multiple temporal scales. As the woodland tree jutting from the circle of figure 16 suggests, the circuits of pictography are not closed or limited. Rather, the pictograph offers the semiotic flexibility necessary for readers to consider the interactions between various sources of temporal centering and movement.

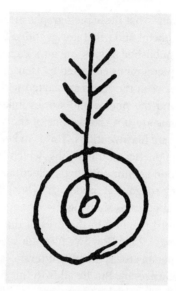

FIGURE 16 A pictograph in Gerald Vizenor's *Summer in the Spring* (1965) that presents "the sacred *midewiwin* stone and tree" (23, 143). The pictograph appears first in Frances Densmore's *Chippewa Music* published in 1910 (1:30).

The poem that provides the title for the book, sourced from a "dream song" in Densmore's *Chippewa Music II* (254), illustrates how the multiplication of space, time, and image can create instances of intellectual and political agency. The poem introduces a speaker who scans the prairie to find the future interpenetrating the present:

> as my eyes
> look across the prairie
> i feel the summer
> in the spring (23)

In this poem, anticipation realizes the prairie in terms of its unrealized flowering, evoking the present in terms of its coming physical conformation. Mark Currie calls this particular kind of crossing of temporal boundaries a "future memory," or an instance in which the future is presented in ways that are more typical of the past—that is, as a force structuring the experience of the present (6). In Vizenor's poem, the structuring force of such a future working itself on the present and the past connects the moment of his poem's writing to the moment when Densmore recorded it. Its summer in his poems was prefigured in the spring of her recording it. Yet if his poem's anticipation elides the boundary between Vizenor's poem and the dream song, then the song's translation is not the archival absencing of native cultures that Vizenor disparages in his introduction as "objective collections" (*Summer* ix) or, elsewhere, as the "preserved metasavages" and "consumable objects of the past" (*Shadow Distance* xi, 143–44). Rather, it is one of those pictographic "dream circles," feeding present into past in a scene of endless presentiment. The view from the vantage of his poem looks through the eye of anticipation to keep the terrain of its present moment always in motion. Rather than be caught in a preliterate premodernity, its voicing is relative, proximal, and responsive to the shifting present of multiple, interacting temporal orientations. Moreover, with its temporal orientation of the future looking back at its past, the poem satisfies the requirements by which the "unmarked present or future anterior" bears the confidence of ongoing time that Povinelli has characterized as a necessary shift for indigenous political activism ("Governance" 23). A mere look toward the future does not secure "a horizon toward which we walk without end"; it only supposes it. The future anterior—the view of the present from the view of its secured futurity—is the more confidently totalizable vision of a world's ongoingness, inasmuch as it refers to a world toward which to walk that is already there ("Governance" 23, 26).

Such scenes of anticipation forefigured recur throughout *Summer in the Spring*, often connecting with scenes of spatial meshing expressed in such lines as, "great mounds of clouds/over there/where i am looking" (26), "going to the south/i will bring/the south wind//in the sky/over there/they have taken pity on me" (33), "let us stand/to see my body/as i would like to be seen" (50), and "i have been waiting/a long time around the drum/for my lover/to come over/where i am sitting" (59). A sense of *over-there-ness* stirs in the poems, linking their anticipatory mood to crossing physical boundaries. The poet's sightline is troubled, time and again, by the other end of what it can see, wishing to see beyond its place in both space and time yet assured in the confidence that that other space and time is there.

These temporal and physical traversals correlate with the movements of the Anishinaabe songs: first through Densmore's ethnography and later through Vizenor's creative reworkings of them. Vizenor accentuates such traversals by repositioning his source songs and the original pictographs with which they were associated. For instance, the source song about the "summer in the spring" was not originally associated with the pictograph in figure 16, alongside which it appears in Vizenor's book. In Densmore's ethnography, that pictograph appears next to a song of initiation into the esoteric *Midewiwin* lodge. Its song has the opposite mood of the anticipatory "dream song," focused instead on feelings of centering and stability: "on the center of a peninsula/I am standing" (Densmore, *Chippewa Music* 30). When Vizenor places this pictograph next to the dream song he creates a new interpretation of the glyph. Its *mide* tree "standing" in the "center" of the concentric circles now moves across those circles, evoking the time-space breaches of the dream song. In changing what the pictograph illustrates, the poem changes the semantic resonance of the image. Pictographic metonymy affects what an image means, making it so that images never have a stable meaning or identity, but are always subject to sensory and semantic difference. Moreover, here, the single centered tree becomes a symbol of traversal, a symbol that comments on the movement of the pictograph from its ritual use in the *Midewiwin* lodge to its circular and ironic voicing in Vizenor's poetry. In the circularity of Vizenor's rewrite, the image implies a self-awareness about its shifting discursive locales. Its movements from ritual to ethnography to poetry hold closely, accurately, and reflexively to the multiperspectival poetics that animate the image to begin with.

Vizenor's self-awareness about the problem of intercultural motion is foundational to his writings. Karl Kroeber calls this the "gruesome irony" at the heart of his thinking: the "disruption is language loss. Vizenor understands how terrible is the burden on a native who is aware of being linked through family to an ancient, impressive, and admirable culture and yet may have no means by herself directly to take advantage of that heritage. She must in all likelihood rely on the research of her culture's destroyers to recover knowledge of its finest capabilities and accomplishments" ("Why" 27). Kroeber adds that Vizenor confronts such irony—here, of writing Anishinaabe poems filtered through Densmore's translations—by means of "unusual linguistic inventiveness" ("Why" 27). Yet even that strategy is enfolded in colonial histories. For instance, his poems must be written in the colonizer's language, English; and they hark as well a Barthean "empire of signs" that gives them their haiku-like quality.

When Vizenor discusses the relation between haikus and his Anishinaabe songs, he invokes indeed the writings of Roland Barthes, for whom haiku could only ever be a mirror reflecting the West. As Barthes experienced it in Japan, the haiku was a poetic refraction of empire, "remind[ing] us of what has never happened to us; in it we *recognize* a repetition without origin, an event without cause, a memory without person, a language without moorings" (qtd. in Vizenor, *Shadow Distance* 32). Vizenor encountered haiku as a serviceman abroad, and his experience reduplicates Barthes's: haikus are evidence of his own imperial alienations.[4] Still, a useful cultural strategy inheres in this relation, since—as he puts it—"haiku enhanced my perception and experience of dream songs, and my consideration of native reason, comparative philosophies, and survivance." "How ironic," he adds, "that my service as a soldier would lead to a literary association of haiku, and an overture to *anishinaabe* dream songs" (*Favor of Crows* xix). Irony's self-reference is instructive here. In casting the colonial mediation of his poetry as ironic, Vizenor prompts us to see—as Hutcheon likewise does for ironic discourse— the whole circuitry of his poems as a verbal problem that resolves into neither empire nor indigeneity. Instead, the poems voice their author's complex multi-temporal position, situated in the traditions, representations, projections, and creative acts of indigeneity, yet never removed from the contexts of imperial alienation.

What fails to satisfy Vizenor is a conception of indigeneity that is diametrically opposed to empire, inasmuch as this opposition grants the linguistic operations of empire sole control over the significations of native people. The term "indigenous" in and of itself is not the problem. What troubles Vizenor is when indigeneity magnifies the indistinct concept of the "Indian," which is—as he puts it in the introductory materials to the White Earth constitution—"a navigational miscalculation, an unintended maritime invention . . . a political simulation of thousands of distinct Native cultures" (Vizenor and Doerfler 31). When it perpetuates a stereotype of "Indians," the misrepresentation of indigeneity strengthens "the notion of Natives as an absence" (Vizenor and Doerfler 32), and not because natives are prevented from identifying with traditions, but because natives are obliged to identify with mediated traditions as if they were unmediated. The task is impossible. In her work on discourses of political recognition of Aboriginal people in Australia, Elizabeth Povinelli notes that "hegemonic domination in . . . (post)colonial multicultural societies . . . works primarily by inspiring in the indigenous subject a desire to identify with a lost indeterminable object—indeed, to be the melancholic subject of traditions" (*Cunning* 39). Responding to the problem pointed out by Povinelli—the liberal calculus in which a person of native background is compelled to conform to colonial fantasies, in order to be recognized politically—Vizenor transforms the object of tradition into a system of transformation.[5] By way of pictography and its anti-isomorphic poetics, he reorients tradition in the continental flow of the intersocietal interactions, migrations, and changes that occurred before, and that have persisted amid, the arrival of Europeans. Against a staid conception of native tradition, his pictographic poetics expose sightlines of ongoing indigenous world making.

In the preamble to the constitution he calls this ordinary right for indigenous people to move in cosmopolitan ways—to move actually and figuratively—the "great tradition of continental liberty" (Vizenor and

Doerfler 63). The denial of this liberty is one inflection point for a control society that has eroded tribal sovereignties; forced migrations; set up internment camps, reservations, and federal schools; monitored tribal economies; appropriated tribal lands; and securitized racial subjects. In support of the liberty to move, which is to say in support of a right to self-determination and self-transformation, he writes:

> Native sovereignty, in this sense, would have a natural ethical and historical presence in the notions and theories of transnational survivance.... Sovereignty as motion and transmotion is heard and seen in oral presentations, the pleasures of native memories and stories, and understood in the values of human and spiritual motion in languages. Sovereignty is transmotion and used here in most senses of the word motion; likewise, the ideas and conditions of motion have a deferred meaning that reach, naturally, to other contexts of action, resistance, dissent, and political controversy. The sovereignty of motion means the ability and the vision to move in imagination and the substantive rights of motion in native communities. (*Fugitive Poses* 182)

Vizenor describes movement as an Archimedean point, a roving vantage from which a viewer could perceive "contexts of action, resistance, dissent, and political controversy" that are embedded in "oral presentations, the pleasures of native memories and stories, and . . . the values of human and spiritual motion in languages" (*Fugitive Poses* 182). Motion on its own has no ethical weight. Rather, the motion Vizenor advocates aspires to a perspectival totalizability, which interpenetrates viewpoints that are native and transnational, natural and historical, biological and symbolic, mnemonic and imaginative, local and cosmopolitan—that is, the *over-thereness* of his poetry. For Vizenor, motion is irony spatialized and pictography literalized. It transforms space into an amalgam of differing perspectives integrating one another from discrepant temporal expressions. With regard to the constitution, the way in which Vizenor ironizes space and time recalls Borrows's uses of the pictograph, whose multiperspectivalism makes possible a multijuridical legal culture. Yet Vizenor's emphasis on *spatial* movement dips differently into the critical framework that Adorno lends to Borrows's idea of multiform subjects. That is, if subjects are loci of interpenetrating legalities, languages, cultures, and material histories, the result of seeing these interpenetrations as spatial ironies is that subjectivity becomes an instance of spatial as well as temporal heterogeneity. Moreover, because we are tracking movement in space, those incoherent conditions must include all of the things that make up space: not only law, language, culture, and history make up the objective basis of a spatial field, but animal, vegetal, mineral, and environmental elements do as well. Through the ironies of movement, subjects are revealed to be constituted by agential, other-than-human beings. Whatever basis for decision making is eked out of such a world must be negotiated from a political assembly of animate, nonhuman objects.

To the extent that language is a domain in which decisionality is made, it is also a field in which animate objects constitute the material conditions for making decisions. Human beings would appear to be privileged agents in such reality. Yet in an essay on metaphor, Vizenor proposes that the world through which we move belongs in actuality to the animate metaphors that constitute it:

> Language, then, is one of the *real* environments of the authored animals, the names, memories, and manners of the real as a narrative. Authored animals are real in the nature of tropes, the figurations that trace and redouble both the imagination of the author and the baited reader in what becomes a marvelous conception, an arcane animal of the shared pleasures of creation. ("Authored Animals" 668)

Language is the source of a pleasure shared, paradoxically, with language. What he calls "authored animals" are both the wellspring and the creatures drinking at the flow of tropes, figures, and signs. Their irony is to be a circular gift, giving what they receive, sharing what they create. As a self-circling gift, the animals of language ask for humans to participate in what Vizenor calls in his constitution "spiritual inspiration" and "reciprocal altruism" (Vizenor and Doerfler 63). Irony participates in (without trying to dominate) the self-circling movement of such gifts. The poem in *Summer in the Spring* associated with the pictograph in figure 17 ratifies these constitutional ironies:

> hunting
> like a little star
> i shine
> the animals
> are held
> staring at my light (23)

In this poem, Vizenor's innervation of irony in pictography comes to life. What he described as "dream circles, visual images and oratorical gestures showing the meaning between the present and the past: word cinemas in the lives of the tribal people of the woodland" takes on visible

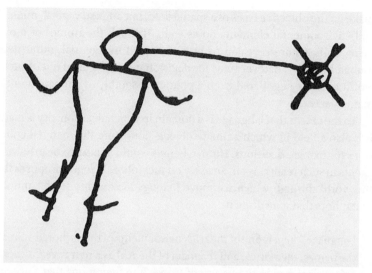

FIGURE 17 A pictograph in Gerald Vizenor's *Summer in the Spring* (1965) that is correlated with a poem about interspecies gazing (51). The pictograph appears first in Frances Densmore's *Chippewa Music* published in 1910 (1:86).

form (*Summer* 15). In the pictograph, the line extending from the human being to the cruciform circle corresponds to a sightline, moving in both directions: the person sees the animals who stare back at the person's shining body. As such, the line is circular, oscillating like the self-circling gift of language.

Yet if we take the idea of "word cinemas" to be also at play here, along-side the "dream circles," then the pictographic perspective reveals its similarity with the perspective of the modern spectatorial subject. Miriam Hansen has described how, early and often thereafter, the ex-perience of cinema was associated with dreaming and the dissolution of the self that happens in dreams. Citing Siegfried Kracauer, she illus-trates the dream logic of cinema: "The viewer's self-abandonment, dis-solution into and incorporation of 'camera-reality' also encourages a perceptual movement away from the film, for instance, when a material detail assumes a life of its own . . . and triggers in the viewer associations, 'memories of the senses' that return the 'absentee dreamer' to forgot-ten layers of the self" (*Cinema* 269). Because those layers of the self are intermingled with "shared historical 'image worlds,'" the experience of cinema viewing is one of dissolving parts, evaporating selfhoods, disin-tegrating identities, and partially recovered, partially invented memories of histories and temporal experiences that may never have existed but whose material presence is absolutely real (*Cinema* 269). In the glow of the cinematic light shared by the hunter and the animal prey in Vizenor's poem quoted above, each becomes an element intermixed with the other's illuminations, reflections, and illusions. When Vizenor interpolates this pictographic pair into a cinematic description— "word cinemas in the lives of the tribal people of the woodland" (*Summer* 15)—he suggests, on the one hand, that the pair's reciprocal relation holds up in a modern context. And, on the other hand, he suggests that experiences of spectatorial evaporation have been present in the poetics of woodland birch bark pictographs since before the arrival of Europeans. In this respect, pictographs have been acting as functional constitutions since time immemorial, awakening "shared historical 'image worlds,'" framing orientations, structuring relations, organizing multiple perspectives, inspiring reciprocity, and negotiating ironies.

Islands of Pictography, Lakes of Paint

Brooks suggests that constitutions are a species of a broader genre of council literature found throughout the native Americas. This genre, she writes, "often emerges during a period of transition, during which 'the people' are undergoing a significant transformation, when there is a pressing need for consolidation and unification and a strong desire for the articulation and formation of principles that can chart the course of the emerging or changing nation" (55–56). For Brooks, the genre of constitutional writing finds its inflection point in crises and the necessary movement of people into new settings and relations. But another distinguishing characteristic emerges when we think about constitutions as a genre of council: that is, their genre status is determined by whoever seeks counsel from the council of a text. The concept of council can be defined as a discourse that governs actions, deliberations, and decisions, disciplining the agency of those in the boundaries of a collective body. The logical outcome to Brooks's suggestion is that when people seek the guidance of such discourse they produce the genre of council literature.

Such is the effect that Erdrich's *Books and Islands in Ojibwe Country* has on the petroglyphs that are its source of council. Her search for their advice is occasioned by her recent venture of opening a bookstore in Minneapolis. This venture summons an anxiety about the necessity of books: "It is the question that has defined my life, the question that has saved my life, and the question that most recently has resulted in the questionable enterprise of starting a bookstore. The question is: Books. Why?" (4). She seeks an answer in an expedition to the "painted islands" of Lake of the Woods, between Minnesota and Ontario, the islands with pictographs on their rocks—some hundreds, others thousands of years old—from which she will inquire what those glyphs have to teach a writer of books (1). These Anishinaabe pictographs are distinct from the birch bark scrolls that serve as source texts for Vizenor and Borrows. Because they are painted on rocks these pictographs are called "petroglyphs" or, when the glyphs are scraped into lichen-covered rock, "lichenoglyphs" (Dewdney and Kidd 41). Part and parcel of their semiotics is their inter-penetration in the biotic material of the islands, a notion that Erdrich emphasizes when she calls the islands "book-islands" and "islands [that she is] longing to read" (1, 3).

For Erdrich, the islands' glyphs are council books. And the council that she seeks from them involves the living materiality of the petroglyphic writing. "The rock paintings are alive," she writes, "This is more impor-tant than anything else that I can say about them" (40). As she investigates these glyphs for their guidance, she focuses on their material composi-tion: the beach plants and oxidized ocher that give them their red hue, the sturgeon's oil used to make the glue that bonds paint to rock (an ad-hesive that has outlasted the flaking synthetic paints used to vandalize the glyphs), and the creviced erosions of the rock that capture the glyphs in natural histories of climatic exfoliation and geological grind.[6] When the signs so thoroughly embody the places they inhabit, their council extends beyond rock, expressing the lake ecology of these islands:

> The paint that is eternal comes from the Eternal Sands. Just down the beach the waves have dragged the sand off the tough roots of a low beach plant. The roots are such a brilliant red that from a short distance it looks as though the leaves are bleeding into the water. This is a component of the sacred paint used in the rock paintings. And the fish who showed itself to me is a part of the atisigan [dye] too. Sturgeon's oil is one of the bonding agents that will not let go, one of the substances that makes the paint eternal. (66)

As Erdrich suggests, the council assembled by the glyphs includes crea-tures of water and earth. Therefore, when this council speaks to Erdrich, it speaks in the first-person plural, making the multiperspectival poetics of the pictograph into an ecological assemblage "that will not let go."

The figure that speaks from the glyphs to Erdrich is that of a "horned man" at Painted Rock Island (fig. 18). For Erdrich this figure represents the writer. In his hand he holds a "sign" of the *Midewiwin*: this pictograph wields a pictograph. In fact, the horned man is surrounded by represen-tations of sign systems: "most of the major forms of communication with the spirit world are visible in this painting—the Mide lodge, the sweat lodge or *madoodiswan*, the shake tent . . . [and the] water drum" (45). His

FIGURE 18 Detail of the "horned man" petroglyph (n.d.) at Painted Rock Island, drawn by Canadian author and artist Selwyn Dewdney. From *Indian Rock Paintings of the Great Lakes*, p. 45, by Selwyn Dewdney and Kenneth E. Kidd © University of Toronto Press 1962. Reprinted by permission of the publisher.

work with these instruments of communication has summoned the bear who "floats over the drum" (45). The line that runs between the horned man and the bear indicates that they are communicating with one another. As Erdrich puts it, "the line is a sign of power and communication. It is sound, speech, song. The lines drawn between things in Ojibwe pictographs are extremely important, for they express relationships, usually between a human and a supernatural being" (45). In this case the communication between the horned man and the bear creates a conduit into the sky, the vertical line "connect[ing] them with the sky world" (45). The pictograph of the horned pictographer expresses the ecological assemblage that Erdrich sees in the making of the glyphs, interconnecting signs and biotic entities. Understanding this horned pictographer to be thus equipped to give counsel on the paradox of writing a book about the island petroglyphs—a situation in which the ecology of the island glyphs is lost when they are published as a book—she asks him, "Books. Why?" And he answers, "So we can talk to you even though we are dead. Here we are, the writer and I, regarding each other" (43). The most striking thing about that sentence is that in Erdrich's book it is not in quotation marks. It is as if the horned man penetrates the text, capturing its voice with his multiperspectival pictography. In doing that, he addresses the paradox of writing books about petroglyphs: this horned man implies that, despite the book's medium, he can create a petroglyphic relation in her writing. That relation is a type of ongoingness that admits him to Erdrich's world and thus admits to that world the "we" of which he consists: the flora, fauna, and geology of the islands' glyphs. As Erdrich says, this rock painting is alive. It lives in both the biotic materials of the rock face and the relational circuitry that it produces in Erdrich's writings.

What the horned man counsels to Erdrich resonates with a foundational principle in Anishinaabe cosmology, a cosmology in which—as Borrows puts it—the earth is not a thing with "no purposes of its own, no discernable thoughts, communication patterns or conscious life-ways." Rather, he adds, Anishinaabe cosmology "characterize[s] the earth as a living entity that has thoughts and feelings, can exercise agency by making choices, and is related at the deepest generative levels of existence. . . . The land's sentience is a fundamental principle of Anishinabek law, one upon which many Anishinabek people attempt to build their societies and relationships." Within such a cosmology it is inconceivable that industrial development would not take into account "earth as having being [that] can be legally recognized." It is in fact "a living being with the power of choice requiring respect for its autonomy, privacy and personal convictions against the liberal frameworks of post-reformation Europe." When the pictographs and petroglyphs of Erdrich's, Borrows's, and Vizenor's writings shed light on nonhuman agencies and perspectives, it is earth coming to life in their books, asking readers "to understand the earth's requirements by observing its interactions with wind, water, fire and other beings with which she relates." Pictographic reading, to continue to use Borrows's words, is a means of "provid[ing] guidance about how to theorize, practice, and order our association with the earth, and [it does] so in a way [that] produces answers that are very different from those found in other sources" (qtd. in Pomedli 227–28). While other sources mediate the constitutions, stories, and dream songs of these writers, their uses of pictography subsume mediation, shaping it in a poetics of transanimate transformation. In their writings, mediation itself is an ecological trace of the pictographs. That ironic detail cracks through colonial mirrors to let shine native constellations of cultural, political, and environmental authority. It even seems to be the case at times that the deeper the details of modernity crack the surface of these painted signs, the more brilliantly their paint that "will not let go" of the rock radiates.

Part Two

METALEPSIS AND HIEROGLYPHS

METALEPSIS AND PROBLEMS

4
HIEROGLYPHIC PARALLELISM

Mayan Metalepsis in Charles Olson's *Mayan Letters*,
Cy Twombly's *Poems to the Sea*, and
Alurista's *Spik in Glyph?*

At the furthest extreme of the deep ecology of signs is the stone. Stone is attributed none of the intention from which a semiotics could be apprehended—or easily imagined. It is far easier to imagine interspecies signifying than it is to imagine a kind of signifying that is abiogenic and crystalline.[1] And still, stone appears time and again in considerations of what it means to make signs. This seems to be the case for at least two reasons. Stones serve a negativizing function, reminding us of the biotic processes that distinguish the living from the larger share of matter in the cosmos, let alone what distinguishes between living beings that do and do not signify. Stones remind us how distinct is the desire to fashion signs from an otherwise lifeless world. They carry that feeling of desertedness that prompts us to signify. Second, the slow mutability of the stone, responding physically to geological conditions, offers the sense of a sign conforming over time to its contexts, while also bearing the invariance of geological processes (Lévi-Strauss thus found the conceptual basis for structuralism in geology: "Probably there is nothing more than that in the structuralist approach . . . to try to understand what is invariant in the tremendous diversity of landscapes, that is, to be able to reduce a landscape to a finite number of geological layers and of geological operations") (*Myth* 8–9; see *Tristes* 56–58; Paz, *Claude* 6–7). The stone has served as an allegory for the substratum on which signification depends: the intensities and extensions of writing are an echo of a stone's tendency to persist. As political theorist Jane Bennett notes, the seeming affinities between those signals of perdurability and intentional signs have stirred philosophers across the ages, from Lucretius and Spinoza to Deleuze and Guattari. In his lyrical essay *The Writing of Stones*, the French philosopher and literary critic Roger Caillois offers one such evocation of how natural stone striations induce a sense of signification: "suddenly you wonder whether this might not be writing instead of images of a thousand other things. . . . Between the inscriptions the dark surface of the stone is covered with a tiny intricate pattern of meandering lines, which fill an unfathomable mineral grief with a mysterious shining life. But it is not an alphabet: it is a pattern without a message, like the wormholes made by insects in dead wood" (70). Here, the traces of stone's tendency to persist—striations and climatic etchings—are its involuntary representation of an existential course of action, a writing of invariant process.

These are the allegories by which stone is made theory, and theory a semiotics of persisting stone. In this chapter, I examine how such conceptual imbrications exist in the carved stone writings of Mesoamerica, especially Mayan glyphs. In those glyphs, the writing of stones is an encounter between enduring mineral legibilities and intentional human script. This encounter helps to define theories of animated dualism in Mayan philosophy. The script is tensioned in the ambiguity of the stone's legible temporality: very old mineral marks appear to say something about continuing existential activity. Yet that existential activity continues only if it conforms to new contexts and conditions, historical and mythical.

In his sensitive analysis of the "ruins poem" of the mid-twentieth century, Harris Feinsod offers a political context for the poetry of stones. Concomitant with "mutually inflected states of ruin—the collapse of political and cultural inter-Americanism in the early Cold War, and the attempt to renew literary aesthetics in the wake of modernism—there emerged a notable poetic genre in postwar hemispheric literary history: the meditation on ruins" (138). As Feinsod describes it, this meditation was an allegory of political disenfranchisement, often situated in the ruins of pre-Columbian societies, whose lost future anterior elicited conceptions of other possible worlds. Poets from North and South wrote ruins poems of a piece with feelings of fractured inter-American political solidarity: Pablo Neruda, Octavio Paz, Alberto Hidalgo, Martín Adam, Ernesto Cardenal, Charles Olson, Allen Ginsberg, Philip Lamantia, and Lawrence Ferlinghetti offer exemplary instances of the genre. In Neruda's hands, the phenomenology of stone was an allegory of dogmatic (i.e., rectilinear) Marxist historiography: present mineral and hieroglyphic illegibilities were evidence of a transcendent process of historical progress. Stone persisted ("*piedra persistente*") to vanquish ideologies of self ("*propio pensamiento*") in the critical present moment of Cold War socialism (Feinsod 146–48, 152, 157). Feinsod notes the limits of such midcentury allegory, particularly when it was mapped onto the stones of Machu Picchu, Tenochtitlan, Teotihuacan, and Yucatan—the megalithic structures of the ancient Americas—whose writing certainly signifies things other than Western self-elegy.

On the other side of ruins are the carved stones themselves. Not only do these bear intentional signs but those signs also comment on the material significations of stone in its temporal ambiguity (are they ancient or presently shifting in geological action?). In the carved stones of the ancient Americas, voluntary and involuntary representations interact to render a double temporality that Javier Sanjinés describes as a "subaltern catachresis." For Sanjinés, the temporality of "ruins" is fractured by "the incorporation of the remote past into the present." Because these two temporalities fail to synthesize, the present becomes an "explosive agent in daily life . . . [a] world turned upside down." Rectilinear conceptions of time (modernist or Marxist) fail to see the irruptions in such temporal ambiguity. But—Sanjinés points out—the time schemes of the cultures that created the glyphs did not fail in that regard. Mayan *kajulew* (mythistory) and Quechuan *pachakuti* (which he translates as world reversal) and *lloqlla* (world avalanche) are frameworks for understanding the irruptive poetics of ruination (34, 33, 32). In these native frameworks, the trope of ruins is temporal catachresis, through which historical multiplicity, melee, and divergence are articulated and perceived as traces of deeper world continuity. For instance, historian Matthew Restall points out that Mayan conceptions of *kajulew* or mythistory—the interanimation of myth and historical change—created cultural continuities for seemingly destroyed sixteenth-century Mayan worlds. In mythistorical Mayan accounts of the so-called conquest, it was a subordinate event in broader temporal structures (Mayan eras that preceded and outlasted the arrival of the Spaniards), making "Conquest into anti-conquest . . . calamity into continuity . . . effectively weak[ening] the impact of Conquest by denying its uniqueness and inexplicability" (43). Mythistory did not serve to deny conquest as such. Rather, it staged the conceptual terms by which conquest could be seen as a catachresis with Mayan dialectical significations of contingency and incompleteness. In mythistory, the ruins are signs of a Mayan world still in motion, present even in the ruptures in which people fail to perceive it.

This chapter examines how the dialectical tropes of the glyphic stone steles in Mexico and Central America impacted the twentieth-century poetry of stones, embedding in that poetry Mesoamerican theories of catachrestical time and living noncontemporaneous contemporaneity. While a midcentury circuitry of state power inflects the visibility, availability, reception, and circulation of such glyphs, my claim is that those glyphs also disclose distinct meanings for that state circuitry and, therefore, that the stone glyphs absorb state apparatuses into times of Mesoamerican signifying. Following Feinsod's point that Charles Olson—in a manner distinct from Pablo Neruda—appreciated the "textual autonomy" of the

Mayan hieroglyphs (167), this chapter offers to that sense of textual autonomy a semiotics by which its impact on Olson's writing can be understood. Aided by the titanic scholar of Mayan cultures Dennis Tedlock's last (posthumously published) book, *Olson Codex*, this chapter argues that Olson knew more about the Mayan hieroglyphs than he is given credit for. While his comments on them are typically taken as a Caillois-like wish for deep mineral mimetic semiosis, in Olson's writing that wish is shaped by the specific semiotic system of the Mayan glyphs—especially by the living minerality of Mayan writing. If he is guilty of an attempt to mineralize or ontologize text, he is abetted in that act by the animated poetics of the hieroglyphic stones.

Not just a delineator of a "human universe," whose goal was "restoration of the human house" by means of the simple dictum that he "who possesses rhythm possesses the universe"—as he writes in one of his manifestos—Olson occasions his "human universe" within "a system of written record, now called hieroglyph, which, on its very face, is verse . . . [and by which Mayans] were able to stay so interested in the expression and gesture of all creatures . . . [and which] disclosed a placement of themselves toward a nature of enormous contradiction to ourselves" (*Collected Prose* 159, 162). My question is: what about this "nature" or system posits an enormous contradiction to Olson? And, in turn, how does that contradiction come to calibrate the rhythm of his "human universe" and "the expression and gesture of all creatures"? Put in terms of classical philology, if Olson's poetic vision was something like the configuration of dynamic lived rhythm that is called *rhusmos*, that *rhusmos* emerged from meaningful interaction with Mayan *rhuthmos* or linguistic rhythm. The rhythms of Olson's "enormous contradiction" appear, then, to be an instance of what James Clifford (quoting William Carlos Williams) called "new form dealt with as reality itself" (*Predicament* 5–6): the new form informing Olson's reality is Mayan catachrestical time. To be clear: I do not think that Olson ever escaped being Olson—grandiloquent, excessive, and ponderous. Rather, what interests me is how Olson's conception of form and reality changes when refracted in the glyph system. What kind of existence does Mayan semiosis induce for his existential throes?

The first person to posit a glyphic framework for understanding Olson's project was Olson himself. In the various research statements that he wrote—in letters to Robert Creeley and Cid Corman in the late 1940s and early 1950s, as well as the 1950 grant application that he submitted to support his research in Yucatan—he frames his work in parallelisms evocative of Mesoamerican *inamic* pairs (see ch. 1). These parallelisms take the form of visually symmetrical planes and motifs of syntactical opposition. In their double format, these elements interact to create what Tedlock calls the "graphic poetry" of Mayan glyphs, by which he means their aesthetic lingering between picture and logographic writing, "on the threshold between sight and sound" ("Drawing" 181; *2000 Years* 113). Olson writes the following in a letter to Creeley that was later republished as part of Olson's epistolary ethnography, *Mayan Letters*:

the glyphs
(their design & rhythms, in addition to
what denotation the scholars have found)

the present Maya lan-	*all surviving tales, records,*
guage (for its sounds &	*'poems,' songs etc: the*
meanings, not its orthog-	*'literature'* (Books of
raphy	Chilam Balam, plus Co-
	dices, plus) (63)

Simply in claiming that design and rhythm, or visuality and temporal measure, play combined roles in the semiotics of Mayan glyphs—that "the glyphs are [to be] seen as LANGUAGE by way of DESIGN" ("Art" 102, 108)—Olson was leagues ahead of contemporaries who were arguing whether the glyphs were writing at all, let alone a writing system able to convey poetic speech (Coe). But a still deeper intimacy is revealed in the way that Olson evokes the workings of the sign system, configuring his ideas into two columns that account for the visual and verbal aspects of the glyphs, apparently aware that their "threshold between sight and sound" involve "dialectics of overlapping or mutual involvement" (D. Tedlock, *2000 Years* 181; B. Tedlock *Time* 204–5). This dialectic—which I discuss in chapter 1 as a type of parallelism—gives his "human universe" a less *human*-centered mooring (that is, "human" here is not understood as the dominant signifier of colonial superordination—the signifier to be policed by racial discrimination), and gives his sense of selfhood a less self-centered footing (that is, "self" here is not understood as the organizing rubric for individualism).[2] With its moorings and footings in the Mayan "nature of enormous contradiction to ourselves," Olson denies certain Western imperial prerogatives that are likewise contradicted in the heterogeneities of Mayan lifeworlds.

In illustrating how the design of Mayan writing carries Mayan worlds into Olson's poetry, this chapter outlines the influence that the conception of "LANGUAGE by way of DESIGN" had on the aesthetic pedagogy at Black Mountain College, where Olson was rector after his return from Mexico. Providing a comparable sense of reality as composite design, Mayan glyphs also helped Chicano poet Alurista—in the 1980s—to reimagine racial embodiment in terms of Mayan dialectical significations of contingency and incompleteness. For these writers, in distinct ways, the Mayan glyph symbolizes historical and formal entanglements: the glyphs provided an era of intercultural anxieties a needed symbol for incommunicability, while also providing an aesthetics that rendered that incommunicability into a metonym for parallelist relational thresholds, that is, relations of nonsynthesizing parts and oppositions. When the dialectics of these signs migrate through midcentury aesthetic discourses, they ramify in secondary and even tertiary ways: while twice removed, the *autonomous textuality* of such Black Mountain works as Twombly's *Poems to the Sea* can also be seen to radiate with the poetry of carved Mayan stones.

Signs of Eroding Cipher-Scripts

The twentieth-century fascination with Mayan glyphs was engorged by nineteenth-century understandings of Egyptian hieroglyphics. In his literary analysis of Egyptomania, *American Hieroglyphics*, John Irwin delineates how Napoleon's military campaign in Egypt and Jean-François Champollion's subsequent decipherment of the Rosetta Stone in 1822 informed concepts of symbolization and representation for Walt Whitman, Edgar Allan Poe, Ralph Waldo Emerson, Henry David Thoreau, Nathaniel Hawthorne, and Herman Melville. These writers were swept up in a craze for Egyptian culture, whose distant mystery was associated with esoteric knowledge and mystical aesthetics. By the same token, in 1841, when John Lloyd Stephens published his account of pyramids and hieroglyphs in Mexico and Central America, his audience was poised to see in such things a kind of Fertile Crescent in the Americas.[3] Poe's review of Stephens's *Incidents of Travel in Central America* concerns itself almost entirely with biblical exegesis and "Arabia Petraea" or Roman Egypt. There and throughout nineteenth-century American literature, the Mayan sign was entangled in fantasies about Nile cultures. This Egyptian symbolism remained grafted onto Mayan hieroglyphs into the twentieth century, inflecting modernist glyph repertoires with spiritual undertones: Robert Stacy-Judd gave the Mayanism phenomenon a theatrical flamboyance, and Frank Lloyd Wright gave it architectural theories. For his part, modernist poet Hart Crane investigated the Mayan signs in Mexico, giving them a sense of potent occultism: "hieroglyphical . . . mysterious cyphers," "the calyx of death's bounty giving back . . . a livid hieroglyph," and intertwining "Tomorrows into yesteryear—[to] link/What cipher-script of time no traveler reads" (24, 73). Situated in modernist affective rhetorics of a world too quickly changing amid technological and capitalist acceleration, the temporally eccentric glyph offered feelings of timeless, centered, unchanging, and transcendent life. Likewise, as Miriam Hansen points out, the filmic reception of Mayan glyphs through such figures as Vachel Lindsay, D. W. Griffith, and Sergei Eisenstein upheld the nineteenth-century craze for transcendent Egyptian glyph morphology (*Babel* 77–78, 190–94). She cites Adorno to characterize the cinematic image of the hieroglyph as a "medium of regression," a means of supplying "archaic images to modernity" (Adorno qtd. in Hansen, *Babel* 188).

While Hansen finds much to critique in Hollywood's hieroglyphics, she also cautiously distinguishes between the hieroglyph as a figure and as a mode of figuration. In tracing the interpenetration of writing systems in Griffith's *Intolerance*, she writes: "we have to confront the difficulty of distinguishing between hieroglyphics as a figure of the film's self-definition and the process of hieroglyphic figuration that seems peculiar to the film's textual activity" (*Babel* 197). The distinction is particularly tricky in cinema because the medium so closely mirrors the methods of hieroglyphic communication. Like film, hieroglyphs combine images and temporal syntax to create what Dennis Tedlock calls their "graphic poetry" ("Drawing" 181"). For instance, the glyph in figure 19 uses its visual features to add meaning to the logographic graphemes that signify the phrase *b'alum pih*, literally nine bundles of 144,000 days, that is, 1,296,000 days or approximately 3550 years. Those graphemes are the patch of jaguar skin on the man's face and the tumpline across his head. Because the word for jaguar in the Mayan K'iche' language, *b'alam*, is a close homophone to the word for nine, *b'alum*, when placed next to the bundling grapheme of the tumpline, the meaning nine bundles (*b'alum pih*) or 3550 years would have been evident to a reader.[4] That is the straightforward meaning of the glyph. But the visual elaboration that encapsulates these basic graphemes complicates their meaning. The man who is also a jaguar is a visual homologue for the image, *b'alam*, that is also a sound, *b'alum*—creating thus a nexus of sight, sound, and syntax. This nexus of mutually animating linguistic parts takes on still greater meaning with the presence of the harpy eagle in the man's tumpline. As the largest predator in the Central American sky, the harpy eagle is the celestial analog to the jaguar, the largest predator on the ground (Miller and Taube 82). In Mayan parlance, such conjuncture of sky and earth denotes the world itself—which is called *kajulew*, literally, "sky-earth," but translated in its philosophical resonance by Tedlock as "mythistory" (*Popol Vuh* 58–60). Representing the conjuncture that is the world itself, the glyph thematizes its figuration as ontological frame setting. That is, its conjunction of heaven and earth is itself conjoined to a system of

FIGURE 19 Dennis Tedlock's analysis (2017) of a calendric glyph at Copan, Honduras, meaning *b'alum pih* or 3550 years (personal communication with author; slightly reworked in *Olson Codex* 19). The glyph appears in Stele D (figure 20), whose date range is 695–738 CE.

mutually animating linguistic elements. As such, the visual poetry of the glyph is a world orientation. The forms of doubling in the glyph (visual and syntactical, as well as heavenly and terrestrial) are instances of the conjunctures that inhere in Mayan reality: not just sky and earth, but—as is brought out by Tedlock's translation of *kajulew*—myth and history, the eternal and the changing, interact in the morphology of the hieroglyph.

Tedlock notes that, from this frame setting, we are to understand that the deep time of the glyph—its 3550-year era—inheres in a minimal scale too: the everyday experience of time, of people bearing their loads in tumplines across city and field, is woven through the time of the gods (*Olson Codex* 19). The glyph's design suggests an author who is eager to disclose a parallelist cosmology or, as Tedlock puts it in another context, "to find the traces of divine movements in [their] actions . . . [and remain] always alert to the reassertion of the patterns of the past in present events" (*Popol Vuh* 59, 60). The author relates writing to a Mayan world frame that, in turn, frames writing as a scene of reflexive figuration, with a dialectic of parts in active relation to one another. In much the same way that film uses scenes of filmic activity to comment on the conceptual aspects of film, or generates filmic figures to explore its mode of filmic figuration, this glyph—which is like a metaglyph—comments on its own process of communicating. This is suggested by an analogy between *muwan* (the harpy eagle) and the material of the glyph itself, etched onto stone. *Muwan* is the deity presiding over 360-day periods called "tun" or stone (the glyph means literally "nine bundles of stone"). With the jaguar-man figure carrying in his tumpline the very material out of which he is carved (stone), this figure carries the linguistic vehicle that carries him. In thus creating a circular relation between a figure and its vehicle, the glyph offers a metaleptic transit point between a sign and its sensual world. In thus drawing out the necessary relation between a sign and material resonance, the glyph makes possible a self-reflection about the distinctly composite semiotics of stone hieroglyphs. While Hansen might not have had the knowledge of glyph morphology to make a claim about its similarity to the film medium, her exploration of the figure of the hieroglyph as a mode of figuration in cinema makes evident the fact that cinema, by virtue of what in 1929 Eisenstein called its "denotation by depiction," incidentally disclosed what Eisenstein likewise called "the principle of the hieroglyph—'denotation by depiction'" (35).

In this regard, filmmakers of the 1920s and 1930s came closer to disclosing the semiotics of Mayan glyphs than their linguist contemporaries. As archaeologist and anthropologist Michael Coe notes, attempts to decipher the Mayan glyphs were plagued by limited conceptions of the nature of writing. The quasi-racist identification of writing with the alphabet and only the alphabet—whose exclusionary force Derrida discussed in terms of Western logocentrism—led to such conclusions as early Mayanist Richard C. E. Long's: "I do not think in any instance there is a real grammatical sentence [in Mayan hieroglyphs]." The thrust of logocentrist quasi-racism here is in the force of the word "real." Or his more aggressive comment, "Writing [marks] the difference between civilization and barbarism . . . and the fact remains that no native race in America possessed a complete writing and therefore none had attained civilization" (Long [1935] qtd. in Coe 138–39). Breakthroughs in deciphering Mayan hieroglyphs would not come until the 1950s, with the scholarship of Soviet linguist Yuri Knorozov, who demonstrated that the glyphs were composite signs of visual and phonetic elements, and Russian American archaeologist Tatiana Proskouriakoff, who identified diachronic elements in the glyphic patterns of image and sound (Coe 146, 167–84). Even so, the effort of Mayan glyph decipherment was a political minefield: because he was a Soviet citizen, Knorozov's research was discredited in the United States, calling into question any scholarship that seemed to build on the idea that the Mayan sign system worked by a combination of visual and sonic features, let alone that it carried a dialectical, reflexive historicity.

In contrast, Olson was up to date with such rogue scholarship and shows—in a carefully crafted proposal that he submitted to the Viking Fund and Wenner-Gren Foundation to fund his fieldwork in Mexico—that he was attracted to these radical approaches to glyph morphology. His project, "The Art of the Language of the Mayan Glyphs," proposed that the glyphs combined visual design and denotative graphemes to create the unique "double nature of this unusual writing":

> The "art" is a matter of the fact that a glyph is a design or composition which stands in its own space and exists . . . both by the act of the plastic imagination . . . and by the act of its presentation in any given case since. Both involved—I shall try to show—a graphic disciplining of the highest order. Simultaneously, the art is "language" because each of these glyphs has meanings arbitrarily assigned to it, denotations and connotations. ("Art" 96, 95–96)

Searching beyond what politically sanctioned scholarship in the mid-century had concluded about the glyphs, Olson intuits how the mechanics and aesthetics of glyph morphology are linked: that is, that the denotative elements of the glyphs are augmented by the pictorial field in which they appear, producing a composite writing that is simultaneously syntactic and visually artistic—and whose composite nature is used to comment on the nature of composite makings. As happened with the hieroglyphic filmmakers of the 1920s and 1930s, aesthetic attention to the glyphs led Olson to his insights about their mechanics. Thus, he imagined that those insights would be best communicated in aesthetic modalities. In his proposal, he adds:

> The value of the writing to my work here would seem to be a matter of the insights which follow from the practice of it as a profession, particularly such graphic verse as a contemporary American poet, due to the work of his immediate and distinguished predecessors, does write. ("Art" 96)

Here he gives his most radical proposition, which is that a poet such as himself is particularly enabled to decipher the Mayan writing and to reveal that decipherment in poetry writing because contemporary trends in poetic experimentalism had awakened a consciousness of "graphic verse." He pins his aesthetic expertise on the fact that his poetry has taken on graphic qualities that could reveal the meanings of the graphic poetry of the glyphs. Elsewhere in the proposal, citing his collaborations and conversations with Mexican artist Hipolito Sánchez, Italian painter Carrido Cagli, Lithuanian American painter Ben Shahn, and German-born Bauhaus artist and designer Josef Albers, Olson suggests that a poetic mode oriented to visual presentation could teach other people how to read the Mayan glyphs. He is more bombastic still with his proposition in his letters to Creeley, to whom he wrote, "Christ, these hieroglyphs.

Here is the most abstract and formal deal of all the things this people dealt out—and yet, to my taste, it is precisely as intimate as verse is. Is, in fact, verse. Is their verse. And comes into existence, obeys the same laws that, coming into existence, the persisting of verse, does" (*Mayan Letters* 41–42). In Olson's view, the persisting graphic poetry of the glyphs would be read by way of the graphic poetics in contemporary resurgence.

The question then must be: did Olson's poetic approach enable him to read the glyphs? In another letter to Creeley, he hints that it did, somewhat. Drawing on his collaboration with Sánchez to be titled "The Glyphs of Copan" (the collaboration in which "the visual presentation [would show]—perhaps for the first time—[that] the glyphs are seen as LANGUAGE by way of DESIGN"), he turns to the glyph in figure 19 to explain to Creeley that "you can see, that time, in their minds, was *mass & weight!*" (Olson and Creeley 102, 108; Olson, *Mayan Letters* 61–62). Letting alone the massification of time, which perhaps is obvious from the glyph's burdened human figure (who carries the stones of time in his tumpline), he tries to crunch the numbers for this massification:

>   that is, Copan D is a date 9 baktuns (400 yrs)
>   15 katuns (20 yrs)
>   5 tuns (year of 360)
>   3905 yrs total   0 uninal (month of 20 days)
>   0 kin (day)
>   it is pictured thus:
>   man 9 carrying baktun (a huge
>   zopalote) on his back (as the
>   woodsmen still carry their baskets,
>   by the band across their fore-
>   head)   (*Mayan Letters* 64–65)

Coming within four hundred years of the glyph's 3550-year span, Olson shows a budding skill in translating the content of Mayan writing. As far as its form is concerned: lineating his calculation alongside a visual description of the glyph that also describes the ongoing everyday experience of contemporary Mayan woodsmen, his translation reaches into the Mayan poetic mode that seeks to frame its cosmology in everyday happenings, to "[reassert the] patterns of the past in present events" (D. Tedlock, *Popol Vuh* 59, 60). In Olson's experimental translation of the glyph, syntactical parallelisms are interlocked with the temporal multiplicities of Mayan conjunctural worlds. What he reads in the glyph appears to be exactly the interrelation of remote and present moments that the glyph expresses by way of language and visual design. Moreover, both original and translation denote by depiction (exploiting the visual field of language to intensify its meanings), and use depiction to examine the nature of denotation (using "graphic verse" to reflect on the present circumstances of writing a poem or glyph-block). Like the figure with the tumpline, Olson's translation has the mass and weight of multiple temporal densities seeking to understand their relation to one another.

The Projectivism of Mayan Glyphs

In the next letter that Olson writes to Creeley from Mexico, he includes one of his earliest poems that could be considered projectivist. As Olson described it in his manifesto, "Projective Verse" (1950), projectivism wished to direct poetic emphasis onto breath, body, field, material solidity, objects, and kinetics. It called on poets to think of verse as a physical construct, whose form was to be self-identical with its object-referents. Its troping was thus circular, emerging from and directed toward its poetic objects; or, as he puts it, "the beginning and the end is breath, voice in its largest sense," "its place of origin and its destination," "of the breathing of the man who writes as well as of his listenings" (*Collected Prose* 247, 245, 239). One way to think about projectivism, then, is as a closed metalepsis. That is, whereas metalepsis is typically the use of a figure of speech in a new context—manipulating an abstract figure to introject or crisscross new meaning into a salient target referent—in projectivism the abstraction and its target object are self-identical, self-introjecting, and closed. Projectivism makes the thing into the word and the word into the thing, creating closed referential circuits that circle endlessly inside their objects. Indeed, while projectivism's most famous dictum—that "form is never more than an extension of content"—has been taken to express an expansive attitude toward form, the opposite seems truer to its semiotics: form is enclosed in content, never able to extend itself beyond content, because thing and word are self-identical. Form only shifts when "the content does—[because] it will—change," when "the material of verse shifts" (*Collected Prose* 247). Only in the moments in which the material content of a poem changes can its forms of verse change.

For a poet pursuing the self-introjection of objects, the task is to be attuned to shifts in the material world. In a letter to Creeley subsequent to the "*mass & weight*" note, Olson draws on the Mayan "glyph-world" to further demonstrate how projective verse finds such shifts in its object-referents. The letter is anchored in a list of glyphs whose form emphasizes the itemized quality of the objects, as if to deny syntactic interconnections and affirm some inherent connectivity in the items:

sunday april 1

What continues to hold me, is, the tremendous levy on all objects as they present themselves to human sense, in this glyph-world. And the proportion, the distribution of weight given same parts of all, seems, exceptionally, distributed and accurate, that is, that

> sun
>> moon
>>> venus
>>>> other constellations & zodiac
> snakes
>> ticks
>>> vultures
> jaguar
>> owl
>>> frog
> feathers
>> peyote
>>> water-lily
> not to speak of
> fish
>> caracol
>>> tortoise
> &, above all,
> human eyes
>> hands
>>> limbs

(PLUS EXCEEDINGLY
CAREFUL OBSERVA-
TION OF ALL POS-
SIBLE INTERVALS OF
SAME, as well as ALL
ABOVE (to precise di-
mension of eclipses,
say, & time of, same
etc. etc.)

And the weights of same, each to the other, is, immaculate (as well as, full)

That is, the gate to the center was, here, as accurate as what you and i have been (all along) talking about—viz., man as object in field of force declaring self as force because is force in exactly such relation & can accomplish expression of self as force by conjuncture, & displacement in a context best, now, seen as space more than a time such (*Mayan Letters* 66–67)

Olson's list is actually a glyph-by-glyph translation of a glyph-block in Copán, Honduras. Its nonligatured form could be read as a symptom of his glyphic illiteracy: what syntax it lacks, it lacks because its translator could not translate the clauses and phrases that arrange the signs into sentences. But the glyphs in this stele are a special kind of sign, one that emphasizes the life within signs. Called "full-figure glyphs," the glyphs of Stele D at Copán (fig. 20, the block that contains the tumpline glyph of fig. 19) are written in a special *style* of Mayan writing, in which signs are expressed as full-figured human and nonhuman bodies. Scholar of Mayan writing Stephen Houston points out that not all styles of Mayan writing were so expressive of human and nonhuman bodies, but, when they were, they served to emphasize that all signs are vital. Their bodily figuration expresses the idea that "writing [is] an animate force" (Mary Miller qtd. in Houston 156). With their tumplines pulling each other, their hands and paws grabbing adjacent signs, pushing and apparently conversing with one another, "the full-figures are texts that push back at the reader. . . . Absent an overt declaration by the Maya that glyphs talk, breathe, and move, the solid bet is that virtuosity, enlivened words, magical creation, and pictorial infusion play equal roles. . . . For the Classic Maya, the full-figure signs seem to be beings in many respects. Endowed with selves, they converse with other signs. . . ." (Houston 118). If it is the case that the glyphs have internal and autonomous vitalities that interact with adjacent signs, readers, and even the "vitality in stones" on which they are carved (Houston 123), then their translation as stand-alone "field[s] of force declaring self as force," whose force is capacity for self-emergent "conjuncture [and] displacement," is entirely fitting and evocative (Olson, *Mayan Letters* 67). Olson's poetic itemization, seen within the lifeworld of its listed items, translates the ligatures, connectivities, disjunctions, and vitalities internal to those items. Seemingly self-involved, the internal interactivity of Olson's translated signs extends ligatures and musculatures that are invisible in the alphabet, but virtually coextensive with the poet's confidence to let them stand on their own.

Such confidence is not held without risks. Houston notes that the full-figured glyphs amplify the tensions and contradictions of Mayan glyphs to a high level. They emphasize fractures and slippage points between the sonic, pictorial, and syntactical aspects of glyphic writing: "as examples of flux, tension, and possibility . . . [the] full-figures invite a blurring of preconceived categories. They interact not just linguistically, but as

FIGURE 20 Stele D, Back (CPN 7). Full-figured inscriptions, whose date range is 695–738 CE. LC 9.15.5.0.0., Ajaw 8 te Ch'en. ISIG: Moon Goddess, patron of the month Ch'en. Erected by Waxaklajuun Ub'aah K'awiil. Drawing by Linda Schele (1996), © David Schele. Photograph: Courtesy of Ancient Americas at LACMA (ancientamericas.org).

embodied, legged, and armed forms. A few seem to go beyond the visual. Open mouths imply speech, song, cries, all in a howling, murmuring, squeaking, orating performance." In their live-action performance of discrepant intentionalities, the full-figured glyphs are a theater of incongruity—an expression of "turbulent identity" in which "a complete union is unattainable" (Houston 107).[5] In other words, they are a semiotic instantiation of Mayan nonsynthesizing dialectics. While not all glyphs are full-figured, the full-figure glyphs serve to remind readers that signs are involved in a parallelist cosmos of mutually intensifying temporal and existential scales.[6] In the glyph-block (fig. 20), the tensioned morphology of visual, phonetic, syntactical, and corporeal elements records a date (9 bak'tun/15 k'atun/5 tun/0 winal/0 k'in or Sunday, July 26, 736 CE) when a Mayan king Waxaklahun-Ubah-K'awil performed a bloodletting ritual to enter a portal-like trance to "the Otherworld where the gods and ancestors lived" (Schele and Mathews 165–69). Therefore, the topmost glyph on the right of the stele—detail in figure 19—is a microcosmic expression of the encompassing dialectic of earth and sky, which the stele as a whole reiterates in the story of Waxaklahun-Ubah-K'awil mediating between human world and Otherworld. That interactivity between scales—glyph-block and single glyph, otherworldy and earthly, mythic and historical, writing and writer, virtuality and actuality—is the kind of metalepsis by which seemingly selfsame things carry the disjuncts that let them connect to other things. While they risk thus what Houston calls "dissipation," they do so to "harness" the possible interactions or shifts internal to things in interpenetrating material, mythic, linguistic, and virtual worlds (123). When writing is alive, its projection permits movement at every scale of being (since signs have already established themselves as perpetually mutable beings), allowing for movement among those scales, blurring thus the stabilizing scalar categories that typically distinguish beings from nonbeings, signs from things, forms from contents, and stones from the life that carves them.

For Olson the risk of translating such full-figured glyphs into a poetics of closed metalepsis is to fall into isomorphy or closed referential circuits. His anxiety about falling into closed representation is expressed in the poem that he writes before he travels to Mexico, "The Kingfishers" (1949), in which he concludes that his strategy will be to "hunt among stones." The poem is an allegory of postwar shock, represented by the poet's hangover in a kingfisher's fetid nest (Maud 26–27; Alcalay 68; Feinsod 137). Olson's 1940s commitment to the ideal of a benevolent American cosmopolitanism had proven ill conceived. Cold War realities of incipient war in Korea, intensified national paranoia about red espionage, and the fractured networks of hemispheric political collaboration intersect in the shattered nerves following excessive intoxication. In the poem, the sought-after stones represent the psychological solidity necessitated by such crisis. But they also represent a desired break in referential solidity—a break through which the poet's words could express not only the present state of affairs (as a kind of hard symptomatic poetry, with the signs of Cold War paranoia manifesting at the level of the shocked bodily symptom) but express the possibility of other worlds as well. With an eye to shifts internal to objects, especially stones, he writes: "What does not change/is the will to change . . . even the stones are split/they rive" (*Collected Poems* 86, 88, 93). With his poem's two senses of stoniness (representing stability and change), Olson is putting pressure on the problem of materiality in poetry: if a poem is to have the solidity of stone, how can it also be responsive to change and how can it engage dynamically with the process of change? The problematic took on a different shape once he was exposed to what Houston calls the "turbulent identity" of signs in Mayan semiosis. In such turbulence, "the object never becomes identical with itself"—Tedlock would add to Houston's reading—eliciting "a poetics in which form is always other than an extension of content" ("Toward" 183, 186, 187). In its aim to be a dynamic poetics of things, the projectivist mode was assisted by the interminability and nonisomorphy of things in Mayan philosophical thought.

Tedlock emphasizes that this philosophical thought is present in contemporary Mayan cultures. Tedlock illustrates this contemporaneity in conversation with Andrés Xiloj Peruch, the K'iche' Mayan "keeper of the days" (diviner and healer) in the Momostenango Highlands of Guatemala with whom he worked closely. "We were discussing dreams," Tedlock writes, "and when I asked him whether the right word to describe a clear dream might be *kajuljutik*, meaning that 'it shines,' he replied, 'Yes indeed. When a clear dream brings news, one can say . . .'" and then Xiloj Peruch switches to poetic speech:

Kajuljutik,	It shines,
kachupchutik	it shimmers
pa ri q'ekum,	in the blackness,
pa ri aq'ab.	In the night. (*2000 Years* 3)

Tedlock explains that the notion of a "right word"—a desire for the naturalistic Flaubertian isomorphy of the mot juste (arriving to poetics via Pound)—is anathema in Mayan conceptions of language, in which "there is no point of rest at which words become isomorphic with objects on a one-to-one basis." To convey that idea—to disperse, as Tedlock puts it, "the essentializing thrust of my question, resisting the search for just the right word to label the phenomenon under discussion"—Xiloj Peruch transforms *kajuljutik* into a point of departure to other descriptions. Tedlock explains that these added descriptions expanded the somatic field of the dream under discussion, giving it visual, sonic, gustatory, and tactile sensations:

> Thus [Xiloj Peruch] produced the word *saq*, "light, white, bright," to make a pair with a word from our question, *q'alaj*, which refers to clarity (as opposed to obscurity) and can be used to describe discourse. Then he took the onomatopoeic verb *kajuljutik*, whose reduplicated stem (*julju-*) gives it the character of small-scale distich, and added a second verb with a reduplicated stem (*chupchu-*). Both verbs indicate some degree of fluctuation in the reception of this "bright and clear" dream, but with a slight difference. *Julju-* carries a sense of acuteness that includes the prickliness of spines and piquancy of chili, while *chupchu-* is less fine-grained, evoking sensations that include the flickering of a candle and the splashing of water. The effect of the sentence as a whole is to raise the discontinuity of the "presence of the same object" to a high frequency.... ("Toward" 184)

Xiloj Peruch signal-jams Tedlock's "essentialist" desire for the right word with a poem that amplifies discontinuity and dis-identification. It does so by translating the referent of *kajuljutik*—a shining and burning thing—into the softened gleam of something that flickers and splashes. The seeming contradiction of a thing that both flickers like fire and splashes like water carries traces of the Mayan cosmos of tensioned oppositions. The poem emphasizes that cosmology in its subsequent lines, when "shines" and "shimmers" are contrasted to "blackness" and "night." Moreover, if we recall that this poem set out to describe a dream, these oppositions take on meanings of memory and loss, or the dream that is remembered through the darkness of a night's sleep. For Mayan daykeepers, nighttime dreams are messages from the ruling divinities of a given day handing over time to the ruling divinities of the next day. Yet in that transfer the divinities on the receiving end also speak, producing an intermixed signal of future and past, a temporal heterogeneity in every night's threshold (Tedlock, *Breath* 208–11). Daykeeper Xiloj Peruch's poetic oppositions stage such heterogeneity, convoking the bright and dark, prickly and spicy, flickering and splashing, and coarse and fine elements of a dream to raise a sense of its fundamental nonidentity and permeability; it is neither this nor that, but also not something in between, which would require a transcendent third position of the middle; and it is certainly anything but "empty" and "homogeneous" (to return to the oft-invoked misquotation of Benjamin, *Selected* 4:402; see ch. 1). The animating quality of things in the Mayan lifeworld is secured in their oscillation into other things—they change because they must, and they must because of the inescapable pull of multiplicity. Like the person whose mind they seize with transposing temporalities, dreams therefore materialize in transfers and transformations. The apparent boundedness of such a thing as a dream, thing, or person disintegrates in Xiloj Peruch's poem as a result of his verbal dis-identifications. In his discussion of dreams, a dream is nothing other than the instances of its changing.

In his *Mayan Letters*, Olson evokes such philosophical nonisomorphy with a poem about a "fish glyph" (figs. 5 and 6 in this book's introduction). In this poem, he calls the glyph a fish because he thought that the glyph depicted K'uk'ulkan—or a Yucatec Mayan equivalent of Quetzalcoatl—with the physical features of a seahorse.[7] Like Quetzalcoatl, K'uk'ulkan was associated with the invention of writing. Hence Olson imagined a Mayan associational matrix between writing, invention, and the sea.[8] The scene of writing was thus rendered a passageway as diversely shifting as ocean currents. The poem reads:

> The fish is speech. Or see
> what, cut
> in stone
> starts. For
>
> when the sea breaks, watch
> watch, it is the
> tongue, and
>
> he who introduces the words (the
> interlocutor), the
> beginner of the word, he
>
> you will find, he
> has scales, he
> gives off motion as
>
> in the sun the wind the light, the fish
> moves
>
> (*Mayan Letters* 52–53)

Like Xiloj Peruch's discourse of dis-identifications, Olson's poem twists incompletion into each word. The first stanza uses rhyme ("what, cut"), alliteration ("stone/starts"), and syntactic echoes (speech. Or . . . // starts. For . . .) in a series of parallels that resonate with the poem's topical paralleling of sight and sound: "The fish is *speech*. Or *see* . . ." This line makes it known that the scene of creation emerges from oppositional relations, that self-differencing inheres in every object, and that this fundamental self-differencing is present at the creation of poetry—in both its mytho-poetic origins and its origination in a present scene of invention. For instance, the word "see" carries its visual referent as well as a homophonic elision into "sea." Working backward from that homophony, "Or see" begins to sound like "hor-sea" or "sea horse," the primary referent of Olson's "fish." Like a tidal eddy, the poem's soundscape pulls into itself while moving forward. That double movement recurs in the poem's repetitions, reversals, and oppositions: what/cut; stone/starts; speech. Or//starts. For; speech/see; or see/[horsey/horse-sea]/[sea horse]; fish/stone; see/sea; watch/watch; watch/[wash]; watch/tongue; [wash]/tongue; he/the; introduces/interlocutor; introduces/beginner; beginner/interlocutor; the /the; the/he; he who introduces the words/the beginner of the word; word/words; you/he; scales/gives; has/he; has/as; will/motion; sun/wind; wind/light; sun/light; light/fish; fish/sun; motion/moves; motion/stone. The sum of this table of oppositions is a poem of interpenetrations between the invention of language and the poet's invention of a linguistic matrix of self-canceling forms, in which each thing presents a threshold into other things, objects are never selfsame, and the influence of Mayan glyph morphology makes salient its semiotics of self-difference in poetic form. If the prosodic problem with "The Kingfishers" was that it was an allegory fishing always for symptomatic representation in closed referential circuits, Olson's response was a poem that staged dissimilarity as a function of identification, a fish or stone emerging always as some other thing.

A fundamental quality of Mayan poetics is that in it identities are not transcendent. Everything becomes, but does not resolve itself in, some other thing. This is what Olson called the "conjunction and displacement" of the glyphs. And it was importantly a means by which he articulated a poetics that was more than poetic or linguistic. In a prosimetric letter to Creeley (many of Olson's letters from Mexico combined poetry, philosophy, ethnography, and everyday epistle in this way), he reflects on how Mayan semiosis theorizes on the medial interstices of which the letter itself is an instance:

CONJUNCTION & DISPLACEMENT, the sense of, C & D, D & C, etc
etc. Is verse.
> Is quite another thing than time.
>> Is buildings. Is
des ign.
> Is—for our trade—

THE DISJUNCT, language
In order to occupy space, *be* object (it being so hugely as intervals TIME)
has to be thrown around, re-assembled, in order that it speak, the man
whose interstices it is the re-make of   (Olson and Creeley 66–67)

Olson writes these thoughts in reference to what he considered the prototypical glyph of Mayan writing—he called it the "first glyph" and "introductory glyph"—because it was the K'uk'ulkan of his sea-horse poem
(figs. 5 and 6). He saw in this glyph not only representation of linguistic origins and invention but also the way in which full-figured glyphs
stage the creative interaction between language and nonlinguistic elements: pictures, bodies, and movement in what Houston calls "flux, tension, and possibility" (107). Their intermedial quality inspired Olson to
think about the relation of verse to habitus, architecture, and schematic
structures of life—"time," "buildings," and "design"—elaborating thus
the Mayan *rhusmos* (or lived dynamics) that is inherent to parallelist Mayan *rhuthmos* (poetic or semiotic rhythm). Mayan media configurations
splinter into ceaseless displacements, only to be conjoined or reassem-
bled into further displacements, disjuncts, and "interstices [they are] the
re-make of." In its description of this semiotics, through its repeated liga-
ture of the verb "to be"—"is . . . is . . . is . . . is . . . ," by which every instance
of a medium is a disjunct into other media—the letter poem characterizes mediality as transmediality.

In a wide-ranging essay, "Stone Thresholds," poet and scholar John Wilkinson elaborates a history of transmedial conceptions of boundary stones
in poetry writing. Yet here, the "threshold experience" of which he writes
is not found in the geography of the stone (on the boundary between
some place and another)(631)—rather, it is present in the semiotic self-
orientation of the stones themselves. The carved stones with which Olson was so deeply engaged were theories of media in which the medium
is never self-identical. Inasmuch as "the stone appears to represent itself"—to quote César Paternosto, artist and scholar of the carved stones
of the pre-Columbian Andes—that representation is a *"piedra abstracta,"*
or "abstract stone" (xv–xvi, 18–19). Paternosto's notion is that such carved
stones were energized with conceptual reflection on the meaning of multidimensional stone writing: they are consciously engaged efforts to understand the contradiction of writing and thinking with stones. In Olson's
hands, such conceptual slipperiness of stone in its transmedial conception would become an aesthetic of artistic collaboration. The unattainable
synthesis of the glyph would continue to work its poetics on collaborative projects and the project of collaboration at Black Mountain College.

Black Mountain Glyphs

When Olson returned from Mexico to the United States, his mind was filled with traces of Mayan forms and worlds. Settling into a position as rector at Black Mountain College, his pedagogical contribution carried a distinct Mayan imprint. He held workshops on glyphs and helped to produce dramatic performances of them, called "glyph exchanges." In these, a person would translate a creative work from one medium to another, thus operationalizing the transmediality of Mayan glyphs. For example, in figure 21 choreographer and dancer Katherine Litz remediates artist Ben Shahn's painting titled *A Glyph for Charles* (propped behind her). The painting's figure of a rectangular, quasi-semaphoric torso was made in response to a poem by Olson. In this performance, Litz dances to the live music of David Tudor and Lou Harrison, whose style drew on the microtonal experiments of Harry Partch and study of Balinese and Javanese gamelan (as well as on ethnomusicological conversations with Jaime de Angulo) (Cohen 203-4; de Angulo, *Music* 6). With this experiment, the group wished to make perceptible the thresholds of seemingly bounded media, as well as to think about artistic works extending across various media platforms, exploring the specificity of a medium as a threshold to other media. Drawing on Olson's aesthetic understanding of the glyphs, Litz explains that "the common idea of a Glyph expressed by the different art forms was simply a compound image contained in a single work" (Litz qtd. in Erickson 330). The single work to which she refers is the virtual content to which the various poems, paintings, and performances each contribute an aspect—creating a nonmedium specific work that media theorist Henry Jenkins has described in terms of "transmediality." Jenkins's conception of transmediality involves virtualized content tracked to narrative practices, whereas at Black Mountain such virtualizability was envisioned in image, poetic form, performance, and design. But what the glyphs offer to the idea of a composite medium is a sense of discontinuity and continuous opposition between its medial elements. The elements do not resolve into synthesis. They continue to examine their disjuncts and hence the possibility for future transformation in new contexts. As Tedlock writes of Xiloj Peruch's poetic speech, the characteristic function of the content virtualizability in the "glyph exchanges" was "to raise the discontinuity of the 'presence of the same object' to a high frequency" ("Toward" 184). Rather than narrative emplotment, Black Mountain transmediality (and the Mayan glyph from which it derived core ideas) was a pedagogy of differencing.

This aesthetic is also present in the stand-alone works that came out of such collaborative pedagogy. Cy Twombly's practice of painting poetry

FIGURE 21 Photograph of *The Glyph* performed at Black Mountain College by Katherine Litz in 1951. Jerome Robbins Dance Division, The New York Public Library, The New York Public Library Digital Collections.

or writing paint distinguished itself precisely by amplifying such ambiguity between media, raising that transmedial noise into a stand-alone artistic content of nonidentity. Mary Jacobus points out that Twombly's attentiveness to the medial noise made when poetry is scrawled in paint was inspired by his study of French symbolism (especially Stéphane Mallarmé's calligrams) and Maghrebi calligraphy, as well as his lesser-known vocation as a military cryptographer in the early 1950s (82–85, 95).[9] But the conception of the Mayan glyph circulating at Black Mountain would have been another rhythm by which to configure a poetics of paint. In explaining Twombly's relation to poetry writing, Jacobus engages with Roland Barthes's essay on Twombly, "Works on Paper," in which Barthes attributes to Twombly symbolist desires to extract the sign from acts of intellection, to have it be a kind of purely embodied "graphism"—in which the sign is the "gesture, not the product . . . decipherable, but not interpretable . . . [in which] writing no longer abides anywhere, it is absolutely in excess." Barthes called this Twombly's distinct attention to the "ductus" or visual gesture of writing (160–61, 170, 185, 190). I understand Barthes's emphasis on gesture (in excess of intellection) to mark off the living textuality of writing. But that vitalization need not come at the expense of words and concepts. On the contrary, in the "graphic poetry" of Mayan glyphs a sense of vitality is intensified by sustained tensions between image, word, and concept. That bolstering of medial tension, and not its sublimation into a homogeneous quality of excess, appears likewise to be at play in Twombly's works.

Particularly in works where Twombly lingers at the threshold between image and text, allowing neither to resolve into the other, a poetics of glyphic discontinuity can be felt. His 1959 series *Poems to the Sea*—whose brushstrokes exude like ocean foam over the wavering scrawl of such water-sounding words as "*What ????*" (plate 8)—recalls Olson's poem about the fish and Olson's associational matrix of Mayan writing, creation, and the sea. As in Olson's poem, the visual field agitates the sound of words, creating conjunctions that destabilize the singular meanings of words. In piece XIX from that series, "What" is scrawled in wave-form across the paper—suggesting a conjunction between "what" and the first syllable of the word "water." Of course, the monosyllable of "what" is like, but also distinct from, the first syllable of "*water.*" As a question—*what?*—this syllable asks to be accentually lifted in the way that the sea surges. Accentually surging, it departs from the midcentral vowel sound of the first syllable of the word "water." Yet in departing from the sound of the word "water," it is closer to the sound effect of water in a rising tide. That sonic tide is pushed back by thick brushstrokes covering the word—brushstrokes that appear like the reverse motion of ocean tides pulling back into the deep. Combined, the sound and sight effects create a circular current that Jacobus describes as the "immutable limen" of Twombly's ductus. She relates this compositional strategy to the blue line that crosses the top of the canvas, which she calls a horizon: a unique "spatial boundary and temporal marker." Unlike other boundary formations, horizons postpone contact, remaining perpetually out of reach. Because a traveler never reaches a horizon, the temporal experience of horizons is one of endless anticipation and liminality—a constant state of deferred excess, or excessive feeling induced by perpetual deferral, indeed a limen of immutability (85–86). Yet such unattainability is countermanded by the thick presencing of materials in Twombly's works. The agitated thickness of paint and writing connotes collision rather than deferral. As each medial element takes on characteristics of the other (paint soaking up poetry and poetry soaking up paint), the composition stages the messy transpositions that happen in boundary zones. More accurately, then, the composition is a limen of mutability designed to denature identification. Its cosmos is one in which things change always into other things. If a defining characteristic of Mayan glyph semiosis is "turbulent identity" (Houston 107), Twombly's compositional strategy elaborates that identity form in adding further turbulence to its contents: it is a Black Mountain glyph in the full incongruity of identification. Such incongruity suffuses the strokes of Twombly's brush and pencil with a sense of life emerging in aesthetic form. What is brought to life in Mayan writing by full-figured glyphs is brought to life in the collisional materiality of Twombly's ductus. Its medial elements remain ever in tension and nonsynthesizing in a visible "howling, murmuring, squeaking, orating performance" (Houston 107).

Chicano Projectivism, Alurista's *Spik in Glyph?*

The North American poetic reception of glyphic dis-identification was not exclusive to Black Mountain. Chicano poet Alurista arrived at a similar aesthetic technique through analysis of Mayan glyphs and deployed it to more sociologically searching ends. Alurista, born Alberto Urista, was the poet laureate of the Chicano movement in the late 1960s and early 1970s. He wrote the poetic preamble to the *Plan Espiritual de Aztlán* (1969), the core manifesto of Chicano nationalism, and published collections of poetry foundational to Mexican American political identity: *Floricanto en Aztlán* (1971) and *Nationchild Plumaroja* (1972). His poetry contributed a mixture of Marxist and indigenist thought to the Chicano movement. "I'm a socialist," he remarked, "with a definite Mayan bent to everything" (qtd. in J. Taylor). In his writings, these two positions are inextricably bound. A 1975 essay, *"La Estética Indigena a Travez del Floricanto de Nezahualcóyotl"* (Indigenous aesthetics in the poetry of Nezahualcoyotl), describes Mesoamerican parallelism as a "dialectic" or a means of understanding social change as opposition and contradiction. Parallelism added to the Marxian dialectical model a necessary imperfectability, offering a system of oppositions that never synthesize but instead remain in the constant oscillation that puts the Mesoamerican world into motion. *"Así pues su pensamiento era serpentino, cíclico, relativo, y dialectico,"* he writes in reference to Nezahualcoyotl, the fifteenth-century poet-king of Texcoco: "his thought was thus serpentine, cyclical, relative, and dialectical" (n.p., my translation). Drawing from such historical models, Alurista's own poetry took on a dialectic of Mesoamerican political economy, at once engaged with contemporary issues while also defined by indigenist, pre-Columbian thought and form.

Yet it was that very aesthetic sensibility that made Alurista unpopular in later years, when scholars accused him of fetishizing and simplifying indigenous cultures (Klor de Alva, "California"; Pérez-Torres 180). Marissa López notes the absurdity that "Alurista has been rejected by the critical community for the very things that brought him favor in the first place" (93). He is said to have materialized the same colonial ideology he set out to demolish, one in which stereotypical representation occludes historical reality. Yet a still deeper absurdity is that his critics themselves oversimplified their analytical object: in avoiding discussion of Alurista's formal experimentation, focusing primarily on the appearance of indigenous themes and symbols in his writing, they sapped his Mesoamerican aesthetic of its intellectual nuance. López thus rightly remarks that the contemporary reception of Alurista's poetry suffers from a lack of the kind of formalist analysis that could bring to light its complex political affordances:

> Alurista's poetry challenges [critical assumptions in Chicano studies] through meditations on the nature of identity and its relationship to language, nation, and time. . . . [His] poetry has critiqued identity politics and cultural nationalism, instead advocating global, anti-imperialist struggle that denies notions of "self" and "other," foundational concepts for much of Chicano/a literature and criticism. This notion of the permeability of the borders between people manifests in his poetry as inventive language play, internationalist themes, and a rejection of linear time. (94)

The concept of identity (a touchstone in ethnic studies) is taken to task by a poetic mode that stages linguistic and temporal dis-identifications— that takes seriously a Mesoamerican poetics of dialectical discontinuity. Rather than take identity as a given, Alurista's poems ask: how is the political category of "identity" an interface for racial and national positionalities? And how do those positions change when cast in the aesthetic forms that are discrepant from normative signs, tropes, and figures? As is the case with Twombly's *Poems to the Sea*, Alurista's poetic experiments—lingering at what López calls the "permeability of borders"— denature identities. Yet here that denaturing also deals with political presuppositions.

To express this political permeability, Alurista often used a Mayan salutation of dialectical lingering: "*in lak'ech*," which he translates as "I am another you." He found this salutation in the scholarship of early twentieth-century Mexican linguist, anthropologist, and philosopher Domingo Martínez Parédez, where it is associated with the response "*a lak'en*," or "you are another me" (Martínez Parédez, *Hunab Ku* 71, 140). While scholars have taken Alurista's use of the phrase to signify a kind of "one[ness] with the world . . . [where] there is no distance between ourselves and anything else" (Bruce-Novoa, *Chicano Authors* 277), the meaning of the phrase—as given by Martínez Parédez—stresses the boundaries and fractures between things, not their fusion. It emphasizes the sense of disconnected connectedness or connection in disconnection. Martínez Parédez illustrates the disjunctive conjunction of "*in lak'ech*" with the figure of a square drawn inside a circle. The circle represents limitless time and the square represents bounded space; together, they represent a dialectic of related but nonsythesizing parts, whose nonsynthesis or restless conjoining puts the world into motion (*Hunab Ku* 40-41). Moreover, the diametric figure of the combined circle and square is meant to connote that Mayan time is neither cyclical nor linear, but rather offers the opposition between circles and lines, repetition and difference, as a way of multiplying possible perspectives—a figural doubling that Restall calls the "multidimensional corkscrew" of Mayan time (42). With this corkscrew all possible oppositional relations are twisted into a dialectic of interanimation: "object and subject; abstract and concrete; the ideal and real . . . religion, science; learning, teaching . . . present, past, and future . . . sun, earth, and moon," and so on (Martínez Parédez, *El Popol Vuh Tiene Razon* 150, my translation). As Martínez Parédez's geometrical figure suggests, these items do not resolve into one another; in their overlap they remain distinct, even as they interact and pull one another into each other's forms. "*In lak'ech*" is a salutation in which self and other configure one another but do not fuse—like a circle and square, or a "multidimensional corkscrew," pulling identities into their opposition and back outward again—as the I who is another you becomes *and* remains the you who is another I.

In his notebooks, "*in lak'ech*" was likewise a means by which Alurista configured identity in oppositional formations (fig. 22). He uses Martínez Parédez's geometrical, glyph-like square-and-circle understanding of Mayan dialectics to analyze relations between the visible and occult, zero and one, nothingness and matter, emotional inertia and intuitive movement, socialist dialectics and capitalist individualism, fascism and anarchism, USA and USSR, history and psychology, and cosmos and atom. By means of this multitiered parallelist analysis, he arrives at the conclusion in the lower right-hand corner of the page:

> Anarcho-socialism that flowers in the dynamic materialist tetralectics across the earth and within one's self gives us a measure of reason in conjunction with the intuitive movement that resides in all beings and sidereal systems. The result is *in lak'ech* at all levels of relation. ("One Bound," my translation)

"Tetralectics," his word for this dizzying method of analysis, refers both to dialectics doubled (Marxist and Mayan) and the four-dimensional space

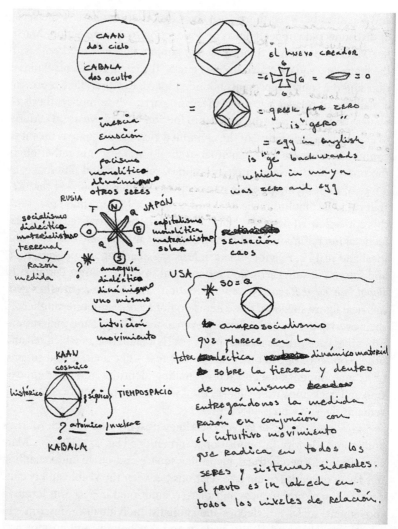

FIGURE 22 A page from Alurista's notebook (1970–72) influenced by Martínez Parédes's geometrical and spatial understanding of Mayan dialectics. Alurista Papers, Benson Latin American Collection, the University of Texas at Austin. Courtesy of Alurista.

in which opposed items interact. In his emphasis on four-dimensional space, he points out that *in lak'ech* is no abstraction: it is reality, configuring things "at all levels of relation"—including atomic, biophysical, interpersonal, symbolic, national, planetary, and cosmic scales. For Alurista, the Mayan concept of being-in-other takes hold at all relational scales, and it also mediates those scales, enabling individual intuition to interact with the movement of such massive and celestial things as "sidereal systems." Tetralectics, then, is a version of what Tedlock called Mesoamerican "mythistory" (a term also used by Martínez Parédez in *El Popol Vuh Tiene Razon* 159)—a temporal structure in which cosmic systems route themselves through the intimacies of everyday happenings and everyday intimacies move through the contortions of cosmic systems. But here those scalar shifts also mediate the Marxist and the Mayan, focalizing its objects in a materialist analysis whose materiality is conditioned by the ontology of interanimating oppositions. Even the social critique that Marxist analysis makes possible—in its attention to exploitative subjectivization—must be refracted by the incompletion that sets Mayan dialectical identities into motion. That motion serves to undermine possible reification or literalization. In Tetralectics, a critique of exploitation must always give way to other possible worlds.

It is important to note that in Alurista's complex dialectic, opposition does not produce alienated essences. Rather, these positions emerge from a Mayan salutation of kinship: "I am another you/you are another me." This salutation plays on pronominal shifters to remind saluter and saluted that kin are as interchangeable as speech positions: in the salutation, two people elide into one another, sharing what Marshall Sahlins calls the "mutuality of being." Yet crucially, Sahlins describes "mutual persons" as something other than selfhood reflexively configured from otherness. Such a dialectic of self "is too much like a commodity notion of exchange in which each party appropriates what the other puts on offer; and in any case, the transaction presumes and maintains the separation of the persons so related, the opposition of self and other." Instead, mutual personhood or kinship consists in the unity of partible selves, a kind of "co-presence" that configures but does not fuse differential positions in an event of intimacy (*What Kinship* 33, 23). If *in lak'ech* is to be taken as a statement of kinship, its relational structure consists of something other than the interchangeability of self and other, yet also not undifferentiated synthesis. Indeed, the arrangement implied in the phrase has motivated scholars—López in particular—to interpret it in terms of borderless belonging in the US-Mexico borderlands, challenging "even the existence of a discrete speaking subject, the very grounds upon which affirmations of chicanismo were built" (López 95). Yet that interpretation gives still too much synthesizing force to the salutation. "I am another you" does not disintegrate the divisions of subject formations; it keeps them at play in order to intensify the communality shared by opposed parts. What is needed is a sense of the duress or turbulence that tensions Alurista's dialectics of identity and kinship.

While Alurista certainly puts the discrete subject under conceptual duress, that subject's boundaries cannot be said to disappear in *in lak'ech* since *in lak'ech* depends upon the subject's solidity for its affinal differencing. Co-presence requires difference to animate its bonding affect (as Godelier points out; see ch. 2 of the present book). When kinship is understood as boundless desubjectification, "we take it for granted that beings are given beforehand and afterward participate in this or that relation" (Sahlins, *What Kinship* 33). A notion of kinship as osmotic being presumes positions and boundaries that it is kinship's task to form and deform. The conceptual difficulty of kinship is that it must be more than identity-in-other but less than open plenitude. More accurately, it is a site of "metamorphosis"—per Godelier—a space where difference and identity are mutual aspects of a single process, whose actants simultaneously interact, consolidate, and diverge. Alurista's poetic experiments in exploring "*in lak'ech* at all levels of relation" denatures the inner solidity of related items while rendering their relational field into sets of pliable boundaries and identities.

These kinship concepts take on the problematics of race in Alurista's 1981 collection of poems, *Spik in Glyph?* The title summarizes its concerns with the racialization of Hispanics, whose transformation into "spics" is enabled by the exploitability of language. By way of language, people are organized and interpellated into a discriminatory racial hierarchy. This hierarchy manifests its totalizability in the everyday expressibility of its markers: racial epithets like "spic" become the easily accessible signifiers by which the subordination of one group to another is confirmed. Yet the title also suggests that—by virtue of the same linguistic pliability—the seeming intractability of that racial order can be upended. That is, "spik" becomes "speak" alongside the adverbial modification of "in Glyph." Moreover, in its phonetic presentation, "spik" expresses the interanimating sonic and visual elements of glyphic writing. The title proposes that by way of a glyphic conception of linguistic pliability, racial formation can be disrupted and disorganized. At the very least, the apparent facticity of race can be posited as a question—one to be answered with the metaphoric force of a collection of poems.

Spik in Glyph? is a watershed work for Alurista, in that its formal experimentalism contrasts with his earlier, more demotic voicing as the premier poet of the Chicano movement. As such, it is concerned with the problems of voicing racial identity without reifying the facticity of race. In describing the book's critical problematic, Urayoán Noel points to an "ironic and radical poetics of signifying density . . . [a] move toward the production of unincorporable texts" (100). Noel's notion of unincorporability refers to texts that stage the "unresolved nature of identity," the way in which poetic voicing can resist incorporation into identitarian categories that reproduce the very discriminations to which one might be opposed. He focuses on poetics of performed embodiment that refuse to leave behind a trace of their physical presence. His primary analytic is thus orality, the poetic element that strains against the orthographical norms of Anglophone writing, yet which expresses a physical presence behind and beyond those lexical constraints—an excess of body amidst its social formations (see Aparicio 798). Yet bilingual orality is only one aspect of the aesthetic of Alurista's book. The book also involves what, on its back cover, is called "hieroglyphic bilingualism." In the book's glyphic poetics, the orality and corporeality of race is subsumed under a performance of differential and turbulent identity, simultaneously real and contingent in its amplification of medial fracture points.

In much the same way that the "glyph exchanges" at Black Mountain drew on the Mayan sign to develop a creative practice between media, Alurista's *Spik in Glyph?* examines how the facticity of race as something manifest between sonic, visual, and figurative elements is both real and unreal, bodily but embodied because of social practices. This conceptual turbulence is brought to life in the next tier of the book's identificational framework: its poem titles, which are a cacographical list playing on the accent patterns of a native Spanish speaker counting in English— "juan," "tu," "tree," "for," "fi," "seex," "se ven," "e it," "na in," "ten," "ee le ven?," "tú él," and "tracy." In these phonetic word games, orality is markedly mediated. It is a formal effect enabled by the phoneticism of alphabetical writing. The visualized sound of alphabetical writing is emphasized by the references to sight in the poem titles—"se ven" and "ee le ven?" which in Spanish mean "they look" and "do they see it?"—as well as by the titles that use orthographic play to denote salient nonnumerical nouns: "juan," "tree," "seex," and "tracy" (the last of these is a cacographical twist back into the Spanish word for 13, *trece*—suggesting a speaker who has exhausted his English language vocabulary). While Alurista's orality is thus encapsulated in the phonetics of the alphabetical sign, that encapsulation is involved in a multidimensional aesthetic that he calls "hieroglyphic." Such multidimensional verbal art is akin to what Doris Sommer has termed "bilingual aesthetics," by which she means the creative abstraction and figuration that happens when speakers stretch their imagination across the norms of two or more languages. Alurista's poem takes such an idea a step further still. It situates the code switch between English and Spanish across the semiotic difference of the alphabet and the hieroglyph. In his "hieroglyphic bilingualism," the visual speech of phonetic writing conveys the visual qualities of the hieroglyph, those qualities that give that sign its sense of tension amid its sonic and syntactic elements. Needless to say, the alphabetical writing is recalcitrantly alphabetical: it does not become a hieroglyph. What the hieroglyph does make possible is an adverbial modification to how the writing happens and how it can be read: it "spiks in glyph" or glyphically. The relation between the writing and its mode corresponds then to the relation between an identity and its performance, or a thing and its dis-identifications. There is something deeply set about Alurista's subject position in the book, racially situated by its ethnolinguistic markers. But that situatedness is also forced to confront its iterability in hieroglyphic identitarian agitation. Thus rather than a coherent whole, the book's poetic voice is a compound of tensioned and inconsistent parts aspiring to a kinship formation.

The contradiction of kinship formation amid the markers of racial difference and social inequality is explored in the poem titled "birth." This poem lingers in the conceptual paradox of birth, which is a scene of presocial natality that is completely interpenetrated by the social constructs that capture a child at parturition. The poem presents birth as a semiotic struggle between unqualified and qualified life, a struggle whose competing values are vying for the ontology of a lifeworld:

> wood u nut
> rather
> b
> bean, being? be in
> born than b
> dye
> in, ing? ang
> s
> t, angst?
> ste, u us dead
> usted, or me four
> that mat
> ër . . . patter
> better than
> tú, two? Too
> also, ass well
> full . .
> thee, thy? (*Spik* 17)

Racial signifiers abound in the poem. Its bilingual vernacular is one such source of race signifying, which nucleates around the epithet "beaner" (to which the poem alludes in its mention of "bean"). And this epithet is immediately connected to the normative force of ontology: "being." The homophony of these words suggests a deep settling of race in the nature of reality: a "beaner" in "being." That is, "bean" becomes "being" with the natural ease by which words equate themselves with their contents. Yet the near homophony of those words is only so near. This is emphasized by the next homophone: "be in," an adverbial modulation of "being," in which "to be" is to be in a relational unit. In this third term, racial being is less inextricably entangled in reality as such. It is mode and performance. In combination, these three terms stage the fundamental contradiction of imagining kinship in its racial contexts, where it must be less than racial but more than relational in all its instances. Theorizing on this problematic, Fred Moten writes of "the ongoing event of an antiorigin and of an anteorigin, replay and reverb of an impossible natal occasion" (14). Moten's point is that kinship (or a sense of deep belonging) in its racial contexts must circulate through the ontological tissue of cultural constructs. The relational surfaces of natality are tinged with the reality of a repressive social order that makes birth into an "antiorigin" or denial of itself. Yet that "antiorigin" also arrives with the self-realizing force of an "anteorigin" or a prepositional relation to the seeming fact of origins—creating the impossible situation in which natality is both qualified and unqualified in race signs. Alurista's poem invests itself in both aspects of race—its reality and its realizability—but it does not settle on one over the other. Its conception of race is most comprehensively invested in the toggle between reality and realizability that social constructs make possible. Like the book itself, the poem is posited as a long-form question on the nature of corporability—or bodily possibility. Not exactly "unincorporability," as Noel has it, Alurista's hieroglyphic modality is a species of bodily iterability when constellated across its constituent parts: sign, sound, sight, figure, and speech.

In its classic contexts, the Mayan hieroglyphic sign was not without ideology. Mayas used hieroglyphs to write history, rewrite it, and bend it to political ends. Often these bends were enabled by engagements with mythological stories of origin—kings associating themselves with origin heros; mythical events subtending warfare and subjugation; and political dynasties claiming immortality. Mayas used the glyphs to record their histories and make propagandistic use of the relation between myth and the historical record (Marcus 8–16). In Moten's words, they had "antiorigin" and "anteorigin, replay and reverb." That is, they had ideology and criticality. Their sense of social reverb or critique can be seen in the very pliability between myth and history, and the shared "turbulent identity" of the versatile signs that communicated those flexible temporalities. In contemporary contexts, the Mayan valuation of systemic heterogeneity appears in such poetic practices as Xiloj Peruch's parallelist frame setting, as well as in Alurista's hieroglyphic toggle between the discrepant codes that meet a body at its birth. Like Olson's fish glyph and Twombly's glyphic sea, Alurista's glyph-as-adverb transports the Mayan sign to new temporal conditions whose specificity it then organizes in its poetics of co-present dissimilars and identificational distortions. In its hieroglyphic mode, Alurista's "birth" creates the noise by which the "impossible natal occassion" is made discontinuous with itself and becomes thus a scene of social and political possibility.

A fundamental quality of Mayan poetics is thus replacement. And with every replacement there is a displacement and erasure. When things change into other things, some things get lost. This formal effect is particularly distressing when it takes place on the uneven terrain of colonial power. Still, the foundational violence of colonial accumulation does not, in itself, preclude anticolonial practices of replacement and transposition. The absencing function of the glyphs can also be a practice of critical signifying, particularly when that negativizability emerges from lifeworlds whose ability to negate is historically negated. The next chapter examines how such forms of forgetting—or what anthropologist Michael Taussig evocatively calls the "death space of signification," when a sign's erasure "challenges the unity of the symbol, the transcendant totalization binding the image to that which it represents" (*Shamanism* 219, 298)—can also take on casts of political resistance to colonial and capitalist violence. In the emergency state of the "death space," all connections and disconnections are emergent and once again available as viable paths forward.

KHIPU AND OTHER ANALEPTIC SIGNS

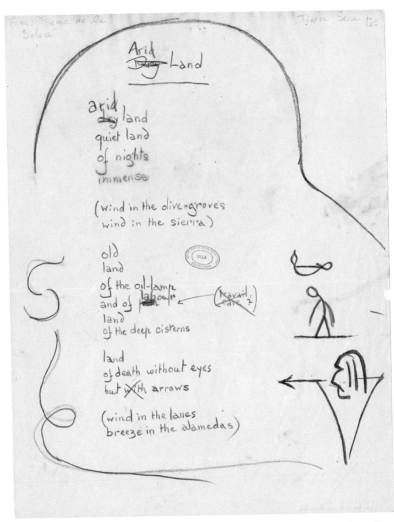

PLATE 2 Jaime de Angulo's pictograph for Federico García Lorca's "Arid Land" (ca. 1950). Jaime de Angulo Papers (Collection 160), UCLA Library Special Collections, Charles E. Young Research Library.

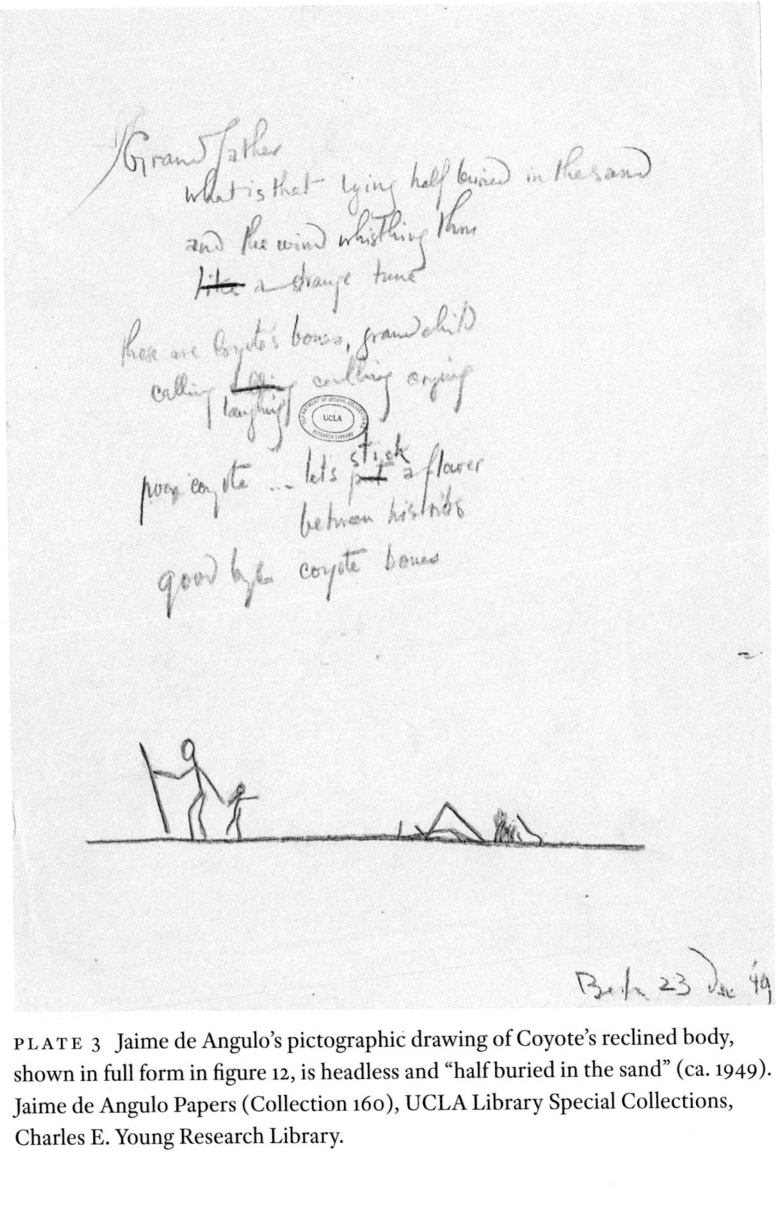

Grandfather
what is that lying half buried in the sand
and the wind whistling thru
~~like~~ a strange tune

those are Coyote's bones, grandchild
calling ~~laughing~~ calling crying
[laughing]

poor coyote ... lets ~~put~~ stick a flower
between his ribs

good bye coyote bones

Berk 23 Dec 49

PLATE 3 Jaime de Angulo's pictographic drawing of Coyote's reclined body, shown in full form in figure 12, is headless and "half buried in the sand" (ca. 1949). Jaime de Angulo Papers (Collection 160), UCLA Library Special Collections, Charles E. Young Research Library.

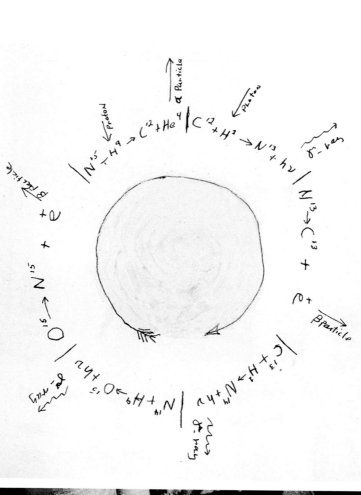

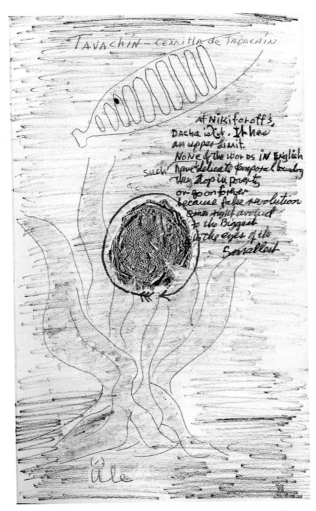

PLATE 4 Ed Dorn, "The Aztec Sunstone" (1972). Drawing from "A Mexico Scrapbook for Kidd and Maya." Notebook "Mex" (unpublished scrapbook) by Ed Dorn, 1972, Box 41, Series II, Subseries C: Notebooks. Photograph: Ed Dorn Papers, Archives and Special Collections, University of Connecticut. Courtesy of Jennifer Dunbar Dorn.

PLATE 5 Ed Dorn's son (1972). Photograph by Ed Dorn from "A Mexico Scrapbook for Kidd and Maya." Notebook "Mex" (unpublished scrapbook) by Ed Dorn, 1972, Box 41, Series II, Subseries C: Notebooks. Photograph: Ed Dorn Papers, Archives and Special Collections, University of Connecticut. Courtesy of Jennifer Dunbar Dorn.

PLATE 6 Ed Dorn, "Collage" (1972). From "A Mexico Scrapbook for Kidd and Maya." Notebook "Mex" (unpublished scrapbook) by Ed Dorn, 1972, Box 41, Series II, Subseries C: Notebooks. Photograph: Ed Dorn Papers, Archives and Special Collections, University of Connecticut. Courtesy of Jennifer Dunbar Dorn.

PLATE 7 Joe Herrera, "Eagles and Rabbit" (ca. 1950), in which Herrera reworks abstract expressionism in a Puebloan visual vocabulary. Paint on board, 15 1/4 × 13 in. Arthur and Shifra Silberman Native American Art Collection. Photograph: © Dickinson Research Center, National Cowboy and Western Heritage Museum, Oklahoma City, Oklahoma.

PLATE 8 Cy Twombly, "XIX" (1959). Oil-based house paint, pencil, wax crayon, 12 3/4 × 12 13/16 in. From Twombly's twenty-four-part series, *Poems to the Sea* (1959). Courtesy of the Cy Twombly Foundation. Photograph: © Cy Twombly Foundation.

PLATE 9 Andean khipu (present day) in the Machu Picchu Museum (Casa Concha), Cusco, Peru. Photograph: Pi3.124, Wikimedia Commons.

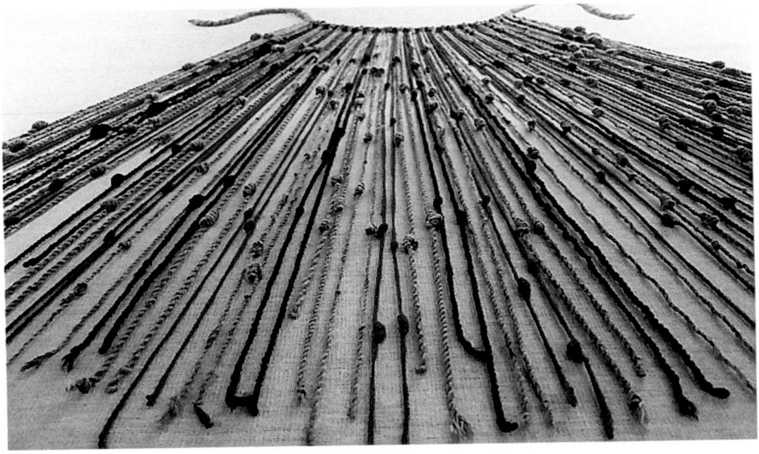

PLATE 10   Cecilia Vicuña, *Cantos del Agua, Chile* (2015). Photograph:
Courtesy of Cecilia Vicuña.

PLATE 11   Roberto Harrison, "escaleras simbólicas de los borrados" ["symbolic
stairs of the erased"], in which the poet and artist engages with the aesthetic form
and semiotics of Kuna molas of Central America. Drawing from *Interface* (2018),
p. 11. Photograph: Courtesy of Roberto Harrison.

5
DEATH SPACES
Shamanic Signifiers in Gloria Anzaldúa
and William Burroughs

Repressive social conditions are typically associated with literary themes of woundedness. Readers expect to read for injury in scenes of colonial violence. But in certain cases the injurious is cast as a source of counter-signifying negativity. In certain scenes of colonial destruction, the power to be captured is the power to destroy. One such repertoire of counter-signifying poetics involves in its historical redress pathologies of healing. That repertoire is what this chapter calls the "shamanic." But this is not the universalist spirit flight that typically goes under the banner of the term "shamanism." Rather than draw its definitional form from the writings of Mircea Eliade, this chapter's conception of shamanism is defined by the practices of deranging colonial signs that anthropologist Michael Taussig situates in states of colonial terror and healing—where the emergency of injury is flipped into a source of emergent signification. Further assisted by the writings of scholar of religion Thomas Karl Alberts, for whom shamanism is a mediation in which modernity negates itself, this chapter defines shamanism as a practice of capturing historical mediation in its instances of social destruction. Practices of shamanic healing are related to the social derangements of colonial and capitalist violence, including the violence carried by such colonial terms as "shaman," "race," "modernity," and "history." To examine how the practice of negating these colonial signs creates historical intelligibility (and therefore a kind of psychic redress)—both a Hegelian criticality in the negative and a Nietzschean instance of empowered metahistoricity—the chapter delves into the writings of Gloria Anzaldúa and William Burroughs. While on first glance these writers seem impossibly incongruent, the superhistorical positioning of their works puts them in conversation with each other and with a broader cultural practice of deranging colonial signs to create critical agency. This chapter examines how Burroughs's cut-up technique adapts the countersignifying practices of shamans whom he encountered in the Amazon basin (the same locales that are the focus of Taussig's work on shamanism), and how Anzaldúa's "imaginal" of creative destruction adapted themes of Mesoamerican shamanism (such as Coatlicue, Coyolxauhqui, and nagualism) to transvalue what she called the "open wound" of the US-Mexico borderlands, "where the Third World grates against the first and bleeds" (*Borderlands* 3). While related to what Lauren Berlant and Wendy Brown describe as a late twentieth-century culture of woundedness—or psychic self-gathering that relies on a sense of injuriousness that then defines the psyche (Nelson 8)—Anzaldúa's "imaginal" holds fast to violence and destruction in its remedy and reparation. In elaborating how her destructiveness carries key political techniques, this chapter develops the concept of the wound beyond the compliant woundedness with which it is typically associated. Alongside Berlant's and Brown's writings on the possible noncompliance and critical creativity of wounds, Anzaldúa casts light on their emphasis on the redemptiveness of certain kinds of negativity.

While such semiotic negativity needs to be understood in its historical contexts, it aims to create superordinate positions to history—that is, points of agency and power over the meanings and effects of time. In this regard, it is a type of analepsis. Analepsis is a trope of discontinuity, when a break in narrative time stages a hiatus in causal relations. In that hiatus, or prying apart of signs from seemingly ineluctable causes and effects, all social and intellectual connections and disconnections are visible and possible once again—they are, in other words, metahistorical.[1] Analepsis is associated thus with states of emergency and emergence: the shamanism discussed here is situated in the neoliberal emergencies of Putumayo, Colombia, in the 1950s to 1970s and the US-Mexico borderlands in the 1970s to 1990s. But that shamanism is *situated* inasmuch as it is a practice of capturing the situations and effects of words in a state of emergence. Anzaldúa and Burroughs fracture the deleterious colonial signs that they themselves embody—in order to find in such self-deletions new social openings—and each characterizes what they find in that rupture as an emergent vital entity: "the imaginal's figures and landscapes are experienced as alive and independent. . . . They speak with their own voices; move about at will. They possess an intelligence and inner knowing" (Anzaldúa, *Light* 36); "[w]ords know where they belong better than you do. I think of words as being alive like animals. They don't like to be kept in pages. Cut the pages and let the words out" (Burroughs, "Literary"). Anzaldúa and Burroughs construe the imagination as a life leaking from the violence of colonialism and capitalism, vitalized by the emergency of those economies while also autonomously emergent inside them.

To understand how states of emergency and the emergent interact in analepsis, this chapter is helped by Taussig's analytical framework of "shamanism," described as "special modes of presentation whose aim is to disrupt the imagery of natural order through which, in the name of the real, power exercises its dominion" (*Shamanism* xiv). Yet because Taussig participates in such modes of presentation as much as he documents them, his writings are also an analytical object in this chapter. They make accessible a third position or triangulation between Anzaldúa and Burroughs that is akin to montage, Taussig's term for describing the formal effects of analepsis: "The nonwhite, nonhomogeneous, fragmentedness of montage . . . on account of its awkwardness of fit, cracks, and violent juxtapositionings can actively embody both a presentation and a counter-presentation of the historical time through which conquest and colonialism matches signs with their meanings" (*Shamanism* 443).[2] With Taussig's racial conception of montage, the triangulation of Anzaldúa-Burroughs-Taussig reveals the ways in which a poetics of temporal hiatus or analepsis breaks apart dominant political signifiers—of race, nature, and natural order—from which colonialism and its capitalist legatees benefit.

Shamanic Tableaux

In his effort of situating shamanic practices in states of colonial terror and healing, Taussig can be said to have taken the "shamanism" out of Putumayo shamans. Inasmuch as the signifier of shamanism is loaded with imperial fictions and settler liberal fantasies, it hides the very terror that necessitates such folk-healing practices. These occlusive fictions emerge in the seventeenth century with the Russian tsar Peter the Great's eastward march into the lands of the Tungusic people of Northeast Asia, whose healers were called shamans. Reports of these healers, as well as their Tungusic name, arrived to Europe in the writings of a German merchant-adventurer, Adam Brand. Brand traveled with the Russian convoys and authored a popular 1698 ethnographic report of his journey to Asia.[3] In it he magnifies the figure of the Tungusic "*Shaman*, which signifies as much as a sorcerer or priest," whose repertoire is a peculiar combination of animal totems, "doleful" drumming, "dreadful" shouting, epileptic fits, and communication with spirits "and other strange birds" (50). Alberts argues that Brand's core template of Tungusic shamanism—configuring animal and atmospheric forces, a cultural sensorium of rhythms and fits, and human disease and unwellness—focalizes twentieth-century Western cognizance of the toxicity of global capitalist governmentality. In Alberts's estimation, the discourse of shamanism is a crucial mediation of modernity, making intelligible the rarified contact points between empire, capitalist statecraft, indigenous deterritorialization, anthropogenic environmental damage, secularist myths of disenchantment, Western lifestyle maintenance, and general human unwellness amid the workings of an exploitative economic system. The spirits poised for shamanism to exorcise are market specters in the psyche of the West.

Alberts hastens to add that such a conception of a mediated shamanism does not mean that shamans—folk healers who work their medicine inside and against the label of shaman—do not exist. In a chapter titled "Imbrications," he turns the figure of the shaman on itself, foregrounding the figural contortion that shamanism forces on shamans: "the figure of the shaman is in fact a figuration, a combination of an individual figure with the discourse that proceeds from, is imposed on, and then circles back to that figure, along the way acquiring new valuations that both expand and intensify this figure in relation to practical domains" (229). The healing work of shamans is "imbricated" in modernist discourses of shamanism with which that healing work must contend. Therefore, the shaman is required to perform magical operations to dispel the discursive specters of modernity that circle around the signifier of shamanism. Shamans are tasked with the tricky operation of purging the colonial signifier traced over their discursively imbricated bodies.

Insofar as the task of the shaman is to make intelligible a certain kind of negativization, anthropologist Juan Obarrio has discussed shamanic practices in terms of "postshamanism":

> the discourse of an ever expanding curved line, an always displacing border. A non-linear horizon that keeps retreating from our tired eyes . . . the shaman was the space where modernity located its dread and desire. . . . "Shamanism," the savant knowledge on those foreign practices, could be considered as another name for the discourse of modernity, along with Cartesianism or Hegelianism. Since the early nineteenth century the shaman was the ever mobile shadowy figure of living death where the Enlightenment found its complete heterogeneity. A starfish, always alert on the outside, submerged in the deepest ocean that Reason can think of. (168)

If "shamanism" is a kind of Hegelian mediation by which modernity becomes self-aware, that intelligibility is won at the cost of stabilizing modernity in its normative commitments. Obarrio characterizes such intelligibility in spatial terms as a receding border, but its relation to time is also pertinent. In her analysis of Hegel's theory of intelligibility, philosopher Rocío Zambrana points out that for Hegel the act of rendering historical awareness—be it in such terms as "modernity" or "shamanism"—is made possible by historically and culturally specific practices that are "precarious" and "ambivalent." Building on Robert Pippin's reading of Hegelian ideality as a process of making norms intelligible and actual, she adds that this process of "form-giving" is inextricable from the negativity of its contents: "Concrete forms of intelligibility are precarious, then, since they are based on commitments whose currency depends on their bindingness within a given shape of *Geist*. They are also ambivalent, given that they accommodate opposite meanings and valences even when enjoying normative authority. They are subject not only to reversals of meanings and effects but also to coextensive positive and negative meanings and effects" (7). If "shamanism" is understood to be an attempt to make intelligible a particular form of history, that attempt is implicated in contents that break apart and reconfigure historicity into discrepant temporal densities, time spaces with "always displacing borders" (Obarrio 168). The cracks and contradictions of the colonial figure of the shaman are a resource with which the shaman can make intelligible the precarity and ambivalence of colonial figuration.

To emphasize this necessity of content in the form of shamanism, Taussig titles his ethnography "A Study in *Terror* and Healing." And he devotes its first part to illustrating the horrendous colonial violence that required shamanic intervention in the Amazon: the twentieth-century rubber business, which brought rights of conquest over the lands and bodies of Putumayo, authorizing slave raids, torture, execution, forced labor and sexual slavery, castration, piecemeal dismemberment, mutilation (genitals, ears, fingers, and feet lopped off with machetes, sometimes kept as souvenirs by overseers), destruction of crops to induce starvation, crucifixions, immolations (on one occasion, to celebrate a birthday), babies smashed against trees, and the use of the elderly as targets in shooting contests by bored officials of the British-financed Peruvian Amazon Company (*Shamanism* 20–32, 51–52). These vile activities constitute a culture of death, whose normative intelligibility persists into the contemporary moment. It persists by way of the practical devaluation of life along racial lines under market economies that pretend to have transcended racial hierarchy but in fact benefit from it the whole way through. Given that the market benefits from racism's occlusion and mystification, the contemporary culture of social death comprises what Taussig calls "the epistemic murk of the space of death" (*Shamanism* 127). The murk of racial signs casting a barely occlusive gloom over the persistent violence of colonial governance is the content of shamanic healing.

Yet in keeping with the idea that the contents of shamanism necessitate themselves in its forms, Taussig adds that "shamanic healing . . . also develops its force" from such "epistemic murk" (*Shamanism* 127). The same morbidity of power that casts a fog over racial life enables its moribundity. The healing work of shamans exploits the "space of death" to drown out the significance of colonial signifiers—"alienating alienation," he adds, "in an endless or almost endless process of connection-making and connection-breaking" (*Shamanism* 329, 460). In Taussig's ethnography, this process takes place in the night-long yagé sessions led by Santiago Mutumbajoy and José Garcia, during which the hallucinatory experience of ingesting yagé is intensified and calibrated by the songs, stories, prayers, imprecations, cries, cajoles, redresses, groans, clicks, and roars of their shamanic performance. In lathering a kind of thick somatic and imagistic froth, these shamans are able to mold new lifeworlds into existence. Never escaping the conditions by which it comes to exist, that form nonetheless informs new conditions for existence. Taussig writes:

> As for the shaman, despite his solidity and caring he is also a strategic zone of vacuity, a palette of imageric possibility. Where he does predominantly swim into focus, however, at least in the eyes of the civilized, is as the alternating, composite, colonially created image of the wild man, bestial and superhuman, devil and god—thus reinforcing the montage technique and in a way its very fount. Just as history creates the fabulous image of the shaman, so the montaged nature of that image allows history to breathe in the spaces pried open between signs and meanings. (*Shamanism* 444)

Glossing Taussig's conception of the shaman as a zone of social possibility, Obarrio calls such a shaman a "remainder" and a "black hole"—an "'empty place' at the core of power, necessary to sustain the rule of law" and "the repository of anti-matter in our world. Our world, which is not this one" (176, 181). Obarrio draws on a Benjaminian conception of the state of exception, in which the vacuity at the core of power is rendered as unrepresentability, a virtuality available for new configurations of responsibility for new forms, bodies, and actions.[4] The "death space of signification" in which the shaman works their magic is a space of possibility for all life (Taussig, *Shamanism* 219). But that plenitude does not "swim into focus" without the focalizing problem of certain colonial tropes and figures. In particular, racial embodiment is a key problematic by which the intensity of shamanic prowess comes into being.

The problematic is put into focus in Taussig's writings when he describes his experience in the night-long yagé ceremony. The opening chapter of the latter half of his ethnography—the half dedicated to "healing"—begins with a description of the animating tensions that whiteness brings to the Putumayo Indian healing ceremonies (referring to Garcia who, like Taussig, is a white man studying under the Indian shaman, Mutumbajoy). This description stages the intensities and mediations that Taussig's discursively imbricated body itself brings to the scene:

> Then the *feo* (ugly). My body is distorting and I'm very frightened, limbs stretch out and become detached, my body no longer belongs to me, then it does. I am an octopus, I condense into smallness. The candlelight creates shapes of a new world, animal forms and menacing. The lower half of my body disappears. I learn to use dissociation as an advantage as a way of escaping from the horror. I am not the person being got at; rather I am the disembodied face-presence calmly peering in and watching this other and unimportant me. I watch my other self, safely now. But then this second me, this objective and detached observer, succumbs too, and I have to dissociate into a third and then a fourth as the relation between my-selves breaks, creating an almost infinite series of fluttering mirrors of watching selves and feeling others. (*Shamanism* 141)

The critical thrust in whiteness studies has been to show that whiteness is a discursive form, neither neutral nor invisible but aligned in a hierarchy of bodies that persists by virtue of its seeming neutrality and invisibility. In this passage and in his drawing that illustrates the scene (fig. 23), Taussig disaggregates the normative body of whiteness—*his* body, construed in its whiteness given the chapter's prefatory note about white intensities in healing ceremonies. In that bodily breaking apart, the racial signifier does not disappear; it reveals itself to be endlessly tessellated. Rather than hold together a racial order or *communitas*, as any racial sign is supposed to do, the bodily dissociation of the yagé ceremony creates the conditions for divisibility and heterogeneity, that is, ruptures in the normative authority of a racial order.[5] He adds: "the yagé nights are the antithesis of this whiteness, this homogeneity" (*Shamanism* 442).

While the shamanic ceremony gives form and meaning to a mediated conception of whiteness, it also prevents that whiteness from negating itself completely. It stays, in Alberts's terms, "imbricated"—in a state of implicated fragmentability that Taussig similarly calls "tableaux": "a fractured format that lobs ill-fitted and therefore likely-to-be-questioned juxtapositions of tableaux into a studied art of difference" (*Shamanism* 329). To follow Taussig's terms, a *tableau vivant* is a living picture, transposing live bodies into the frozen posture of a painting or photograph. In its medial contradiction, the tableau recalls Benjamin's conception of the dialectical image, a written picture twitching with critical awareness of the "ill-fitting" mediality in which it appears (see Richter). The shamanic tableaux of whiteness are one such instance of emergent

FIGURE 23 Michael Taussig's drawing of a "disembodied face-presence" (1987) that appears above him amid the performances of Santiago Mutumbajoy and José Garcia, two shamans who play prominent roles in his *Shamanism, Colonialism, and the Wild Man* (411).

self-consciousness, specifically of modernity becoming self-aware in its contradictions. Here that same modernity is undermined and disorganized by the "ill-fitting" form in which its dominant symbol (whiteness) is forced to confront itself: distorting, frightening, stretching out, and becoming detached, the poetics of the body in shamanic performance are a "death space" for racial norms and the hierarchies they carry. These are critical features of shamanic technique that have been underexamined in Burroughs's cut-up technique.

Shamanic Whiteness: Burroughs and Malinowski

It will come as no surprise that Taussig has written about Burroughs. The two share an immersive style of writing in the interruptions, juxtapositions, imagistic overlaps, and diagetic shocks of a colorful prose. Color as such is heavily emphasized in both writers' repertoires. Taussig makes note of this in his *What Color is the Sacred?* as he writes: "Burroughs is drawn to color as an organic entity, alive and intimately related to the human body. His writing oozes color that serves him as an agent of metamorphosis" (8). Taussig likely has in mind Burroughs's writings under the influence of Amazonian yagé sessions. Called *pintas*—which is the Spanish word for "paint" but denotes "hallucination" in Amazonian slang—the color-flushed visions of yagé are laced with the racial signifiers that the color-flush is supposed to swirl and wash out. In this regard, the yagé *pintas* often take the shape of a labyrinthine cityscape, crowded with people and anthropomorphic entities of diverse cultures, historical eras, and racial composition, dripping with the chromatic details of far-off lands, countries, and times.[6] In his description of a yagé vision of 1953, Burroughs calls it "The Composite City"—a precursor of his later "Interzone"—and makes note of the way in which the *pintas* invade the flesh, much like racial signifiers: "The room takes on a Near Eastern aspect with blue walls and red tasseled lamps. I feel myself turning into a Negro, the black color silently invading my flesh. My legs take on a well rounded, Polynesian substance. Everything stirs with a writhing, furtive life. The room is Near Eastern and South Pacific in some familiar but undefined place" (*Naked* 97). Color or *pinta* is equivalent here with race, and there is no instance in Burroughs's writings in which color does not take on racial tones. The polychromatic "ooze" of the "Composite City" and "Interzone" is the leakage of a racial hierarchy in which Burroughs's whiteness emits its abjection.

Taussig does not directly address this aspect of Burroughs's attraction to "color as an organic entity" (*What Color* 8). But he does offer an indirect analysis of it by way of a reading of Polish British anthropologist Bronisław Malinowski's complex relationship to colorful writing. Malinowski is known as a modernist anthropologist—a pioneer in the field—inasmuch as he advocated fieldwork and intercultural dialogue over armchair analogy and Victorian racial science. These commitments to culture as a living text shaped by fieldwork are evident in such ethnographies as *Argonauts of the Western Pacific* (1922) and *Coral Gardens and their Magic* (1935)—works in which description is felt to be alive with implication and consequence. As he put it, he wished to be the Joseph Conrad of ethnographic writing. Not until the publication of his private journals in 1967—published as *A Diary in the Strict Sense of the Term*—was it revealed that he also had something of the shadowy Kurtz from Conrad's *Heart of Darkness* in him as well. Along with the colorful descriptions that he felt were too novelistic for his ethnographies, the journals are pocked

FIGURE 24 Bronisław Malinowski shielded in whiteness amid the potent coloration of the Trobriand Islands (1929), "talking to Togugu'a, a sorcerer of some repute" (*Sexual Life of Savages*: plate 68, n.p.).

with expressions of racial paranoia, jealousy, lust, hatred, anger, and violence. In the controversy that ensued from their publication (with which the writings of James Clifford, Clifford Geertz, and George Stocking engaged, all of whom subsequently became central to a reflexive movement in anthropological studies, a disposition that itself was catalyzed by the publication of these journals), a discipline encountered its sordid subconscious. But, as Taussig notes, what remained underdiscussed in this disciplinary self-examination was the relation between lurid raciality and thickly colorful description.

To depict this tension, Taussig juxtaposes Malinowski's descriptive chromatism with his sartorial self-presentation as a consummate colonial anthropologist: colors explode wildly in the writing but, in contrast, Malinowski walks these same color-filled atmospheres dressed in a clinical and defensive shield of total whiteness (fig. 24). A sample passage from the journals even stages him walking around the island, as if to dramatize the distinction between walker and environment, between Malinowski and the potent color of the nonwhite world: "*Thursday 22 November 1917:* Walked around the island a second time; marvelously rich coloured sunset. Roge'a: dark greens and blues framed in gold. Then many pinks and purples. Sariba a blazing magenta; *fringe* of palms with pink trunks rising out of the blue sea.—During that walk I rested intellectually, perceiving colours and forms like music, without formulating them or transforming them" (qtd. in Taussig, *What Color* 83–84). Cut from the published ethnography, Malinowski's uses of color are both repressive and purgative; denied because effusive, and effusive because denied. That repressive dialectic of denial is stated most literally in the white outfit of the nineteenth-century explorer-anthropologist, which casts its wearer in a purity that must be protected, yet that must be protected because its vulnerability is everywhere manifest. Such outfits are doubtless impossible to keep clean in the field. Their "colorless purity," in Taussig's words (*What Color* 83), is evidence of that which could never be: colorlessness and purity. As the controversial publication of the journals showed, another version of such a colonial outfit was the genre of the realist ethnography, presupposing an objective stability clean of racial horror, overpowering color, and other para-analytical "impurities."

Whereas Malinowski buries these impurities in the pages of his private journals, Burroughs presents them as the phenomenon to be engaged in field writing. Burroughs would have encountered Malinowski's work while studying anthropology at Harvard in the early 1930s,[7] but he was ambivalent about the discipline and only engaged it to undermine its insitutional formation and principles. He characterizes such institutional norms as "stasis horrors," which induce both the nervous dissatisfaction that leads him to seek other worlds in the Amazon and the subcutaneous sickness that resists relief in those other worlds (*Yage* 40). Burrowed beneath his white skin is the curse of Conrad's Kurtz, an accretion of social "horrors" that he elsewhere calls "virus," "ugly menace," and "ugly spirit." The homophony of "ug-ly" had special resonance for Burroughs, whose hated uncle Ivy Lee represented the "horrors" of US capitalist institutions. Lee was an antilabor propagandist for big corporations, putting spin on unsightly facts for Standard Oil, IG Farben, Union Pacific Railroad, and others. Biographer Ted Morgan thus characterizes the relationship between uncle and nephew as a corrective construct: "his uncle had debased the language, turned it to purposes of trickery and deceit. [Burroughs] would, in his own writing, restore integrity to language" (25). While Morgan's reading of the antipathy to an uncle whom Burroughs called "a real evil genius" is spot-on, less on the mark is the idea that Burroughs's response restores integrity, undivided wholeness, or any other principle of unifying totality to language ("William Tells" 71). On the contrary, Burroughs's entire cut-up project aims to disarticulate the reifications that his uncle's work had made possible: the aim of the cut-up is to cut up, to split signs from their seemingly intractable, socially calcified, and literalized meanings. That project effectively begins with the search for the visionary derangements of yagé in *The Yage Letters*, which is tellingly Burroughs's first work that drops the "ug-ly" pseudonym under which he had published his first two books: Lee.

Leading scholar of Beat literature Oliver Harris consequently has singled out the importance of Putumayo for Burroughs's literary experiments. He points out that Burroughs's time in South America has been read either as (1) an aberration in the biographical continuity between early genre works (*Junky* and *Queer*) and later postmodern textual experiments (*Naked Lunch* and *The Nova Trilogy*) or (2) a continuous iteration of the overarching metaphor of addiction, in which yagé derangement is a brief stand-in for junk sickness. He notes that these readings fail to satisfy because they do not address the literary techniques that Burroughs develops between *Queer* and *Naked Lunch*, 1952 to 1959—the time in which he works on the ethnography of Amazonian shamanism, *The Yage Letters*. To elaborate the importance of this work, Harris focuses on its "epistolarity," or its distinct structure as a series of letters to friend and collaborator Allen Ginsberg. Harris shows that these letters were not actually written as letters—they were ethnographic vignettes to which the epistolary format was later added for publication, thus freeing the material from the need for "regular beginnings, continuities, and conclusions." And this decision reveals another aspect of Burroughs's writerly attitude: narrative and intersubjective continuities matter less than the talismanic communicability of literary and linguistic figures. Harris suggests that Burroughs characterized this one-way communicability as a kind of "black magic," in which "the empty shell, the dry husk of the letter form, its formal tops and tails" works like a kind of charm upon its readers (146, 176–78). But Harris does not elaborate how the magical presuppositions of such literary technique might be related to the indigenous magical practices described in *The Yage Letters*.

While Harris mentions Taussig's work, he does so to emphasize that Putumayo was a source of unbounded terror for Burroughs—a complete "death space"—without examining the decolonial uses of such negativization. As does Taussig, Burroughs's *pintas* foreground the gruesome and even apocalyptic disaster of the rubber trade: "black marketers of World War III . . . epidemics of violence and the untended dead [who] are eaten by vultures in the street . . . people eaten by unknown diseases [who] spit at passersby and bite them and throw pus and scabs and assorted vectors (insects suspected of carrying a disease) hoping to infect somebody . . . doctors skilled in treatment of diseases dormant in the black dust of ruined cities. . . ." (*Yage* 52). And Burroughs does not hesitate to cast himself as a culpable signifier for such misery: like Malinowski, he presents himself in the pith helmet, canvas shirt, and khaki safari pants of a colonial anthropologist (fig. 25), adding a certain miasma to these sartorial airs with his observations that the "rubber business is shot . . . [so] the whole Putumayo region is on the down grade," even speculating

FIGURE 25 Burroughs dressed the part of a colonial anthropologist in Putu-mayo, Colombia, surrounded by yagé vines in 1953.

on pharmaceuticals as the next boom commodity for the region (*Yage* 25). Burroughs is magnifying a kind of image, that of the "ugly" white ghost to be husked in the yagé ceremony. He is the semiotic blight to be skinned and disarticulated, a signifier of the material conditions that re-quire negativization. In his erasure—literalized by the cutting out of the "Lee" surname—is the wish to give space to a repertoire of nonwhite, non-homogeneous color and motion. One description of a *pinta* reads like a manifesto of global human mobility:

> Yage is space time travel. The room seems to shake and vibrate with mo-tion. The blood and substance of many races, Negro, Polynesian, Moun-tain Mongol, Desert Nomad, Polyglot Near East, Indian—new races as yet unconceived and unborn, combinations not yet realized passes through your body. Migrations, incredible journeys through deserts and jun-gles and mountains (stasis and death in closed mountain valleys where

plants sprout out of your cock and vast crustaceans hatch inside and break the shell of the body), across the Pacific in an outrigger canoe to Easter Island. The Composite City where all human potentials are spread out in a vast silent market. (*Yage* 50)

In the flow of race and migrations Burroughs imagines the possibility of yet unimagined races, evoking the kind of normative open-endedness in which Benjamin construed the utopic possibility of the state of exception. For Benjamin, the state of exception beckoned a kind of responsibility for possible difference existing outside the normative commitments of the law—the "possible righteousness" of an "unforeseeable future" (de Wilde 198). While that degree of ethical commitment is not present in Burroughs's *pinta*, the template for its realization is. The "stasis" or "death" of racial ideology is fragmented like a shell into embodiments still to be imagined and seen, recalling Taussig's "tableaux" or "fractured format" by which race tesselates in a self-critical or "likely-to-be-questioned . . . studied art of difference" (*Shamanism* 329).

A few pages later, that template takes on a properly temporal element when *The Yage Letters* enters the analeptic mode that prefigures the cut-ups. This mode stages the responsibility for time-as-history that comes to characterize Burroughs's later writings:

> Followers of obsolete unthinkable trades doodling in Etruscan, addicts of drugs not yet synthesized, pushers of souped-up Harmine, junk reduced to pure habit offering precarious vegetable serenity, liquids to induce Latah, cut antibiotics, Tithonian longevity serum; black marketeers of World War III, pitchmen selling remedies for radiation sickness, investigators of infractions denounced by bland paranoid chess players, servers of fragmentary warrants charging unspeakable mutilations of the spirit taken down in hebephrenic shorthand, bureaucrats of spectral departments, officials of unconstituted police states. . . . (*Yage* 53)

This passage dwells in the imagistic shards of subjunctive moods, virtual aspects, and anticipatory temporalizations. And it also dabbles in geological (i.e., Tithonian) and human (i.e., Etruscan) deep history. Pitching distantly forward and back in its temporal moods, this is the chronological equivalent to the "fractured format" of Taussig's shamanic tableaux. Its time is multiple and broken, continuous only in discontinuities and hiatuses. Such analepsis creates a heightened state of temporal emergency or a state of affairs in which anything could happen because everything is happening all at once. Its sense of radical possibility is further emphasized by the scalability of each imagistic shard. Each shard represents a world that can absorb the significations of surrounding shards. Are the many signals of world calamity subsumed under the mental break of hebephrenia? Are the syntactical cues of psychosis and schizophrenia metonyms for the madness of endless war? Or are these mental and social breaks shorthand for a technique of syntactical splintering, designed to manipulate the mental cost and social need of disorganizing dominant signifiers? If these are totalizable fragments, their totalizability does not come without the expenditure of self, nature, and society. In the Composite City, the social possibility of the negative is bound to the conditions that necessitated such negativity. There are no "empty shells." The violence of colonial governance in Putumayo, which finds its emblem in the body of colonial anthropologist, beckons the form of Burroughs's disorienting and self-destabilizing prose. If "Yage is space time travel," it is implicated in its material conditions in every instance, exploding the colonial horror in which it is constellated. With this shamanic method the form of Burroughs's writings deranges the colonial signifier whose content is Burroughs himself.

When he formalized the Composite City as a technique of cutting up texts, rearranging the cut portions into new compositions (introducing much redundancy in his writing, but by the same token installing tableaux of temporal transposition into it), Burroughs continued to make magical claims about the process. He groans in an audio recording of a cut-up session: "when you cut into the present the future leaks out" (*Break*). Divination is a constant theme in Burroughs's writings; with the cut-up technique, it finds its signal strategy. His claim is that the splicing and sequencing of textual bits offer prophetic insight. To understand such a claim, it is helpful to turn to the conception of the sign in a divinatory context. One such context is offered in critical genealogies of the sign in Greek classical antiquity, in which the idea of the sign as such emerged from reflections on divination. Semiotician Giovanni Manetti explains that the sign or *semeion* emerged from reflections on divination because it is in acts of divination (be it oracle, dream interpretation, auspicy, reading the folds on a goat's liver, or the various other modes of casting the future) that language arrives in a state of emergency. Its emergency is brought about by the *semeion* of the gods (who exist outside time) appearing in the temporally bound form of human language, a form in which such *semeion* is *ill fitting* and therefore *likely to be questioned*, examined, and pondered over. Practices of divination are scenes of temporal crisis and interpretation, in which a querent must constellate their moment amid discrepant temporalities and returns (Manetti 14–35). Such act of coordination or *rhusmos* with an eye to the future makes possible a conscious participation in historical unfolding. Divination is a kind of magical trick by which multiple temporalities are made present—with an epiphenomenal effect of cutting the present open to newly possible and different futures.

In making time pliable to present uses, divination recalls Nietzsche's writings on "the uses and abuses of history for life." This is the short essay that Benjamin likely has in mind when he conceptualizes temporal states of exception (analepsis) as sources of political redemption. For Nietzsche, redemption was not to be found in the sheer defense of historical facts and figures. Rather, the uses of historical facts and figures to create "superhistorical standpoints" were the source of political agency and restorative justice. Superhistoricity was Nietzsche's rebuke to conceptions of time that alienate historical experience. Instead, he argued, history is present in the perception of life, where "the past and present is one." In those instances, in which the past is made present, the past is made presently reflective—that is, "super-" or "meta-". The aim is to not allow perception to become desensitized in historiographical models that create "the remarkable opposition of an inside to which no outside and an outside to which no inside corresponds." History is worth studying because, present on the surface experience of being, it is waiting to be cut into new "plastic" forms and "eternalizing powers" (*On the Advantage* 13, 24, 62). Burroughs's cut-up is an attempt to technologize such metahistoricity. It wishes to make the creative act of writing divinatory, insofar as divination is the art of making the various temporal elements of language readily emergent. If "when you cut into the present the future leaks out," that future leaks like blood because the scene is construed with the critical urgency required by its contents (*Break*). Superhistoricity is not an escape from colonial realities; it is an encounter with, and responsibility for, those realities in the urgency of their presence.

Such colonial urgencies of the cut-up would have had another resonance in Tangier, where Burroughs's "Composite City" took on the name "Interzone." "The Interzone City" of *Naked Lunch* inserts the above quoted yagé vision of Composite City into its body text but calls it "Interzone." Whereas "Composite City" refers to a textual strategy, Interzone refers to the Tangier International Zone (the neutral demilitarized zone jointly administered by European nations between 1924 and 1956, where Burroughs lived in the mid-1950s). Burroughs changes the name of his montage city to emphasize not a composition but a landscape of fractured sovereignty. Interzone is a locus split between nations, a zone of overlapping and mutually undermining jurisdictional spaces. Brian Edwards describes the midcentury Tangerian glut of nations as "a space that exposed the nation form as a fiction." The Tangier International Zone did so because its plurinational governance created legal ambiguities that "repeated the multiplicity of Tangier's spatial and experiential environ-ment" (138). Edwards argues that this "supranational" atmosphere nour-ished the anticolonial independence movement (notwithstanding that the movement itself took a nation form). In considering its origination in Burroughs's montaged yagé *pintas*, the fractured spatial sovereignty of "Interzone" takes on temporal superpositions as well. As the Bolivian scholar Javier Sanjinés notes on the constitutionally ratified and indigenously oriented "plurinational" state of Bolivia, plurinational governance not only mandates overlapping jurisgenerative spaces but involves the overlap of uneven temporal densities. People existing in various, disaligned rhythms of labor and cultural organization make up the divisible Bolivian nation-hood whose divisibility is a mark of its decolonial commitments to dis-crepant presents and unknown future possible forms of belonging. Even as Burroughs's racial embodiment (white, privileged, even colonialist) must be the object of the cut-ups, that process carries emancipatory va-lences in the disarticulation of its objects. Its divisibility and negativizabil-ity are of a piece with the temporal heterogeneity from which it became conscious, self-reflective, superhistorical, and plastic.

Borderland Analepsis

If Burroughs's uses of the negative fail to achieve a sense of decolonial negativizability, it is because the positions of its enunciations are so sticky. It is that stickiness of colonial signs, which Burroughs embodies, that requires the force of derangement, negativity, and divisibility found in the cut-ups of Amazon and elsewhere. Such process is driven by similar conditions in Anzaldúa's writings, except that in her case what Jonathan Eburne has called the "privileged experience of cultural sub-version" is not so privileged (qtd. in Harris 141–42). Readers tend not to think of Anzaldúa as an experimental writer—let alone as a writer of negativizability—because there is an overarching tendency to emphasize her various precarities as a brown, lesbian, disabled woman living in the injustices of the Texas borderlands. But the way in which she construes the border as a space of annihilation and transformation calls for readings that see these markers of identity in their negation. The test is whether such negation and disorganization can do the work of restorative justice that the emergency of the border's "open wound" requires of its writer. In the same way that Nietzsche's concept of superhistoricity is not an escape from history, Anzaldúa's concept of Borderlands is not an escape from the US-Mexico borderlands. While she writes that "Borderlands" is her metaphor for "psychic and emotional" transitions, her psychic and emotional transitions are grounded in the racial violence of the Texan

borderlands in the 1970s and 1980s (*Light* xxiv). The conflicts of that locale—as well as its longer colonial history—are the critical hinge for her
writings that gave voice to dispossessed subjectivity in the US-Mexico
borderlands. Yet as with Nietzsche's superhistoricity, the redemptive element of Anzaldúa's writing depends on a negation of identities within a
given historical model. Like Burroughs, she is paranoid about the "ugly
menace" of ideological entrapment. She writes about her fear:

> She has this fear   that she has no names   that she
> has many names   that she doesn't know her names   She has
> this fear   that she doesn't know her names   that she comes and goes
> clearing and darkening   the fear that she's the dreamwork
> inside someone else's skull   She has this fear   (*Borderlands* 43)

Anzaldúa called this anxiety or even paranoia about deep interpellation
the "Coatlicue State," which is also what she called the poetic practices
of linguistic evisceration by which she could "cross over" into "conscious
awareness" (*Borderlands* 48–49). Coatlicue is an Aztec goddess of earth
in its transitions—encompassing fertility, maize, the moon, seasons, and
stars—who was dismembered by her children. Aztec representations of
the goddess emphasize this gruesome aspect, suggesting that transitions
of life involve death, sacrifice, and loss. Anzaldúa thus pointed out that
"*Coatlicue* depicts the contradictory . . . life and death, mobility and immobility, beauty and horror" (*Borderlands* 47), and she uses this contra-
dictoriness to give agency to such states of seemingly intractable political negativity as racism, the police state, and the free market cultures of
the borderlands. In Anzaldúa's hands, these violences of the state also
become aspects of the destructive goddess of transitions and transformations. With Coatlicue thus defining its negativizability, the threshold
between the United States and Mexico is made into an Aztec trope for
movements into and out of the signifiers of the US-Mexico borderlands.

Alicia Schmidt Camacho calls this Anzaldúa's "body-as-bridge" metaphor, explaining that Anzaldúa converted "a condition of absolute negation" into "the source of a differential agency." In Schmidt Camacho's
account, this conversion was helped by Anzaldúa's lesbian sexuality intersecting with her racial subjugation. Forced as a queer woman of color
to confront discrimination on two fronts—racism and Mexican American
family patriarchy—she "anchored" the possibility of a "borderless subjectivity" in the "articulating capacity of a coalitional, feminist practice in
the body as a site of racial and gendered wounding" (262–63).[8] Anzaldúa
thus reclaims "the liminal space of the borderlands as a site from which to
intervene in nationalist and patriarchal discourses" (261). As is the case

in the story of Coatlicue, the wound becomes a source of change and strength. But the process by which a wound is transvalued into a source of political agency is more complex than that suggested by the metaphor of a bridge. A bridge is a stable intersection between worlds, when what Anzaldúa seems to value about the border is its negativity, disjuncture, and emergency. She writes: "The U.S. Mexican border *es una herida abierta* [is an open wound] where the Third World grates against the first and bleeds. And before a scab forms it hemorrhages again, the lifeblood of two worlds merging to form a third country—a border culture" (*Borderlands* 3). In Anzaldúa's words, the "border culture" is characterized by its constant state of violent emerging. As soon as it starts to scab, it bleeds again. That does not evoke a bridge so much as it does the river rushing under the bridge, cracking and bursting its foundations. Likewise, in her writings and drawings (see fig. 26), bodily emancipation is associated with fissures, flows, ruptures, and wounds. Just as Coatlicue embodies both violence and generativity, Anzaldúa conjoins the borderlands to both its state horror and transformational possibility.

Such a complex dialectic was similarly at play in Benjamin's "state of emergency," which was both inherited from Carl Schmitt's apology for fascism by way of the "state of emergency" and tracked to the utopic potential of what Benjamin called "a *real* state of emergency [that] will improve our position in the struggle against Fascism" (*Illuminations* 257). What Benjamin must mean by "a *real* state of emergency" is deeply contradictory because what is "real" about his antifascist state of emergency is that it is virtual. He refers to the imaginative open-endedness by which the state could have a form of belonging that is expansive and differential, rather than contractive and homogenizing. His "*real* state of emergency" is meant to convey a condition of possibility for a radically inclusive politics. Yet because he describes this state of political emergence in terms of a state of emergency, Benjamin suggests that the imagination cannot escape its material conditions. Those conditions are the substance of an impassioned and transformative politics because they make necessary the forms of negativizability that Anzaldúa calls fissures and wounds. The actual conditions of a state of emergency are the necessary content of emancipatory political form—a form that carries into its articulation the disarticulated violence of state force, of a literal Coatlicue state.

Anzaldúa's version of Benjamin's "*real* state of emergency" was the US-Mexico border, in all of the "magic of the state" in which this border is cast. This magic involves a rite of passage in which some live and some die, some are polluted with criminality and some are cleansed of it, some are permitted to pass through and some are detained, some flow into a community while some are singled out in the violence of exception (Taussig,

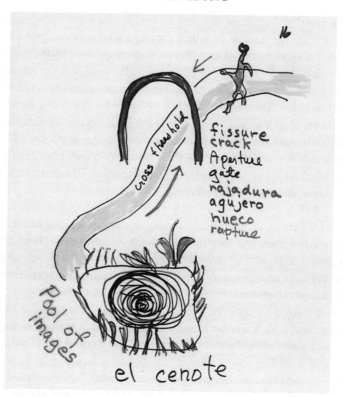

FIGURE 26 Gloria Anzaldúa's drawing of the "travesía" (or "crossing") at the Rio Grande, in which she transvalues the "open wound" and its "wetbacks" into sources of shaman-like imagistic transformation (*Light in the Dark* 99). © 2004 by Gloria Anzaldúa and The Gloria E. Anzaldúa Literary Trust. By permission of Stuart Bernstein Representation for Artists, New York, NY, and protected by the Copyright Laws of the United States. All rights reserved. The printing, copying, redistribution, or retransmission of this Content without express permission is prohibited.

Magic 148–49). In each of these instances, the state affirms its sovereignty over life and death, as well as its control of the ritual of passage as such. In controlling the passing, the state is spiritualized as a source of transformation. Recognizing the actual power involved in that act, as well as its proliferation in a neoliberal economy that benefits from the split labor markets created by more and more borders (Mezzadra and Neilson), Anzaldúa seeks to claim such power and proliferation for herself.

While her biography is a story of constant deprivation by "U.S. colonizing companies"—in the form of landowners, owners of the factories or *maquiladoras*, and currency manipulators who all exploit labor immobility across a secured border (*Borderlands* 10)—Anzaldúa does not argue for a borderless world. On the contrary, the border is a necessary source of possibility for her. She describes critical consciousness itself as a kind of border crossing:

> It is only when she is on the other side and the shell cracks open and the lid from her eyes lifts that she sees things in a different perspective. It is only then that she makes the connections, formulates the insights. It is only then that her consciousness expands a tiny notch, another rattle appears on the rattlesnake tail and the added growth slightly alters the sounds she makes. Suddenly the repressed energy rises, makes decisions, connects with conscious energy and a new life begins. It is her reluctance to cross over, to make a hole in the fence and walk across, to cross the river, to take that flying leap into the dark, that drives her to escape, that forces her into the fecund cave of her imagination where she is cradled in the arms of *Coatlicue*, who will never let her go. If she doesn't change her ways, she will remain a stone forever. *No hay más que cambiar* [there is nothing else to do but change]. (*Borderlands* 49)

Scholars have regularly commented on Anzaldúa's relentless commitment to the critical possibility of the border. From Anzaldúa's transvalued border, Edward Soja developed his concept of "thirding as othering" (127–34); Chela Sandoval articulated her relational sense of Latinidad as a condition "*entremundos* [between worlds] . . . constituted always-in-relation to" (xiii); Walter Mignolo and Madina Tlostanova exfoliated the epistemic frontier that they called "border thinking," in which critique is seen as "languaging practices [that] fracture the colonial language" (Mignolo and Tlostanova; Mignolo, *Local* 237; see also J. D. Saldívar 15–19); and Emma Pérez limned Latinidad as a "cultural identity [that] is inextricably enmeshed with ambiguity . . . always already transforming" (5). Yet it remains important to emphasize that in Anzaldúa's writings the border continues to be *the* border. She asserts its violence even as she seeks to think through it and past it. And even in thinking past it, she wishes to capture its political energies for critical consciousness. The implicit claim appears to be that the state does not hold exclusive rights over threshold and transformation. But even if that is the case, it would not require her to hold forth on the spiritual atmosphere of the US-Mexico border. In her commitment to the spiritual aspects of that locale of racial violence and exclusion, Anzaldúa pushes to make its emergency a source of emergent identities and communities. The border becomes a border onto itself, relating the material history of the borderlands to the spiritualizing force by which the borderlands seem both necessary and exceptional, intractable and even transcendental. Such magic is too powerful to abrogate, so she captures it as an affirmation of *real* agency amid the political deadlocks of a state formation that can recapture and administer its negative remainders—that perpetuates its violence by way of *its* exclusions and erasures. Whereas the state of the borderlands seeks to control negativizability, Anzaldúa claims such uses of the negative for herself.

While Anzaldúa has been critically chastised for her slipperiness with historical facts and statistical data, these are not as central to her writing as is the possibility of historical imagination. Her tendency to leap across time in creative engagements with the historical archive is evident in the structure of her books—which (as the above quoted passages from *Borderlands* show) swing abruptly across poetry and prose in multiple languages, testimonial autobiography (in first and third person), polemic, philosophical speculation, critical theory, visual art, and iconography—while drawing loosely on discourses of sociology, history, speculative fiction, religious studies, and mythology. She does not present herself as a uniformly disciplined scholar of history or sociology. Rather, she examines the premises by which intellectual border norms are made—that is, the norms by which disciplines are policed at their edges[9]—and captures in a composite form the energies by which those norms can be negated. She reflects on this quality of her writing in the book itself:

> This almost finished product seems an assemblage, a montage, a beaded work with several leitmotifs and with a central core, now appearing, now disappearing in a crazy dance . . . rough, unyielding, with pieces of feather sticking out here and there, fur, twigs, clay. My child, but not for much longer. This female being is angry, sad, joyful, is *Coatlicue*, dove, horse, serpent, cactus . . . a flawed thing—a clumsy, complex, groping blind thing—for me it is alive, infused with spirit. I talk to it; it talks to me. (*Borderlands* 66–67)

Like Burroughs's "Interzone," Anzaldúa's *Borderlands* performs the overlap of multiple discursive and political spaces. But, unlike Burroughs's montage city, Anzaldúa's overlap is one and the same with her experience of structural violence. Her body is not just a signifier to be disorganized; it is also the precarious target of racial governance. Its disorganization comes at a cost incurred in the author's struggle for redemption and restorative justice—a fact that is emphasized by the montage imagined as a living being speaking to her in a dissociative split.

Nonetheless, Anzaldúa insists that for her work this is a dangerous but necessary cost. She writes:

Soy un amasamiento, I am an act of kneading, of uniting and joining
that not only has produced both a creature of darkness and a creature of
light, but also a creature that questions the definitions of light and dark
and gives them new meanings . . . a new story to explain the world and
our participation in it, a new value system with images and symbols that
connect us to each other and to the planet. (*Borderlands* 80–81)

The *amasamiento* or kneading is her way of describing both the accumulation of history and its plasticity. It is plastic because it is amassed,
involving the density of violence and exclusion that accumulates in the
border conflict, as well as the pliability of that mass when consolidated
with those critical remainders and contradictions that it cannot absorb
into its strategy of control. That is, the failure of state control is evident
in Anzaldúa proposing to give new meanings, stories, and values to the
borderlands.

One value that she proposes to give the borderlands is a principle of
temporal mastery. Anzaldúa's "snap out of the paralyzing states of con-
fusion, depression, anxiety, and powerlessness" consists in "extracting
the old dead metaphors" that have accumulated in a seemingly natural
order of things (*Reader* 121–22). The seeming nature of racial subjugation is a signifier suspended outside time, presenting itself thus as literal
and self-evident; whereas to see it in time, bending with renewed metaphoricity and plasticity, is to gain mastery over it (Taussig, *Magic* 186–
87). In this, Anzaldúa prefigures political theorist Wendy Brown's reading of Nietzsche's Zarathustra in her *States of Injury*. Brown writes:
"Zarathustra's own relationship to the will as a 'redeemer of history' makes
clear that this 'angry spectatorship' can with great difficulty be reworked
as a perverse kind of mastery, a mastery that triumphs over the past by
reducing its power, by remaking the present against the terms of the
past—in short, by a power of self-transformation that arrays itself against
its own genealogical consciousness" (72). In this work, Brown examines how a sense of woundedness sustains race and gender formations,
encoding a kind of helplessness in those forms. Zarathustra offers her
a critical model in which the wound is reworked into a source of historical agency. In allowing for self-transformation against history, Zarathustra's woundedness is—like Benjamin's "*real* state of emergency"—a
source of emergent identities and collectivities. It is a means of rendering
a sense of history into a workable mass. Anzaldúa's own "open wound"
is likewise a source of self-transformation: affirming a genealogy in racial
violence that it reworks into a promise of redemption. As such, her conception of the wound is less like a bridge than—to quote Brown quoting

Nietzsche—"a future himself and a bridge to the future—and alas, also, as it were, a cripple at the bridge: all this is Zarathustra" (72). Like the body in her drawing of the "crossing" (fig. 26), which looks as though it is constituted by the waters that make the fissure and wound, cracking the bridge at its base, Anzaldúa possesses herself as an "eddy in the stream of becoming" (Benjamin, *Origin* 45)—a master of temporal thresholds and the transformations they make possible.[10] Yet that mastery remains in every instance a reflection of a wound that is open and exposed.[11] She does not escape historicity or the material conditions of a racist political order. Rather, she creates the semiotic conditions by which she can control its frictions and flows.

The nearness of Anzaldúa's "superhistorical" positioning to Taussig's understanding of shamanism (especially in its relation to metaphoricity) is further emphasized in her essay "Metaphors in the Tradition of the Shaman," in which she describes the agency that comes with breaking the literality of colonial and racial identities: "People in possession of the vehicles of communication are, indeed, in partial possession of their lives" (*Reader* 122–23). That self-possession is obtained in countersignifying practices, in which the separability of signs from their meanings is manipulated to introject new meanings and values into signs and identities. As does Taussig, she compares that analeptic hiatus to the aesthetics of film and montage:

> When I create stories in my head, that is, allow the voices and scenes to be projected in the inner screen of my mind, I "trance." I used to think I was going crazy or that I was having hallucinations. But now I realize it is my job, my calling, to traffic in images. Some of these film-like narratives I write down; most are lost, forgotten.... But, in reconstructing the traumas behind the images, I make "sense" of them, and once they have "meaning" they are changed, transformed. It is then that writing heals me, brings me great joy. (*Borderlands* 69–70)

For Anzaldúa, the necessity of such harmful signifiers as "borderlands" is that—like cinema—they make imaginable the jump cuts, transitions, and temporal layering by which a traumatic history is made pliable and contingent. Taussig goes so far as to say that this imagistic quality is *itself* the agent of healing in the shamanic act: "the curer-spirit relationship . . . is basically a curer-picture relationship" ("What Do" 273). On the one hand, he means that there is a correspondence between the spirit and the "song, dance, prayer, or picturing" used to invoke it ("What Do" 273); but, on the other hand—in light of Anzaldúa's emphasis that montage must be seen as a living being, if its struggle for justice and redemption will matter at all—Taussig's words can also be reckoned to signify the necessary embodiment of the content in the forms of shamanism. Its underlying political terror is inescapable. But, in its analeptic techniques, that historical terror lying beneath the pictured surface is transfigured as a pool of possible change, a *real* state of emergency.

Certainly, the concept of an *unnatural* sign begins to exhaust itself here. Such imagining of possible life in the borderlands of signs has a ring of animism to it. But that is precisely the intellectual risk that is necessitated in politically expansive conceptions of belonging—in that open-endedness that Benjamin called the possible "*real*." Describing the necessary hazard of a *natural* sign, Taussig writes: "Recognizing that while it is hazardous to entertain a mimetic theory of language and writing, it is no less hazardous not to have such a theory. We live with both things going on simultaneously. Try to imagine what would happen if we did not in daily practice conspire to actively forget what Ferdinand de Saussure called the arbitrariness of the sign. Or try the opposite experiment. Try to imagine living in a world whose signs were 'natural'" (*Corn Wolf* 10). Without a natural sign what is missing is the necessity of content to form—a problem that is most pressing when that content wishes to undo the terms of its relation to the form. Whereas such negativity is enacted in analeptic discontinuities in the writings of Anzaldúa, Burroughs, and Taussig, in other places that negativity is evidence of a deep colonial violence. What is "natural" to the colonial sign would seem—on first glance—to be a totalized practice of supersession and elimination. In the case of such a sign as khipu or Andean knot writing, whose meanings have been lost across a violent colonial interdict, analeptic discontinuity is already there in the present material conditions of the sign system. Yet even in that sign system, analepsis makes possible a view of nature that is not colonial nature, and makes possible meanings that encompass colonial erasures in the natural orders of indigenous lifeworlds. To understand how such a sign makes its meanings across colonial silencing—to see how it brings its creative contents to bear upon the attempted erasure of its form—requires a reconsideration of its *nature* within the indigenous orders of nature in which it comes into being.

6
KHIPU, ANALEPSIS, AND OTHER NATURAL SIGNS
Cecilia Vicuña's Poetics of Weaving and Joaquín Torres-García's *La Ciudad sin Nombre*

A poetics of discontinuity has a different resonance in khipu, a sign system whose literacy remains under colonial erasure. *Its* analepsis is, in a sense, a simple expression of historical loss. After the violent colonial destruction and interdict of the knot writings of the Andes, nobody today can read the khipu. Yet, the loss notwithstanding, its expression has continued to take shape within the aesthetic form of that which is felt to be lost. In the writings and performances of Cecilia Vicuña, the khipu is a structure in which to comprehend historical violence, as well as to think past it. While the semantics of the sign system remain a mystery, its semiotics or linguistic patterns have been a topic of generative analysis. In Vicuña's works, those patterns represent rhythms of life in resistance to a colonial historiography that would deny such life, as well as a resistance to the market culture that continues to find new ways to destroy such life and its generative possibility.

Her works therefore carry an important question: if the meanings of this sign system are lost, how can its forms continue to affect the meanings of contemporary reality? As if to insist that a sign is *not* dead without its semantics—but, on the contrary, that it is animated by the challenge of having to make its meanings across such loss—she writes: "the quipu that remembers nothing, an empty cord—*is the core*/the heart of memory—/the earth, listening to us . . . Piercing earth and sky/the sign begins/ To write from below, seeing the efface" (*QUIPOem* q.8–12). If the khipu remembers nothing, if it is subsumed under the absencing of the colonial archive, the question is how that "empty cord" could have a "heart of memory." How could it be that the sign's memory persists because it can "write from below," emerging from colonial erasures to rewrite those erasures into an "earth and sky" of its own making? If the khipu remembers nothing, can Vicuña's poetry be the living khipu that she proposes it is—"an empty cord" that is also where "the sign begins"? Can the khipu animate speech across its colonial interdict, and, as she suggests that it does, how does that interanimation *define* colonial interdicts and amnesias? What is this khipu that "remembers nothing" yet holds inside itself the ability to remake everything?

The materiality of knot writing—knots that are read tactually, as they move between the fingers—has been a means to shed light on Vicuña's khipu poetics. The tactility of knots gives a kind of archival immediacy to the khipu. Its semantic losses are lost in the sensuousness of the knots (see plate 9). This way of reading Vicuña's knot works nucleates in a figural trifecta of texture, textile, and text (see plate 10). The *texturality* of khipu helps Vicuña to disclose the materiality of poetic texts. Art historian and curator M. Catherine de Zegher thus correlates Vicuña's textual wovenness with enhanced perception of social and ecological networks (qtd. in Vicuña, *QUIPOem* 17–45), and art critic and activist Lucy R. Lippard reads these "words [in] a weaving vortex" as a feminist bulwark against the "dematerialization" of conceptual art (qtd. in Vicuña, *QUIPOem* 13).[1] Literary scholar Juliet Lynd focuses on the "precarious resistance" present in the raw materiality of Vicuña's works in order to develop a historical materialist reading. In Lynd's analysis, Vicuña's opposition to Augusto Pinochet's free market dictatorship (from which she was exiled) is expressed by way of a resistant "diary of objects . . . [and] objects of resistance" that include material evidence of the socialist democracy that Salvador Allende led in the pre-Pinochet years of 1970 to 1973, as well as material evidence of the state violence that came with the US-backed ouster of Allende and the torture, murder, and disappearances that sustained Pinochet's seventeen-year dictatorship (1596–97). The resistant materiality of people and objects during the dictatorship finds an aesthetic form in the khipu bundles, which have outlasted colonial torture, murder, and erasure to make a poetics of resistance present to this day.

Lynd thus characterizes khipu as a contemporary aesthetic strategy for giving presence to absence, giving the khipus a compensatory quality: "As part of the contemporary social imaginary, then, quipus connote an irrevocably lost way of life, and as a constitutive element of Vicuña's poetry, they represent at once the desire to know the precolonial past and the aporia of memory in the postcolonial world" (1591). To be sure, the khipus have suffered from colonial silencing. But to suggest that they are thus captive to such silence only amplifies the colonial noise around them. "The system of which they once formed an integral part has disappeared," she writes,

the reinvented quipu does not so much suggest a desire to recuperate that lost code as it signals the emptiness of the traces of the forgotten and unknowable. . . . [Vicuña's khipu works affirm] that writing now has the authority that the quipu once had in the structuring of memory, but the alphabetic text lacks the visual, tactile, and spatial dimensions of older forms of encoding memory, of representing the past. . . . [Its] memory is the trace of an absence, the consciousness of something irrecoverably disappeared. (1591, 1593)

Khipu defined in terms of totalized absence or irrecoverable loss is innocent of the conceptual trouble of living experience. While Lynd's emphasis on Vicuña's materiality is important, the emphasis on total loss— wherever it is found—gives way to that Lévi-Straussian melancholia for the always already lost native object, for the condition of hopelessness in which native things must exist, caught in a kind of necessary death.

Another way of taking seriously Lynd's emphasis on the "irrecoverable" without giving way to colonial totalization is through philosopher Paul Ricoeur's theorization of irrecoverability. In his writings on memory and forgetting, Ricoeur unraveled a living dialectics of absence that the rhetoric of the "irrecoverable" hides. The irrecoverable, whose French verb tense is "'*n'être plus*' (being no longer)," is a special ideological construct of historical representation, in which "the ontology of being-in-the-world . . . [is] placed under the sign of a past as being no longer and having been." When historical representation inhabits this domain of the *irrecoverable*, it creates the conditions in which "past things are abolished" and "the absent thing itself gets split into disappearance into and existence in the past" (280). Ricoeur's point is that such rhetorical strategies of historical representation hide the work that historical representation itself does to make the past present and to recover the past for present experience. He reminds readers of an Aristotelian relation between an absent thing and its presence in representation: "absence [is] the other of presence!" he writes, insofar as representations elicit the absence of the represented thing (a thing is never so absent as when it is virtualized), while the absence of the represented thing is elided into felt presence in the instance of its representation (a thing is never so present as when we are forced to feel its absence) (17). In Ricoeur's finessed dialectic of memory and historicity, this means that absence is a condition for the possibility of presence. If there must be anything like *n'être plus*, that irrecoverability must be understood in implicit relation to the constant recoveries it makes possible.

The difference between the irrecoverable and its implicit recoveries has to do with the redemption of the search itself. In this regard, Ricoeur distinguishes the *pragmatics* of absence from its *semantics*—by way of a classical Greek distinction between *anamnesis* and *mneme*:

The Greeks had two words *mneme* and *anamnesis* to designate, on the one hand, memory as appearing, ultimately passively, to the point of characterizing as an affection—*pathos*—the popping into mind of a memory; and, on the other, the memory as an object of a search ordinarily named recall, recollection. Memories, by turns found and sought, are therefore situated at the crossroads of semantics and pragmatics. To remember is to have a memory or to set off in search of a memory. In this sense, the question "How?" posed by *anamnesis* tends to separate itself from the question "What?" more narrowly posed by *mneme*. (4)

The mnemonic activity of *mneme* has a simple circuit between sign and historical referent, while the activity of *anamnesis* involves reflexive engagement with the processes, techniques, and poetics of recollection. That reflexive engagement makes the historical referent a situated effect of historical making. It brings historicities into the present of historical representation, emphasizing the *how* of memory rather than the *what*, the *search* rather than the *sought-after* thing. In the formal effects of *anamnesis*, the irrecoverable disappears in the blasting persistence of its poetic, narrative, affective, or intellectual recoveries. In this sense, Vicuña's question for the khipu is not a *what*—as in, *what* does this or that khipu mean?—but rather a *how*: as in, *how* does khipu make meaning? *How* is khipu "the earth listening to us," and, in its listening, *how* is it a sign system "piercing earth and sky/[a] sign [that] begins/To write from below, seeing the efface" (*QUIPOem* q.8–12)? *How*, in seeing itself effaced, does the khipu make meaning today?

In regard to khipu, such systematicity of *how* is neither lost in the sands of history nor completely imaginary. Much work has been done to describe the aesthetics and semiotics of the sign system, work that orients Vicuña's writings. But, more pertinent, what needs emphasis is that her writings are not just meditations on the raw material of a vacated signifier. They are investigations into *how* the poetics of that signifier provide access to otherwise "irrecoverable" history; *how* khipu allows for historical experience and interpretation today. She puts her khipu in the present tense. Her claim is bold: her works do not comment on the poetics of khipu. In engaging the poetics of khipu—poetics that go beyond the etymological links between texture, textile, and text—her works become primary material contents for an ongoing khipu archive. This poetic move from external commentary to content internalization—that is, from the simple referential circuit of *mneme* to the immersive recollection of *anamnesis*—is a version of what I have called *analepsis*. Analepsis, the trope of retroprojection, is the poetic technique of capturing what Ricoeur calls "the living experience of recognition," where absence is refigured in "the sort of presence proper to *anamnesis*" (410). Analepsis—a trope of anamnesis—fills the emptiness of semantic absence with the creative effects of semiotic and aesthetic recognition. *How* Vicuña gets to anamnesis through analepsis is a leap made possible by the poetic structures of khipu.

While Ricoeur does not discuss analepsis as such, he does rely on poetic analysis to observe the workings of anamnesis. Here, I briefly follow him in this—specifically, an interpretation of Charles Baudelaire's *"Le Cygne"* or "The Swan"—before returning to Vicuña's writings to extend Ricoeur's observations into a discussion of the anamnesic poetics of khipu. *"Le Cygne"* is a poem about the "Old Paris" that (in urban planner Georges-Eugène Haussmann's modernizing rush circa 1861, when the poem was written) no longer existed for Baudelaire. Yet in the poem, that transformation of the city is hapless and incomplete. Wherever he looks, old Paris bursts out "as heavy as a stone." That constant burst of the foregone into present life is embodied in the roaring wings of "A swan who had escaped his cage, and walked/On the dry pavement with his webby feet" (80). Ricoeur points out that the homophony of *le cygne* with *le signe* (sign) "invites the reader to seek out the ruses hidden in the games of representation intended to signify loss" (391). In its homophony of *cygne* and *signe*, the poem suggests that signs of loss or even lost signs call forth a present recognition that contravenes such loss. The swan breaking free from the cage of new Paris reminds the poet that the old signs await new bursts of recognition and recovery—forms of attention whose poetic trope is the temporal leap of analepsis. Much as Baudelaire makes old Paris burst through a hapless sign with "mad gestures, foolish and sublime,/As of an exile whom one great desire/Gnaws with no truce" (83), the analeptic leap is intensified by the desire to recover that which is supposed to be irrecoverable, but which in every instance presses for its recognition.

Vicuña's gnawing "great desire" is to know the sign work and aesthetics of pre-Columbian South America. In this respect, Baudelaire's poem also prefigures her works, particularly as it reckons with the losses of the colonized people of the world. "Andromache, I think of you!" the poem begins, referencing the twice-conquered wife of the Trojan Hector.[2] Andromache's symbolic relationship to modern colonialism is amplified at the poem's end. "And then I thought of you," it reads,

> Widow of Hector—wife of Helenus!
> And of the Negress, wan and phthisical,
> Tramping the mud, and with her haggard eyes
> Seeking beyond the mighty walls of fog
> The absent palm-trees of proud Africa;

Of all who drink of tears; all whom grey Grief
Gives suck to as the kindly wolf gave suck;
Of meagre orphans who like blossoms fade.
And one old Memory like a crying horn
Sounds through the forest where my soul is lost . . .
I think of sailors on some isle, forgotten;
Of captives, vanquished . . . and many more.   (83)

In these last lines, the sign work of the swan poking through historical erasure takes on figures of slavery, territorial expropriation, cultural erasure, and people captive to the devastation of colonial modernity. What the swan promises is not a promise for a nostalgic and existential *flâneur* of the corroded metropole (as Baudelaire tends to be read). It is, more forcefully, a promise for people whose memories must see through the rubble and haze of colonization. These promises are what Ricoeur calls "mnemonics of dispossession" (391), quoting Richard Terdiman. Terdiman's reading of the poem focuses on the crisis of signifying regimes that surrounded its writing (Haussmann's triumphant respatialization of Paris and the capitalist system it represented). But this reading does not address the poem's colonial significations (140)—significations for which I adapt the phrase here. In the poem's "mnemonics of dispossession," the poet is reminded of a promise of other worlds resounding like a "crying horn" in the hapless and incomplete spatial project of modernity and its colonial formations—which is how Walter Benjamin read the poem's "illumination" (a reading to which I will return later). To hear the "crying horn," Baudelaire has recourse to remembering by way of semiotic form—hearing the *signe* in the *cygne*. This analeptic leap across seemingly lost memories, even memories dispossessed of semantic contents, present only in a kind of sound and rhythm, is likewise the entry point for Vicuña's promise of signification. Even if Vicuña cannot read the khipu, her work proposes that the poetics of that sign burst through the ruses of colonial signs.

In Ricoeur's terms, the promise of signification in Vicuña's khipu could be described as *anamnesis* sounding through the cracked *mneme* of colonialism. Javier Sanjinés examines such "violent, impatient form" that I call analepsis with a Quechua concept of *pacha*, which refers to a present time dense with multiple possible pasts and futures (110–12). *Pacha* denotes a "world-moment" that consists of the interactions between sky, earth, and inner worlds—when those worlds collide in a "specific configuration of matter, activity, and moral relationship—a state of experience" (Catherine Allen 22). Drawing on the Andean-inspired Marxism of philosopher José-Carlos Mariátegui, Sanjinés distinguishes the adaptable temporal heterogeneity of *pacha* from the inflexible "accumulative process" of Western historiography. In Sanjinés's estimation, rather than absorb everything into a singular, inescapable process of wealth expropriation, *pacha* makes possible acts of "skipping over the continuum of history," particularly in places where "the suffering and humiliated masses enter history." When the spurned enters the present, it forces a reconsideration of time in its unequal and multiple dimensions, because those peripheralized states of experience must be reckoned with in their centrality. Moreover, *pacha* itself has a means of organizing that inequality and multiplicity. What was "spurned, humiliated, scoffed at" presents itself in *pacha* as necessarily present, integral in its contradictory conceptions of time and reality, at once whole and constituted by totalizable fractures. If the phenomenological concept for such an experience of memory is *anamnesis*—the whole experienced from a part—the experience of memory in *pacha* gives those parts the ability to create their wholes: *pacha* is "not satisfied with calling up the events of the past; it seeks to transform them, to reinterpret them in the present" (Sanjinés 110–12). In *pacha*, Vicuña's khipu—the scorned and subordinated sign system of the Andes—gains the impatient immediacy in which it was philosophically articulated. This chapter examines that Andean philosophy in its contemporary contexts, in order to explain how the temporal leaps that Sanjinés suggestively describes as "stubborn knots, as knotted cords, disturbing the smooth surface of historical events" are in fact congruent with a poetics of knot writing (97). In allowing for the khipu to offer the theories of time and reality embedded in its knots and twists, this chapter elevates it from figure to trope and concept. In keeping with Vicuña's assertion of the khipu's capacity to "write from below, seeing the efface," my reading embraces the analepsis by which her work bursts through the occlusive ruses of colonial signs. In offering a final instance of such anticolonial poetics, this book concludes with a theory of the natural sign emerging from the spurned Americas—a contexualized theory that helps me to return to the Andean-inspired works of Joaquín Torres-García.

The Prose and Poetry of the In-Khipu World

Khipu, which means "knot" in the Quechua language of the central Andes, is a system of knotted cords that the Incas and other Andean people used to record numerical, demographic, religious, legal, historical, and other kinds of information (plate 9). Because the camelid fiber with which these cords are made deteriorates in all but the driest parts of the moist Andean climate, relatively few texts of the once widespread semiotic system survive (this is not to mention the purposeful destruction of the cords during the Spanish colonization). Yet, while widespread, it was not a uniform system. Different knot patterns were used in different parts of the Andes to communicate distinct things, almost as if there were different languages in the knots. Scholar of khipu Galen Brokaw calls this the "semiotic heterogeneity" of Andean knot writing and points out that it extended and varied in space *and* time. Knot writing began (insofar as the oldest dateable surviving cords suggest) sometime in the first millennium CE, emerging from the semiotic practices of such pre-Inca cultures as the Moche, Chimu, and Wari. Related to *tocapus* and *yupanas* (polychromatic checkerboard notation systems prevalent in the pre-Inca Andes), khipu developed as thread wrapped into polychromatic squares. It is possible that this development was instigated by a need to make the abacus-like notation system of the checkerboards (the *tocapus* and *yupanas*) more portable and usable.[3] The Wari culture of the Peruvian coast and south-central Andes (500–1000 CE) appears to be the first to have "transposed" the polychrome squares into a system of knots (Brokaw 1–21, 84–89).

Brokaw borrows the term "transposition" from Julia Kristeva's writings. He notes that Kristeva came to use the term as a replacement for "intertextuality," which she believed was being used in more simplistic ways than she had intended. Rather than the account of literary interanimations that intertextuality came to denote (i.e., "study of sources"), she used the Freudian concept of transposition to describe "the passage of one sign system to another." Transposition was a tertiary poetic process, in addition to metaphor and metonymy, whose Freudian equivalents in the work of the unconscious were condensation and displacement. This third poetic process was the psychoanalytic equivalent of "the thetic position: the destruction of the old position and the formation of a new one." The thetic or thesis position is a self-reckoning within the changes of sign systems. It is the "enunciative and denotative positionality" that emerges when a person is forced to mark out their meaning amid a stream of changing semiotic regimes. Kristeva notes that it is therefore related to a kind of "anamnesis," inasmuch as changing sign systems induce "considerations of representability" (59–60). That consideration takes place in a consciousness of contradiction between sign systems, a kind of criticality that emerges from the self-aware shifts in the meaning of signs—conscious shifts that Brokaw calls "semiotic heterogeneity." Woven into the first Wari transpositions of *tocapus* and *yupanas*—that is, woven in the first khipus—was thus an occasion to meditate on the nature of the changing sign, on its *hows* as well as its *whats*.

While Brokaw does not give as much granularity to his interpretation of "transposition" as I have here, he does show how the pragmatic shifts of knot writing gave rise to theories of representability. Inasmuch as "transposition" refers to a kind of criticality within "semiotic heterogeneity," Brokaw delineates such transposed formations in the Quechua-language concept of *quilca*. *Quilca* is a complex theory of mediation that helps to shed light on how khipu can be conceptually laden. In an essay on the concept of *quilca*, Brokaw begins by demonstrating the multifarious use of the word in the colonial period. In colonial-era texts, *quilca* refers to color, paint, painting, embroidery, sculpture, writing, book, khipu, checkerboard notations, and other media. He demonstrates that any analysis of the term that has associated it with a single medium has come up short because the term refers to semiotics and aesthetics in a general sense: "*Quilca* reflects a kind of metonymy, by which the literal meaning of the term referring to a semiotics/aesthetics of color also refers by association to the media that employ it" ("Semiotics" 181). In its multitiered denotation—referring to different media and their semiotic and aesthetic codes—*quilca* appears to be an indigenous media concept. Brokaw emphasizes that this media concept preceded the arrival of the Spaniards, inasmuch as it was ready to hand when these foreigners arrived with their books and alphabets. In the crisis of representability that Walter Mignolo calls "colonial semiosis" (*Darker Side* 7–20), *quilca* was available as a conceptual tool for understanding representational heterogeneity.

This use of the concept is evident in colonial catechisms where *quilca* is used to think through the representability of Christ. Transposed into a Christian context, *quilca* reveals how distinct its philosophical lifeworld is from the Christian one. For example, the Third Lima Council's Quechua-language *Catecismo* of 1583 reads:

> And the Christians know very well that Jesus Christ, and Our Lady, and the Saints are in heaven alive and glorious, and that they are not in those bundles, or Images . . . and they revere the Images, and kiss them, and they bare themselves before them, and kneel down on their knees, and they beat their chests; it is because of what those Images represent, and not for what they are in themselves. Just like the Corregidor kisses the provision and Royal seal and puts it on his head, not because of the wax or the paper [*quillcata quellca*], but rather because it is the King's *quilca* [*Reypa quellcan*]. (qtd. in Brokaw, "Semiotics" 193–94)

The italicized terms demonstrate the problematics of *quilca*. Whereas the speaker wishes to instruct the student in the difference between image and representation (and thus to abstract the divine from its earthly picturings), the Quechua language translates all of these representational aspects into variants of *quilca* ("*quillcata quellca . . . quellcan*"). Rather than clarify the difference, *quilca* problematizes the continuity between media and their messages. In thus presenting representability as an array of materials and modalities, *quilca* reveals the contradictions of the Spaniards' worship of images (which the Spaniards argue are not images but abstract devotional icons)—while it also insists on the animating intimacy between representational materials and abstractions. In its insistence on the intimacy shared by pictures and the immateriality of the thing they represent, the use of *quilca* in the passage offers a sense of representability that is opposed to that of the Spaniards, and it also offers a provocative conceptual rationale for reframing the contradictory Spanish episteme. In *quilca*, the material and conceptual—a medium and its messages, the visible and invisible, even the earthly and divine—are interwoven into necessary aspects of one another, interanimating rather than mutually repressive.

Scholar of khipu Gary Urton has argued that these philosophical considerations—properly speaking, transpositions or "considerations of representability"—gave khipu certain structural properties. Khipu was not only a way of communicating and was not only a way of thinking about communication; it was importantly also a means for thinking about the relation between media and material reality. For instance, in an analysis of the uses of khipu to map kinship structures, Urton describes the relation between knots and social structure in terms of "the great synthesizing and synchronizing structure at the heart of the empire." "Seen in this light," he adds, "khipus can be understood as a medium for discourses of power"—discourses that are ultimately "concerned with history." Grounding his interpretation in philosophical debates about structure and historical change, he describes the khipu as a means of comprehending history in its invariant structures and those structures in the pulls of historical flow. In its concerns with the representability of the material world (and therefore of the mutual impact that representations and things have on one another), "khipu history took the form of structural history or, more accurately, the history of structures" (153, 258, 5). Urton's observation about khipu structuralism recalls Michael Taussig's writings on the "animated structuralism" of the Andes. His *The Devil and Commodity Fetishism*—a work focused on the dialectic of indigenous Andean myth and the commodity fetishism of mining in the Andes—describes an Andean worldview that is sensitive to the interplay between structure and historical change. Taussig explains how this interplay remains "animated" because it takes place in a consideration of "pattern[s that] not only exist but have to be continuously preserved" (161). Unlike the coldly abstract sense in which "structuralism" tends to be invoked, the native structuralism described by Urton and Taussig points to a broader

sense of reciprocity and responsibility for the structures that hold together a material world. These reciprocities can be considered a logical extension of a media concept that does not alienate signs from their
materials or abstractions. That is, if khipu designs are conceptually en-
twined with their tactility (*quilca* in all aspects and scales), then built
into that sign system is a relational circuit between a design and its physical twining—which is to say between structure and material iteration,
a "world-moment" or "specific configuration of matter, activity, and . . .
relationship—a state of experience" (Catherine Allen 22, 25). In this distinct structuralism, reciprocity is not a matter of simple exchange between individuals; it is a mutual interpenetration or weaving of individual actions and the structure of the world—threading into a tight knot
what would be incorrectly (in terms of that structure) distinguished as
"culture" and "nature."

It is no accident that Urton and Taussig both arrive to their conclusions about the "animated structuralism" of the Andes in a discussion of
kinship. As Marshall Sahlins has noted, kinship is a place where biology
and symbols intersect, offering a handy instance in which to consider the
relation between "*physis* and *nomos*, nature and law" (*What* 14). Yet (as
Sahlins also notes) that relation is inextricable from its cultural contexts.
It matters where and how that relation is articulated. In the Andean instances with which Urton and Taussig are concerned, kinship takes on
the same problematics of representability that animate khipu structuralism. In this sense, khipu is a kind of overarching trope of weaving that
characterizes all levels of relationality in the Andean world, from interpersonal to cosmological—as well as acting as an interface that relates
the personal and cosmic. In its priority over all aspects of relationality,
this structure is called *ayllu*.

While Urton and Taussig both write about *ayllu*—as does Brokaw,
who associates it with "principles of reciprocity" (*History* 89)[4]—its most
encompassing description appears in the work of Peruvian anthropologist Marisol de la Cadena. In her *Earth Beings*, a decade-long study of
practices of Quechua political community building, de la Cadena situates a study of *ayllu* in the contemporary Pacchanta village southeast of
Cusco, Peru. While she does not discuss khipu as such, in her informants'
descriptions of *ayllu* the metaphors of thread and weaving dominate.
Descriptions of relations are so completely determined by principles of
reciprocity or mutual interdependence (like threads in a weaving) that
relationality itself seems to be a khipu structure. She calls this structure
of a world that is woven in its relationships "being-in-ayllu" or "ayllu-
relationality" (44). And its most evocative descriptions are given in the
words of a bilingual Quechua-Spanish grade school teacher named Justo

Oxa, one of her primary informants. She quotes him at length, and offers a helpful gloss on the distinct modality of weaving that is active in *ayllu*:

> The teacher explained: "Ayllu is like a weaving, and all the beings in the world—people, animals, mountains, plants, etc.,—are like the threads, we are part of the design. The beings in this world are not alone, just as a thread by itself is not a weaving, and [as] weavings are with threads, a runa [a person] is always in-ayllu *with* other beings—that is ayllu." In this understanding, humans and other-than-human beings do not only exist individually, for they are inherently connected composing the ayllu of which they are part and that is part of them—just as a single thread in a weaving is integral to the weaving, and the weaving is integral to the thread. . . . [C]omposing the ayllu are entities *with* relations integrally implied; being at once singular and plural, they always bring about the ayllu even when appearing individually. Thus viewed, the ayllu is the socionatural collective of humans, other-than-human beings, animals, and plants *inherently* connected to each other in such a way that nobody within it escapes that relation. . . . (44)

De la Cadena points out that the reciprocity of *ayllu* implicates humans in nonhuman relations, integrating individuals in a weaving that involves animals, plants, and other other-than-human beings. That modality is meant to elicit responsibility for one's actions, inasmuch as any one person's actions are intimately linked to the well-being of other beings, whose actions in turn are congruent with the given individual's welfare. With such relations intrinsically implied, individuals are fractals of a larger design; that is, entities whose form does not make sense outside of the pattern in which they are threaded and woven.[5] De la Cadena goes on to observe that such woven relationality has many conceptual implications beyond kinship, including the conception of representability.

Contrasting *ayllu* to sociologist John Law's apothegm that "'to represent is to practice division' . . . to separate represented from represented, signifier from signified, subject from object," de la Cadena notes that *ayllu* construes representability in the same intense reciprocity that binds individuals to broader ecological networks (44). In *ayllu*, the concerns of *quilca* are expanded to considerations of human and other-than-human interwovenness. Oxa emphasizes this in his assertion that in *ayllu* people are both "like the threads" and "part of the design." This tight correlation between materials and design leads him—and de la Cadena—to speak of "being-in-ayllu" and the "in-ayllu world," in which the names of things and things themselves are entangled and mutually affective (44, 116). That is, signs are not inert vehicles for the transmission of knowledge about things. Instead, signs are present and active in their scenes of enunciation, imposing their veridictional force on the world and its happenings. This leads in turn to de la Cadena's conclusion about the temporal and ontological leaps made possible by *ayllu*: "in the prose of the in-ayllu world, where there is no separation between the event and its narration, eventfulness can be ahistorical. Far from the events not having happened, this means that events are not contained by evidence as requirement" (116).

De la Cadena's conclusion draws boldly on Michel Foucault, whose writing on the "prose of the world" offered a critique of the natural semiotics that de la Cadena associates with *ayllu*. Yet de la Cadena's point—which will help to explain how khipu poetics work in Vicuña's writings—is that not all the natures of natural signs are the same. The nature of signs in *ayllu* is distinct from the nature of the sixteenth-century ecclesiastical European natural sign with which Foucault was concerned. For Foucault, the problem of the natural sign was one of infinite iterability and singular reference. Nature is enclosed in signs whose secrecy stirs human language to life. Yet, once stirred, speaking humans come to find that natural language "is everywhere the same: coeval with the institution of God." In this version of a natural sign, "the *general configuration* of nature" refers in every instance, explicitly or implicitly, to the order of a Christian God (*Order of Things* 31–33). Nature is nothing but a code hiding the messages of a singular divinity. De la Cadena emphasizes that this is not the version of nature that informs signs in *ayllu*. Rather than instantiate a singularity of signified, the "prose of the in-ayllu world" prioritizes multiple domains of possible authority and reference. That is, in the reciprocal entanglements of *ayllu*, "storytelling creates the jurisdiction of the earth-beings whose story is being told" (114–15). Because representability is not limited to humans (or even animals and plants) but is coextensive with the materials and designs of a world, the crowd of possible sources of authority for what a world can be is more vast than that offered in sixteenth-century ecclesiastical semiosis. In the world of in-*ayllu* narration, the beings of stories, as well as the earth-beings that they represent—which de la Cadena describes as "different entities emerging in more than one and less than many worlds and their practices"—can effectuate their own "jurisdictions" or spaces of authority. What she calls the "prose of the in-ayllu world" is a *specific configuration* of nature in which multiple iterability is associated with multiple reference and authority. In this configuration of nature, seeming fragments carry the possibility of whole worlds inside them.

Staying with Foucault for another moment, it is evident also how such representability in *ayllu* affects the possibility for a contemporary poetics of khipu. De la Cadena rather perversely quotes Foucault's critique of the hiddenness of meaning in natural signs—but in order to reveal how such hiddenness is changed when considering the signs of the Americas in their native and colonial contexts: "it is not possible to act upon those marks without at the same time operating upon that which is secretly hidden in them" (Foucault qtd. in de la Cadena 115; see Foucault, *Order of Things* 32–33). In Foucault's critique, such marks are dangerous because they tantalize people with a lost similitude between human language and the divine meaning of things. But even he concedes that not all similitudes are the same.

Elaborating this idea in his introduction to erotic novelist and artist Pierre Klossowski's *The Baphomet*, Foucault explains that the natural sign in and of itself is not the problem; the problem is the ideology through which such a sign is apprehended.[6] The doctrines of the Christian church "constituted one of the great causes of vertigo" for the natural sign whose nature is never its own: "what [such a sign] says, it says by virtue of a profound belonging to an origin, by virtue of a consecration. There is not a single tree in the Scriptures, not a single living or dissicated plant which does not refer back to the tree of the Cross—or to the wood cut from the First Tree at the foot of which Adam succumbed . . . [and] the tree of the Fall one day becomes what it has always been, the tree of the Reconciliation" (*Baphomet* xxvii). Foucault explains that, in contrast to this closed analogical circuit, Klossowski imagines a situation in which language no longer seeks to redeem a fallen world or to discover a hidden one, but can create one. Heavily influenced by Nietzsche's assertion that "God is dead"—while interpreting that assertion to mean that the analogical or ecclesiastical conception of the natural sign has given way to the conception of the sign as convention and pragmatics—Klossowski developed a theory of "fabulation" that is compatible with the "thread" and "design" of *ayllu* described by Oxa and de la Cadena. He offers his theory in an extended comment on Nietzsche's aphorism, "How the 'True World' Finally Became a Fable" (which appears in *The Twilight of the Idols*):

> The fable, I said, is an event that is narrated; it happens, or rather, it must make something happen; and in effect an action takes place and narrates itself. . . . The re-fabulation of the world also means that the world exits historical time in order to reenter the time of myth, that is, eternity. Or rather, it means that the vision of the world is an apprehension of eternity. Nietzsche saw that the mental conditions for such an "exit" [*sortie*] lay in the *forgetting* (of the historical situation) that was preliminary to the act of creating: in *forgetting*, the past is remembered [*sous-vient à*] by humans as their *future*, which takes the *figure of the past*. It is in this way

that the *past comes to* [*advient*] them in what they create; for what they believe they create in this way does not come to them from the present, but is only the pronunciation of a prior possibility in the momentary forgetting of the (historically determined) present. ("Nietzsche, Polytheism, and Parody" 88)

Just as we find in Ricoeur, in Klossowski's Nietzsche, *forgetting* makes possible a kind of sign that is creative of the situations in which it finds itself. In the fable—a genre characterized by legendary creatures, speaking animals, and other anthropomorphic beings—audiences are asked to forget their entanglement in historical time and to accept the possibility of the disaligned time of myth and animal life. Klossowski's concept of "fabulation" suggests that such practices of temporal disalignment are also found outside the genre conventions of the fable. Wherever *forgetting* is induced with the aim of making possible the disaligned time of myth and animals, he sees "fabulation." And, wherever such fabulation reflects on its relation to time, it becomes a hermeneutics for the sign, revealing the vying temporal densities at play in language.

As if written to echo de la Cadena's analysis of Oxa's words, Klossowski's considerations of representability with regard to time, event, myth, and history are congruent with a poetics of *ayllu* in which "eventfulness can be ahistorical." When de la Cadena locates in *ayllu* Foucault's cryptic assertion that "it is not possible to act upon those marks without at the same time operating upon that which is secretly hidden in them" (Foucault qtd. in de la Cadena 115; Foucault, *Order of Things* 32–33) she uncovers a confluence between the Klossowski hidden in Foucault and the "thread" and "design" of representability in the "in-ayllu world." Indeed, she so asseverates that world that Foucault is made to signify within its configuration of nature. What is "secretly hidden" in his words is a consideration of representability within the reciprocal entanglements and multiple authorities of *ayllu*. Missing from those words, however, is a consideration of how the *forgetting* involved in remembering the hidden meanings of signs is affected by the problem of uneven development. Whereas *forgetting* takes on an imperative and even heroic cast in the writings of Nietzsche and Klossowski (as well as Ricoeur)—where it is an intellectual imperative obligated by a need to make creativity impactful—in the colonial contexts of the Americas, *forgetting* is already woven into the conditions of engagement. In this situation, in which the memory of the past has been forcibly erased, and in which such signs as khipu have been effaced and eliminated from the archive, the condition for engaging such signs is already ahistoricity, loss of forgotten content, and ruptured rhythm—eventfulness *is* ahistorical. This enforced forgetting begs the adjectival modifier that Saidiya Hartman offers to fabulation with her description of "critical fabulation," or that "re-presenting" whose re-duplicative prefix "re-" denotes the effort of returning to "matters absent, entangled, and unavailable" because of colonial destruction (11). In this broader sense, analepsis can be seen as the principal trope of the Americas, inasmuch as the archive of the Americas is encompassed by erasures. Even in the embrace of the temporal heterogeneity that Sanjinés celebrates in its Quechua conception as *pacha*, whenever the "suffering and humiliated masses enter history" they reveal the amnesia and partiality of the historical record (110–12). The *pacha* of these lands is a *pacha* riven with the reckless violence of primitive accumulation—yet it is *pacha* nonetheless. That is, tactics of organizing inequality, fragmentation, and multiplicity can still be configured within the cultural lifeworlds of the humiliated and seemingly superseded. Insofar as the presence of the humiliated insists on a right to time, these subjugated embody *anamnesis*, filling out the content of the present with the necessity of remembering amid so much loss. In the signs of the Americas, the *how* of memory is definitive and encompasses that encompassing erasure.

Colonial loss thus instantiates a condition for seeing how creativity implicates memory, as well as for observing how such implication is folded into the conceptions of time and reality in which it happens. This is Vicuña's fundamental insight—and helps to explain her assertion that a "quipu that remembers nothing" could be "*the core*/the heart of memory" (*QUIPOem* q.8–12). In investigating the form, techniques, and conceptual contours of this sign system, she amplifies its semiotic *how*, "piercing earth and sky" with the sound of khipu representability considering itself. Whereas Klossowski might call this an instance of "fabulation," for Vicuña—who recognizes the uneven terrain of colonial forgetting—it is simply "memory" in its active political form. Her most explosive political act is to be creative in the so-called mnemonics of dispossession. When she insists on an *irrevocable* contemporaneity for the khipu, she countermands the principal colonial order, which is to remain dispossessed of creative agency.[7] As Klossowski suggests, such creativity dispels the colonial trance of historicity and the historical inevitability of one's subjugation and self-loss. Moreover, when considered within the representability of *ayllu*, such creativity entwines in the material reality of everyday life.

In *ayllu*, the threads of everyday life are a part of the ever-shifting (never referentially singular) design, and that design gives a form and meaning to the threads. To return to the epigraph with which the present book opened—Benjamin's critique of the concept of origins, amid the "eddy in the stream of becoming"—Vicuña's work resonates with a reading of this passage by philosopher Howard Caygill. Caygill writes that the sense of Jewish loss and endangerment in an ethnonationalist context (Germany in the 1930s) led Benjamin to replace concepts of "substance and subject with *transitivity* . . . [and to replace the] Kantian transcendental deduction of the categories of quantity, quality, relation, and modality from the pure unity of the apperceptive 'I' [with] such categories of modern experience as 'porosity,' 'threshold,' and 'shock' from the impure dispersal of transitivity." Caygill explains that Benjamin never gave up on an idea of origins. Instead, he configured origins within modalities of impurity, dispersal, and transitivity. Rather than signify a search for an originary and fallen world (whose lost greatness warrants the necessity of deathly purifying violence—and whose "pure unity" is related to the policing of divisiveness, heterogeneity, imperfection, and "undesirables" in a social group), Benjamin's "origins" are "intricately woven into the weft of everyday life" (Caygill, *Colour* 119). Caygill's metaphor of weaving is consonant with de la Cadena's description of *ayllu*: as with the "in-ayllu world," Benjamin's sense of origins is a means by which to see the past as the handiwork of present threads and design. But Benjamin distinctly offers to that social formation an emphasis on the necessary fray and imperfection of such a woven world.

With regard to a search for origins, fray and imperfection necessitate themselves because only in their emphasis can origins be something other than a warrant for purification. Fray and imperfection challenge the possible purity of thread and design—to always, as Vicuña has it, "write from below/seeing the efface." Benjamin and Vicuña do not deny the violent history from which everyday life extends. On the contrary, they write from its present flows. But in doing so, they offer that historicity the generative problem of its fray in other cultural configurations and ontological entanglements. In a manner reminiscent of Benjamin's writings on origins, Vicuña forces the political and temporal problem of origins on the khipu. That is, upon its historical silencing, she forces the problem of present creativity. How could it be that the khipu "write[s] from below/ seeing [its] efface" (*QUIPOem* q.12)? How indeed is the analepsis of the Americas fulfilled in the imperfect totalizability of khipu? How is that totalizability made real in her writings? And how does its realization remain totalizable—that is, a source of possibility, virtuality, and imagination—by virtue of the semiotics of the khipu itself?

Khipu that Stands for Itself: Analeptic Languaging

The point to be emphasized is that Vicuña not only writes poetry about khipu. More incisively, she writes within khipu, complicating a distinction between the form and content of this sign system in her works. To remain with the poem through which the present chapter has been think-ing, a turn to the visual presentation of that poem in its book—the collec-tion aptly titled *QUIPOem* (1997)—reveals how the poem works inside khipu semiosis. This book, like Vicuña's other published collections, is a collage-like amalgamation of writing, images, and objects that she calls a "diary of objects" (*QUIPOem* q.34). As her description suggests, in these books materiality is a key feature of their testimonial-like corroboration of an enduring self. In Vicuña's case, exiled from Chile after Pinochet's coup in 1973, the self that endured witnessed the shock of the coup and the violent political repression that followed. That repression was carried out through an infamous secret police, torture, and the "disappearing" of opponents to Pinochet's extreme rightist regime. These forced disap-pearances—in which the state abducted political enemies who were tor-tured and killed, and the bodies hidden or destroyed—were widespread in the right-wing military dictatorships of Latin America throughout the 1960s, 1970s, and 1980s (and indeed occurring in many locales to this day). Because the aim of such regimes is to make political opponents com-pletely nonexistent, it is not sufficient to kill them. They must be erased from the records of life and death (the bodies must be removed from the possibility of legal representability)—or, as the Argentinian dictator Jorge Rafael Videla put it, "they are neither dead nor alive. They are disappeared" (qtd. in Bilbija et al. 113). Against this institutionalized culture of disap-pearance (and the debilitating fear it instills in a population), Vicuña's books bear materiality as a trace of representability resistant to disappear-ance. Her "diary of objects" is a metonym for the necessary material re-presentability of the bodies and objects erased by these dictatorial re-gimes. In this way, their materiality finds kinships in the bodies and objects erased by the colonial regimes that prefigured the right-wing dictator-ships. That is, her books' material emphases are also a source of relation to the resistant representability of the indigenous cultures of the Andes, where—Taussig reminds us—"preconquest institutions still flourish" (*Devil* 159). And it is by way of such still flourishing preconquest cultures that Vicuña's materiality takes its cast of representability in khipu semiosis.

The poem itself ("the quipu that remembers nothing, an empty cord—*is the core*/the heart of memory—/the earth, listening to us . . .") is spread in a khipu-like material structure over six pages (see figs. 27, 28, and 29). In those pages, what I have been presenting as a text of poetry is actually a combination of typographic text, calligram-like handwriting, and a pho-tograph of her sculpture in sand (which she calls a "precario" or fragile object). For instance, what I have translated as an em dash followed by italics—"cord—*is the core*"—is in Vicuña's text a drawn line that continues into a line of cursive writing. Likewise, what I have rendered as poem

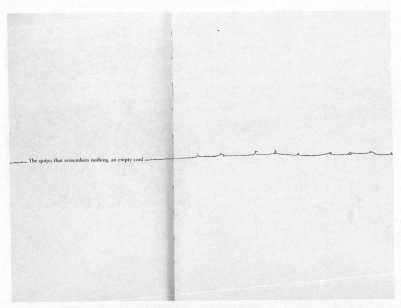

The quipu that remembers nothing, an empty cord

FIGURE 27 Opening pages from Vicuña's multimedial book of poetry and art, *QUIPOem* (q.8–9) (1997). Photograph: Courtesy of Cecilia Vicuña.

heart of memory.

the earth, listening to us. Con-cón.

FIGURE 28 Pages following the first pages of Vicuña's *QUIPOem* in figure 27 (q.10–11) (1997). Here, the text is revealed to be a thread that runs through the book. Photograph: Courtesy of Cecilia Vicuña.

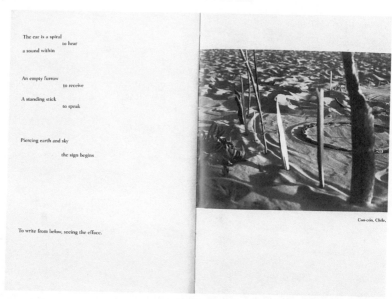

The ear is a spiral
                    to hear
a sound within

An empty furrow
                    to receive
A standing stick
                    to speak

Piercing earth and sky

                    the sign begins

Con-cón, Chile,

To write from below, seeing the efface.

FIGURE 29 A view of the sand sculpture in figure 28 from another angle in Vicuña's *QUIPOem* (q.12–13) (1997). Photograph: Courtesy of Cecilia Vicuña.

line breaks with forward slashes—"*is the core*/the heart"—are breaks between media and representional materials. The poem has three such breaks: separating it across a foldover page from figure 27 to figure 28, across a photograph of the sand sculpture from figure 28 to figure 29, and across the page of text that separates a textual line that runs across the photographs from figure 29 to figure 27 (I will explain what I mean by this below). That multitextuality—bringing various instruments of representation to bear upon one another, and thus to complicate a consideration of their representability—could be interpreted as a kind of *quilca* awareness. Much as *quilca* made possible a critical investigation of conflicting representational regimes in the colonial catechism, the composite text of Vicuña's book begs a consideration of how a poem might extend into drawing, photograph, sculpture, and sand.

Yet inasmuch as that extension involves both the technological instruments of modernity (book and photograph) and preconquest techniques of organizing time and space (weaving and sculpture), not to mention the nonhuman materials of the natural world (sand, grass, and sticks), this extension also begs consideration of what colonial aporias and amnesias interfere in the act of remembering described in the poem. What Ricoeur (via Terdiman) called the "mnemonics of dispossession" are active in every leap that the poem takes from one medium to the next: in each one it reminds readers of a lost connection between these signs and their signified things. That constant reminder entails what Benjamin—in his analysis of the same Baudelaire poem that motivates Ricoeur—called a "mimesis of death." Benjamin does not mean that the apparently foregone objects of Baudelaire's world are dead. Rather, he means to point out that in Baudelaire's poem those objects of a seemingly foregone era cannot be disappeared because the poem itself reveals their enforced disappearance to be "as brittle as glass—and as transparent" (*Selected Writings* 4:50–51). In the breaks and separations of Vicuña's poem, Benjamin would have seen the glass of enforced disappearances cracking amid the presence of that which the dictatorships could not disappear: the persistent creativity of the writer. In Vicuña's hands, the seeming fractures of colonial historicity are the looped fissures where the relational wovenness of the khipu is made.

In a way that recalls Oxa's suggestion that the thread is actively involved in making the design, Vicuña's poem coheres its various media elements in a series of lines and angles that are khipu-like in their design, as if held together by a fabric that holds the book together. For instance, figure 29 presents the same sculpture shown in figure 28, but from another angle. The angle from which the viewer sees the sand sculpture in figure 29 is the same angle from which the line of written poetry arrives to the sand sculpture shown in figure 28. In giving the reader a sightline that takes place from the angle of the poem's "view" of the sculpture in figure 28, the photograph in figure 29 invites the reader into the interior of the poem, treating its text like a habitable vantage. That treatment of the text—in which it has a kind of "view" on its surroundings—suggests as well that the text has perception of some kind. We are given *its* view on the sand sculpture. If readers are invited thusly to enter the text, whose textual elements are interwoven with the materials of the sculpture, then by extension readers are invited to enter the sculpture (which is coextensive here with text)—as well as to enter the khipu-like topology of warp and weft that holds all of these materials together. Woven into its interior, a reader's relation to the poem they have just read retroactively changes. A reader's position becomes internalized to the "quipu that remembers nothing," introjecting that seeming vacancy with the experience of reading. In this introjection, the act of reading bypasses two temporal rifts: most presently, it skips backward from the effects that figure 29 plays on figures 27 and 28; yet also, by virtue of this formal retroprojection, skips backward to the other side of the colonial silencing by which khipu is supposed to remain unread.

Here, analepsis plays upon the spatial relations of the book in order to transgress its linear structure. In doing so, the book subverts chronological distance.[8] Readers are put in a position of *reading in khipu*, which—much like *being in-ayllu*—sutures multiple temporal threads. In reading Vicuña's *quipoem*, readers are in the relational wovenness of khipu and *ayllu*, while also inescapably in a book of contemporary poetry and art. To return to de la Cadena's repositioning of Foucault's cryptic Klossowskian statement that "it is not possible to act upon those marks without at the same time operating upon that which is secretly hidden in them" (qtd. in de la Cadena 115; see Foucault's *Order of Things* 32–33), we can understand how that repositioning itself participates in a kind of shifting in *ayllu* or the relational topology by which things have relational values in a design. Foucault becomes a node in the woven world that encompasses and holds him in place. Likewise, in Vicuña's poem, readers are put inside the elements that are "secretly working" in signs, only to find that those secrets are external to the signs and not very secret at all, inasmuch as they are the open system of reciprocities that holds the elements of the book together—and, insofar as we are introjected in the poem in its reading, that holds readers in khipu-*ayllu* as well.

The poem that extends from the left of the photograph in figure 29, and whose shape horizontally mirrors the sticks vertically propped in the sand in the sculpture (as if the poem's lines were shadows cast behind the sticks by the sunlight), supports such comparison of khipu and woven textual topology:

> The ear is a spiral
>   to hear
> a sound within
>
> An empty furrow
>   to receive
> A standing stick
>   to speak
>
> Piercing earth and sky
>   the sign begins
>
> To write from below, seeing the efface. (*QUIPOem* q.12)

The poem is a meditation on the relation between signs and things. It is organized around two referential poles: the "ear" of the first line and the "sign" of the penultimate line. The ear is the subject with which "spiral," "empty furrow," and "standing stick" are associated. Therefore, the actions of spiral, furrow, and stick are all extensions of what an ear does:

"hear," "receive," and "speak." While the last of these actions seems alien to what an ear does, this is because the actions and their actors (spiral, furrow, and stick) are also drawn into the gravitational pull of the poem's second referential pole: "the sign . . . piercing earth and sky." Enacting what it references, the signifier "sign" acts as if *it* were the subject with which the spiral, furrow, and standing stick were identified. In so doing, it extends upward and backward in the poem—from earth to sky, but also backward in time or analeptically—to do what stick, furrow, and spiral do. The sign "speaks," "receives," and "hears." While the last of these actions seems alien to what a *sign* does, this is because—conversely—the proximity of the ear returns to assign meanings to the poem's actors and actions. In its multidimensional syntax (a grid interrelating various media in the text), the poem weaves into a single knot the ear and sign— perhaps represented by the spiral in the middle of the sand sculpture (fig. 28). In offering the sand spiral as the visual icon of ear and sign, the whole poem twists into this icon—while also ostensibly emanating from it, if it indeed is the case that the poem is "writing from below."

Congruent with the multidirectionality of the spiral, the poem gives neither "ear" nor "sign" full control of actions and objects. Indeed, the poem's meticulous design complicates distinctions of sign and thing. In straddling sign and ear across a variety of actions and actors, like the knots hanging from the main cord of a khipu rope, the poem locates their relation in an always-suspended orthogonality. They intersect but pull in their own directions as well, giving a woven form to the world that holds these items and their names in place. Its final line, "writing from below, seeing the efface," reminds readers that the text at hand is very literally a text at hand: the discrete signs, media, and objects of the poem are elements of a situation in which erasure is countermanded by the khipu text in a reader's hand, evidence of a woven form written from below. Or, as Vicuña puts it in a Benjaminian meditation titled "Origin of Weaving," the textile is the context for the text—that is, the khipu is the world-making form from which the content of her poetry emerges. First textile, then poem:

> textile, text, context
> from *teks*, to weave, to fabricate, to make wicker or
> wattle for mud-covered walls . . . (*Unravelling* 10)

This passage highlights the idea that the textile is the primary form for Vicuña's writings, as well as more generally for her sense of what writing is. Rather than the product of alphabetic accumulation, her notion of writing focuses on a topology or a study of positions in a framework of intersecting positions. Vicuña's abstract and systematic understanding of khipu as topology "inspired"—in his own words—Argentinian-born visual artist and scholar of Andean aesthetic form César Paternosto to describe khipu in terms of a "structural paradigm" that he called "the *tectonic* principle" (165). Relating khipu to Andean cultural mastery of sculpture, engineering, architecture, mathematics, and textile weaving, he insists on a master principle of positional logic in the Andes. While he calls it "tectonic" to relate Vicuña's network of etymologies in *teks* to *"tekton"* or builder, the topological is more direct in emphasizing what Vicuña emphasizes: any builder or maker begins in a network of positionalities whose aesthetic and ontological nature is a kind of weaving (plates 9 and 10). And in the Andes weaving is indeed the aesthetic form on which other arts—sculpture, writing, poetry, masonry, and even government—are modeled. First textile, then text.

As if they were written to describe the philosophical nuances of Vicuña's hard emphasis on the wovenness of the in-khipu world, the words of Gilles Deleuze and Félix Guattari are worth dwelling on momentarily. In their critique of simplified distinctions of "word and thing," they write, "a form of content is not a signified, any more than a form of expression is a signifier. . . . We are never a signifier or signified. We are stratified" (67). Scholar of semiotics Paul Bains explains that Deleuze and Guattari suggest here that the consistency of language emerges from "multiplicity and its social/cultural stratifications. . . . They analyze language in terms of actions that produce transformations, rather than in terms of words and things or signifiers and signifieds" (104). This is of import because the *symbolic* aspect of language, what inheres in the notion of an abstract and transcendent sign, obscures the *relational* nature of linguistic activity. Language is related to action in all domains and, according to Bains on Deleuze and Guattari, is thus coterminous with it. Its unqualified immanence in action means that pragmatics comes closest to elaborating its "nature." Yet, Bains notes, pragmatics fails to appreciate certain actions immanent to language, especially the way in which language "specifies the space in which it exists" (101). In extending the creative effects of language beyond "pragmatics and context" to consider its "ethological, ecological, corporeal, and incorporeal dimensions"—its ontologies—he puts Deleuze and Guattari into conversation with theories of natural semiotics in the writings of Chilean biologists Humberto Maturana and Francisco Varela.

Like Deleuze and Guattari, Maturana and Varela coauthored important works on the possible semiosis of nonhuman systems. What Maturana and Varela termed "autopoiesis" refers to a structural coupling between a system and a medium that can be observed in living organisms. In the terms of the present chapter, they describe a kind of *quilca* that is coextensive with the natural world. In cellular structure, for instance, "the product is the same as the network of processes involved in production" (Bains 88). That is, organisms and environments are completely interdependent and mutually determining. Bains describes how these ideas implicate semiotic systems: "the *flow of interactions* between participants" (the system of language) is immanent to the medium in which they interact (a medium relation that Maturana and Varela call "languaging"). In turning the noun of language into a verb they emphasize that the linguistic medium is constituted in the interactive system: "notions such as transmission of information, symbolization, denotation, meaning or syntax, are secondary to the constitution of the phenomenon of languaging in the living of the living systems that live" (qtd. in Bains 109–10). For the purposes of the present book, they give to the decolonial sense of "languaging"—as developed by Walter Mignolo to denote creativity in the transcultural exchange of language and culture—a sense of nature-bearing form. That is, in their hands, rather than a modified transculturation, languaging is ontology configured in its most complete sense. Languaging is not only a tactic for "thinking and writing between languages" (Mignolo, *Local* 226); it is a way of carrying, orienting, manipulating, and effectuating the real worlds in which thinking and writing happen.

Moreover, Maturana and Varela are emphatic about the livingness of language in nonhuman domains. The worlds carried in languaging are not limited by human interactions. Relational effects between living systems create the patterns of conduct that linguists have separated from life by way of the symbolic theory of language. But that symbolic theory cannot explain how "the *flow of interactions*" moves between materials and linguistic elements and effects. Khipu can "write from below"—as Vicuña says—because its materials have a system that organizes the patterns of conduct around it, as well as a present shaping force on human memory, perception, imagination, and forgetting. This is its autopoiesis and its means of continued creativity and ramification in contemporary experience. The system is immanent to the medium in which Vicuña entwines herself and her readers (see plate 10). In imposing its structural coupling or topology on readers, organizing their experience of time by organizing their spatial and temporal relations (indeed, in acting as the topological system that Taussig calls an "animated structuralism"), Vicuña allows khipu to act as an autopoietic natural sign.

To put it another way: if readers do not assume that language obtains its defining feature from representational, informational, archival, or even strictly epistemological functions, if we can perceive that it is in some meaningful basis an interactive phenomenon and system of positions (as the in-*ayllu* or in-khipu conception of language insists; and as the idea of language as languaging reaffirms), then the silence of the colonial archive is cracked. Such silencing is indeed—as Benjamin put it in his reading of Baudelaire's poem—"as brittle as glass—and as transparent" (*Selected Writings* 4:50–51). In its continued making of positions and perspectives, the khipu speaks. It gives form and content to Vicuña's poetry within its own topological design. Her languaging is the representability of khipu representing itself.

This is the feature of autopoiesis in khipu that resists enforced disappearance and thus can be described as a kind of resistant representability. In a different context, Jerome McGann likewise drew on Maturana and Varela's notion of autopoiesis for understanding the autonomous representability of texts, employing the concept to explore textuality as "feedback systems that cannot be separated from those who manipulate and use them" (15). In his works, he has expanded a sense of textuality beyond language and print to involve the generative effects of electronic and informational technology. But he does not move laterally in semiotic interfaces to examine something like khipu. His sense of textuality did not exactly take stock of autopoietic *texturality*. In khipu, the "feedback system"—which encloses user and text in a shared effort of producing, maintaining, and defining the system that organizes their effort—is continuous with *threads* and *design* that have resisted colonial silencings. Moreover, the semiotics and aesthetics of that resistant thread and design have persisted in the resistant words and makings of people like Oxa and Vicuña. To rephrase McGann's uses of Maturana and Varela: it is not only that feedback systems cannot be separated from those who manipulate and use them; feedback systems *resist* separation from those users. Those users in turn become expressions of the resistance of the semiotic and aesthetic system.

The meaning of *resistance* is used in its full political resonance here. Poetics of resistance are typically understood as positional statements in a state of war. Benjamin scholar Caygill thus begins his study "on resistance" with Carl von Clausewitz, reasoning that "the ambivalent experience of a blocking or aporia that is also an uprising or insurrection—an experience that might be called the state of resistance—locates it on the crossroads between violence and speech" (*On Resistance* 9). The economy of war frames the discourse of resistance. Its poetics implies speech in refusal of death, silence, or what I have called here the enforced disappearance of khipu (so as to compare its colonial destruction to the political terror of twentieth-century free market regimes). With respect to khipu, its representability has resisted that destruction by eliciting voice. In animating and structuring poetic acts to this day, its "feedback systems" not only have resisted the colonial interdict but have come to shape and define it as well.

The title of this section is drawn from anthropologist Roy Wagner's phrase, "the symbol that stands for itself." Wagner describes how the formal and aesthetic properties of signs effectively allow for signs to create their own meanings. I repurpose the phrase here to emphasize not meaning but relational structure. Relating itself in a colonial context, the formal properties of khipu encompass and give definition to that context, giving it another nature in which to understand itself. Interconnecting that context into a text that is textile, khipu subsumes relations into a *textural* structure of reciprocal warp and weft—the social fabric called *ayllu* in Quechua, a type of reflexivity reaching into nonhuman domains. Indeed, its embededdness in animated materiality has kept khipu resistant. That materiality brings to life anticolonial significations of ongoing resistance—positions in a topology that extends into nonhuman worlds. In distilling the political message that interconnects Maturana, Varela, Deleuze, and Guattari, Bains could have been writing as well about Vicuña's khipu:

> This autonomy of language is also creative, allowing its participants to describe, imagine, and conjure up the past and invent the future. Order-worlds may constrain and determine subjectivity, in particular as one is born into regimes of signs. *However*, there is always the possibility of unpredictable encounters and novel interactions leading to previously unimagined observations, statement-acts, and networks of conversations. . . . "Accordingly, all coercive political systems aim, explicitly or implicitly, at reducing creativity and freedom by specifying all social interactions as the best means of suppressing human beings as observers and thus attaining political permanence. . . ." The Achilles hell of absolute domination = relations. (130–31)[9]

Ultimately, the political explosiveness of Vicuña's khipu is that it is creative. Written amidst the double political shock of colonial governance and its continuance in Pinochet's dictatorial regime, Vicuña's khipu functions not only as remembrance but as relation making as well (see plate 10 for a literalization of this idea). Khipu is not only subject to normative positions, spaces, and temporalities of history. It shapes positions, temporalities, and spaces as well, transforming historical experience in a deixis of present creativity. Rather than serve simply as a shadow symbol for market regimes and colonial power, it sheds light on the communitarian philosophies and ecological reciprocities that lurk immanently in the materials of these Andean signs.

Such is the political possibility of the signs studied in this book. They are more than traces of a foregone and conquered past. They allow for people in the present to confront and determine colonial legacies. The autopoietic sign itself confronts and determines its past, present, and future. Not only humans move subsumption in multiple directions; the signs that stand for themselves also subsume. They subsume because their constellation of poetic effects—in metonymy, metalepsis, amphiboly, introjection, montage, and analepsis—flashes like lightning over the landscape of thought and feeling through which people move.

Cosmoplasty

The texturality of the sign was also woven into the outfit that Joaquín Torres-García wore to the artists' ball at the Waldorf Astoria in 1921. In his drooping cartoonish overalls (see fig. 1 in the preface and fig. 30 in this chapter), the motif of the city took on tones both dismal and clownish. The outfit is a kind of combination of the costume of a court jester and an abject human billboard—the wearable cityscape is thus an amalgamation of commodity and critical ridicule. Luis Pérez-Oramas (poet, art scholar, and curator of the Museum of Modern Art's 2015-16 Torres-García exhibit) analyzes this tension by way of Jean-François Lyotard's "distinction between the textural and the figural." As Pérez-Oramas argues, in Torres-García's outfit the figure of the clown is disrupted by the textures of the market, eliciting a disruption found throughout Torres-García's works: a rift between "the space of the text and the space of the figure." In this book I have explored a similar rift—but I have articulated it from world structures other than that of capital. In doing so, the present chapter has arrived to something other than what Lyotard describes as the "ontological separation" between figures and texts, or signs and things (qtd. in Pérez-Oramas 28, 36). As in Vicuña's works, in Torres-García's writing and art the signifier is not constrained or alienated by the capitalist system it encounters, subverts, and just as often subsumes. Its totalizability is also generated from the cultures of the native Americas. Torres-García called this totalizability "*cosmoplastia*" or "cosmoplasty," a neologism that blends the words "cosmos" and "plasticity" in order to reference the pliable consolidation of word and thing.[10] "*Signo: Estructura*," he affirmed, later adding, "reality is only a symbol . . . and we all know that form is only a mask" (qtd. in Pérez-Oramas 11). If it is the case that such a relational in-*ayllu* realizability of signs guides his sense of the sign, it is no surprise then that in his works the plasticity of signs bears the densities of whole worlds, temporalities, and processes of change. Crossing the threshold of the Waldorf Astoria, the outfit bears some sense that it wishes to channel that building, its geography, and the historical panorama of the city. Rather than simple superstructural expression of New York City infrastructure, the outfit is a source of transitivity for those material bases,

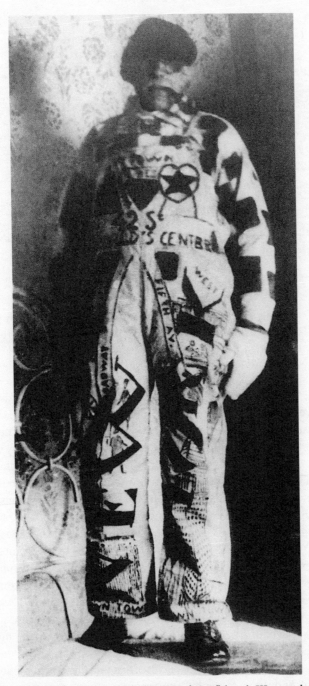

FIGURE 30 Joaquín Torres-García, "New York Suit" (1921). Worn at the Artists' Ball (Society of Independent Artists) at the Waldorf Astoria Hotel, New York, 1921. Photograph: Courtesy of the Estate of Joaquín Torres-García.

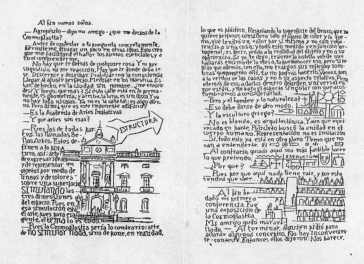

FIGURE 31   Adjacent pages from Torres-García's *La Ciudad sin Nombre* (Montevideo: Asociación de Arte Constructivo, 1941), n.p. Photograph: Courtesy of the Estate of Joaquín Torres-García.

wearing and shaping them, while also making possible their disrobing and divestment.

Decades later, in 1941 back in Montevideo, Torres-García writes an allegory of transitive cosmoplasty, *La Ciudad sin Nombre*. "The City without a Name" tells the story of an anonymous *flâneur* walking an unnamed city, observing its bustling activity, architectural and aesthetic objects, literary coteries and cultures, and general sociological scene. At various points in the manuscript, this anonymous writer inscribes the mantra of "structure" and "sign" into the text, most certainly to signal the book's commitment to cosmoplasty. That commitment is manifest in the texture of the manuscript itself, which is a handwritten manuscript, not a typescript (see fig. 31). Moreover, like a combination of de Angulo's pictographic ethnography, Ortiz's and Geyer's multilayered multiliteracy, Twombly's hieroglyphic ductus, and Vicuña's khipu texturality, this manuscript is an instance of semiotic heterogeneity. The text itself visualizes the materiality of the alphabet: reproducing the shape, slope, size, and style of the author's handwriting. But it also encloses that visualization in the aesthetic norms of Andean pictography. Torres-García offers a straightforward example of this tactic in his work "Indoamérica" (fig. 2 in the preface), which presents such words as *"pacha mama"* (Andean Earth goddess—literally, world mother), "*vida*" (life), and "Indoamérica" in the shape and style of the surrounding pictographs. Pictography is not asked to operate alongside alphabetical writing. It is presented as a texturality that can absorb and carry the meaning-making function of the alphabet. It is the aesthetic in which the alphabet appears.

In the visualized text of *La Ciudad sin Nombre*, pictographic visual characteristics have a shaping effect on the alphabet *and* the representation of urban modernity. The seen city is seen through the lens of pictographic writing. Such pictographic urbanity contravenes Uruguayan literary critic Ángel Rama's conception of a "lettered city" that is coextensive with modernity. In the pages of Torres-García's book, the urban motif of the modern world is experienced as a pictograph. To be sure, the urban motif itself captures the pictograph in the kinds of amnesias, losses, and dispossessions that Baudelaire made vivid in his poem "*Le Cygne*." But, as Benjamin's Baudelaire suggests, those amnesias interlock in acts of remembering—acts that crack the totality of the modern scene. From such opened crevices is emitted the plasticity of a cosmos, as well as the heterogeneous structures in which that plasticity is given distinct shape. In Torres-García's book, the shaping structure is pre-Incan Andean pictography—derived principally from the stonework of the ancient Tiwanaku, Chavín, and Cerro Sechín metropoles from around 2000 BCE. Any examination of these pictographs must peer across the seemingly impossible temporal distance of four millennia. Yet in examining the unique temporal density of these signs Paternosto has noticed how such distance is flattened at the touch. In his *The Stone and the Thread*, a study of the contemporary impact of ancient Andean art, he notices that the stonework of the Andes is distinctly fabric-like. Unlike the stonework of Mesoamerica, which is driven primarily by "iconographic aims," "the flat, synthetic, lithic iconography of [the Andes cultures] first evolved in the reductive, geometrizing matrix of the textile medium . . . the monoliths of Tiwanaku [for instance] are entirely covered by filigreed reliefs that reproduce textile designs." He calls this the "*plectogenic* nature" of the Andean world, which is to say a natural world "first developed in textiles" (18–19).[11] This textile-based sense of textuality infuses the pre-Incan Andean icons with the same values of in-*ayllu* mesh, by which the texture of the text is a contact point between different times and places.

Moreover, if those intersections and interstices are conceptualized—as they are in *ayllu*—as resources for reciprocity between memory and imagination (the past in its present fashioning), then the icons in Torres-García's book also stand as the evidence of a woven world. In such a world, semiotic structures reaching across the seemingly impossible temporal distance of four millennia are surfaced into present tactility. In their surface effects, they channel the depth of time and world. In this way, a "nature" first developed in textiles continues to subsume nature in the present moment. Torres-García's pictographs do not illustrate the text but rather reveal its plectogenic nature. Like the geometric icons in the stone reliefs of Tiwanaku, the pictographs in Torres-García's book express a model of time that disrupts the rectilinear course of colonial historiography, and it also infuses that disruption with the in-*ayllu* conception of resistant reciprocal representability. The implicit threads holding the book together carry the design of an Andean cosmos. And, by plectogenic extension, those threads implicate themselves in the appearance of the wearable pictographs at the Waldorf Astoria in 1921. The city of New York becomes a "city without a name" and is held together instead by pictographic threads and designs.

But while the textures of Torres-García's works bring the city into a kind of woven structuralism, the contradictions of such intercultural animation do not go away. Not quite a pure pictograph, the visualized text in Torres-García's works bends and folds in the traces of modernity, urbanism, commodity, and the alphabet. In this complexity, the pictographs work, rather, as what Benjamin would have called "*Denkbilder*" or thought pictures. As Gerhard Richter explains, the *Denkbild* was a strategy developed by the Frankfurt School of Critical Theory for staging dialectical encounter: when an object is seen as the complex combination of image and thought that it is, its various other contradictions and problematics are likewise made perceptible. In other words, *Denkbilder* are means of transforming objects into situations, and objecthood into the site of transitivity and transformation that it in fact is (1–43). In its aspect as a philosophical "picture puzzle," the pictograph of the Americas stages the problem of multiple epistemologies, ontologies, temporalities, and mnemonic and creative priorities. Yet in its particular coordination of thought and image—not quite a picture, not quite a word either—the pictograph arrives with certain capacity for organizing the *Denkbilder* of the Americas. As Theodor Adorno puts it with reference to the poetics of the "picture puzzle" or *Denkbild*, pictographs "get thought moving . . . they strike sparks through a kind of intellectual short-circuiting that casts a sudden light on the familiar and perhaps sets it on fire" (qtd. in Richter ix). Resonating with Sanjinés's description of the totalizable archival fragment as a kind of "ember," waiting to set fire to situations in the living present, Adorno's description of the *Denkbild* insists upon the necessary historical context that the pictograph nonetheless wishes to enkindle and cast into new light.

Inextricable from historical contexts, the signs of the Americas also burn through those contexts with their distinct semiotics and worlds.

Such a contradiction makes possible their criticality and creativity. That creative criticality is blazed into a passage from Chicano novelist Miguel Méndez's *Pilgrims in Aztlán*, a story set in the US-Mexico borderlands where people suffering racial governance seek redemptive justice in the mythic Aztec homeland of Aztlán. Like the Aztec priests whose defiant speech at Tenochtitlan subsumed a semiotic chaos into the resilient signs of the Americas, Méndez writes:

> When amnesia began to sow shadows in our memory, we went to our ancient lakes, seeking in the depth the faces we had lost. We saw through the mist of the ages that they were blurred and no longer the same. We reached the ancient bed of a river, facing the mountain of granite. We shouted for the echo to give back to us the names and the voices that had departed . . . leaving us empty. We came down from the hills, along the trails and roads, dragging our roots against the thorns, the snow, and the fire. We inquired after our destiny, but no one wanted to understand us because our signs were so strange. . . . We descended to the bottom of the sea, where the stars descend to their nests, to ask if the heavens know where we are headed or where we come from. . . . *Know, those who have been immolated, for in this region you will be the dawn and you will also be the river.* . . . (178)

The passage narrates the losses of colonial violence through a series of failed apostrophes. The speaker seeks contact with their past in addressing lake, river, mountain, and foothill valley. But in all of those places their speech fails them because the signs have been estranged. In the murk of colonial semiosis, the speaker's signs have been alienated from redemptive pasts and futures. Yet that amnesia also induces the intensity of the speaker's search. In that search, Méndez's speaker takes on the intensity of the stars burning above, descending into the watery nest of the lake to cool in a critical investigation of their pasts and possible futures. If this is a *Denkbild*, it is one into which the speaker walks—as if it were a landscape over which a new constellation burns bright. It feels at times like the murky lands of colonial historicity. But the night atmosphere is clear with the possibility of other forms, rhythms, and worlds. In entering the image, the signs finally resonate. They promise a dawning and rivering. They promise light liquefied.

AFTERWORD
Anthropological Poetics

In *Poetics of Relation*, Martinican poet and philosopher Édouard Glissant touches on pictographs as he moves through a broader explanation of what he calls "*échos-monde*" and "*chaos-monde*." The "chaos of the world" is the global turbulence of intercultural contacts, ruptures, catachreses, derangements, and reckonings that give rise to the "echoes" in which a world hears and understands itself. These echoes are the resonance of a globalizing process hearing itself in "archipelegic agglomerations," "*métissage*," hybrid baroquisms, "composite languages," and the various other creoles of the contemporary *chaos-monde*. Wondering how non-alphabetic sign systems will sound themselves in this chaos, Glissant asks: "Will ideograms, pictograms, and other forms of writing show up in this panorama? Do translations already allow perceptible correspondences between language systems? . . . Lists of this sort are not innocent; they accustom the mind to apprehending problems in a circular manner and to hatching solutions interdependently" (99–100). Glissant wonders whether such a sign as the pictograph will resonate in an increasingly turbulent globality—and, if so, how. While *Signs of the Americas* responds to such a question in the affirmative, it does so by challenging the idea of a singular *monde* in which such resonance is heard. The chaos of the world is incomplete and imperfect because it is a chaos of worlds. And each world has its own structures, forms, rhythms, and orders by which it organizes and gives meaning to chaos. In considering whether the pictograph will "show up in this panorama," this book affirms that there are topographies other than the singular abyss of capitalist modernity to consider.

While Claude Lévi-Strauss has been a hobbyhorse throughout, he is also present in these pages because of his fundamental contribution to an intellectual legacy in which this book (as well as Glissant's writings) is

situated. The sincerity of the opening sentence of his *Tristes Tropiques*—
"I hate traveling and explorers"—is strangely complicated by the book's
arresting thrill for language, form, poetics, narrative, cultural grammar,
creative patterning, myth, and so many other instances of what he called
"transient efflorescence." While he might despise the ethnographic project, he commits himself to it out of an apparent desire to echo the many
worlds of a nonsingular *chaos-monde*. This echoing effect gives his writings a quality of transmutation, removed yet involved in the cultural
rhythms he sets out to hear. Octavio Paz thus pointed out that Lévi-
Strauss's writings are challenging because they take place in "the relations between the universe of discourse and nonverbal reality, thought
and things, meaning and nonmeaning . . . constantly shifting between
the concrete and the abstract, between direct intuition of the object and
analysis: a thought which sees ideas as perceptible forms and sees forms
as intellectual signs" (*Claude* 16, 5). In according world-making power to
the forms and signs he set out to understand, Lévi-Strauss became implicated in those worlds. In his works, the analysis takes form as a repetition
of the studied form and sign, especially myth: "Myth engenders myths:
oppositions, permutations, mediations, and new oppositions. . . . Each
myth reveals its meaning in another one, which, in its turn, refers to another, and so on in succession to the point where all these allusions and
meanings weave a text" (Paz, *Claude* 38). In the case of *Tristes Tropiques*,
the text is a "repetition and variation" (Paz, *Claude* 39)—or rooting and
extension (to echo the Deleuzian rhizome that gives rise to Glissant's poetics of relation)—of the native signs and forms. Its "transient efflorescence" is the power of these signs and forms to define and transform the
world-moments in which they find themselves.

Lévi-Strauss thus can be credited thus for helping anthropology think
about the world as a text and the text as a world. His sensitivity to how
the plurality of entextualizations induces worlds in the plural is what
gives *Tristes Tropiques* its composite, crowded, hebephrenic, and even
montaged quality—even as its author proposes exactly the contrary, that
is, that the world is closing in on itself in a silencing singular modernity.
In short, the book's content is contradicted in its form, with the dynamic
energies of the latter outpacing the former at every instant. In like manner, the present book has sought to show how the forms of world poetics enthusiastically destabilize and disintegrate the stale notion that the
colonial abyss is *all* that there is.

Inasmuch as it seeks to understand how worlds are made with words,
this work has been prefigured in the concerns and strategies of the so-
called writing cultures movement. More of a disciplinary attitude than
a movement as such, the group of anthropologists that later became as-

sociated with that name shared a concern with anthropological entextualization. In this regard, I was stunned to find in the first pages of James Clifford's *Predicament of Culture* the extended analysis of William Carlos Williams's poem "To Elsie." The poem helps to stage Clifford's main claims about the compositionality of experience, the political stakes of exposition, and the aesthetics of intercultural contact. But he does not mention why a poem, in particular, should lead the examination of such issues. If Glissant is indeed correct that our methods are "not innocent," inasmuch as they "accustom the mind to apprehending problems" in a certain way, it is essential to consider what the formal specificity of the poem offers to Clifford's analysis. More recent work by anthropologists working in the object-immersive mode of "fictocriticism"—that is, the mode in which a writer reckons *in* the reality of the world they set out to describe, "giving oneself over to a phenomenon rather than thinking about it from above" (Taussig, *Nervous* 10)—gives a finer tuning to the resonance of poetics in the intercultural composition. Such thinking emerges in the works of such anthropologists as Michael Taussig, Kathleen Stewart, and Alphonso Lingis, who access the interior of worlds by way of the compositionality of words. And in their compositions the key strategy is a frictional calibration (calibration within intercultural frictions and flows) that is a kind of rhythm. Yet they do not write poetry or discuss poetry as such. It is important to do so because poetry is the art of rhythm, and rhythm is the form of time when time must organize its heterogeneity. The intercultural composition is therefore a rhythmic effort in its attempt to apprehend and inhabit the living and conflicting temporalities of worlds in the plural (within what Glissant might have called their *Créolité*, but which is specified here as a more consciously anthropological project and problematic).[1] In poetry *as such*, that rhythmic effort presents itself still more boldly because a poem not only represents an event but also brings that event into a persistently present moment. Intercultural rhythms and world echoes are afforded the possibility of a present life when staged within what poet and anthropologist Renato Rosaldo calls "the ambition of poetry [which] is indeed 'to *be* the event itself'" (102). This ambition is lined in the very form of poetic language, making it so that a study of poetics is effectively a study of the forms, rhythms, and temporal measures of a world. The power of Clifford's presentation of Williams's "Elsie" is that in it her apprehensibility in the ongoing event of the poem refutes (or at least seriously challenges) the sense of "entropic modernity," "endangered authenticities," or "pure products always going crazy" that might be projected upon her (Clifford, *Predicament* 4–5). Her rhythm in the rhythm of the poem begets the possibility for new rhythms, and thus new permutations, mediations, and oppositions.

In his probing study of native poetics, *Trans-Indigenous*, Chadwick Allen offers a view of what such a multi-ontologized poetic formalism might look like—especially in the chapter titled "Pictographic, Woven, Carved." This chapter interprets a poem by Kiowa poet and novelist N. Scott Momaday through the three distinct hermeneutical frameworks of Plains Indian pictography, Diné textile design, and Māori sculpture. Allen's claim is not that Momaday sourced his aesthetic decisions in the poem from these traditions. Instead, with much more emancipatory force, Allen proposes that these traditions offer frameworks by which meaning is given to worlds and, thus, by which the meanings of a poem can be felt and known. Indigenous and minority cultures are not only content for interpretation by way of the theories of white Western men. They are also the framework and form by which interpretation and experience can be had and understood. Calling the absorption of indigenous and minority cultures into mere content a kind of "aesthetic apartheid," he advocates instead "the possibility for appreciation and interpretation of Indigenous literatures informed by multiple, distinct systems of Indigenous aesthetics across tribal, national, geographic, and cultural borders." Allen hastens to add that he is not advocating a pan-indigenous aesthetic. Rather, he is interested in taking seriously the worldviews of distinct indigenous aesthetic systems "as an index of their intrinsic value" as well as "within the contexts of resistance to multiple forms of ongoing colonialism [as] a defiant assertion of enduring cultural and communal distinctiveness" (103, 106). Whereas the intercultural reception of native arts often has negated the value of those aesthetic and semiotic systems, Allen affirms that value by letting these systems bear their own theories on the scene of interpretation. Colonial history does not disappear in his analysis—but neither does it enslave the terms, aims, and ambits of interpretation, critique, and imagination. Native and minority forms also inform the form of world reality.

In allowing for aesthetics to take on world-making, world-framing, and world-breaking force, the present book follows Allen's impetus, which echoes Gloria Anzaldúa's emphasis that "it is vital that we occupy theorizing space, that we not allow white men and women solely to occupy it . . . [because by] bringing in our own approaches and methodologies, we transform that theorizing space" (qtd. in Soja 129). In the pages of this book, I have taken such an approach to poetic objects, striving to allow them to theorize on the situations in which they find themselves and, in recognizing themselves there, to which they give situational definition. My personal relation to this approach aligns itself with fellow Central American scholar Arturo Arias's observation—akin to Anzaldúa's and Allen's—that Central American signs, words, rhythms, and stories are emerging (from a subalternity to which they continue to resist absorption) as a critical inflection for the contemporary hemispheric "theorizing space." Arias discusses the double eccentricity of Central American Americans, at once alienated in the hierarchy of hemispheric Latinidad, which is itself alienated within the racial hierarchy of US national belonging. Yet this is not a point of complaint for Arias. On the contrary, he sees it as an intellectual possibility in "the alternative knowledges generated by exploring this eccentricity" (xvi). In Central American Americans he sees a regionalism in critical apprehension of itself—a critical regionalism—reflecting on the politics and poetics of origins as constellated in Mesoamerican cultural repertoires, shared colonial experiences, pervasive US military intervention, and contemporary diaspora amid devastating poverty and state violence—that is, a "region that has outgrown neither its origins nor its heavy indigenous cultural imprint" (xix).[2] When these regional signs encounter themselves circulating in the United States looking southward, they carry the very contradiction that defines hemispheric belonging. Their "cultural remittances" are a consciousness of contradiction in which the hemispheric space becomes a theorizing space, or an attempt to reckon in and resolve such social contradiction (Juan Flores qtd. in Arias xiii).

My book occupies that space not only in native-to-native circuits of relation but in the movements of indigenous signs and tropes across racial and national boundaries, with special attention to how those bounded categories are altered or eliminated when cast in the distinct aesthetics of the signs themselves. Not wishing to limit itself to a "study of sources"—which was Julia Kristeva's term for what she saw happening to her idea of "intertextuality"—this book concludes by returning to that sharper and more troubled notion of the intertext as the problematic activity of a sign when it interacts with another sign system, perhaps even as its users bring about that interaction unwittingly or blindly (59–60): a conception of the sign that we see in the Quechua concepts of *quilca* and *ayllu*—but also more generally in the emergent natures of unnatural signs. When a person is forced to mark out their meaning amid a stream of changing semiotic regimes, it is not necessarily the case that the sign with more military might behind it conquers. The repertoires of pictography, hieroglyphs, and khipu in contemporary poetics, aesthetics, and jurisgenerative and sociogenerative practices demonstrate how signs and the worlds of their tropes persist. And they persist because they continue to problematize, forcing a reconsideration of social categories, figural logics, disciplinary norms, and even what constitutes objects and situations—aesthetic, political, and otherwise.

Thus, in the pages of this book, the Adornian-Benjaminian dialectical image is transposed into the pictograph, the intractability of colonial conflict into the double nature of hieroglyphic writing, and Foucault's natural sign into the philosophical textures of Andean thread and design. But there are still other sign forms whose occupation of the contemporary "theorizing space" beckons itself and, in many cases, whose theorization is already in place: wampum belts and sashes, totem and ceremonial poles, Pacific Northwest formline design, ceremonial boxes, Andean *tocapus* and *yupanas*, fetishes, button blankets, medicine bundles, winter counts, ledger art, earthworks and modified trees, dance, crests, heraldry, Ainu bark dresses, Chamorro *sainas*, Aotearoa tattoos, oracle bones, calendars, divinatory practices, dream interpretation, Mayan day-keeping practices, textiles, New Guinea *koteka*, archaeoastronomy, sand painting, Aboriginal songlines and dreaming, mandalas, masks, Gunai possum-skin cloaks, ceramics, Inca feather tabards, Santeria and Vodoun altars, banners, rattles, Fon statues and king aprons, Dogon painted stones, Oceanic tapa or barkcloth, and the list could go on.

For instance, in plate 11 is an artwork by the Panamanian American poet and visual artist Roberto Harrison, whose work is influenced by the aesthetics of Kuna molas. Molas are a type of indigenous Panamanian sewn appliqué that characteristically engages with themes and figures of the surrounding world, including the seemingly colonial or capitalist. As literary scholars and anthropologists Dina Sherzer and Joel Sherzer note, the appearance of Western symbols in molas "should not be taken as a sign of acculturation, degeneration, or imminent disappearance of the mola—anything but. In fact, it is part of the lack of fear of novelty and change characteristic of Cuna culture and apparent in ordinary day to day life. . . . Central to Cuna social and esthetic life is the creative and dynamic ability to make foreign, non-Cuna objects, themes, and ideas function in and become part of Cuna culture . . . to transform it into something Cuna, into *Cunaité*" (34; see Taussig, *Mimesis* 131–35, 182–92, 212–35). In Harrison's work, this transformative power is translated into a "bone window interface. escaleras/simbólicas de los borrados" (10). These lines of poetry accompany the drawing in plate 11, whose labyrinth thereby gains a winding path: its radiant lines and colors are the *symbolic stairs of the erased*, a pathway out of disappearance. In Harrison's work, the apparently erased is revealed to be the teeming interface it always already is, giving resonance to his writing and art which itself echoes Kuna worlds, removed yet involved in the sounding of those worlds. Rather than a semiotic or aesthetic system deceased in the transcultured pages of a book, the mola captures the scene of its apparent disappearance with a dynamic configuration. Designed to do so, it lives in Harrison's book with the confidence characteristic of Kuna appliqué.

While a critique of colonial power can never relent (especially when contemporary political life remains so contaminated by colonial legacies of racial and sexual subjugation), the endurance of these signs reveals the imperfection of that power; its contradictions are canalized into the affirmation of worlds other than that singular modernity of the commodity form.

To maintain a critical disposition in such methodology is to be a kind of text positivist; but, in doing that, to affirm the lifeworlds of texts other than the top-down, left-to-right, phonetically entextualized type—with special attention to those living texts that cast what poet and anthropologist Michael Jackson calls the ambiguous "open, complex, and never self-contained" nature of a lifeworld (xi); and which another poet and anthropologist, Robert Bringhurst, in describing the world of Haida mythtellers, calls "form [that] as much as substance, in the mythworld, can and does embody knowledge. . . . The forest of language [that] in its entirety forms an ecology in which ideas feed and hide. . . . The mythworld is structured like a forest or an animal. It wakes and feeds and sleeps and dreams and changes. And it is made of separate parts that live and die. . . . [Poems do] the same. The poems themselves [are] ecological components of the world they describe" (102, 164, 134). These forms of simultaneous attention to worlds and words—the living forest of language in which ideas and feelings feed and hide—require a coordination of anthropology and poetics.

As Ivan Brady notes in a touchstone essay that inspired the title of this afterword, the possibility that words carry worlds was the implicit rationale behind the ethnopoetics project ("Anthropological Poetics" 951–53).[3] Rather than turn to types of "deep hanging out" (Geertz's wry way turning Clifford's own words on him, to critique a certain kind of ethnographic solipsism), ethnopoetics sought to understand how linguistic forms (especially rhythms, syntactical patterns, and other modes of linguistic temporal configuration) inform a variable reality. In the works of Dennis Tedlock, the notion of a world-bearing poetics took on sharp formalistic dimensions: from his first book (*Finding the Center: Narrative Poetry of the Zuni Indians*) to his last (*The Olson Codex: Projective Verse and the Problem of Mayan Glyphs*), Tedlock experimented with the visual presentation of text to convey other kinds of literacies, aesthetics, and semiotic repertoires. Not just oral poetries but pictographs, hieroglyphs, textiles, archaeoastronomy, chirography, daykeeping (Mayan calendrics), and divination informed the form of his investigation and presentation. Each book is an analysis steeped in the shape and measure of linguistic creativity. Therefore, this book finds in Tedlock's work a foundation but it departs from Tedlock's work—and the ethnopoetics project—in its anthropological poetic emphasis on the unevenness, ambiguity, and complex uncontained nature of worlds, especially in their temporalization. Rather than hold onto such worlds for scholarly presentation, it wishes to offer entry points into their knowledge, experience, and contradiction by way of poetic form, flow, and friction. Its anthropological impetus is a desire to hear worlds in the chaos they carry inside, and the echo in which we resonate in encountering them.

From a similar viewpoint, anthropologist Paul Stoller remarks how poetics necessitates itself in the anthropological project. He quotes Roy Wagner: "'A Cartesian scientist aims to discover what is there; the surprise of poetics is that it is here. The industries of Cartesian science have labored to make the time of creation interminably long; the surprise of poetics is that it is now. . . .' It is now that anthropologists . . . must return to poetics, to re-center themselves, to confront the challenges of ethnographic subjectivity and representational politics" (qtd. in Greenhouse 28). But Stoller's words remind us as well why anthropology necessitates itself in the poetic project. Without an affirmation of the world-making power of words, a poem such as Whitman's "Mannahatta" can never reach beyond whatever political contagion attaches to its author at any given moment. In spite of Whitman's modernist bombast, the fact remains that the Lenape word *Mannahatta* designates an indigenous orientation for the island. This is more than can be said for most American place naming in its enthusiasm for replacement and supercession (*New York*, for instance). The challenge is not only to see in *Mannahatta* a trace of the foregone but a source of present signifying too—a "surprise of poetics that is now." In Whitman's poem that surprise happens in the fifth line, when we learn that the poem's central object is not exactly an island, but "that word nested in nests of water-bays, superb." "Rich, hemm'd thick all around with sailships and steamships" (585), this word presides like an island over the movements and changes that "*function in and become part of*—to adapt Sherzer and Sherzer's words—that word "Mannahatta." In that word—"musical, self-sufficient"—is the ambition to be the event itself, a structure of feeling and thought by which to perceive hemispheric continuity and change.

The ambition to be the event itself is not the *end* of the problem of intercultural knowledge and feeling; it is the entry point to it. When that entry point is found in the world-bearing fragments of a ruinous archive, its contradictions necessarily create a theorizing space: how, it forces us to ask, is the fragment totalizable? How is *its* now *now*? In such questions are inherent resistances. They resist what Bertolt Brecht—one of Benjamin's preferred poets—describes as the danger of unalterable nature:

"Let nothing be called natural/In an age of bloody confusion/Ordered disorder, planned caprice,/And dehumanized humanity, lest all things/ Be held unalterable" (qtd. in Taussig, *Shamanism* 466). The anthropological necessity of the signs of the Americas is their world poetics by which our worlds remain interminably unmade.

NOTES

Preface

1. "Sign: Structure" and "the temporal is no more than symbol" are written in works of art that appear in Pérez-Oramas's *Arcadian Modern* (54). The second statement is written in Catalan, a native language for Torres-García alongside Spanish, as his father immigrated to Montevideo, Uruguay, from the town of Mataró in the province of Barcelona, Catalonia.

2. This work has been authenticated by Cecilia de Torres and is currently in the process of being included in the Online Catalogue Raisonné of Joaquín Torres-García.

Introduction

1. Sapir presented this idea anecdotally, suggesting that linguistics—like physics in his day—was undergoing a quantal shift: "Have we been talking verse all our lives without knowing it? . . . Verse, to put the whole matter in a nutshell, is *rhythmically self-conscious* speech or discourse. . . . Opening [the book that lies nearest to hand] at random, the first sentence that strikes my eye is: 'uniforms and badges promote brotherhood.' I am convinced that this is meant to be prose. Nevertheless, when I read it many times . . . I gradually find myself lulled in the lap of verse" (Sapir qtd. in Friedrich 28). Poetry is the event in which a language user becomes aware (here, forces themself to become aware) of the indeterminacy of meaning making.

2. Warburg and Nordenskiöld offer their fullest accounts of pictographic writing in their books *Images from the Region of the Pueblo Indians of North America* and *Picture-Writings and Other Documents by Néle, Paramount Chief of the Cuna Indians and Ruben Pérez Kantule, His Secretary*, respectively.

3. Here, Gombrich quotes his own famous *Story of Art* (1950) to make a point about the "illiterate" modality of pictographic communication. It is worth noting that, in that earlier work, he draws on an ecclesiastical distinction between literacy and illiteracy that is tracked (by such authors as Ignace Gelb and John DeFrancis) to an evolutionary timeline for global human development (95, 122). "Painting can do for the illiterate what writing does for those who can read," says Pope Gregory

the Great in the sixth century CE (qtd. in Gombrich, *Story* 95), setting the terms by which nonalphabetical writing is sidelined as a signal outside of present time. This is the timescape that Fabian critiques as "allochronicity" or "denial of coevalness" to the other (ix), and which Foucault further takes to task in his writings about the ecclesiastical "natural sign" in his *Ideas of Order*, and which in the final chapter I reconfigure in terms of a natural sign whose nature it is to always make new natures.

4. Another work of the Warburg-Gombrich school worth considering, in its own light, is Frances Yates's *Art of Memory*. While it also interlocks pictographic inscription into closed relations of icon and memory, it takes into account the distortions that spatial systems enact on those relations. Chapter 2 of the present book explores how those distortions are negotiated in the metonymy of pictographs, that is, how they are enacted as deliberately creative—and not just mnemonic—acts.

5. It should be noted that among the Pueblo communities, with whom he conducted fieldwork, there was a great distrust about disseminating ritual pictography, after anthropologist Elsie Clews Parsons had published pictures of sacred pictographs to the great offense of her informant communities. De Angulo was not interested in repeating the offense: "It is all right to talk about it in a general way, with certain reservations," he writes to Ruth Benedict, "the necessary care that must be always used in handling all esoteric knowledge. It is as powerful and dangerous as the lightning. . . . But the actual details of ceremonies, that must never be told. . . . They have a real, actual meaning and value, as secrets, for the members of the society" (G. de Angulo 247–48). By "a general way" de Angulo means prosody, and he goes on to discuss this prosody as the "chance" and "acrobatic performance" of ritual pictography ("What"). But he does not publish or keep (in his archive) any sacred materials.

6. I draw on the writings of linguist Zoltán Kovecses, who explains that the metonymic shuttle transits specifically from the concrete to the abstract; that is, metonymy occurs when "a more concrete or salient vehicle entity is used to give or gain access to a more abstract or less salient target entity" (176). His comments are of a piece with Jacques Lacan's description of metonymy as a type of linguistic straying, displacement, desiring, and deviation.

7. "The particular meaning articulated at a given moment—i.e., water, wind, journey in search of the Center—depends on the context, the situation, in which that meaning is given voice," writes Young (154), asserting the idea that the semiotics of pictography are contextualized in nonhuman networks. See also Munn (217), K. Kroeber (*Artistry*), and Morrison. Young's point also recalls the important search for centers in Puebloan cosmology (see D. Tedlock's *Finding the Center*, B. Tedlock's *The Beautiful and the Dangerous*, and Severin Fowles's *Archaeology of Doings*).

8. I draw here on Elizabeth Povinelli's concept of geontology, or the life-nonlife distinction, on which such biopolitical segmentations as race are built (*Geontologies*).

9. Anderson's helpful contextual elaboration of the links between indigenous resistance movements and anarchist political philosophy is provided in his *Under Three Flags*.

10. Andrew Schelling's recent biography of de Angulo brings these networks to life, as does the biography written by de Angulo's daughter's, Gui Mayo, about her father, *Old Coyote of Big Sur.*

11. In addition to what is republished in the present book, I have also gathered a larger selection of these materials for the *Chicago Review,* as part of a special issue on Jaime de Angulo and West Coast modernism (Spring 2020).

12. Duncan's full quote also bears the point that de Angulo's sense of gender was ecological: "I think that the transvestite role was certainly keyed to Jaime's constant fascination with what was a shaman. I have a very pronounced pelt on my back and neck, and Jaime told me that I would qualify in the Sur community as a were-bear, and he was fascinated because in my poetry bears had already appeared" (*Poet's* 230). Before hormone therapy changed his body, de Angulo occasionally dressed as a woman to cavort in bohemian circles of San Francisco and Oakland. And for de Angulo these elisions of gender and sex were connected to deeper themes of interspecies metamorphosis and ecological reciprocity, as I examine in chapter 2.

13. Sanjinés is not the only scholar of Bolivia to emphasize the value of Benjamin's writings for understanding the cultural and ontological heterogeneity of the region. Essays by Luis Antezana, Guadalupe Valencia García, and Maya Aguilez Ibargüen that appear in the Bolivian collection *Pluralismo Epistemológico* (published by the editorial collective *Muela del Diablo*), take a similar approach. In his essay appearing in that collection, Antezana further compares the works of Benjamin to those of influential Bolivian politician and philosopher René Zavaleta (whose ideas I explore more closely later in this book) (121).

14. Here, I adapt the words of historian of Mayan mythistory Matthew Restall. But in a broader sense, the centering of North American experimental poetics— particularly Olson's influential "projectivism"—in the semiotics of Mesoamerica gives those poetics fuller exposure in the world system that Guillermo Bonfil Batalla has called "*México profundo,*" José David Saldivar "greater Mexico," and Gordon Brotherston "*Anahuac,*" each of which refers to the transhistorical and transnational impact of classical, colonial, and contemporary Mesoamerican cultures. Heriberto Yépez's controversial polemic against Olson's entry to "greater Mexico" misconstrues this entry as absolutely imperialistic, in that Yépez misses the important point that while Olson might have invaded *México profundo,* *México profundo* invaded North American experimental poetics as well by way of Olson.

15. For instance, in figures 5 and 6 Olson can be seen to engage with the thirteenth-century *Dresden Codex*—which survived the Allied firebombing of Dresden in 1945, and which is the oldest extant book of the Americas (made in Yucatan). (Olson's version in figure 6 engages with the original glyph from the *Dresden Codex* in figure 5.) Its antiquity resonated contemporary possibilities for Olson: the codex's the seahorse-human-god amalgam glyph shown here, which in his *Mayan Letters* he called its "fish glyph," evidenced social and ecological kinships that totalitarianism could not achieve and that transnational capital (in Yucatan and Gloucester, Massachusetts) was poised to destroy.

Chapter 1

1. For a more extensive analysis of Marx's ethnographic engagements, see Kevin Anderson's *Marx at the Margins*.

2. Diana Taylor notes that sixteenth-century Nahuatl conceptions of representation, *ixiptlatl* in Nahuatl, connoted constructedness and transmission, so that Quetzalcoatl's "representation" or transmission in Spaniard bodies would have been a familiar "making/unmaking" of embodied performance (38–39): as it were, an image and a spokesperson that embodies that image. I discuss this in greater length below.

3. The necessity for scaling down to "counterplots" is—as Nash puts it in her analysis of the relationship between the discipline of anthropology and world system theory—twofold: "1. the outcome of [a world systems approach] seems predictable in the model, and 2. the mobilization of counterforces is doomed to failure [in that model]." Therefore, she adds, "it is precisely for that reason that the anthropological quest for cultural diversity should be pursued" ("Ethnographic Aspects" 408).

4. Linda Tuhiwai-Smith, Margaret Kovach, and Shawn Wilson argue that indigenous stories, music, art, and metaphor are ontological repertoires or "quintessentially intersubjective activity that brings the social into being" (Jackson, *Politics* 16). My point in this chapter is that poetic form is also a world-making repertoire.

5. Nash draws on the writings of Ulf Hannerz for her concept of the "global ecumene." Yet, whereas Hannerz sees it as a multisited proliferation of a homogeneous globality (haunted, perhaps, by the ghosts of Lévi-Strauss), Nash sees it as a messier heterogeneous process with multidirectional pulls (*Mayan Visions* 221).

6. Shifting scale in this way also affects what the object of criticism will be. A passage from Nash's book encapsulates how a methodological shift in scale affects not only how we see analytical objects but also what objects we choose to observe: "In order to rescue ourselves from what Jean Comaroff and John Comaroff (1992: 37) call the 'vapid theoreticism' derived from 'our current conceptual obsession with agency, subjectivity, and consciousness,' a key to reconnect with the field might be found within postmodernist strategies for developing the 'reflexivity,' 'polyphony,' and 'dialogue' that Steven Sangren (1988) poses as their core values. Recalling an earlier crisis of representation in the eighteenth century that Giambattista Vico bridged with his interpretations of 'pagan' myths in his *Scienza Nuova* (1725, revised 1744), we are turning again to mythopoetic imagery to find insights. Gary Gossen (1999), Nathaniel Tarn (1997), and Dennis Tedlock (1984) are among those interpreters who succeed in imaginatively recreating the Mayan world while drawing on sound ethnographic research of their imagery and metaphors" (*Mayan Visions* 19). The converse problematics that emerge when the anthropologisms of literary studies are amplified are examined in the present book's afterword.

7. As I suggest, the concept of subsumption extends from the problematic of primitive accumulation to contemporary sociogenerative cultural practices, and it gives temporal characteristics to what Carl Schmitt called "political theology." The friars' demands on the Aztec priests exemplify how the exploitation administered

by the church translated itself, without much secularization, into the political theology of global capitalism administrated by the state (especially in the homologous subjectivization of personal body to Christ and state).

8. Sahagún composed his *Coloquios* at the library of the first European university in the Americas, the Colegio de Santa Cruz de Tlatelolco, which was built on the site of a *calmecac*, an Aztec institute of learning for its elites. A core rationale for founding the Colegio in 1536 was to assimilate these scions in the European way of seeing and making the world. It was not enough to merely religiously convert the Aztecs. The Colegio—and other institutions of its kind in the colonial Americas— sought to integrate indigenous minds in historiography and philology that put Europe at the center. Yet this conversion was rough and incomplete; the Colegio was a site of deep ideological conflict. Walter Mignolo notes that while the "discursive frames" of the Colegio served to "colonize Amerindian languages and memories," they nonetheless conflicted with "the forces of the [indigenous] traditions (both in the content of their memories as well as in the way of remembering and transmitting them)" (*Darker* 203–4). Sahagún relied on these very students for help in reconstructing the events of the conquest and the cultural richness of the world that preceded it, as he documents at length in his *General History of the Things of New Spain* (also known as the Florentine Codex). Considering that he interacted with students on the subject of culture and conquest, one can imagine how the ideological conflict tensioning the Colegio might have further inflected the poetic resistances found in his *Coloquios*—that is, the Aztec priests' reply.

9. I draw on Erving Goffman's conception of framework in my claim that the poetic markers stage a particular genre, which itself arrives with institutional norms (21).

10. While such dis-identification resonates with what Walter Benjamin characterized as dialectic in standstill and Theodor Adorno as negative or interminable dialectic (both effectively drawing on Hegel's concept of "determinate negation"—the classic Western Marxist use of Hegel as method rather than content), here I bracket the Frankfurt critical theorists to foreground the alternative origination of such ideas in Nahuatl and Mesoamerica philosophy. For closer analysis of such parallelist philosophy in contemporary Nahuatl cultures, see Taggart (55–66). And for the same in relation to contemporary Mayan cultures, see Hull and Carrasco (esp. 339–476).

11. Dorn uses the same poetic strategy in conveying the cultural distance and human nearness of the Apache people in his epic of Geronimo and the Apache Wars, *Recollections of Gran Apacheria*: "the winde driving the wild fire of their loyalties/and in the cruel vista/I can see the Obdurate Jewell/of all they wanted, shining/without a single facet/upon our time/and yet the radiance marks everything/ as we unweave this corrupted cloth" (*Collected Poems* 370). I return to this point in the chapter's conclusion.

12. As I have noted, Taylor suggests that sixteenth-century Nahuatl conceptions of representation (*ixiptlatl*) connoted constructedness and transmission, so that Quetzalcoatl's "representation" or transmission in Spaniard bodies would have been a familiar "making/unmaking" of embodied performance (38–39)—or, as I have argued here, a concept with a conception of its own mediality. Building on

this idea of mediality (or sense of removable skin or husk embedded in the particle root of the word—*xip*) in the Nahuatl word *ixiptla*, contemporary visual artist Mariana Castillo Deball has edited a journal of artistic anthropological mediations of Mesoamerica named *Ixiptla*—a journal that examines the skins, husks, and masks of anthropology and their artistic potential.

13. The interwoven pronouns in Nahuatl are the second-person plural object pronoun (*amech*) to refer to the friars, the second-person singular pronoun (*ti-*) to refer to Quetzalcoatl, and the blending of alternative second-person plural and singular pronouns (*ami* and *xi-*) in the line "*ca ami xiplava, amjipatilloa*" ("because you are made in his image, his representation"). The sense of the alternative pronouns used in the final line is akin to the English-language pronoun "you," which makes no distinction between the singular and plural second person. The interweaving of pronouns in the line, which has the effect of eliding its second-person plural and second-person singular, in effect weaves the friars into the representational tapestry that is Tezcatlipoca-Quetzalcoatl.

14. Gérard Genette describes metaleptic transit as transgression: as the "intrusions [that] disturb . . . the distinction between levels" (88). He suggests that metaleptic figures disrupt the stratigraphic boundary between words and worlds, between meanings and events, and thus collapse the linguistic thresholds of existential orders. Drawing on Genette's view that poetic tropes and ontological orders become indistinguishable in practice, Brian McHale and Werner Wolf analyze metalepsis as a theorem of possible worlds. John Pier provides the overview of these analyses from which I draw my citations.

15. There is a debate as to whether it is Tonatiuh in the middle of the Aztec sunstone, or *Piedra de Sol*, also called the Calendar Stone. David Stuart summarizes this debate in a post for his scholarly blog, *Maya Decipherment*, as follows: Carlos Navarrete and Doris Heyden argue that the face represents the Living Earth, Tlalteuctli; Cecilia Klein argues that it represents the Night Sun, Yohualteuctli; and Stuart argues that it represents the Mexica ruler at the time of the Spanish invasion, Moctezuma II. Because the Tonatiuh interpretation (made by Eduard Seler and Herman Beyer) would have been the one available to Dorn, and is still the best known, I align my interpretation with it. But I note that, in spite of the debates, the idea of world ages as represented by moving suns is consistent in each interpretation. The referent of the face is always subordinate to the disc's use as a calendar, that is, a temporal diagnostic of solar movement and entropy.

16. For this deciphering I thank Sky Russell, majoring in physics and architecture at Harvard University, who helped me to crack the code of Dorn's drawing and offered enlightening notes about CNO cycles.

17. Brotherston explains the rationale for comparing the Aztec and Mayan cosmogonies: "the *Sunstone* of Tenochtitlan and the *Popol vuh* of Quiché complement each other in affirming the shape of Mesoamerican cosmogony, one that has its literary roots in the pre-Cortesian books, encompasses the main languages of the region—Nahuatl, Maya, Otomanguan—and remains an important political element in the lives of native people today. Availing itself of the resources of native

script to produce an ingenious visual statement of five Suns in one, the *Sunstone* actually shows how deeper levels of time may inhere in the present (the four humiliations remembered by the maize people) and employs *tonolamatl* Numbers and Signs to suggest not just their story but their rhythms and phases in time, again like the *Popol vuh*" (Brotherston 244–45). Arias also gives a compelling and related rationale for the regional coherence of a Mesoamerican cultural complex (xvii).

Chapter 2

1. I offer a closer study of Anishinaabe petroglyphs in the next chapter of this book. Here, I look forward to that chapter by introducing the idea that petroglyphs make their meaning in relation to the landscape in which they exist.

2. While it is beyond the scope of the present work, it is important to note that as enmeshed as this institutional mandate was in the nationalistic program of American pluralism, it spawned a scholastic desire for difference that blighted encounters with indigenous societies as mere data collections of "the other" (Deloria, *Custer* 78–100; Biolsi and Zimmerman) in the works of various—but, needless to say, not all—cultural anthropologists.

3. For examples of the trope of the mythic prehuman animal people in native California, see *Surviving Through the Days*, a collection edited by Herbert Luthin. Andrew Schelling notes that in addition to his fieldwork one of de Angulo's most important sources for imagining this prehuman animal world was the *Annikadel* myth as told by Istet Woiche to C. Hart Merriam (Woiche and Merriam; Schelling, private correspondence). The theme is also emphasized in Robert Bringhurst's *A Story as Sharp as a Knife: The Classical Haida Mythtellers and their World*. Anthropologist Eduardo Viveiros de Castro provides a theoretical analysis of cosmologies in which animal people precede human people in "Exchanging Perspectives"; see also his "Cosmologies: Perspectivism" (in *Cosmological Perspectivism*) and "Some Reflections on the Notion of Species in History and Anthropology"; see also Philippe Descola's *Beyond Nature and Culture*.

4. In his biography of de Angulo, Andrew Schelling gives a vivid account of this singing session (98–102), with special attention to what Michael Taussig might call the uses of skepticism and tricks in the magical systems of shamanic healing ("Viscerality"). While Schelling focuses on de Angulo, here I venture a longer historical context for Kate Gordon's song, whose themes seem inextricable from histories of colonial violence in northern California.

5. See Carroll (33–37); Margolin (22–24); Dixon (189–93); Harris Block and Gifford (201–3); Swann (728–36); and Kinkade (270–73).

6. The song is in the Pit River language of Achumawi, not Modoc, because Gordon had been living and healing in the Achumawi community of Alturas when de Angulo participated in the ceremony that he transcribes as both "Pit River Medicine Song" and "Old Kate's Medicine Song."

7. De Angulo's primary sources for knowledge about pictography were conversations with Tony Luhan; Ochwiay Biano (Mountain Lake) aka Antonio Mirabal;

and people from Taos Pueblo, with whom he discussed "the translation of certain powerful elemental forces into safe symbols" (*Jaime* 87–93; qtd. in G. de Angulo 226–37). Yet, as mentioned in the introduction, de Angulo was sensitive to the sacred nature of the symbols. Unlike "[Frank Hamilton] Cushing [who] killed Zunyi," he writes, "or [Elsie Clews] Parsons [who was] doing her best to kill Santo Domingo" by publishing the secrets of those tribes, de Angulo discerned that the secrets "have a real, actual meaning and value, as secrets, for the members of the society." When he wrote about pictography or invoked the semiotics of the pictograph for his creative work, he did so, as he puts it, "in a general way, with certain reservations," careful that his poetic reflections not expose "the actual details of ceremonies" (qtd. in G. de Angulo 92, 93).

8. The concept of mythistory recalls Lévi-Strauss's idea that the character of myth is to evoke a dialectic between structure and history—a "mythological history" or "animated structuralism": "Is it not the character of myths . . . to evoke a suppressed past and to apply it, like a grid, upon the present in the hope of discovering a sense in which the two aspects of his own reality man is confronted with—the historic and the structural—coincide?" (qtd. in Taussig, *Devil* 161, 227). In distinguishing mythistory from Lévi-Strauss's conception of myth, my point is to specify a type of mythological thinking within the plurality of possible systems in that nonsingular, historically dynamic, and formally diverse body of thought that is world poetics. But, to give credit where credit is due, Lévi-Strauss recognized the criticality and intellectuality of mythical thinking, and thus made possible the study of myth as poetics, philosophy, and theory (see Paz, *Claude*).

9. In chapter 5, I examine Victor Turner's ideas about the ritual use of dominant symbols—particularly as they connect to Edith Turner's writings on "*communitas*," or the social unity that the act of protecting dominant symbols provides. My entry point to that idea is Taussig's writings on shamanism which I interpret as necessarily engaged with the dominant symbol of whiteness that the shaman must derange, disaggregate, de-homogenize, and pluralize into states of signification undisciplined by the purity of racial wholeness.

10. My implicit point here is that such worlds have specific features. If these are beings of metamorphosis, they are not of the unqualified, semi-Hegelian sort to which Bruno Latour opposes ideologies of reproduction in his *Inquiry into Modes of Existence* (202–5). I am concerned with particular colonial contexts and the cultures that configure them, even as such configuration at times takes on Hegelian themes or patterns (e.g. the comparability of *inamic* pairs and determinate negation in chapter 1).

11. These are Duncan's words, remembering de Angulo's conceptions of gender: "Hidden in what we view as disorders of bestiality or fetishism is the suggestion of a polymorphic sexuality that operates in more than two genders. Male and female, Jaime de Angulo once enlightened me, are only arbitrary genders. Gender has to do with what you are permitted and not permitted to fuck. Moose, fox, pine tree and ocean might also be genders. Thus in such a language, you could fuck your mother, your nude, a dog, or fall in love with a tree, providing each was of the right

gender: if your mother was 'fox,' nude 'fox,' the said dog 'fox,' and tree 'fox' in gender" (Duncan, "Aug 1 1969"). The idea that gender involves nonhuman bodies and forms is a persistent theme in Duncan's memories of de Angulo, and thus bears repeating: "I think that the transvestite role was certainly keyed to Jaime's constant fascination with what was a shaman. I have a very pronounced pelt on my back and neck, and Jaime told me that I would qualify in the Sur [Indian] community as a were-bear, and he was fascinated because in my poetry bears had already appeared" (Duncan, *Poet's* 230). De Angulo's influential role in shaping Duncan's thought and aesthetic is beyond the scope of this chapter. While Duncan's biographers gesture at the significance that de Angulo had in Duncan's life, each limits the place of de Angulo to three short pages (Faas 282–85; Jarnot 115–18). I hope with this chapter to make broader analysis of that relationship possible for future researchers. There are places in Duncan's poetry where de Angulo's ideas are amplified. One is the poem "An Essay at War" [1950] (*Collected Early* 381–96). Another is the more subtle prose poem "Source": "And vast as the language is, it is no end but a resistance thru which the poem might move—as it flows or dances or puddles in time—making it up in its going along and yet going only as it breaks the resistance of the language.//When I was about twelve—I suppose about the age of Narcissus—I fell in love with a mountain stream. There, most intensely for a summer, staring into its limpid cold rush, I knew the fullest pain of longing. To be of it, entirely, to be out of my being and enter the Other clear impossible element. The imagination, old shape-shifter, stretcht painfully to comprehend the beloved form" [1954] (*Letters* 671–72). Still another avenue for further research would be de Angulo's relationship as instructor in linguistics to Jack Spicer, beginning with Spicer's gay-rights poem "An Answer to Jaime de Angulo" [1947] (13).

Chapter 3

1. The quote appears in an interview published by his alma mater, the University of Minnesota: "Up Close with Gerald Vizenor."

2. More recent ethnographies and histories of pictographic writing have emphasized this improvisational feature. See Munn; Young; Brotherston; Davis; Hill Boone and Mignolo; and Severi, *Chimera Principle*.

3. This self-surety is an expression of alphabetical chauvinism or the hegemonic metaexistence of the alphabet as such (Rama 43–44; Mignolo, *Darker* 127).

4. Vizenor also discusses the relationship between Anishinaabe dream songs and haiku in the introduction to his book of haikus, *Favor of Crows* (xi–xxxv). Barthes's short essay on haiku, "The Incident," appears in *Empire of Signs* (77–80).

5. While Povinelli's subject is different from that of Vizenor and Borrows (and Coulthard)—that is, the politics of recognizing Aboriginal discrimination and difference in the Constitution of Australia—these authors overlap in their concerns with the problem of native political recognition. In being required to request recognition within the framework of colonial governance, Aboriginal people of the Australian continent must make kin with national institutions and authoritative

imaginaries. Yet Povinelli, as well as Vizenor and Borrows, suggests that that act need not result in isomorphic stabilities: the work of cunning, irony, and performative nonisomorphy can signal-jam such interpellations.

6. A more intensively literal version of this idea can be found in the "living pigment" of the Gwion Gwion petroglyphs of Kimberley, Australia—whose synthetic biofilm of the red bacteria and black fungi used to paint them is actually alive (they are thought to have been composed or put into ongoing symbiotic relation at least forty-six thousand years ago). See Pettigrew et al.

Chapter 4

1. For signature studies of interspecies signifying, see Kohn; Tsing; Haraway; Viveiros de Castro.

2. Regarding Mayas and humanhood, Restall notes that the Mayas who met the Spaniards certainly had a conception of humanity, in which they included the Spaniards: "Mayas saw the Spaniards as fellow human beings, not as gods to be admired, demons to be feared, or dogs to be disdained; the invaders, like the natives, earned admiration, fear, or disdain on an individual basis" (39). As Restall adds, the significant difference between Mayan and Spaniard conceptions of the human is that—for the former—the human was not attached to a taxonomy of racial subjugation.

3. Byron Ellsworth Hamann gives a detailed study of how the Mayan sign system came to be closely associated with Egyptian hieroglyphs in his "How Maya Hieroglyphs Got Their Name."

4. Regarding the tumpline's denotation of bundled time, J. Eric S. Thompson—a leading scholar of Mayan glyphs in the mid-twentieth century (whom Olson read)—wrote, "The Maya concept of time was something which in its broad outlines is not unfamiliar to us, but which in its philosophical aspect reflects a very different mentality. The Maya conceived of the divisions of time as burdens which were carried through all eternity by relays of bearers . . . for time was not portrayed as the journey of one bearer and his load, but of many bearers each with his own division of time on his back" (59). In their multiplicitous system of time Mayas have a conception of time that prefigures (and indeed informs) what I have called here temporal heterogeneity.

5. In an article published in the literary magazine at Black Mountain, Olson theorizes Mayan sculptural faciality as also expressive of the conceptual tension of full-figured glyphs. Supplementing a photo essay of Mayan head sculptures in the *Black Mountain Review*, he writes: "I want to tell you that the language these same people cut into stone was chiefly made up of intervals of the face, human and animal. . . . The signs, I mean. Two things, then: (1) that the face was such a study that it was the meat of the written language, stayed, as our alphabet once was, representative . . . [and] (2), that color: for example, that these all were covered over with paint once, as was every single passage of the writing daubed, with, red" ("Mayan Heads" 27).

6. The Mayan parallelist cosmos or dialectic of nonsynthesizing oppositions is to Mayan poetics of parallelism as *rhusmos* is to *rhuthmos*, the former an embodied configuration of the latter. It is as though Viktor Shklovsky's conception of parallelist poetry were taken to be the lifeworld that, in many cultures that are characterized by parallelist poetry, it is: "the perception of disharmony in a harmonious context is important in parallelism. The purpose of parallelism, like the general purpose of imagery, is to transfer the usual perception of an object into the sphere of a new perception—that is, to make a unique semantic modification" (220). What poetic parallelism sets out to reveal is that objects are not selfsame, that they are continuously self-differencing, and that this self-differencing is worth marking out because it gets at the nature of things.

7. Olson was obsessed with the idea of seafaring Mayas, arguing that maize alone could not have provided the adequate protein for sustaining such civilizational growth (i.e., they needed fish as a food supply). Incidentally, he is indebted to Carl Sauer and certain strains of contemporaneous Marxist anthropology (especially Soviet) for such protein-count civilizational growth paradigms (see Bloch). While he failed to appreciate that the Mesoamerican treatment of maize in lye increases its nutritional value (a process called nixtamalization, which creates hominy), he was more perceptive than most scholars at the time in simply noticing the oceanic iconography in Mayan culture. Scholars of the midcentury largely denied the possibility of seafaring Mayas. Restall's vivid description of Mayan seaports and oceanic trade and migrations shows how far the scholarship has come, and in many ways how canny Olson was in his unorthodox observations (Restall 22).

8. Olson's excitement about K'uk'ulkan's association with writing is expressed in a letter to Creeley: "I remain wholly fascinated that K's [K'uk'ulkan's] reputation was not the invention of maize, calculations of Venus, or the hieroglyphic system (which, wld seem, any one of them, to be sufficient reason for the arising of a humanistic god-figure. . . . K's reputation (he comes late, as 1st HUMAN god) was something else: WRITER, actually—or so the hints seem to be, that, he made Maya language & astronomy available to *others*" (Olson and Creeley 67). K'uk'ulkan both invented language and symbolized its uses. He was the first writer and god of writing present at every scene of writing (Séjourné). See also chapter 1 of the present book, in which I explore the relationship between the Nahuatl K'uk'ulkan (Quetzalcoatl) and Tezcatlipoca in the creation of language, as manifest in Edward Dorn's poetry, translations, and visual art.

9. French symbolism, surrealism, and modernism had its own trans-Atlantic encounters with Mesoamerican glyphs. Guillaume Apollinaire's calligram "*Lettre-Océan*" translates the Aztec sunstone into a set of messages sent via telegram from Mexico across the Atlantic Ocean to France. It ends: "*Tu ne connaitras jamais bien les Mayas*" ("You will never know the Mayas well"), teasing readers while giving them a taste of the visual and textual amalgamations of Mayan glyphs (143). Similarly, late symbolist playwright and poet Antonin Artaud—who documented his experiences with the Tarahumara or Rarámuri people of northwestern Mexico in his *Voyage to the Land of the Tarahumara*—described the glyphs as a multidimensional

semaphore, a sign that amalgamates image, text, gesture, and sensation: "These actors with their geometric robes seem to be animated hieroglyphs. . . . [O]nce aware of this language in space, language of sounds, cries, lights, onomatopoeia, the theater must organize it into veritable hieroglyphs, with the help of characters and objects, and make use of their symbolism and interconnections in relation to all organs and on all levels. . . . To know the points of localization in the body is thus to reforge the material chain. And through the hieroglyphs of a breath I am able to recover an idea of the sacred theater" (54, 90, 140–41). Mirroring Olson, as well as the hieroglyphic filmmakers of the 1920s and 1930s, Apollinaire and Artaud caught glimpses of the semiotics of the glyphs by means of an aesthetic approach to their interpretation. Focusing on the glyphs as aesthetic objects, these poets and filmmakers discerned how the sign system was impacted by visual design. Another such hieroglyphic poet whose name bears mentioning, but whose reworkings of the glyphs are beyond the scope of this book, is American anthropologist, linguist, translator, and poet R. H. Barlow. Barlow's method took hold at the intersection of linguistics (he was chair of the department of anthropology at Mexico City College) and H. P. Lovecraft–influenced gothic symbolism. During this chairmanship in the 1940s, he published prodigiously on Mesoamerican codices, maps, and languages, while also writing a rhizomatic poetry: "field sprouted/with several kinds of flower/& a mushroom/N., N.E., E., S.E.;/spokes of grass/rimmed with a/(1.) red beetle sawing his tongue through trunks of violets/(2.) palaeontology of sparrow bones/(a.) their hilts/(b.) their shafts/(3.) arabic of a tunnel written underground. Feelers dodged into dark" ([1947] 184). Barlow's aesthetic attention to the glyphs appealed to experimental writers. William Burroughs took classes with him at MCC while avoiding his prison sentence in Louisiana. And Olson— who praised Barlow's aesthetic approach or "combination that of documentarian & selectivity of the creative taste & mind"—intended to meet him there too. But Barlow killed himself (at the young age of thirty-two) before he could see the impact that Mayan glyphs would have on the poetry of the twentieth century. Olson mourned his death as "very much of a loss . . . to all contemporary America" (*Letters* 28).

Chapter 5

1. While "analepsis" is a word typically used to denote "flashback," I use the term to encompass the various practices of making and managing discontinuous time—a form of both "*ameipsirhusmein*" (changed configuration of time or changed "*rhusmos*") and "*ameipsikosmie*" (world change) (Most 223). These terms are reconfigured in chapters 4 and 6 by Javier Sanjinés's translation of Quechuan *pachakuti* (world reversal) and *lloqlla* (world avalanche) (33, 32).

2. Here Taussig writes about the relation of Benjaminian montage to Amazonian poetics of disorganization. Benjamin explores the tension in his writings between linguistic convention and natural language in his essay, "On Language as Such and the Language of Man," where he twists argumentative positions into

highly montaged sentences (amplifying the tension between the argumentative positions so as to break them into analytical rupture points): "There is a language of sculpture, of painting, of poetry. Just as the language of poetry is partly, if not solely, founded on the name language of man, it is very conceivable that the language of sculpture or painting is founded on certain kinds of thing-languages, that in them we find a translation of the language of things into an infinitely higher language, which may still be of the same sphere. We are concerned here with nameless, nonacoustic languages, languages issuing from matter; here we should recall the material community of things in their communication" (*Selected Writings* 1:73). In this intentional intensifying of the incommensurable contradiction between positions, twisted into the same sentence, Benjamin prefigures the poetic strategy by which Taussig sheds light on shamanic poetics of Putumayo and which the present chapter focalizes through the border techniques of Burroughs and Anzaldúa.

3. In addition to its rapid translation into the major European languages— English (1698), French (1699), Dutch (1699), and Spanish (1701)—an extract of Brand's German-language work was translated by Leibniz into Latin and included in his compendium on Asia, *Novissima Sinica* (1697). The Latin translation would have given the work its widest circulation among European intelligentsia of the time, as well as a heightened scholarly legitimacy in such circles.

4. For a fuller elaboration of Benjamin's "state of exception," see chapter 2 of the present book.

5. I draw, as does Taussig, on anthropologists Edith Turner's and Victor Turner's writings on *communitas*. As the Turners described it, *communitas* is a sense of social unity that emerges from the act of protecting dominant symbols (*Image* 254–55; E. Turner, "Communitas" 143–49). The purported purity of such symbols as milk, blood, semen, maleness, whiteness, or homeland creates the conditions for policing divisiveness, heterogeneity, aberrance, and undesirables in a social group. Taussig's yagé nights cut against such states of shrinking and policeable belonging by disaggregating the basic unity of symbols.

6. Taussig also mentions this feature of the yagé *pintas*, calling them the "cities of Yagé." Likewise, in a letter to Allen Ginsberg, Burroughs reveals that he had been prepared to see such cityscapes by the shamans—whom in actual terms of urban real estate he calls "brokers": "Incidentally you are supposed to see a city when you take Yagé" (qtd. in Taussig, "Cities of Yagé" 122).

7. In the 1930s, Malinowksi and British social anthropology were in high regard in US academia (especially as an alternative to Boasian cultural anthropology). Malinowski held various academic appointments in the United States, and the "direct influence of British Functionalism" could be seen in the appointments of Malinowski at Yale, Alfred Radcliffe-Brown at Chicago, and British-functionalist trained W. Lloyd Warner at Harvard. Malinowski was awarded an honorary doctorate at Harvard at its tercentenary celebration in 1936, on which occasion he delivered an address about his work (Stocking, *Ethnographer's Magic* 131). Considering the chronology, it is possible that Burroughs was present at this lecture.

8. One passage from Anzaldúa's *Borderlands* that brings Schmidt Camacho's reading to light is: "As a *mestiza*, I have no country, my homeland casts me out; yet all countries are mine because I am every woman's sister or potential lover. (As a lesbian I have no race, my own people disclaim me; but I am all races because there is the queer of me in all races.) I am cultureless because, as a feminist, I challenge the collective cultural-religious male-derived beliefs of Indo-Hispanics and Anglos" (80-81).

9. For an evocative description of such disciplinary policing and the countervailing work of transgressing those norms at the edges of a discipline, see Clifford (*Edges* 8-12).

10. The drawing also depicts a descent to the underworld pool of images. With regard to the psychogeography of such an underworld journey or *katabasis*, Anzaldúa writes: "There's always a monster in the cave . . . the deeper you go, the sharper its fangs. If you don't find a way in it will find a way out" (*Light* 98). She thus suggests that the pool of images is also a kind of monster. As Donna Haraway notes, "monsters have the same root as to demonstrate; monsters signify," and what they uniquely signify is "the limits of community in Western imaginations" (Haraway 117, 37). Congruent with Edith Turner's conception of *communitas* as a body policed by dominant signifiers, Anzaldúa's and Haraway's sense of the monstrous reveals the work that such liminal creatures do in organizing national and state formations. In this way as well, the cave symbolizes an ideological borderland through which she must cross—and a monster she must confront (in counterritual)—to break the spell of the racial order of US *communitas*.

11. Brown similarly writes, quoting Nietzsche: "This past cannot be redeemed *unless* the identity ceases to be invested in it, and it cannot cease to be invested in it without giving up its identity as such, thus giving up its economy of avenging and at the same time perpetuating its hurt—'when he then stills the pain of the wound *he at the same time infects the wound*'" (73).

Chapter 6

1. Lippard and de Zegher's essays appear in Vicuña's book *QUIPOem/The Precarious*. It is a unique object, inasmuch as it is two books presented in opposite directions: one side is paginated with the numbers given for Lippard and de Zegher's essays, and the other side is paginated with q.pp format (a designation that I follow in this chapter).

2. First, Andromache is orphaned at Thebes, which Achilles sacks while killing her father; then, saved by Hector, she is again dispossessed when the Achaeans sack Troy and Achilles kills her Trojan spouse.

3. A *yupana* is visible alongside a khipu in the lower-left corner of figure 8 in the present book's introduction. This image from the Quechua nobleman Felipe Guaman Poma de Ayala's famous intercultural, colonial-era (ca. 1615) chronicle of the Americas reminds its readers of the relationship between the checkerboard system and the knot writing.

4. Brokaw suggests that ideas of reciprocity were embedded in khipu media aesthetics because khipu was dedicated to "handling the intricate relationships involved in community-level administration . . . quadripartite division, *ceque* system, dual organization of authority . . . [and] the details of the communal administration at the local *ayllu* and moiety levels" (*History* 89). He uses the term *ayllu* to denote "the local economies of Andean communities," distinguishing the "principles of reciprocity" in those communities with the Quechua word *ayni*. Yet these two elements (*ayllu* and *ayni*) are inextricable in every instance: khipu carries concepts of social reciprocity (*ayni*) by way of its association with the local economic organization of *ayllus*—economic organizations that in turn depend on principles of reciprocity or mutual interdependence (like threads in a weaving) perceptible in the khipu. To return to the logic of *quilca*: *ayni* is *ayllu* in action, as a painting is paint painted or khipu is thread threaded.

5. Anthropologist Roy Wagner has developed the concept of fractal personhood (to which I allude here) to describe such relational reciprocities. In her gloss of *ayllu*, de la Cadena compares Wagner on fractal persons to Oxa's description of *ayllu*: "never a unit standing in relation to an aggregate, or an aggregate standing in relation to a unit, but always an entity with relations integrally implied" (Wagner qtd. in de la Cadena 44). Both Wagner and Oxa emphasize the impossibility of fragmentation in fractal personhood, in which seeming fragments are implicitly related to a whole from which they gain their meaning and form.

6. Foucault spoke of his debt to Nietzsche as interpreted by Klossowski in the 1957 *Collège Philosophique* lecture "Nietzsche, Polytheism, and Parody"—which Gilles Deleuze characterizes as a watershed in the contemporary study of Nietzsche—and in such essayistic fantasies as *Diana at her Bath* (1956) and *The Baphomet* (1965). With respect to Klossowski's antiecclesiastical conception of the sign (see below), it is worth noting that this French writer (descended from Polish petty nobility, whose older brother was the modernist painter Balthus) was an associate of the Collège de Sociologie and attempted to reconcile a search for the sacred in seminary education, before turning finally to studies and translations of Nietzsche and others, as well as to painting and the writing of novels.

7. Haitian anthropologist Michel-Rolph Trouillot describes the colonial project in terms of "continuous creation." The effort of erasing that which preceded and subtends the colony is a constant effort of creation because that which subtends has not gone away. Therefore, to control the past is to control its everyday making in the present. This involves more than just "summoning representations of what happened." It is a stringing together of "positions" in relation to strategic "pastness." To be effective, the constant effort of creating a past cannot be challenged by the creativity of competing pasts and historicities—colonial power must decidedly control a "single-sided historicity" (4, 4–16). To possess creative agency in relation to one's past is thus to countermand colonial mnemonics.

8. Another resource for thinking about the heterogeneous temporalities of analepsis is the work of Robert Graves. Graves claimed to have recovered lost mythologies and historical memories by immersing himself in the prosody and rhythms

of those myths and times. This mythopoetic method, which indeed he called an "analeptic method"—in which objects were recovered by the "historical grammar of the language of poetic myth"—allowed for the "intuitive recovery of forgotten events by a deliberate suspension of time" (qtd. in Woodrow Presley 167). In Benjaminian sentences, he explained that such temporal leaps were made possible by the "riverwise" effects of poetic rhythm (something that the "prose men" could not understand)—rhythm which he also called a "wibble-wobble" and "stream/ of discontinuity" (qtd. in Kohli 55, 56). Influenced by the writings of the interwar English philosopher of time (and proponent of a theory of precognition) J. W. Dunne, Graves understood time to be a kind of gelatinous mass, through which the vibrations of causes and effects could move in every direction. Such an image of time as a block of wobbling jelly is analogous to the idea of time as a fabric of interpenetrated threads, in which activity on one thread of the fabric pulls on the other intersected threads, constituting a tensile whole that responds to movement across the grid. I have called such a grid "mythistory" in previous chapters, but Vicuña imagines it as a weaving. Her weaving most certainly carries ideas of multidirectional movement in time that Graves calls a "wibble-wobble." Yet Graves alienates himself from discussion here because of his investments in a possible purification of poetic language, whereby (influenced by a particular reading of J. G. Frazer's *The Golden Bough*) he insisted that true poetry is worship of what he called the "White Goddess."

9. Bains quotes Maturana in the middle of this passage.

10. Here and throughout I take as standard the classical definition of *kosmos* as an "ordered world," "world order," or "the world inasmuch as it is ordered and arranged" (Most 239).

11. In addition to elaborating the textile aesthetics of Andean abstraction, Paternosto's book goes on to explore the influence of these aesthetics on the formal strategies of such visual artists as Torres-García, Anni Albers, Josef Albers, and Barnett Newman, while showing as well much broader interconnections between indigenous aesthetics and postmodern abstract art.

Afterword

1. These thoughts about the value of rhythm for object-immersive analysis came together for me in a symposium that was organized by Lauren Berlant and Kathleen Stewart at the University of Chicago in 2018. Called "The Soup is On" in reference to Lyotard's distinction between discourses and metadiscourses—the former exemplified by the phrase "the soup is on," and the latter exemplified by the phrase "it's true, the soup is on"—the symposium discussed how (according to Berlant) criticality might be had in the discursive framework of "the soup is on." That is, in what ways does criticality move through its object—not so much capturing it in a metadiscourse but really thinking *through* it, allowing it to bear *its* theories on the act of interpretation? As I suggest here, in my own work such an entry point is found in the rhythm and calibration of varying temporal densities (by which I mean worlds).

2. Arias gives a vivid sense of the indigenous contours of this critical regionalism of Central America, akin to that of the Andes: "Central America is marked by its indigenousness, an indigenousness that has yet to be fully theorized and critically grasped in terms of how, in its marginality, it relates to such other unrecognizable margins as the Garífunas. Nonetheless, in Guatemala alone there are still over twenty-two different Maya groups, and their own rivalries can be fierce. El Salvador has Lencas and Pipiles, who are Nahuatl speakers. Nicaragua has Miskitos, Sumus, and Ramas. Costa Rica had the Chiriquí, Chorotega, and Chibcha, who were culturally closer to the Incas and related to the Rama of Nicaragua. Panama has the Kuna of San Blas. It is clear, then, that to this day the Central American region has outgrown neither its origins nor its heavy indigenous cultural imprint" (xix). Elsewhere in his work, Arias situates the indigenous cultural contours of this critical regionalism in the persistent influence of Mesoamerican cultures, especially the form, structure, and content of the Mayan *Popol Vuh*.

3. The essay develops an idea of "anthropological poetics" that was first put forward in an edited collection of that name in which Wagner's essay appears and to which Stoller's review—both mentioned here—enthusiastically responds.

REFERENCES

Adorno, Theodor. *Critical Models: Interventions and Catchwords*. Translated by Henry Pickford. New York: Columbia University Press, 2005.

Alberts, Thomas Karl. *Shamanism, Discourse, Modernity*. New York: Routledge, 2015.

Alcalay, Ammiel. *A Little History*. Edited by Fred Dewey. Los Angeles: Re:Public/UpSet Press, 2013.

Allen, Catherine J. "When Utensils Revolt: Mind, Matter, and Mode of Being in the Pre-Columbian Andes." *RES: Anthropology and Aesthetics*, no. 33 (1998): 18–27.

Allen, Chadwick. "Productive Tensions: Trans/national, Trans-/Indigenous." In *The World, the Text, and the Indian: Global Dimensions of Native American Literature*, edited by Scott Richard Lyons, 239–56. Albany: State University of New York Press, 2017.

———. *Trans-Indigenous: Methodologies for a Global Native Literary Studies*. Minneapolis: University of Minnesota Press, 2012.

Alurista. *Floricanto en Aztlán*. Los Angeles: Chicano Studies Center, UCLA, 1971.

———. "La Estética Indígena a Través del Floricanto de Nezahualcoyotl." *Revista Chicano Riqueña* 5, no. 5 (1977): 48–62.

———. *Nationchild Plumaroja, 1969–1972*. San Diego: Centro Cultural de la Raza, 1972.

———. "One Bound Journal of Poetry, 1970–1972." Alurista Papers, Collection Accession No. 1984-36, OCLC No. 22717658, Benson Latin American Collection, University of Texas at Austin.

———. *Spik in Glyph?* Houston: Arte Público Press, 1981.

Anderson, Benedict. *Under Three Flags: Anarchism and the Anti-Colonial Imagination*. New York: Verso, 2007.

Anderson, Kevin. *Lenin, Hegel, and Western Marxism: A Critical Study*. Champaign: University of Illinois Press, 1995.

———. *Marx at the Margins: On Nationalism, Ethnicity, and Non-Western Societies*. Chicago: University of Chicago Press, 2016.

Anzaldúa, Gloria. *Borderlands/La Frontera: The New Mestiza*. San Francisco: Aunt Lute Books, 1987.

———. *The Gloria Anzaldúa Reader*. Edited by AnaLouise Keating. Durham, NC: Duke University Press, 2009.

———. *Light in the Dark/Luz en lo Oscuro: Rewriting Identity, Spirituality, and Reality*. Durham, NC: Duke University Press, 2015.

Aparicio, Frances. "On Sub-Versive Signifiers: U.S. Latina/o Writers Tropicalize English." *American Literature* 66, no. 4 (1994): 795–801.

Apollinaire, Guillaume. *Calligrammes*. Paris: J. Touzot, 1984.

Arias, Arturo. *Taking Their Word: Literature and the Signs of Central America*. Minneapolis: University of Minnesota Press, 2007.

Artaud, Antonin. *Theatre and Its Double*. Translated by Mary Caroline Richards. New York: Grove Press, 1958.

Arteaga, Alfred. *Chicano Poetics: Heterotexts and Hybridities*. Cambridge: Cambridge University Press, 1997.

Asad, Talal. "The Concept of Cultural Translation in British Social Anthropology." In *Writing Culture: The Poetics and Politics of Ethnography*, edited by James Clifford and George E. Marcus, 141–64. Berkeley: University of California Press, 1986.

Ascher, Marcia, and Robert Ascher. *The Code of the Quipu: A Study in Media, Mathematics, and Culture*. Ann Arbor: University of Michigan Press, 1981.

Bains, Paul. *The Primacy of Semiosis: An Ontology of Relations*. Toronto: University of Toronto Press, 2006.

Barker, Joanne. *Native Acts: Law, Recognition, and Cultural Authenticity*. Durham, NC: Duke University Press, 2011.

Barlow, R. H. *Eyes of the God: The Weird Fiction and Poetry of R.H. Barlow*. Edited by S. T. Joshi, Douglas A. Anderson, and David E. Schultz. New York: Hippocampus Press, 2002.

Barthes, Roland. "Cy Twombly: Works on Paper." In *The Responsibility of Forms: Critical Essays on Music, Art, and Representation*, 157–76. Translated by Richard Howard. New York: Hill and Wang, 1985.

———. *Empire of Signs*. Translated by Richard Howard. New York: Hill and Wang, 1982.

Batalla, Guillermo Bonfil. *México Profundo: Reclaiming a Civilization*. Translated by Philip A. Dennis. Austin: University of Texas Press, 1996.

Baudelaire, Charles. *The Flowers of Evil*. Edited by Marthiel and Jackson Mathews. New York: New Directions, 1955.

Belting, Hans. *An Anthropology of Images: Picture, Medium, Body*. Princeton, NJ: Princeton University Press, 2011.

Benhabib, Seyla. *The Rights of Others: Aliens, Residents, and Citizens*. Cambridge: Cambridge University Press, 2004.

Benjamin, Walter. *The Arcades Project*. Translated by Howard Eiland and Kevin McLaughlin. Cambridge, MA: Harvard University Press, 1990.

———. *Illuminations: Essays and Reflections*. Translated by Harry Zohn. New York: Schocken Books, 2007.

———. *The Origin of German Tragic Drama*. Translated by John Osborne. New York: Verso, 2009.

———. *Selected Writings*. Vol. 1, *1913–1926*, edited by Marcus Bullock and Michael W. Jennings. Cambridge, MA: Harvard University Press, 2002.

———. *Selected Writings*. Vol. 2, pt. 1, *1927–1930*, edited by Michael Jennings, Howard Eiland, and Gary Smith. Cambridge, MA: Harvard University Press, 1999.

———. *Selected Writings*. Vol. 2, pt. 2, *1931–1934*, edited by Michael Jennings, Gary Smith, and Howard Eiland. Cambridge, MA: Harvard University Press, 2005.

———. *Selected Writings*. Vol. 4, *1938–1940*, edited by Howard Eiland and Michael Jennings. Cambridge, MA: Harvard University Press, 2006.

Benn Michaels, Walter. *Our America: Nativism, Modernism, and Pluralism*. Durham, NC: Duke University Press, 1995.

Bennett, Jane. *Vibrant Matter: A Political Ecology of Things*. Durham, NC: Duke University Press, 2010.

Berkeley, George. *The Theory of Vision, or Visual Language, Vindicated and Explained*. 1733.

Berlant, Lauren. "The Subject of True Feeling: Pain, Privacy, and Politics." In *Cultural Pluralism, Identity Politics, and the Law*, edited by Austin Sarat and Thomas Kearns, 49–84. Ann Arbor: University of Michigan Press, 1999.

Bernstein, Charles. *My Way: Speeches and Poems*. Chicago: University of Chicago Press, 1999.

Bilbija, Ksenija, Jo Ellen Fair, Cynthia Milton, and Leigh Payne, eds. *The Art of Truth Telling About Authoritarian Rule*. Madison: University of Wisconsin Press, 2005.

Billitteri, Carla. *Language and the Renewal of Society in Walt Whitman, Laura (Riding) Jackson, and Charles Olson*. New York: Palgrave Macmillan, 2009.

Biolsi, Thomas, and Larry J. Zimmerman, eds. *Indians and Anthropologists: Vine Deloria, Jr., and the Critique of Anthropology*. Tucson: University of Arizona Press, 1997.

Bloch, Maurice. *Marxism and Anthropology*. Oxford: Oxford University Press, 1987.

Bloom, Harold. "Whitman's Image of the Voice: To the Tally My Soul." In *Walt Whitman: Bloom's Modern Critical Views*, edited by Harold Bloom, 91–110. New York: Chelsea House, 2006.

Borrows, John. *Canada's Indigenous Constitution*. Toronto: University of Toronto Press, 2010.

———. *Drawing Out Law: A Spirit's Guide*. Toronto: University of Toronto Press, 2010.

Bost, Suzanne. "Messy Archives and Materials that Matter: Making Knowledge with the Gloria Evangelina Anzaldúa Papers." *PMLA* 130, no. 3 (2015): 615–30.

Brady, Ivan. *Anthropological Poetics*. Lanham, MD: Rowman and Littlefield, 1991.

———. "Anthropological Poetics." In *Handbook of Qualitative Research*, 2nd ed., edited by Norman K. Denzin and Yvonna S. Lincoln, 949–81. Thousand Oaks, CA: Sage, 2000.

Brand, Adam. *A Journal of the Embassy from Their Majesties John and Peter Alexievitz.* D. Brown, 1698. https://archive.org/details/BrandAJournalFromTheMajesties, accessed 22 Dec. 2017.

Brightman, Robert. "Jaime de Angulo and Alfred Kroeber: Bohemians and Bourgeois in Berkeley Anthropology." In *Significant Others: Interpersonal and Professional Commitments in Anthropology.* Edited by Richard Handler, 158–95. Madison: University of Wisconsin Press, 2003.

Bringhurst, Robert. *A Story as Sharp as a Knife: The Classical Haida Mythtellers and Their World.* Madeira Park, BC: Douglas and McIntyre, 2011.

Brokaw, Galen. *A History of the Khipu.* Cambridge: Cambridge University Press, 2010.

———. "Semiotics, Aesthetics, and the Quechua Concept of *Quilca.*" In *Colonial Mediascapes,* edited by Matt Cohen and Jeffrey Glover, 166–202. Lincoln: University of Nebraska Press, 2014.

Brooks, Lisa. "The Constitution of the White Earth Nation: A New Innovation in a Longstanding Indigenous Literary Tradition." *Studies in American Indian Literatures* 23, no. 4 (2011): 48–76.

Brotherston, Gordon. *Book of the Fourth World: Reading the Native Americas Through Their Literature.* Cambridge: Cambridge University Press, 1992.

———, and Edward Dorn, eds. *The Sun Unwound: Original Texts from Occupied America.* Berkeley, CA: North Atlantic Books, 1999.

Brown, Wendy. *States of Injury: Power and Freedom in Late Modernity.* Princeton, NJ: Princeton University Press, 1995.

Bruce-Novoa, Juan. *Chicano Authors: Inquiry by Interview.* Austin: University of Texas Press, 1980.

———. *Chicano Poetry: A Response to Chaos.* Austin: University of Texas Press, 1982.

Brugge, Doug, Timothy Benally, and Esther Yazzie-Lewis, eds. *The Navajo People and Uranium Mining.* Albuquerque: University of New Mexico Press, 2007.

Burroughs, William. *Break Through in Grey Room.* Sub Rosa, 1986.

———. *Junky.* New York: Penguin Books, 1977.

———. "The Literary Techniques of Lady Sutton Smith." *Times Literary Supplement,* August 6, 1964. https://www.the-tls.co.uk/articles/public/burroughss-beat/.

———. *Naked Lunch.* New York: Grove Press, 1992.

———. *Queer.* New York: Penguin Books, 2010.

———. *The Soft Machine.* New York: Grove Press, 1966.

———. "William Tells." *Spin* 7, no. 7 (1991): 68–73.

Burroughs, William, and Allen Ginsberg. *The Yage Letters Redux.* San Francisco: City Lights Books, 2006.

Bush, Christopher. *Ideographic Modernism: China, Writing, Media.* Oxford: Oxford University Press, 2010.

Byrd, Jodi. *The Transit of Empire: Indigenous Critiques of Colonialism.* Minneapolis: University of Minnesota Press, 2011.

Caillois, Roger. *The Writing of Stones.* Translated by Barbara Bray. Charlottesville: University Press of Virginia, 1985.

Carroll, Michael. "The Rolling Head: Towards a Revitalized Psychoanalytic Perspective on Myth." *Journal of Psychoanalytic Anthropology* 5, no. 1 (1982): 33–37.

Casanova, Pascale. *The World Republic of Letters.* Translated by M. B. DeBevoise. Cambridge, MA: Harvard University Press, 2007.

Castoriadis, Cornelius. *L'Imaginaire selon Castoriadis: Thèmes et Enjeux.* Edited by Sophie Klimis and Laurent van Eynde. Saint-Louis, 2006.

Caygill, Howard. *On Resistance: A Philosophy of Defiance.* London: Bloomsbury Academic, 2015.

———. *Walter Benjamin: The Colour of Experience.* New York: Routledge, 1998.

Caygill, Howard, Alex Coles, and Richard Appignanesi. *Introducing Walter Benjamin.* London: Totem Books, 1998.

Chakrabarty, Dipesh. *Provincializing Europe: Postcolonial Thought and Historical Difference.* Princeton, NJ: Princeton University Press, 2000.

Cheah, Pheng. *What Is a World? On Postcolonial Literature as World Literature.* Durham, NC: Duke University Press, 2016.

Cheyfitz, Eric. "The (Post)Colonial Construction of Indian Country." In *The Columbia Guide to American Indian Literatures of the United States Since 1945,* edited by Eric Cheyfitz, 1–126. New York: Columbia University Press, 2006.

Clifford, James. *On the Edges of Anthropology (Interviews).* Chicago: Prickly Paradigm Press, 2003.

———. *The Predicament of Culture: Twentieth-Century Ethnography, Literature, and Art.* Cambridge, MA: Harvard University Press, 1988.

———. *Routes: Travel and Translation in the Late Twentieth Century.* Cambridge, MA: Harvard University Press, 1997.

———. *Returns: Becoming Indigenous in the Twenty-First Century.* Cambridge, MA: Harvard University Press, 2013.

Clifford, James, and George E. Marcus, eds. *Writing Culture: The Poetics and Politics of Ethnography.* Berkeley: University of California Press, 1986.

Coe, Michael. *Breaking the Maya Code.* London: Thames and Hudson, 1992.

Cohen, Brigid. "Musical Cosmopolitans at Black Mountain College: John Cage, Lou Harrison, and Stefan Wolpe." In *Leap Before You Look: Black Mountain College 1933–1957,* edited by Helen Molesworth with Ruth Erickson, 202–07. New Haven, CT: Yale University Press, 2015.

Cohen, Matt, and Jeffrey Glover, eds. *Colonial Mediascapes: Sensory Worlds of the Early Americas.* Lincoln: University of Nebraska Press, 2014.

Conrad, Joseph. *Heart of Darkness and Other Tales.* Oxford: Oxford University Press, 2008.

Coulthard, Glen Sean. *Red Skins White Masks: Rejecting the Colonial Politics of Recognition.* Minneapolis: University of Minnesota Press, 2014.

Crane, Hart. *Complete Poems and Selected Letters.* Edited by Langdon Hammer, New York: Library of America, 2006.

Culler, Jonathan. *The Pursuit of Signs: Semiotics, Literature, Deconstruction.* Ithaca, NY: Cornell University Press, 1981.

———. *Theory of the Lyric.* Cambridge, MA: Harvard University Press, 2017.

Currie, Mark. *About Time: Narrative, Fiction, and the Philosophy of Time.* Edinburgh: Edinburgh University Press, 2010.

Damrosch, David. *What Is World Literature?* Princeton, NJ: Princeton University Press, 2003.

Davis, Whitney. *Masking the Blow: The Scene of Representation in Late Prehistoric Egyptian Art.* Berkeley: University of California Press, 1992.

———. *Replications: Archaeology, Art, History, Psychoanalysis.* University Park: Penn State University Press, 1996.

De Angulo, Gui. *The Old Coyote of Big Sur: The Life of Jaime de Angulo.* Berkeley, CA: Stonegarden Press, 1995.

De Angulo, Jaime. *Coyote's Bones: Selected Poetry and Prose.* Edited by Bob Callahan. Berkeley, CA: Turtle Island Foundation, 1974.

———. *Home Among the Swinging Stars: The Collected Poems.* Albuquerque: La Alameda Press, 2006.

———. *Indian Tales.* New York: Farrar, Straus, and Giroux, 1997.

———. *Indians in Overalls.* Berkeley, CA: Turtle Island Foundation, 1973.

———. *A Jaime de Angulo Reader.* Edited by Bob Callahan. Berkeley, CA: Turtle Island Foundation, 1979.

———. *Jaime in Taos: The Taos Papers of Jaime de Angulo.* San Francisco: City Lights Books, 1985.

———. *Lariat and Other Writings.* Edited by David Miller. Oakland, CA: Counterpoint, 2009.

———. *The Music of the Indians of Northern California.* Edited by Peter Garland. Santa Fe: Soundings Press, 1988.

———. *Old Time Stories.* Pacifica Radio Archives, 1949 and 1991. https://archive.org/details/canhpra_000044.

———. *Shabegok.* Edited by Bob Callahan. Berkeley, CA: Turtle Island Foundation, 1976.

———. "What is Language?" Jaime de Angulo Papers (Collection 160), Department of Special Collections, Charles E. Young Research Library, University of California, Los Angeles, n.d.

De Certeau, Michel. *The Practice of Everyday Life.* Translated by Steven Rendall. Berkeley: University of California Press, 2011.

DeFrancis, John. *Visible Speech: The Diverse Oneness of Writing Systems.* Honolulu: University of Hawaii Press, 1989.

De la Cadena, Marisol. *Earth Beings: Ecologies of Practice across Andean Worlds.* Durham, NC: Duke University Press, 2016.

Deleuze, Gilles, and Felix Guattari. *A Thousand Plateaus: Capitalism and Schizophrenia.* Translated by Brian Massumi. Minneapolis: University of Minnesota Press, 1987.

Deloria, Vine, Jr. Afterword to *America in 1492: The World of the Indian Peoples Before the Arrival of Columbus,* edited by Alvin M. Josephy Jr., 429–43. New York: Vintage Books, 1993.

———. *Custer Died for Your Sins: An Indian Manifesto.* Norman: University of Oklahoma Press, 1969.

De Man, Paul. "Anthropomorphism and Trope in the Lyric." In *The Rhetoric of Romanticism*, 239–62. New York: Columbia University Press, 1984.

Densmore, Frances. *Chippewa Music*. Washington, DC: U.S. Government Printing Office, 1910.

———. *Chippewa Music II*. Washington, DC: U.S. Government Printing Office, 1913.

Descola, Philippe. *Beyond Nature and Culture*. Translated by Janet Lloyd. Chicago: University of Chicago Press, 2013.

Dewdney, Sewlyn H., and Kenneth E. Kidd. *Indian Rock Paintings of the Great Lakes*. Toronto: University of Toronto Press, 1962.

De Wilde, Marc. "Violence in the State of Exception: Reflections on Theologico-Political Motifs in Benjamin and Schmitt." In *Political Theologies: Public Religions in a Post-Secular World*, edited by Hent de Vries and Lawrence Sullivan, 188–200. New York: Fordham University Press, 2006.

Dimock, Wai Chee. *Through Other Continents: American Literature Across Deep Time*. Princeton, NJ: Princeton University Press, 2006.

Dixon, Roland. *Maidu Texts*. Leyden: E. J. Brill, 1912.

Dorn, Edward. *Collected Poems*. Edited by Jennifer Dunbar Dorn. Manchester: Carcanet, 2012.

———. *Derelict Air: From Collected Out*. Edited by Justin Katko and Kyle Waugh. London: Enitharmon, 2015.

———. *The Poet, the People, the Spirit*. Vancouver: Talonbooks, 1976.

———. *The Shoshoneans: The People of the Basin-Plateau*. Albuquerque: University of New Mexico Press, 2013.

Douven, Igor. "Peirce on Abduction." In *Stanford Encyclopedia of Philosophy*, 2017. https://stanford.library.sydney.edu.au/entries/abduction/peirce.html.

Dresman, Paul. "Internal Resistances: Edward Dorn on the American Indian." In *Internal Resistances: The Poetry of Edward Dorn*, edited by Donald Wesling, 87–111. Berkeley: University of California Press, 1985.

Dunbar-Ortiz, Roxanne. *An Indigenous Peoples' History of the United States*. Boston: Beacon Press, 2015.

Duncan, Robert. "Aug 1 1969, reading notes." Robert Duncan Papers (collection not cataloged), Poetry Collection and Special Books, Special Collections, Lockwood Memorial Library, State University of New York at Buffalo.

———. *Bending the Bow*. New York: New Directions, 1968.

———. *The Collected Early Poems and Plays*. Edited by Peter Quartermain. Berkeley: University of California Press, 2012.

———. *The H.D. Book*. Edited by Michael Boughn and Victor Coleman. Berkeley: University of California Press, 2011.

———. *Letters: Poems, 1953–56*. Chicago: Flood Editions, 2003.

———. *The Truth & Life of Myth: An Essay in Essential Autobiography*. Amsterdam: House of Books, 1968.

———. *A Poet's Mind: Collected Interviews with Robert Duncan, 1960–1985*. Berkeley, CA: North Atlantic Books, 2012.

Dussel, Enrique. "Beyond Eurocentrism: The World-System and the Limits of Modernity." In *The Cultures of Globalization*, edited by Fredric Jameson and Masao Miyoshi, 3–31. Durham, NC: Duke University Press, 1998.

Eagleton, Terry. *Walter Benjamin: Or Towards a Revolutionary Criticism*. New York: Verso, 1981.

Eburne, Jonathan Paul. "Trafficking in the Void: Burroughs, Kerouac, and the Consumption of Otherness." *Modern Fiction Studies* 43, no. 1 (1997): 53–92.

Edwards, Brian T. *Morocco Bound: Disorienting America's Maghreb, from Casablanca to the Marrakech Express*. Durham, NC: Duke University Press, 2005.

Eisenstein, Sergei. *Film Form: Essays in Film Theory*. Translated by Jay Leyda. New York: Harcourt, 1969.

Eliade, Mircea. *Shamanism: Archaic Techniques of Ecstasy*. Princeton, NJ: Princeton University Press, 2004.

Erdrich, Louise. *Books and Islands in Ojibwe Country: Traveling through the Land of My Ancestors*. New York: Harper Perennial, 2014.

Erickson, Ruth. "Between Media: The Glyph Exchange." In *Leap Before You Look: Black Mountain College 1933–1957*, edited by Helen Molesworth with Ruth Erickson, 328–35. New Haven, CT: Yale University Press, 2015.

Faas, Ekbart. *Young Robert Duncan: Portrait of the Poet as Homosexual in Society*. Boston: Black Sparrow Press, 1984.

Fabian, Johannes. *Time and the Other: How Anthropology Makes Its Object*. New York: Columbia University Press, 2014.

Feinsod, Harris. *The Poetry of the Americas: From Good Neighbors to Countercultures*. New York: Oxford University Press, 2017.

Foucault, Michel. *The Order of Things: An Archaeology of the Human Sciences*. New York: Vintage Books, 1994.

Fowles, Severin. *An Archaeology of Doings: Secularism and the Study of Pueblo Religion*. Santa Fe: School for Advanced Research Press, 2013.

Frazer, James George. *The Golden Bough: A Study in Magic and Religion*. Oxford: Oxford University Press, 2009.

Freeland, Anne. "Notes on René Zavaleta's 'Abigarramiento' as Condition of Constitutive Power." *Alternautas* 1, no. 1 (2014): 65–70.

Friedrich, Paul. *The Language Parallax: Linguistic Relativism and Poetic Indeterminacy*. Austin: University of Texas Press, 1986.

Ganguly, Debjani. *This Thing Called the World: The Contemporary Novel as Global Form*. Durham, NC: Duke University Press, 2016.

Geertz, Clifford. "Deep Hanging Out." *New York Review of Books*, October 22, 1998. https://www.nybooks.com/articles/1998/10/22/deep-hanging-out/.

Gelb, Ignace. *A Study of Writing: The Foundations of Grammatology*. Chicago: University of Chicago Press, 1952.

Gell, Alfred. *Art and Agency: An Anthropological Theory*. Oxford: Oxford University Press, 1998.

———. *Metamorphosis of the Cassowaries: Umeda Society, Language, and Ritual*. London: Athlone, 1975.

Genette, Gérard. *Narrative Discourse Revisited*. Translated by Jane E. Lewin. Ithaca, NY: Cornell University Press, 1988.

Ginsberg, Allen. *Reality Sandwiches*. San Francisco: City Lights Books, 1963.

Glissant, Édouard. *Poetics of Relation*. Translated by Betsy Wing. Ann Arbor: University of Michigan Press, 2010.

Godelier, Maurice. *The Metamorphoses of Kinship*. Translated by Nora Scott. New York: Verso, 2012.

Goffman, Erving. *Frame Analysis: An Essay on the Organization of Experience*. New York: Harper and Row, 1974.

Gombrich, E. H. "Action and Expression in Western Art." In *Non-Verbal Communication*, edited by Robert A. Hinde, 373–92. Cambridge: Cambridge University Press, 1975.

———. *Art and Illusion: A Study in the Psychology of Pictorial Representation*. Princeton, NJ: Princeton University Press, 2000.

———. *The Story of Art*. London: Phaidon, 1995. First published 1950.

Graves, Robert. *Claudius the God*. New York: Vintage International, 1989.

———. *I, Claudius*. New York: Vintage International, 1989.

———. *King Jesus*. New York: Farrar, Straus, and Giroux, 1981.

———. *The White Goddess: A Historical Grammar of Poetic Myth*. New York: Farrar, Straus, and Giroux, 2013.

Greenhouse, Carol J. *The Paradox of Relevance: Ethnography and Citizenship in the United States*. Philadelphia: University of Pennsylvania Press, 2011.

"Greenwich Village Tops Artists' Ball." *New York Times*, March 12, 1921.

Guaman Poma de Ayala, Felipe. *El Primer Nueva Corónica y Buen Gobierno*. 1615. http://www.kb.dk/permalink/2006/poma/info/en/frontpage.htm.

Guha, Ranajit. "The Migrant's Time." *Postcolonial Studies* 1, no. 2 (1998): 155–60.

Guillory, John. "Genesis of the Media Concept." *Critical Inquiry* 36, no. 2 (2010): 321–62.

Hallyn, Fernand, ed. *Metaphor and Analogy in the Sciences*. Dordrecht: Kluwer Academic, 2000.

Hamann, Byron Ellsworth. "How Maya Hieroglyphs Got Their Name: Egypt, Mexico, and China in Western Grammatology since the Fifteenth Century." *Proceedings of the American Philosophical Society* 152, no. 1 (2008): 1–68.

Hanneken, Jaime. "José Carlos Mariátegui and the Time of Myth." *Cultural Critique* 81 (Spring 2012): 1–30.

Hansen, Miriam. *Babel and Babylon: Spectatorship in American Silent Film*. Cambridge, MA: Harvard University Press, 1994.

———. *Cinema and Experience: Siegfried Kracauer, Walter Benjamin, and Theodor W. Adorno*. Berkeley: University of California Press, 2011.

Haraway, Donna. *The Haraway Reader*. New York: Routledge, 2004.

———. *Staying with the Trouble: Making Kin in the Chthulucene*. Durham, NC: Duke University Press, 2016.

Hardt, Michael, and Antonio Negri. *Empire*. Cambridge, MA: Harvard University Press, 2000.

Harootunian, Harry. *Marx After Marx: History and Time in the Expansion of Capitalism.* New York: Columbia University Press, 2015.

Harris, Oliver. *William Burroughs and the Secret of Fascination.* Carbondale: Southern Illinois University Press, 2006.

Harris Block, Gwendoline, and Edward Gifford, eds. *California Indian Nights.* Lincoln: University of Nebraska Press, 1990.

Harrison, Regina. *Signs, Songs, and Memory in the Andes: Translating Quechua Language and Culture.* Austin: University of Texas Press, 1989.

Harrison, Roberto. *Interface.* Des Moines: Oxeye Press, 2018.

Hartman, Saidiya. "Venus in Two Acts." *Small Axe* 12, no. 2 (2008): 1–14.

Hill Boone, Elizabeth, and Walter D. Mignolo, eds. *Writing Without Words.* Durham, NC: Duke University Press, 1994.

Horkheimer, Max, and Theodor Adorno. *Dialectic of Enlightenment: Philosophical Fragments.* Translated by Edmund Jephcott. Stanford, CA: Stanford University Press, 2002.

Houston, Stephen. *The Life Within: Classic Maya and the Matter of Permanence.* New Haven, CT: Yale University Press, 2014.

Hull, Kerry, and Michael Carrasco, eds. *Parallel Worlds: Genre, Discourse, and Poetics in Contemporary, Colonial, and Classic Maya Literature.* Boulder: University Press of Colorado, 2012.

Hutcheon, Linda. *Irony's Edge: The Theory and Politics of Irony.* New York: Routledge, 1994.

Irwin, John T. *American Hieroglyphics: The Symbol of the Egyptian Hieroglyphics in the American Renaissance.* New Haven, CT: Yale University Press, 1980.

Jackson, Michael. *How Lifeworlds Work: Emotionality, Sociality, and the Ambiguity of Being.* Chicago: University of Chicago Press, 2017.

———. *The Politics of Storytelling: Variations on a Theme by Hannah Arendt.* Copenhagen: Museum Musculanum Press, 2013.

Jacobus, Mary. *Reading Cy Twombly: Poetry in Paint.* Princeton, NJ: Princeton University Press, 2016.

Jakobson, Roman. "Grammatical Parallelism and its Russian Facet." *Language* 42, no. 2 (1966): 399–429.

Jameson, Fredric. *A Singular Modernity: Essay on the Ontology of the Present.* New York: Verso, 2002.

Jarnot, Lisa. *Robert Duncan: The Ambassador from Venus.* Berkeley: University of California Press, 2012.

Jenkins, Henry. *Convergence Culture: Where Old and New Media Collide.* New York: New York University Press, 2008.

Jung, Carl Gustav. *Psychology of the Unconscious.* New York: Moffat, Yard, 1921.

Keating, AnaLouise, ed. *EntreMundos/AmongWorlds: New Perspectives on Gloria Anzaldúa.* New York: Palgrave MacMillan, 2008.

Keen, Benjamin. *The Aztec Image in Western Thought.* New Brunswick, NJ: Rutgers University Press, 1990.

Kinkade, M. Dale. "Bluejay and His Sister." In *Recovering the Word: Essays on Na-*

tive American Literature, edited by Brian Swann and Arnold Krupat, 255–96. Berkeley: University of California Press, 1987.

Klor de Alva, J. Jorge. "California Chicano Literature and Pre-Columbian Motifs: Foil and Fetish." *Confluencia* 1, no. 2 (1986): 18–26.

Klor de Alva, J. Jorge, H. B. Nicholson, and Eloise Quiñones Keber, eds. *The Work of Bernardino de Sahagún: Pioneer Ethnographer of Sixteenth-Century Mexico*. Albany: Institute for Mesoamerican Studies at SUNY-Albany, 1988.

Klossowski, Pierre. *The Baphomet*. Translated by Sophie Hawkes and Stephen Sartarelli. Hygiene, CO: Eridanos Press, 1988.

———. *Diana at Her Bath/The Women of Rome*. Translated by Steven Sartarelli and Sophie Hawkes. New York: Marsilio Press, 1998.

———. *Nietzsche and the Vicious Circle*. Translated by Daniel W. Smith. Chicago: University of Chicago Press, 1997.

———. "Nietzsche, Polytheism, and Parody." *Bulletin de la Société Américaine de Langue Français* 14, no. 2 (2004): 82–119.

Kohli, Devindra. "The Necessary Trance and Graves's Love Ethic." In *Graves and the Goddess: Essays on Robert Graves's The White Goddess*. Edited by Ian Firla and Grevel Lindop, Selinsgrove, PA: Susquehanna University Press, 2004.

Kohn, Eduardo. *How Forests Think: Toward an Anthropology Beyond the Human*. Berkeley: University of California Press, 2013.

Kovach, Margaret. *Indigenous Methodologies: Characteristics, Conversations, Contexts*. Toronto: University of Toronto Press, 2009.

Kovecses, Zoltán. *Metaphor: A Practical Introduction*. New York: Oxford University Press, 2010.

Kristeva, Julia. *Revolution in Poetic Language*. Translated by Margaret Waller. New York: Columbia University Press, 1984.

Kroeber, Alfred, and Edward Sapir. *The Sapir-Kroeber Correspondence*. Edited by Victor Golla. Survey of California and Other Indian Languages, Report 6. Berkeley: University of California, 1984.

Kroeber, Karl. *Artistry in Native American Myths*. Lincoln: University of Nebraska Press, 1998.

———. "Why It's a Good Thing Gerald Vizenor Is Not an Indian." In *Survivance: Narratives of Native Presence*, edited by Gerald Vizenor, 25–38. Lincoln: University of Nebraska Press, 2008.

Kusch, Rodolfo. *Indigenous and Popular Thinking in América*. Translated by Joshua M. Price. Durham, NC: Duke University Press, 2010. First published 1971.

Lacan, Jacques. *Écrits: The First Complete Edition in English*. Translated by Bruce Fink. New York: Norton, 2006.

Latour, Bruno. *An Inquiry into Modes of Existence: An Anthropology of the Moderns*. Translated by Catherine Porter. Cambridge, MA: Harvard University Press, 2013.

Leeds-Hurwitz, Wendy. *Rolling in Ditches with Shamans: Jaime de Angulo and the Professionalization of American Anthropology*. Lincoln: University of Nebraska Press, 2004.

León-Portilla, Miguel. *Aztec Thought and Culture: A Study of the Ancient Nahuatl Mind.* Translated by Jack Emory Davis. Norman: University of Oklahoma Press, 1990.

———. *Bernardino de Sahagún, First Anthropologist.* Norman: University of Oklahoma Press, 2002.

Levine, Caroline. *Forms: Whole, Rhythm, Hierarchy, Network.* Princeton, NJ: Princeton University Press, 2015.

Lévi-Strauss, Claude. *Myth and Meaning.* New York: Schocken Books, 1979.

———. *Tristes Tropiques.* New York: Penguin Classics, 2012.

Lincoln, Kenneth. *Native American Renaissance.* Berkeley: University of California Press, 1983.

Lingis, Alphonso. *Excesses: Eros and Culture.* Albany: State University of New York Press, 1984.

LiPuma, Edward. *Encompassing Others: The Magic of Modernity in Melanesia.* Ann Arbor: University of Michigan Press, 2001.

López, Marissa. "The Language of Resistance: Alurista's Global Poetics." *MELUS* 33, no. 1 (2008): 93–115.

Luthin, Herbert, ed. *Surviving Through the Days: A California Indian Reader.* Berkeley: University of California Press, 2002.

Lynd, Juliet. "Precarious Resistance: Weaving Opposition in the Poetry of Cecilia Vicuña." *PMLA* 120, no. 5 (2005): 1588–1607.

Mackey, Nathaniel. *Discrepant Engagement: Dissonance, Cross-Culturality, and Experimental Writing.* New York: Cambridge University Press, 1993.

Maffie, James. *Aztec Philosophy: Understanding a World in Motion.* Boulder: University Press of Colorado, 2014.

Malinowski, Bronisław. *Argonauts of the Western Pacific: An Account of Native Enterprise and Adventure in the Archipelagoes of Melanesian New Guinea.* London: Routledge, 1932. First published 1922.

———. *Coral Gardens and Their Magic: A Study of the Methods of Tilling the Soil and of Agricultural Rites in the Trobriand Islands.* Bloomington: Indiana University Press, 1965. First published 1935.

———. *A Diary in the Strict Sense of the Term.* Stanford, CA: Stanford University Press, 1989.

———. *The Sexual Life of Savages in North Eastern Melanesia.* New York: Harcourt Brace, 1929.

Mallery, Garrick. *Picture-Writing of the American Indians.* New York: Dover, 2012. First published 1888.

Manetti, Giovanni. *Theories of the Sign in Classical Antiquity.* Translated by Christine Richardson. Bloomington: Indiana University Press, 1993.

Marcus, Joyce. *Mesoamerican Writing Systems: Propaganda, Myth, and History in Four Ancient Civilizations.* Princeton, NJ: Princeton University Press, 1992.

Mariátegui, José Carlos. *Seven Interpretive Essays on Peruvian Reality.* Translated by Marjory Urquidi. Austin: University of Texas Press, 1988.

Margolin, Malcolm. *The Way We Lived: California Indian Stories, Songs, and Reminiscences.* Berkeley, CA: Heyday, 1992.

Martínez Parédez, Domingo. *El Popol Vuh Tiene Razon: Teoria Sobre la Cosmogonia Preamericana*. Mexico City: Editorial Orión, 1968.

——. *Hunab Ku: Síntesis del Pensamiento Filosófico Maya*. Mexico City: Editorial Orión, 1973.

Marx, Karl. *Capital*. Vol. 1. Translated by Ben Fowkes. New York: Penguin, 1990.

Maud, Ralph. *What Does Not Change: The Significance of Charles Olson's "The Kingfishers."* Madison, NJ: Fairleigh Dickinson University Press, 1998.

Mbembe, Achille. "Necropolitics." *Public Culture* 15, no. 1 (2003): 11–40.

McCaffery, Steve. *Prior to Meaning: The Protosemantic and Poetics*. Chicago: Northwestern University Press, 2001.

McGann, Jerome J. *The Textual Condition*. Princeton, NJ: Princeton University Press, 1991.

McHale, Brian. *Postmodernist Fiction*. London: Methuen, 1987.

Méndez, Miguel. *Pilgrims in Aztlán*. Tempe, AZ: Bilingual Review Press, 1992.

Mezzadra, Sandro, and Brett Neilson. *Border as Method, or, the Multiplication of Labor*. Durham, NC: Duke University Press, 2013.

Mignolo, Walter. *The Darker Side of the Renaissance: Literacy, Territoriality, and Colonization*. Ann Arbor: University of Michigan Press, 2003.

——. *Local Histories/Global Designs: Coloniality, Subaltern Knowledges, and Border Thinking*. Princeton, NJ: Princeton University Press, 2000.

Mignolo, Walter, and Madina Tlostanova. "Theorizing from the Borders: Shifting to Geo- and Body-Politics of Knowledge." *European Journal of Social Theory* 9, no. 2 (2006): 205–21.

Miller, Mary, and Karl Taube. *The Gods and Symbols of Ancient Mexico and the Maya: An Illustrated Dictionary*. London: Thames and Hudson, 1993.

Mircan, Mihnea, and Vincent W. J. van Gerven Oei, eds. *Allegory of the Cave Painting*. Milan: Mousse, 2015.

Mitchell, Stanley. "Introduction to Benjamin and Brecht." *New Left Review*, no. 77 (1973). https://newleftreview.org/I/77/stanley-mitchell-introduction-to-benjamin-and-brecht.

——. Introduction to *Understanding Brecht*, by Walter Benjamin. Translated by Anna Bostock. New York: Verso, 2003.

Mitchell, W. J . T. *Iconology: Image, Text, Ideology*. Chicago: University of Chicago Press, 1986.

Molesworth, Helen, and Ruth Erickson. *Leap Before You Look: Black Mountain College, 1933–1957*. New Haven, CT: Yale University Press, 2015.

Momaday, N. Scott. *The Way to Rainy Mountain*. Albuquerque: University of New Mexico Press, 1976.

Moore, Jason W. *Capitalism in the Web of Life: Ecology and the Accumulation of Capital*. New York: Verso, 2015.

Moretti, Franco. "Conjectures on World Literature." *New Left Review*, no. 1 (2000): 54–68.

Morgan, Ted. *Literary Outlaw: The Life and Times of William S. Burroughs*. New York: Henry Holt, 1988.

Morrison, Kenneth M. "The Cosmos as Intersubjective: Native American Other-Than-Human Persons." In *Indigenous Religions: A Companion*, edited by Graham Harvey. London: Cassell, 2000.

Most, Glenn W., and André Laks, eds. and trans. *Ancient Greek Philosophy*. Vol. 1. Cambridge, MA: Harvard University Press, 2016.

Moten, Fred. *In the Break: The Aesthetics of the Black Radical Tradition*. Minneapolis: University of Minnesota Press, 2003.

Muela del Diablo, eds. *Pluralismo Epistemológico*. La Paz: Muela del Diablo Editores, 2009.

Munn, Nancy. *Walbiri Iconography: Graphic Representation and Cultural Symbolism in a Central Australian Society*. Ithaca, NY: Cornell University Press, 1973.

Nancy, Jean-Luc. "Vox Clamans in Deserto." In *Multiple Arts: The Muses II*, 38–49. Translated by Simon Sparks. Stanford, CA: Stanford University Press, 2006.

Nash, June. "Ethnographic Aspects of the World Capitalist System." *Annual Review of Anthropology* 10 (1981): 393–423.

———. *Mayan Visions: The Quest for Autonomy in an Age of Globalization*. New York: Routledge, 2001.

Nelson, Deborah. *Tough Enough: Arbus, Arendt, Didion, McCarthy, Sontag, Weil*. Chicago: University of Chicago Press, 2017.

Nietzsche, Friedrich. *On The Advantage and Disadvantage of History for Life*. Translated by Peter Preuss. Cambridge, MA: Hackett Classics, 1980.

Noel, Urayoán. *Invisible Movement: Nuyorican Poetry from the Sixties to Slam*. Iowa City: University of Iowa Press, 2014.

Nordenskiöld, Erland. *Picture-Writings and Other Documents by Néle, Paramount Chief of the Cuna Indians and Ruben Pérez Kantule, His Secretary*. New Haven, CT: Human Relations Area Files, 1998. First published 1928.

Obarrio, Juan. "Postshamanism (1999)." *Cultural Studies Review* 13, no. 2 (2007): 166–89.

Olson, Charles. "The Art of the Language of the Mayan Glyphs." *Alcheringa* [1], no. 5 (1983): 94–100.

———. *Collected Poems*. Edited by George Butterick. Berkeley: University of California Press, 1997.

———. *Collected Prose*. Edited by Donald Allen and Benjamin Friedlander. Berkeley: University of California Press, 1997.

———. *Letters for Origin, 1950–1956*. Edited by Albert Glover. London: Cape Goliard Press, 1969.

———. "Mayan Heads." *Black Mountain Review* 1, no. 2 (1954): 26–36.

———. *The Mayan Letters*. London: Jonathan Cape, 1968.

Olson, Charles, and Robert Creeley. *The Complete Correspondence*. Vol. 5. Edited by George F. Butterick. Boston: Black Sparrow Press, 1983.

Ortiz, Fernando. *Cuban Counterpoint: Tobacco and Sugar*. Translated by Harriet de Onís. Durham, NC: Duke University Press, 1995.

Ortiz, Simon. *Song, Poetry and Language—Expression and Perception*. Tsaile, AZ: Navajo Community College Press, 1978.

————. "Speaking-Writing Indigenous Literary Sovereignty." In *American Indian Literary Nationalism*, edited by Jace Weaver, Craig Womack, and Robert Warrior, xii–xiv. Albuquerque: University of New Mexico Press, 2006.

————. "Towards a National Indian Literature: Cultural Authenticity in Nationalism." In *American Indian Literary Nationalism*, edited by Jace Weaver, Craig Womack, and Robert Warrior, 253–60. Albuquerque: University of New Mexico Press, 2006.

————. *Woven Stone*. Tucson: University of Arizona Press, 1992.

Ortiz, Simon, and Andrea Geyer. *Spiral Lands*. In *Kindred Spirits: Native American Influences on 20th Century Art*, edited by Carter Ratcliff and Paul Chaat Smith. New York: Peter Blum Edition, 2011.

Palumbo-Liu, David, Nirvana Tanoukhi, and Bruce Robbins, eds. *Immanuel Wallerstein and the Problem of the World: System, Scale, Culture*. Durham, NC: Duke University Press, 2011.

Paternosto, César. *The Stone and the Thread: Andean Roots of Abstract Art*. Translated by Esther Allen. Austin: University of Texas Press, 1996.

Paz, Octavio. *Claude Lévi-Strauss: An Introduction*. Translated by J. S. Bernstein and Maxine Bernstein. Ithaca, NY: Cornell University Press, 1970.

————. *Sunstone/Piedra de Sol*. Translated by Eliot Weinberger. New York: New Directions, 1990. First published 1957.

Pérez, Emma. "La Gran Nueva Mestiza Theorist, Writer, Activist-Scholar." *NWSA Journal* 17, no. 2 (2005): 1–10.

Pérez-Oramas, Luis, ed. *The Arcadian Modern: Joaquín Torres-García*. New York: Museum of Modern Art, 2015.

Pérez-Torres, Rafael. *Movements in Chicano Poetry: Against Myths, Against Margins*. Cambridge: Cambridge University Press, 1995.

Pettigrew, Jack, Chloe Callistemon, Astrid Weiler, Anna Gorbushina, Wolfgang Krumbein, and Reto Weiler. "Living Pigments in Australian Bradshaw Rock Art." *Antiquity: A Review of World Archaeology* 84, no. 326 (2010). http://antiquity.ac.uk/projgall/pettigrew326/.

Pier, John. "Metalepsis." In *The Living Handbook of Narratology*, edited by Peter Hühn et al. Hamburg: University of Hamburg. Revised March 13, 2013. http://www.lhn.uni-hamburg.de/article/metalepsis-revised-version-uploaded-13-july-2016.

Pocock, J. G. A. "Burke and the Ancient Constitution: A Problem in the History of Ideas." *Historical Journal* 3, no. 2 (1960): 125–43.

Poe, Edgar Allan. "Review of the Incidents of Travel in Central America." *Graham's Magazine*, August 1841, 90–96. http://www.eapoe.org/works/criticsm/gm41083.htm.

Pomedli, Michael. *Living with Animals: Ojibwe Spirit Powers*. Toronto: University of Toronto Press, 2014.

Pound, Ezra. *ABC of Reading*. New York: New Directions, 1960.

————. *The Cantos*. New York: New Directions, 1970.

————. *Gaudier-Brzeska*. New York: New Directions, 1970.

————. *Guide to Kulchur*. New York: New Directions, 1970.

———. Letter to Jaime de Angulo. Jaime de Angulo Papers (Collection 160), Department of Special Collections, Charles E. Young Research Library, University of California, Los Angeles, n.d.

———. *Pavannes and Divagations*. New York: New Directions, 1958.

Pound, Ezra, and Ernest Fenollosa. *The Chinese Written Character as Medium for Poetry*. Edited by Haun Saussy, Jonathan Stalling, and Lucas Klein. New York: Fordham University Press, 2011.

Povinelli, Elizabeth. *The Cunning of Recognition: Indigenous Alterities and the Making of Australian Multiculturalism*. Durham, NC: Duke University Press, 2002.

———. *Geontologies: A Requiem to Late Liberalism*. Durham, NC: Duke University Press, 2016.

———. "The Governance of the Prior." *Interventions: International Journal of Postcolonial Studies* 13, no. 1 (2011): 13–30.

Presley, John Woodrow. "Robert Graves's Other Obsession: *King Jesus, the Nazarene Gospel Restored* and *Jesus in Rome*. In *Graves and the Goddess: Essays on Robert Graves's* The White Goddess. Edited by Ian Firla and Grevel Lindop. Selinsgrove, PA: Susquehanna University Press, 2004.

Rama, Ángel. *The Lettered City*. Translated by John Charles Chasteen. Durham, NC: Duke University Press, 1996.

Ramazani, Jahan. *The Hybrid Muse: Postcolonial Poetry in English*. Chicago: University of Chicago Press, 2001.

———. *A Transnational Poetics*. Chicago: University of Chicago Press, 2009.

Rappaport, Joanne, and Tom Cummins. *Beyond the Lettered City: Indigenous Literacies in the Andes*. Durham, NC: Duke University Press, 2011.

Rasmussen, Birgit Brander. *Queequeg's Coffin: Indigenous Literacies and Early American Literature*. Durham, NC: Duke University Press, 2012.

Restall, Matthew. *Maya Conquistador*. Boston: Beacon Press, 1998.

Revel, Jacques. *Jeux d'Échelles: La Micro-Analyse á l'Expérience*. Paris: Gallimard, 1996.

Richter, Gerhard. *Thought Images: Frankfurt School Writers' Reflections from Damaged Life*. Stanford, CA: Stanford University Press, 2007.

Ricoeur, Paul. *Memory, History, Forgetting*. Translated by Kathleen Blamey and David Pellauer. Chicago: University of Chicago Press, 2004.

Rifkin, Mark. *Beyond Settler Time: Temporal Sovereignty and Indigenous Self-Determination*. Durham, NC: Duke University Press, 2017.

Rosaldo, Renato. *The Day of Shelly's Death: The Poetry and Ethnography of Grief*. Durham, NC: Duke University Press, 2014.

Rosen, Bryan. "On Attributive Adjectives in Ojibwe and Cinque's Phrasal Movement Analysis of Adjective Orders." *Linguistic Inquiry* 47, no. 1 (2016): 158–68.

Rothenberg, Jerome, ed. *Technicians of the Sacred*. New York: Anchor, 1969.

Sahagún, Bernardino de. *Coloquios y Doctrina Cristiana*. Mexico City: Universidad Nacional Autónoma de México, 1986.

Sahlins, Marshall. "Cosmologies of Capitalism: The Trans-Pacific Sector of 'The World System.'" In *Culture in Practice: Selected Essays*, 415–70. Brooklyn: Zone Books, 2000.

————. "Interview with Marshall Sahlins." *Anthropological Theory* 8, no. 3 (2008): 319–28.

————. *Islands of History*. Chicago: University of Chicago Press, 1985.

————. *Stone Age Economics*. Chicago: Aldine-Atherton, 1972.

————. *What Kinship Is—And Is Not*. Chicago: University of Chicago Press, 2014.

Saldaña-Portillo, María Josefina. *The Revolutionary Imagination in the Americas and the Age of Development*. Durham, NC: Duke University Press, 2003.

Saldívar, José David. *Trans-Americanity: Subaltern Modernities, Global Coloniality, and the Cultures of Greater Mexico*. Durham, NC: Duke University Press, 2011.

Saldívar, Ramón. *The Borderlands of Culture: Américo Paredes and the Transnational Imaginary*. Durham, NC: Duke University Press, 2006.

Sandoval, Chela. "Unfinished Words: The Crossing of Gloria Anzaldúa." In *EntreMundos/AmongWorlds: New Perspectives on Gloria E. Anzaldúa*, edited by Ana-Louise Keating, xiii–xvi. New York: Palgrave MacMillan, 2005.

Sanjinés, Javier C. *Embers of the Past: Essays in Times of Decolonization*. Translated by David Frye. Durham, NC: Duke University Press, 2013.

Sapir, Edward. *Language: An Introduction to the Study of Speech*. New York: Harcourt, Brace, 1921.

Schele, Linda, and Peter Mathews. *The Code of Kings: The Language of Seven Sacred Maya Temples and Tombs*. New York: Scribner, 1999.

Schelling, Andrew. *Tracks along the Left Coast: Jaime de Angulo and Pacific Coast Culture*. Berkeley: Counterpoint, 2017.

Schmidt Camacho, Alicia. *Migrant Imaginaries: Latino Cultural Politics in the U.S.-Mexico Borderlands*. New York: New York University Press, 2008.

Schmitt, Carl. *Political Theology: Four Chapters on the Concept of Sovereignty*. Translated by George Schwab. Chicago: University of Chicago Press, 2006.

Schoolcraft, Henry Rowe. *Information Respecting the History, Condition and Prospects of the Indian Tribes of the United States*. Philadelphia: Lippincott, 1851–57.

Scott, James C. *Against the Grain: A Deep History of the Earliest States*. New Haven, CT: Yale University Press, 2017.

Sedley, David. *Plato's Cratylus*. Cambridge: Cambridge University Press, 2003.

Séjourné, Laurette. *El Universo de Quetzalcoatl*. Mexico City: Fondo de Cultura Economica, 1962.

Severi, Carlo. *The Chimera Principle: An Anthropology of Memory and Imagination*. Translated by Janet Lloyd. Chicago: Hau, 2012.

————. *La Memoria Rituale: Follia e Immagine del Bianco in una Tradizione Sciamanica Amerindiana*. Scandicci: Nuova Italia, 1993.

Sherzer, Dina, and Joel Sherzer. *Mormaknamaloe: The Cuna Mola*. Austin: Offprint Series, Institute of Latin American Studies, the University of Texas at Austin, 1976.

Shklovsky, Viktor. "Art as Technique." In *Modernism: An Anthology of Sources and Documents*, edited by Vassiliki Koloctroni, Jane Goldman, and Olga Taxidou, 217–20. Chicago: University of Chicago Press, 1998.

Sinclair, Niigaanwewidam James, and Warren Cariou, eds. *Manitowapow: Aboriginal Writings from the Land of Water*. Winnipeg: HighWater Press, 2011.

Soja, Edward. *Thirdspace: Journeys to Los Angeles and Other Real-and-Imagined Places*. Malden, MA: Blackwell Press, 1996.

Sommer, Doris. *Bilingual Aesthetics: A New Sentimental Education*. Durham, NC: Duke University Press, 2004.

Spicer, Jack. *My Vocabulary Did This To Me: The Collected Poetry*. Edited by Peter Gizzi and Kevin Killian. Middletown, CT: Wesleyan University Press, 2010.

Stanford Friedman, Susan. *Planetary Modernisms: Provocations on Modernity Across Time*. New York: Columbia University Press, 2015.

Stocking, George W., Jr. *The Ethnographer's Magic and Other Essays in the History of Anthropology*. Madison: University of Wisconsin Press, 1992.

———. *Race, Culture, and Evolution: Essays in the History of Anthropology*. Chicago: University of Chicago Press, 1982.

Stoler, Ann Laura. *Along the Archival Grain: Epistemic Anxieties and Colonial Common Sense*. Princeton, NJ: Princeton University Press, 2010.

———. *Duress: Imperial Durabilities in Our Times*. Durham, NC: Duke University Press, 2016.

Strathern, Marilyn. *After Nature: English Kinship in the Late Twentieth Century*. Cambridge: Cambridge University Press, 1992.

Stuart, David. "The Face of the Calendar Stone: A New Interpretation." *Maya Decipherment* (blog). June 13, 2016. http://decipherment.wordpress.com/tag/nahui -ollin/.

Swann, Brian, ed. *Coming to Light: Contemporary Translations of the Native Literatures of North America*. New York: Vintage Books, 1996.

Sweet Wong, Hertha Dawn. *Sending My Heart Back Across the Years: Tradition and Innovation and Native American Autobiography*. New York: Oxford University Press, 1992.

Taggart, James. *Nahuatl Myth and Social Structure*. Austin: University of Texas Press, 1983.

Taussig, Michael. "Cities of Yagé." *Anthropology and Humanism* 36, no. 1 (2011): 122–29.

———. *The Corn Wolf*. Chicago: University of Chicago Press, 2015.

———. *The Devil and Commodity Fetishism in South America*. Chapel Hill: University of North Carolina Press, 1980.

———. *The Magic of the State*. New York: Routledge, 1997.

———. *Mimesis and Alterity: A Particular History of the Senses*. New York: Routledge, 1993.

———. *The Nervous System*. New York: Routledge, 1992.

———. *Shamanism, Colonialism, and the Wild Man: A Study in Terror and Healing*. Chicago: University of Chicago Press, 1987.

———. "Viscerality, Faith, and Skepticism: Another Theory of Magic." *HAU: Journal of Ethnographic Theory* 6, no. 3 (2016): 453–83.

———. *What Color Is the Sacred?* Chicago: University of Chicago Press, 2009.

———. "What Do Drawings Want?" *Culture, Theory, and Critique* 50, no. 2–3 (2009): 263–74.

Taylor, Diana. *The Archive and the Repertoire: Performing Cultural Memory in the Americas*. Durham, NC: Duke University Press, 2003.

Taylor, J. Douglas Allen. "Wizard of Aztlán." *Metro: Silicon Valley's Weekly Newspaper*, August 5–11, 1999. http://www.safero.org/books.html.

Tedlock, Barbara. *The Beautiful and the Dangerous: Encounters with the Zuni Indians*. Albuquerque: University of New Mexico Press, 1992.

———. *Time and the Highland Maya*. Albuquerque: University of New Mexico Press, 1992.

Tedlock, Dennis. *2000 Years of Mayan Literature*. Berkeley: University of California Press, 2010.

———. *Breath on the Mirror: Mythic Voices and Visions of the Living Maya*. New York: HarperCollins, 1993.

———. "Drawing and Designing with Words." In *Parallel Worlds: Genre, Discourse, and Poetics in Contemporary, Colonial, and Classic Period Maya Literature*, edited by Kerry M. Hull and Michael D. Carrasco, 181–94. Boulder: University Press of Colorado, 2012.

———. *Finding the Center: The Art of the Zuni Storyteller*. Lincoln: University of Nebraska Press, 1999.

———. *The Olson Codex: Projective Verse and the Problem of Mayan Glyphs*. Albuquerque: University of New Mexico Press, 2017.

———, trans. *Popol Vuh: The Definitive Edition of the Mayan Book of Dawn of Life and the Glories of Gods and Kings*. New York: Simon and Schuster, 1996.

———. "Toward a Poetics of Polyphony and Translatability." In *Close Listening: Poetry and the Performed Word*, edited by Charles Bernstein, 178–99. New York: Oxford University Press, 1998.

Terdiman, Richard. *Present Past: Modernity and Memory Crisis*. Ithaca, NY: Cornell University Press, 1993.

Thompson, John Eric Sidney. *Maya Hieroglyphic Writing: An Introduction*. Washington, DC: Carnegie Institute of Washington, 1950.

Tomba, Massimiliano. *Marx's Temporalities*. Chicago: Haymarket Books, 2013.

Torres-García, Joaquín. *La Ciudad sin Nombre*. Montevideo: Asociación de Arte Constructivo, 1941. Republished by Ministerio de Educacion y Cultura de Uruguay, 1974.

Trouillot, Michel-Rolph, *Silencing the Past: Power and the Production of History*. Boston: Beacon Press, 1997.

Tsing, Anna Lowenhaupt. *The Mushroom at the End of the World: On the Possibility of Life in Capitalist Ruins*. Princeton, NJ: Princeton University Press, 2015.

Tuhiwai-Smith, Linda. *Decolonizing Methodologies: Research and Indigenous Peoples*. London: Zed Books, 1999.

Turner, Edith. "Communitas, Rites of." In *Routledge Encyclopedia of Religious Rites, Rituals, and Festivals*, edited by Frank A. Salamone, 143–49. New York: Routledge, 2004.

Turner, Edith, and Victor Turner. *Image and Pilgrimage in Christian Culture: Anthropological Perspectives*. New York: Columbia University Press, 1978.

Twombly, Cy. *Poems to the Sea*. Munich: Schirmer-Mosel, 1990.

Urton, Gary. *Inka History in Knots: Reading Khipus as Primary Sources*. Austin: University of Texas Press, 2017.

Vicuña, Cecilia. *QUIPOem/The Precarious: The Art and Poetry of Cecilia Vicuña*. Middletown, CT: Wesleyan University Press, 1997.

———. *Read Thread: The Story of the Red Thread*. Berlin: Sternberg Press, 2017.

———. *Saborami*. Oakland, CA: ChainLinks, 2011. First published 1973.

———. *Unravelling Words and the Weaving of Water*. Minneapolis: Graywolf Press, 1992.

Vicuña, Cecilia, and Ernesto Livon-Grosman, eds. *The Oxford Book of Latin American Poetry: A Bilingual Anthology*. New York: Oxford University Press, 2009.

Viveiros de Castro, Eduardo. *Cosmological Perspectivism in Amazonia and Elsewhere*. London: Hau Books, 2012.

———. "Exchanging Perspectives: The Transformation of Objects into Subjects in Amerindian Ontologies." *Common Knowledge* 10, no. 3 (2004): 463–84.

———. "Some Reflections on the Notion of Species in History and Anthropology," translated by Frederico Santos Soares de Freitas and Zeb Tortorici, *e-misférica* 10, no. 1 (2013).

Vizenor, Gerald. "Authored Animals: Creature Tropes in Native American Fiction. *Social Research* 62, no. 3 (1995): 661–83.

———. *Favor of Crows: New and Collected Haiku*. Middletown, CT: Wesleyan University Press, 2015.

———. *Fugitive Poses: Native American Indian Scenes of Absence and Presence*. Lincoln: University of Nebraska Press, 2000.

———. *Manifest Manners: Narratives on Postindian Survivance*. Lincoln: University of Nebraska Press, 1999.

———. *Shadow Distance: A Gerald Vizenor Reader*. Middletown, CT: Wesleyan University Press, 1994.

———. *Summer in the Spring: Ojibwe Lyric Poems and Tribal Stories*. Minneapolis: Nodin Press, 1981. First published 1965.

———. "Up Close with Gerald Vizenor." *Legacy Magazine*, University of Minnesota, August 19, 2015. https://cla.umn.edu/news-events/news/close-gerald -vizenor.

Vizenor, Gerald, and Jill Doerfler. *The White Earth Nation: Ratification of a Native Democratic Constitution*. Lincoln: University of Nebraska Press, 2012.

Von Hallberg, Robert. *American Poetry and Culture, 1945–1980*. Cambridge, MA: Harvard University Press, 1985.

Wagner, Roy. "The Fractal Person." In *Big Men and Great Men: Personifications of Power in Melanesia*, edited by Maurice Godelier and Marilyn Strathern, 159–63. Cambridge: Cambridge University Press, 1991.

———. *Symbols that Stand for Themselves*. Chicago: University of Chicago Press, 1986.

Wallerstein, Immanuel. *World-Systems Analysis: An Introduction*. Durham, NC: Duke University Press, 2007.

Warburg, Aby. *Images from the Region of the Pueblo Indians of North America.* Translated by Michael P. Steinberg. Ithaca, NY: Cornell University Press, 1995. First published 1923.

Warwick Research Collective. *Combined and Uneven Development: Toward a New Theory of World-Literature.* Liverpool: Liverpool University Press, 2015.

Weaver, Jace, Craig Womack, and Robert Warrior, eds. *American Indian Literary Nationalism.* Albuquerque: University of New Mexico Press, 2006.

Weber, Samuel. *Benjamin's -abilities.* Cambridge, MA: Harvard University Press, 2008.

Whitman, Walt. *Poetry and Prose.* New York: Library of America, 1982.

Wilkinson, John. "Stone Thresholds." *Textual Practice* 34, no. 1 (2017): 631–59.

Wilson, Shawn. *Research is Ceremony: Indigenous Research Methods.* Black Point, NS: Fernwood, 2008.

Woiche, Istet, and C. Hart Merriam. *Annikadel: The History of the Universe as Told by the Achumawi Indians of California.* Tucson: University of Arizona Press, 1992. First published 1928.

Wolf, Werner. "Metalepsis as a Transgeneric and Transmedial Phenomenon: A Case Study of the Possibilities of 'Exporting' Narratological Concepts." In *Narratology Beyond Literary Criticism: Mediality and Disciplinarity*, edited by Jan Cristoph Meister. Berlin: de Gruyter, 2005.

Wynter, Sylvia. "Columbus, the Ocean Blue, and Fables that Stir the Mind: To Reinvent the Study of Letters." In *Poetics of the Americas: Race, Founding, Textuality*, edited by Bainard Cowan and Jefferson Humphries, 141–63. Baton Rouge: Louisiana State University Press, 1997.

Yates, Frances. *The Art of Memory.* New York: Routledge, 1966.

Yépez, Heriberto. *The Empire of Neomemory.* Translated by Jen Hofer, Christian Nagler, and Brian Whitener. Oakland, CA: ChainLinks, 2013.

Young, M. Jane. *Signs from the Ancestors: Zuni Cultural Symbolism and Perceptions of Rock Art.* Albuquerque: University of New Mexico Press, 1988.

Zambrana, Rocío. *Hegel's Theory of Intelligibility.* Chicago: University of Chicago Press, 2015.

Zavaleta Mercado, René. *Towards a History of the National-Popular in Bolivia.* New York: Seagull Books, 2018.

INDEX